About the author

Kate began her working life as an insurance clerk and later went on to university where she studied to become an early childhood teacher, a career she describes as challenging, interesting, rewarding and fun. She began writing at the insistence of friends and discovered a new love – words. Stunned by the interest in her first book, *The Long Way Home: the Story of a Homes Kid*, Kate now writes full time in the Blue Mountains where she lives with her partner, Dave, the first homes' kid she met as an adult. She relaxes through bush care, sculpture and the company of friends.

Praise for *The Long Way Home*

'A moving story that both breaks the heart and lends it courage'
– Caroline Jones AO

'Profoundly moving, tinged with ineffable sadness'
– THE CANBERRA TIMES

'A moving memoir that highlights another lost generation of Australian children'
– ELLE MAGAZINE

'A moving life story [that] documents a little-known period in Australian welfare history'
– AUSTRALIAN BOOK REVIEW

A TUESDAY THING

KATE SHAYLER

RANDOM HOUSE AUSTRALIA

Random House Australia Pty Ltd
20 Alfred Street, Milsons Point, NSW 2061
http://www.randomhouse.com.au

Sydney New York Toronto
London Auckland Johannesburg

First published by Random House Australia 2004

National Library of Australia
Cataloguing-in-Publication Entry

   Shayler, Kate.
   A Tuesday Thing.

   ISBN 1 74051 268 5.

   1. Shayler, Kate. 2. Foster children – New South Wales –
   Biography. 3. Social acceptance. I. Title.

   362.733092

Cover photograph: Getty Images
Internal design and typesetting by
Midland Typesetters, Maryborough, Victoria
Printed and bound by Griffin Press, Netley, South Australia

10 9 8 7 6 5 4 3 2 1

'It does not matter how slowly you go,
so long as you do not stop.'

– CONFUCIUS

CONTENTS

PROLOGUE
THE CURTAIN

'Come on, little Charlie Onions. Let's peel you.' Haley is eager to let me help her out of her winter warmers. She's beaming, full of anticipation. Peel off the outer layers and there you have the perfect four-year-old, at home anywhere because she's loved and wanted.

I would have been like her once, if my mother had lived beyond my fourth year. Now, seeing the child I was is not as simple as peeling off a few soft layers. The fabric of my life has formed a curtain that obscures her almost entirely.

There are a few glimpses of the child who was lost when her centre vanished. Little girl. Standing alone in a cold room. Crying. Best to keep away from that child. But there are silly memories that make me laugh too, like folding squares of toilet paper with the other kids at the children's home on Sunday afternoons before Sunday school. Freezing memories of picking up every frosty leaf off the lawn at five o'clock on dark winter mornings. Visits from my father with his big leathery hands and string bag of goodies. Dark father memories that I stay completely away from.

1

I can see the threads that make the curtain that hides my perfection. Some are hard, knotted and tangled. Some are colourful and smooth. They're woven together with self-doubt and a search for something I haven't understood or been able to name. Is the curtain beginning to disintegrate? Should I turn from the window or stay?

Sometimes I've taken a risk and told close friends about the children's home I grew up in. They are shocked to hear that someone with a university degree and a successful teaching career could have had a background like that. My self-confidence is an act, though. Inside there are innumerable insecurities and a loneliness that I think is about wanting a family of my own. I thought it was. Until now.

'Have you been to your mother's grave?' Tony Benton, my psychologist, asked.

'No,' I replied incredulously. 'What good could possibly come from a visit to my mother's grave?' She died thirty-four years ago and she's just an idea, a word, not a person. I don't need to say goodbye to a mother I hardly knew.

Yet here I am at her grave now feeling as if I could fly on the memories of having been loved so thoroughly by her. No need to question my perfection. I'm home, at last, in the certainty that I am whole. Always have been. My wholeness was just lost. Hidden behind the curtain. In every thread, even the brightly coloured ones, there's been loneliness that now I recognise and understand: I miss my mother to my very core.

How could the child who had lost her mother and her sense of self, understand that when she didn't even understand the finality of death? How could the teenager, who'd learnt that she was a lesser being than those whose world she'd been thrust into, understand the loneliness that goes far, far deeper than being alone? But can I, the adult, pull the curtain right back and see the child I was?

No. I must keep the other from drifting out from behind the curtain. Hold on to the euphoria of knowing my mother and my perfection, my wholeness, where there are no dark shapes or wolves or bruises or tears.

Here's the grief threatening again. Tony said I need to grieve so that I can put it to rest at last and reach my full potential. Well, I have grieved. I've sat at the grave for hours doing just that but I don't want it to come home with me. I only want the euphoria. Why does the grief have to come back and back? And the confusion and emptiness, and my perpetual need to try to be acceptable. Normal. I just want the euphoria.

I can't wait for Tuesday, therapy day with Tony Benton. I'll tell him all about the visit to the grave and thank him for sending me there. It was the best advice I've ever had. I don't think I'll need to see him much now, if he can just show me how to stop the grief getting in my way.

Will I tell my brother and sister, Ken and Kerry, about the grave? Strange to see our names joined in a family on the head-stone *Norma Shayler. Beloved mother of Kenneth 6, Katherine 4 and Kerry 2.* Not just because they're on a headstone but because we haven't felt like a family for all those years that the stone has stood there marking the disintegration of our family.

I haven't seen Ken for ten or more years but I lost him, in effect, when Dad put us in Burnside Homes. I suppose the little girl behind the curtain loved Ken, hero worshipped him, but now I'm just curious about where he is. I need to know he's safe and happy enough. I rarely see Kerry either and I have the same feelings for her. We try to be sisters sometimes, not to just say the word, but I don't think we succeed. She lives interstate with her family and it's as if she lives in another country and speaks a foreign language when she talks about her husband and kids. Will I learn the language soon? Now that I know what's behind the curtain.

Well, some of it.

NORMAL ACT

Out here, in the world away from Burnside Homes, everyone seems to have a rule book that us homes kids didn't get. I suppose the other kids didn't get one, though I don't know any of them now. Apparently I'm never going to get that book, so I'll have to keep watching the outsiders to find out what to do, say and pretend I think, so they'll think I'm a normal seventeen-year-old.

Show that you are sad when your father dies but don't cry in public. I am sad. Dad was my only hope of family to belong to when I left Burnside, but it all went wrong when his terrible dark side resurfaced and made me leave his house and live in the hostel. Now he's gone, the only person who loved me, and I'm struggling to fit in and to find a place to belong. I haven't found out how long I have to show my sadness but I think it's all right to move on and learn more rules now.

Don't blush. That's one rule I just can't keep. I blush any time I meet a stranger or don't know the answer or get a compliment.

There's a rule for getting compliments but it's tricky because at

4

Burnside we dished out lots of insults but rarely gave compliments. I don't know what people are really doing when they say I look nice. Are they teasing me or just being kind? Val, a tall, graceful girl in the church fellowship I go to, gives me a lesson. 'You have trouble accepting compliments, don't you?'

I break the don't-blush rule straight away.

'Just say thank you.' She smiles. 'Don't disagree or say it's just ordinary.' Then her smile turns to a grin, she puts her nose in the air and adds, 'Or just say, I concur.'

'But you shouldn't, you know, get a swelled head.' I try to explain the rule from the other world. Then I add a bit for church: 'God isn't pleased with people who are vain or conceited.'

'Yeah, but you don't have to put yourself down or say you don't look nice or you don't have lovely eyes or a good figure or whatever. Surely God gave you all that!'

'Yeah, but . . . oh! I mean thank you. I concur.' *But I don't.*

There's a rule for going to parties too. Or not.

'Are you going to John's party, Kate?' someone at church might ask.

'Don't know. When is it?'

'Oh. Er. Sorry. Weren't you invited?'

'No. Can I go?'

'Um. You, uh, you can't unless you were invited. Sorry. Shouldn't have mentioned it.'

'That's all right.'

But it's not. It hurts.

Sometimes people try to plumb the depths behind the red face.

'What was it like growing up in Burnside?'

'All right,' I usually say.

Crumbs! What's the rule for that? We weren't allowed to talk about it to outsiders when we lived there but what about out here? I don't want to talk about it now, anyway. I hate people looking at me and making me the centre of attention. I just say, 'It was all right.'

Being so shy is crippling but it's useful sometimes. It stops them trying to get me to talk. I'm a freak who needs explaining. The others aren't. There's still a lot for me to learn apparently.

Act normal. That's the main rule, I think. I haven't got my normal act working properly yet. I'll just keep watching and trying to copy. Wish I had an invisible Val to follow me around dropping hints or just plain bossing me about.

My secrets go deeper than even she could reach, though. Dark secrets and secret fears. So deep down that eventually I forget they are there.

At the hostel where I live I'm not shy. Sometimes I make the others laugh, especially when I play a Burnside matron.

'Winsome, get in there right this minute and turn that dreadful racket off! And wipe that smile off your face.' If there's a wet washer handy I might throw it at her to help with the wiping.

But when I'm sad about Dad and the others are cheerful, I try to be alone so I can cry. Emily, my roommate, keeps coming and going and I'd be so embarrassed if she caught me bawling my head off. I cry quietly in bed.

Most girls here gets heaps of letters from their friends and family in the country but I rarely get letters. Today is different. A beautiful envelope embossed with doves holding fluttering ribbons and rings is waiting for me. The handwriting looks familiar. Jenny, my outsider friend, best friend, at school! Jenny and school seem so far away and disconnected from me now. Jenny's sent an invitation to her wedding. Her wedding? She's caught a boy already! How did she do it? She must have got beautiful. Skinny enough to be a bride. She was the same shape as me . . . oh but she doesn't wear glasses and her skin is rosy and smooth. But how did she catch a boy to marry so soon? There's not an inkling of a nice boy within fifty miles of me. But Jenny is normal, with a mother and father and a sister who she was bridesmaid for when we were at school. She knows about all that.

Kate and friend, the invitation says. What friend? Do I even know anyone who'd pretend, even if I was game to ask him?

'Go by yourself, then,' Brenda suggests.

I've tried to get brave and go to new places on trains by myself. Like the time I went to see Kerry at her foster home. What if that thing happened again that happened that day?

Kerry's foster parents invited me for a weekend. I found out how to get there and I'm on my way. I squeeze past an ordinary-looking man to sit next to him in the only seat left in the carriage. Wham! His fist suddenly slams into the seat in front of him. He starts mumbling angrily. Is he talking to me? I steal a look. No, he's talking to the seat. Now both his fists are slamming into it. The people sitting there move away. Wish I could. But he might hit me. Trapped! Train rattles on. Can't breathe.

'Poor sheila,' a boy a few seats away says. Wish he'd rescue me. Wish someone would. Sit rigid. Don't look at him.

Nearly at my stop. He's still punching. Have to get out.

'Excuse me, please,' I squeak. He stops punching, moves his feet aside. Squeeze past quickly expecting to dodge or feel punches.

On the platform I cry.

I hate going on trains, except to work. That's become all right if I ignore touches that don't feel right.

Will I go by train to Jenny's wedding?

When the other girls at the hostel send *Inability to Accept* cards, they are sorry, but I'm not when I send mine to Jenny. Not really. I'd love to see her but I don't want her to see me, to see what I've become. That's the real problem. I'm ashamed that I won't fit in and I don't know what to do or what to wear or anything. Wish I could go and see her but not be seen.

Jenny doesn't write again. I imagine she's too happy and busy being a married woman.

Although I get anxious about going out, I don't get anxious much at work. I know I'm a good worker and that gives me confidence. People who come to make claims on their life insurance policies can be sure that I'll get their money through as soon as is humanly possible. They smile at me and thank me. Mostly. Some people come in angry.

'There has to be a mistake here, Miss. They can't really be serious offering me two hundred dollars. I've been paying in for twenty years!'

'I'll check the quote,' I tell them, then I add the bit that I've been taught to say, to try to intimidate them: 'They calculate the value on a computer at head office in Melbourne.' Computers are mysteries that don't make mistakes.

Some people shrug and leave when I tell them about our infallible intimidation machine but others get more angry and yell at me. I freeze, then I back away slowly.

'You'll have to learn how to talk to them, Kate,' Dorina says. She's efficient and calm and can cope with anything. 'They won't bite your head off.' I know they won't but anger makes me so frightened. I'm better than I was when I first started counter work. I force myself not to cringe when customers shove papers at me and not to twitch when they thump the counter.

If Dorina isn't in the office, I go to Daniel, but he talks to people with his nose in the air, puffing smoke around them and they get angrier. It's better to ask Mr Mansouriani. It's embarrassing asking the boss but he's good at talking to customers.

Sometimes Mr Mansouriani tells me to bring him a file and he holds my hand and looks in my eyes for too long when I pass it to him. I have to pull my hand away and pretend it didn't happen, because I don't know what else to do. Why does he do it? He's old, about thirty or something. Surely he doesn't like me. I'm only seventeen. I'm supposed to meet a nice boy, not an old man.

I will meet one. One day. I suppose. Some girls at work go on cruises to meet boys but I'd be so shy of all those cruising strangers. What do you say to them? If they wanted to talk about claims on their life insurance policies, calmly, I'd be all right, but what about the rest of the time? Oh well, can't afford it anyway.

Dorina has a budget. She organises little labelled envelopes on her desk each pay day. After the paymaster has handed out our pay packets she puts the exact amount of cash into each envelope. There's one each for board, fares, entertainment, holiday, savings and so on. I can't imagine needing all those envelopes. I just pay board and fares and put the bit that's left in the bank.

Denise, who works in the department next to ours, loves shopping for clothes and shoes. She loves to be fashionable and must spend all her money on that. Sometimes when we go shopping at lunchtime she helps me pick out new clothes, but am I allowed to wear short skirts or blouses with the top button open? We weren't allowed to at Burnside and the girls at church don't leave the top button open. And do I want things that show my breasts are big? No I don't, even though Denise wishes she could swap with me.

'Can't afford it,' I tell her. That stops her trying to make me buy things she reckons I should get.

We go to the cosmetics counter and Denise tries some makeup on her hand.

'Would you like a demonstration?' the sales woman asks. 'It will only take half an hour.'

Denise agrees.

'But we'll be late back to work,' I whisper.

'Doesn't matter. Phyllis's away.'

'Yeah, but Mr Mansouriani isn't.'

'Oh well, stay 'til it's time to get back.'

When Denise arrives back at work she looks beautiful. She always wears lipstick but now she's got mascara, blush and eyeshadow, all the right colour for her skin.

'Busy are we, Miss Shayler?' Mr Mansouriani asks with a grin as he catches a small group of us inspecting Denise's face. 'You look lovely, Miss Wickens, but this is not a beauty parlour.' I think he's nice not to yell at us. We should be working because they pay us for that, not for talking about makeup. I go to my desk determined to get some of that stuff Denise has got.

The lady at the cosmetics counter is old and she tells me what to get. It doesn't feel like a bad thing to do when she says I should buy it. I wish she could come to some clothes shops with me. I practise putting the lipstick, foundation, powder and blush on at home, when Emily isn't in our room. She thinks makeup is sinful and it makes you look cheap. The girls at work think it looks good.

On weekends I still go back to Dad's house because I can go to fellowship and church close by. My brother, Ken, still lives there but he's often out. We seem to be getting on all right when we meet.

On Sunday I get ready for church and decide to wear my makeup. Boys at fellowship say hello to me but they don't try to talk any more. Maybe if I look nice they will and they won't care that I'm shy. Most girls there don't wear makeup but they don't need improving like I do.

Cheryl sits beside me like she's been doing since I started coming here. I like her quiet humour and gentleness. She kneels to pray and when she's finished she sits again and says her usual quiet hello. Suddenly she looks again and whispers, 'Wow. You look more lovely than usual! Where did you learn to put makeup on?'

'Makeup counter in town,' I whisper. 'Is it all right?'

'It's great. Mum won't let me have any. You're lucky that way.'

No mum to stop me but no mum to tell me it's all right either. The boys don't treat me any differently with my makeup on and it starts to feel like glue as the temperature rises. Oh well, you must just have to grin and bear that. Scraping it off feels good but I'm going to keep wearing it.

Mr and Mrs Jenson have invited me to lunch at their place on Sundays after church. They live near Dad's house and have four sons. The three eldest are in fellowship. The elder one goes out with one of the girls from church and the next two don't have girl-friends. I like Gavin but he hardly knows I exist.

They all like joking and I don't have to say much at lunch because they're so busy talking. Mrs Jenson knows I'm shy and she doesn't put too much pressure on me to talk. Mr Jenson talks to me about doing more study and improving myself. Makeup isn't enough for him.

'Have you thought about going back to school to do your HSC?'

'I have to work! I haven't got any money.' I don't add that I'm too dumb to study.

'There must be some sort of government funding you can get. You look into it. A girl like you should be entitled to some kind of support.'

A girl like me? Why would the government have anything to do with me?

Soon I'm able to tell Mr Jenson that I'm studying insurance. Dorina wants promotions but it's hard for girls to get them so she's decided to study for the Insurance Institute exams and become an associate, whatever that is.

'Do it with me,' she suggests. 'It'd help you get ahead.'

Everyone thinks I still need improving to get ahead. Do I want to study and get ahead? Don't know. I'm too dumb, aren't I? Anyway, when I meet a nice boy I'll just leave and have babies. That's what girls do.

'Come and keep me company,' Dorina pleads. 'They're all blokes. Come on. Please. What have we got to lose?'

The course is easy and we both pass the exams with no trouble. Mr Mansouriani is pleased and he recommends us for a pay rise.

The girls from church are going out to dinner at the Island Trader restaurant at Circular Quay and they invite me to come too. I've never been to a restaurant but I know you have to get dressed up in better clothes than your work or weekend ones.

'Come on,' Denise says. 'We'll find you something nice.' It takes them a while but Denise and a shop assistant persuade me to buy a white suit and Denise says to wear my pink polo-neck singlet under it.

After work I change into my new outfit and walk to the Quay. I'm early so I wander around looking at ferries and ships and people. There are lots of sailors in funny-looking uniforms, speaking what sounds like French, exploring the Quay too. I like listening to them because sometimes I can pick up words I know from school French.

Suddenly a sailor is too close, mumbling beery words in my face. Panic. Want to shout, 'Go away.' Didn't learn that at school. 'You want good time?' Hand on my bottom. Struggle to get away. Darkness. Walk fast. Sailor follows. In my face, beer words. 'Kiss me.' Stinking mouth too close. Turn away. 'You come with me, 'ave good time.' Hand on my breast! Dying of embarrassment. Fear. Shame. Dark shame. Want to vomit. Pull away. Walk fast. People watching. Doing nothing. Want to die. Run. Swallow bile. At the restaurant at last. Run to ladies room. Wash. See tear-smudged mascara. Wash again. Try to calm down. Cheryl beside me.

'G'day, Kate. We were waiting out the front but you ran right past. Oh! Are you all right?'

'Yeah. No. A man just tried to . . . to . . . bother me.'

'Oh the creep! Are you okay?'

'Yeah.' Splash water over my face. Rub off the rest of my makeup. I am all right. I am all right.

But none of the other girls got pawed by a sleazy sailor. Why did I? There must be something about me . . . Is it because I'm bad inside and it shows on the outside? Church boys don't like me but sleazy sailors do. I hate the lot of them.

'You should have yelled at him.'

'Yes, and kicked him where it hurts.'

'Called the police. Who do they think they are!'

They all have ways of handling it. I didn't think of any of them. I just felt small and frightened. Didn't know what to do. Still a lot to learn.

We get off the subject and I start to calm down and watch and listen. I learn how to choose and order a meal. As we eat, someone asks me about my job and as the others join in I realise that being a clerk is the one thing I know more about than anyone else here. They are all uni students. All the same, I'm glad when attention is off me and I can listen to the chatter and explore the delights of a Matterhorn Waffle. I like these girls and I start to relax with them.

Today Dorina is beaming and flashing a diamond ring. She and Neil are to be married in six months time. Now her payday parade of envelopes is different. She shifts from 'holiday fund' to 'wedding fund'. She starts bringing wedding magazines to work and we all discuss wedding dresses. Gowns not dresses. I try to imagine wearing one myself but none of the brides in the magazines wears glasses and they're so skinny. Jenny must have got like that. Why hasn't even a tiny hint of it happened to me yet?

'Do you think you could handle Dorina's job, Kate?' Mr Mansouriani asks when she gets her promotion. 'Get her to show you the ropes before she goes. I think you could do it with no trouble. You're doing your Institute courses, aren't you?'

I don't tell him that they were so boring I've decided not to do any more next year. I get my first promotion and say goodbye to Dorina, though we remain friends after she moves on. Our fellowship groups meet close to each other and we have some combined outings.

'Kev wants to ask you out,' Neil tells me. 'Come on. I'll introduce you.'

'No!' What's happening to me? Kev has seemed nice and normal from a distance but I'm in a panic now.

'What's wrong?' Neil asks.

'I don't want to,' is all I can say.

'Don't you like him?'

'Don't know him.'

'Well, he wants to know you. Come on.'

'Don't want to.'

Later Dorina asks what the problem was. 'He's a lovely guy. A really nice man. He's a crop duster so he's really rich too.'

I have to come up with an explanation.

'Crop dusters are high risks. Remember, we learnt that in Risk Assessment. High premiums because they get killed easily.'

'Oh statistics!' Dorina scoffs. 'What's really the matter?'

'He's bald!' I think he looks nice regardless of his shiny head but I'm still afraid of something I can't explain.

'Yeah, but he's only twenty-four.'

'He's too old for me.'

Dorina can't work me out. She knows I want to find a nice boy, yet I won't even meet this one. I can't work myself out either. I can't just say that I'm frightened. Especially when I don't understand why.

Doing my job well continues to feed my confidence in the office.

'Cleared your in-tray again, eh,' Roy remarks. He's older than me and came to our department a year ago.

'Yes. Verna's up to date too. Do you have anything I can do?'

'Really? You can do my filing, if you like.' He hands me a bundle of papers and I file them.

'What are you doing?' Daniel asks when he sees me at the wrong filing cabinet.

'Helping Roy. I've finished my work.'

'Can't you just slow down? You make the rest of us look bad when you're always finished and looking for something to do. Can't you read a book or something?'

Read a book? They pay me to do insurance work, not read books. If Daniel didn't make phone calls all day he'd get through his work too. I'm too scared to say that to his face. 'I like working,' I tell him.

'Well, when you finish that I'll give you some. You can go through my files and take out ones where I'm waiting for documents before I can settle.'

I have to read the files and they're intriguing. Who needs books! These files are much more interesting than my boring ones. Daniel does death claims, so he has to find out who the beneficiaries are and what the causes of death were.

I don't like reading books because I'm too slow but Daniel's files are like short stories and I become an avid reader. Mr Tihu died in his homemade sauna while drunk. The coroner, whoever he is, can't decide if it was an accidental death, suicide or something sinister related to the person who went into the sauna with the deceased but went home and left him asleep in there. Or there's Mr Rivett who was found dead in his kitchen with his gas oven turned on but not lit. Was it suicide or did the unidentifiable substance in his stomach cause him to faint before he could light the gas? I want to read more and more. Help Daniel with his work.

Daniel doesn't want me to help him much but I've had a glimpse into his job and I know it's more interesting than mine. He's been here for ages. I wonder if he'll get promoted. His position is the most senior in our department except for Mr Mansouriani's so I probably wouldn't get it.

Mr Mansouriani gains promotion next and he moves to an office around the corner. I won't have him striding past me every morning, grinning and demanding, 'Righto, Miss Shayler. What's on the agenda?' Or striding out in the afternoons with, 'All right, Miss Shayler. Let's go home.' We've got into the habit of getting the lift down to Martin Place together in the afternoons. I've forgotten I was ever afraid to be alone with John, the lift driver, or with he and Mr Mansouriani together.

It's a few years now since my father died and his estate still isn't settled.

'Kate, it's Ken. Uncle Jack says we have to clear the house out so it can be sold.' Uncle Jack is our half-sister Zelda's ex-husband. We hardly ever see Zelda, who is very beautiful but cold and harsh. Uncle Jack, who stayed friends with Dad after the divorce and is now his executor, had been a regular, jovial visitor at Burnside. We rarely see him now because he moved out of Sydney.

He said Ken, Kerry and I can take what we want from Dad's house and the rest will be sold. I want to keep everything as it is and pretend our family never fell apart. But it has and now I'm collecting mementos of what might have been. What might be too. I take two of each dinner set item, ones that aren't cracked, and some cutlery because I'll need them in my glory box. I take a milk jug and sugar bowl, as well as some doilies that my mother might have made. I'd like a clock but where would it fit in my room at the hostel? We clean the house and, because we don't know what to do with all the stuff, Ken digs a huge hole in the long backyard and we bury everything we don't want except the furniture. We bury pots and pans, crockery, photos of people we don't know, books and some mysterious craft things. Uncle Jack will have to deal with the furniture and the clocks that I haven't got room to keep.

Ken moves to a boarding house. I hope he'll be happy there. I hope there won't be too many rules, because he's done what he likes for years and if there's rules like the ones at the hostel, he'll hate it.

Hostel rules seemed reasonable when I first came to live here. I hadn't been out of Burnside long and I needed rules to show me how to fit in. Now, a few years later, they're becoming a pest, especially the one that says we must be home by ten thirty at night. Or is it a blessing? Sometimes it's hard to tell.

Lots of the girls at church swoon when Charles, so handsome and charming, comes. He's a flight steward, so he might be in Paris or London or Hong Kong instead of Marrickville. He's just moved into a new flat not far from the hostel but he still comes to church, in his sports car, when he's home.

'Hey, Kate, can I give you a lift home?' he asks.

Red hot face replies without thinking that Mrs Jenson has

invited us all around for supper and I've told her I'll be there.

'Good. We'll go there first and then you can have supper with me.'

Red hot face replies, 'Oh all right.' Blundering girl wondering if it's at all possible that this perfect man could like her. We say goodnight to the Jensons after supper and Charles escorts me to his car.

He opens the car door and I wish he hadn't heard me gasp.

'Yes, it's like a lounge or bed or something, isn't it?' he laughs as I try to relax into my seat.

Why did I worry about what to talk about on the way home? The car is so noisy we give up talking unless we come to a red light.

'Nothing seems to be open. How about coming to my place and I'll make supper?' Charles suggests.

Your place! I can't. You're a man. I can't go to a man's place for supper! What if it's as scary as it feels? What will I do? I tell myself that he's a Christian, so he couldn't be bad. It'll be all right.

'Have a seat,' he says, guiding me to the lounge. 'Now, let's see. We could have a cold drink or would you like coffee?'

'Coffee, please.' I've never had it but sophisticated people drink coffee and I hope Charles is impressed.

'Coffee it is, then. In fact, let's have cappuccino. Would you like that?'

'What is it?' I ask too quickly to be impressive.

'You'll love it. Wait and see.'

He disappears into the kitchen but soon he's heading for the door saying, 'Be right back. Just have to dash out and get some cream. Won't be long.'

I gaze around not game to get up and wander in case he comes back and catches me snooping. I wait and try to stay calm. What on earth is cappuccino? Is it alcohol? Or some kind of special cake that goes with coffee? Eventually I wonder what the time is. I find the clock. It's ten thirty! I should be home and Charles is out there somewhere searching for cream to make cappo something. He'll think I'm so boring when I tell him I have to go home.

'Why?' he asks.

'It's the hostel rule. You get locked out if you're late.'

'Well, can't you say you were at church supper or something? Is it really that strict? What happens after you're locked out?'

'You throw dirt at the windows and hope one of the girls lets you in. Then you say you were in earlier but forgot to cross your name off the book as you came through the door.'

'But ten thirty's so early! It's crazy. Who gets home at ten thirty?'

'I do. Or should. I'll have to go.'

'Coffee first. Might as well be hung for a sheep as a lamb.'

I want to go now but I want to appear to have some control over my life.

'Stay for a quick coffee. We won't do cappuccino. One quick cup of coffee.'

'All right.'

Soon Charles is dropping me off and letting the car roll slowly away so Miss Driver, the matron in charge of the hostel, won't hear the motor. I wake Brenda by throwing pebbles at her window and she lets me in. I cross my name off the book at the door. Sue isn't in yet either. I leave the chain off for her and go to bed wondering if Prince Charming will ever invite me anywhere again. He doesn't but he's always warm and charming.

These days people talk about 'nasho' and being 'called up'. I wonder why, in the 1970's they're talking about war. It ended in 1945! I listen to the fellowship lot and think how clever they are to know what it's all about. They say if any of the boys is called up he'll have to join the army. They wouldn't be, though, would they? They're so young and they've got jobs or training to do. They don't seem like people who'd go off somewhere and kill people or become part of 'our glorious sacrifice' that we learnt about at primary school. People talk about Viet-something too. I've seen it on the newspaper posters. Some people think our army shouldn't go and others think they should. I don't know what to think, so I stay quiet. The government is in charge and don't you just have to do what they say? None of the boys gets called up.

Some of them with cars start doing shift work, so sometimes there's no-one to drive me home. I think I'm becoming a nuisance as the novelty of having to go to the hostel before they go joy riding to milk bars or to the Cross wears off.

'It'd be good if you had a car,' someone says.

'How much do they cost?' How do you buy one? How do you know what sort to get? How do you drive them?

'Depends what you get. But we could help you look.'

'Yeah. The boys could help you find a secondhand one. Cost much less.'

'But I don't know how to drive!'

'I could teach you,' Lance says quietly. I hardly know Lance. He doesn't come to fellowship regularly but I've heard him say he'll have to register for nasho in the next draft. He seems too gentle and smiling to go to a war. Even so, the thought of being in a car alone with him, or any boy, makes me anxious. My mouth sticks shut after I squeeze a 'Thanks' from it.

On the train home I imagine having a car of my own but my imagination gets stuck after I get in. How do other people learn to drive? The boys at fellowship learnt from their older brothers or their fathers. Ken rides a motorbike but I don't know if he can drive a car. I've heard of driving schools but they're incredibly expensive.

'Cheryl, do you know how much secondhand cars cost?'

'Oh don't get a secondhand one. You'll have no end of trouble.'

'What do you mean?'

'You'll be breaking down all the time and depending on who-ever comes along to help you. Dad reckons you're just buying someone else's garbage.'

'But if the boys found a good secondhand one, how much would it be?'

She guesses an amount that equals about five years' salary for me. I'm relieved. I don't have to explore the idea any more, because it is out of the question. I'll just have to give up fellowship and night church and stay home. By myself.

When Lance offers to teach me to drive again, I tell him, 'Um, it wouldn't be any use. Can't afford a car.'

'You wouldn't need much. We could get a really cheap one and work on it. I've got a friend who was selling one for five hundred bucks and it only needed a bit of work. Not that you'd want that one but . . .'

'I can't work on cars!' I interrupt.

'No, but I could and the others would help out.'

'I haven't got five hundred dollars.'

'Well, let Lance teach you and in the meantime you could save up,' Cheryl suggests.

They're all keen for me to learn to drive and I've run out of excuses. Wish I wasn't so worried about being alone with Lance. By the time he arrives, I'm a tight ball of nerves who forces her arm to straighten enough to hand over the L plates. Lance is cheerful as we drive off and I think he's describing what he's doing to make the car work. I'm too tense to understand. Then he's saying, 'How about you get in the driver's seat now?'

'What! Me! No, I don't know what to do. What if I crash?'

'You'll be all right. We'll just stay in the side streets. You know your way around here, don't you?'

'Not much.' I've only been on the road to the station and the shops, roads I need to know for walking, not for driving.

'Can't I watch you a bit more?' And maybe hear what you're saying next time. Maybe even understand some of it.

'You could, but if you want to learn, the sooner you start, the better. This is a quiet street. Come on. Give it a go.'

We change seats and Lance waits. 'How?' a feeble voice asks.

'Turn the key.' I don't look but I think he's enjoying himself.

I turn the key. The motor starts! 'Help! Oh it's not moving.'

'Put it in first.'

'First what?'

'Gear!'

Oh yes. I remember gear, gear stick, top of the aitch is first. It still doesn't move.

'Now the clutch,' Lance says gently.

Clutch? Oh clutch! 'Which one is it again?'

'Remember A, B, C. Accelerator, brake and clutch.' I look down at the pedals and press the clutch one. 'You're in first. Yep. Now let the clutch pedal . . . Uh! Slowly . . . Mm. Start again. It stalls if you let your foot off too quick.'

Stall. That must be what lurching forward and stopping suddenly with your head a fraction off the windscreen is.

I do a few more stalls but at last the car is slowly moving forward. This is all right. It'd take a long time to get to fellowship . . .

'Now into second. Foot on the clutch, move the gear to second. Yeah, straight down. Foot off . . . Not too fa . . . ast. It's all right. Start again. Don't worry, this happens to everyone.'

Driving around quiet streets in second gear is quite a challenge, especially for drivers stuck behind me. Eventually we come to an intersection where I need to make a right-hand turn across heavy traffic. There are no lights.

'Can you do this?' I ask Lance. 'I'm too scared.'

'You'll be right. Just concentrate.'

'But there's cars on the road!'

'Yeah. They go on roads. Stay calm. There'll be a break soon. Just do what you've been doing so far. Only quicker.'

My arms and legs forget what they've been doing as we wait for the break.

'Okay. After this blue car. You'll need to be quick. Oh stop!'

Sitting in a cloud of grit. Grit in my mouth. Open eyes. Smashed bricks all around. Lance's shaky voice. 'Are you all right?'

Who am I? Where am I? What's all this mess? Old man wandering around shaking his head.

'Is she all right?'

'Can you get out?' Lance's voice breaks through the daze and I move in slow motion with him into a lounge room. I can hear the old man telling him it's happened so many times before and something has just been repaired after the last one.

'Did I do that to the fence?' I whisper to Lance.

'Yeah. But you're all right, aren't you?'

'Yeah. Are you?'

'I'm okay.'

'I'm so sorry. Look what I've done to your car! I'm sorry.'

'It's a bit of a mess but I'll get it fixed. Brother's a panel beater. You're really all right, are you?'

'Yeah, but what did I do wrong?'

'Hit the accelerator instead of the brake, I think. Went straight across and through the fence.'

I'll die of embarrassment when everyone finds out what an idiot I am, that my first driving lesson ended with me being dropped off in a tow truck and Lance disappearing down the road in the same truck with his battered car dragging along behind. I'm buying a brick fence instead of a car.

Lance is going out with Cheryl but he still smiles and chats with me. He doesn't hold a grudge against me and didn't embarrass me by telling everyone what I did to his car.

A better solution to my travel problem might be to move. I'll have to ask someone how to find a flat. I'll be twenty-one soon and, although Miss Driver has let me have the one single room at the hostel because I've been there the longest, she thinks it would be good for me to follow up on my plan to find a flat. The hostel is meant to tide you over until you find your feet in the city. It's not a long-term thing.

'One of the others might like to share with you. Like Kerry and Jocelyn did,' she says. 'That would reduce your rent bill.' Kerry came to live here for a while and became friends with Jocelyn who lived here too. They went off to a flat together. But this little sunny room I have now has shown me that being by myself is bliss. Imagine a whole place of my own! Bathroom. Kitchen. The lot. And best of all, no pretending to be normal. Just be myself and do what I like.

Kerry is married with a baby now. I can't understand how she managed to find a boyfriend so quickly. Her husband Mike is in the army and he's going to Vietnam. I met him once and we didn't click. I think he thought I was a snob or something. That must be the impression I gave by not knowing what to do with a brother-in-law or a baby nephew. To be honest, I hardly know what to do with a little sister who feels more like someone I know than a close friend like most people's sisters seem to be. I don't go and see my brother-in-law off to Vietnam. He wouldn't care if I was there or not. The girls at work think I should have gone. Now I feel bad. It's all so confusing. I still don't know what to think about the war either.

A dreadful mood is about at church today. 'Lance's been called up,' Cheryl says, her red eyes starting to fill with tears.

'Oh no!' I exclaim, wishing I could think of something to make the red and the tears go away. Wish I'd read newspapers or watched the news and knew more about what the wretched war was for.

'It mightn't mean he has to go to Vietnam, but he might.' Cheryl tries very hard not to cry.

'He can't go to the war!'

'I know. But we've prayed about it and he thinks if God wants him to go, he'll go.'

How could God want Lance to go? Or any of our lot? Or anyone, including my brother-in-law? How can the government decide that Lance has to change himself into a different kind of person and go to war? *Please God, please don't send Lance to war.* That's my prayer every night and morning and any other time of the day I think about it. I don't look at the Cenotaph in Martin Place as I go to work.

Mr and Mrs Jenson want to give me a party for my twenty-first birthday. I don't want one because I hate being the centre of attention. I say, 'No thanks,' when they ask. It's months away so maybe they'll forget.

'Let them give you one,' Helen says. Helen is a Sunday school teacher who invites me to lunch at her place sometimes. She lives with her parents and is a legal secretary. I'm getting comfortable in my friendship with her and because she is ten years older than me, I ask her opinion sometimes. She gives good advice. 'You'll be all right and they'll just love doing it for you,' she tells me. I agree to have the party.

Denise and I ransack material shops at lunchtimes until we find the perfect dress pattern and fabric. I bought a sewing machine a couple of months ago so I set about making my very modern dress for my party and I dye some shoes to match.

Helen says she'd like to give me a watch for my twenty-first. I've wanted one for ages but they cost so much! I've got a little alarm clock at home and there are clocks on stations and a clock in the office. There's also the huge clock on the GPO in Martin Place that chimes every quarter hour, so I don't really need a watch. But, oh how I want one! I've been trying to save up but I won't get myself one 'til I'm thirty-five or something.

'But they cost so much!' I tell Helen. 'Parents usually do that, don't they, buy watches for people's twenty-firsts?'

'Yes, but you only turn twenty-one once.'

'But I've looked at how much they —'

'Once ever,' she interrupts. 'In your whole life. Let me do it. I'd really like to and I wouldn't offer if I couldn't afford it. No. I won't go bankrupt and be carted off to gaol.'

We go to town and I pick out a watch with a gold mesh band. Helen is pleased and I feel grateful but secretly ashamed of how much I want to be worthy of having that watch. I don't know why Helen likes me enough to do this.

Invitations for the party go out and I finish making my dress and put a last coat of dye on my shoes. I should have made the dress short-sleeved so my watch would show.

Lots of people come to the party and I'm amazed at all the presents I'm getting. I've never had this many! Just as well they can't see what I'm thinking. I want to rip them open greedily and see what I've got! Instead I do it like other people do. Read the card first and say how nice it is. Undo the ribbon and sticky tape slowly so they won't think you're greedy. Say what a beautiful cut-glass vase it is and don't blush too much when they say I can put it in my glory box.

I'm glad Ken has come even though I'm the only person he knows. He looks very suave in his suit and his modern hairdo and dark moustache. Kerry couldn't come. She's busy with the babies.

Being the centre of attention is agony but I only have to be there while the speeches are made. I feel so proud of my brother when he makes his. I'm too nervous to listen to what he says but he smiles a lot and sounds so confident, as if he makes speeches every day. I couldn't do that. I wonder how he learnt. He seems to know his way around his life. Mr Jenson makes a nice speech too. They've got me a beautiful cake like the ones Dad used to bring us at Burnside. After I cut it, the games go on and I fade from the centre. People laugh and chat and then it's time to go home. I wonder why I didn't want a party so much. It was fun mostly.

People say that when I have a flat of my own I'll be able to have parties all the time. Will I? Why? Anyway, I haven't found out how to get a flat yet. I went to look in a real estate window once but the prices for flats were about three times my wage! There must be some other place people like me go to find them.

Helen saves me.

'Gillian is moving to Broken Hill parish. Have you been to her flat? It's at the back of a house in Clyde Street. Why don't you have a look? It's cheap rent, so you could afford it. You'd be closer to all of us then too.'

Soon I'm packing my belongings and loading them into the boot of Helen's car. The biggest item is my sewing machine. Girls at the hostel will miss it. Miss Driver wishes me well and tells me that my dad and Burnside would be proud of how well I've worked through my life since I left the home. That feels like a lifetime ago but I like that someone would be proud of me.

'You come back and have lunch with us sometimes, won't you?' She smiles.

'Thank you. That would be good,' I say.

Now I'm on my own. No-one around to ask for an opinion or advice.

Now that I'm twenty-one I have to confront a problem I haven't thought much about. Voting. The government is in charge. I'd feel so guilty voting against it, because you don't criticise authority figures. Big trouble happens if you do. Once I asked Dad who he voted for and he said Labor, the working man's party. That's who I'll vote for, but I hope they're already the government, because I won't have to go against the ones in charge then. It's unimaginable that a whole lot of people do.

FLAT

My new landlady is Mrs Thomas. She is ancient and is followed everywhere by her equally ancient collie, Prince. When he pants, his breath is enough to bowl me back to the hostel. His general odour is not much better. Someone ought to tell him about doggy deodorant if there is such a thing. Luckily I don't have to spend much time with them. The flat is self-contained. Its front door is the only trap. It's inside Mrs Thomas's laundry, where I have to leave the rent each fortnight so I don't disturb her.

Got to get my key out before I get to the laundry. Prince has taken it upon himself to bound from the house into the laundry and huff a greeting at me when I'm coming or going. 'Dodge the dog,' is my homecoming chant.

'Gosh, you've got it looking nice. Fancy having your own place with no rules!' Cheryl remarks. 'You can do whatever you like here.'

I don't know what she has in mind but she seems impressed and, what? Jealous? Jealous of me? I'd rather have a family to live in, rules or no rules, or a plan to make one like she and Lance have. But maybe it'll just take time for me to learn what exciting things happen in a flat.

Meanwhile, it's fun going to the supermarket and buying whatever food I want, including tomato sauce, Burnside's biggest gourmet item, without permission from anybody. I feel uneasy about spending my money without approval but I have to eat and clean, don't I? Cooking is fun. At Burnside I helped cook meals for thirty but meals for one are so small. I soon learn that tomato sauce doesn't go with everything after all. Not really. It's just a symbol of my freedom. Coming home to be alone is wonderful. No expectations. No limits. No timetable. As long as I don't think about wanting a family.

Sunday lunch with the Jensons is a tradition now and the table is extended to include the boys' girlfriends, who are fellowship girls too.

Today Mrs Jenson has cooked a casserole which soon disappears and after the table is cleared she brings out a huge fruit salad in a bowl.

'Not the Stuart crystal one, dear?' Mr Jenson asks.

'This is the only one big enough,' she replies. 'Anyway, the crystal one is so heavy.'

A discussion begins about Stuart crystal and I'm relaxed enough to join in.

'I don't like crystal. I like plain glass with no pattern.'

The silence makes me look up and that is when I remember that just about everyone in the room gave me crystal for my twenty-first birthday!

Eventually someone thinks of a new conversation topic and I don't, can't, join in.

Helen lives with her parents and I've met them when I've had lunch at their house. I'm not as nervous of them as I was when I first met them.

'You could do more study and improve your position,' Mr Belling tells me.

'She's all right where she is, aren't you, love?' Mrs Belling says kindly.

When people look like they're about to argue, I want to disappear. I reply quickly, 'Some other people have said that too but I can't afford to.' And I'm too scared to try. Too dumb. I'm safe as I am.

Why does everyone still want me to improve myself anyway? I'm doing all right, aren't I? I feel good when they tell me I'm intelligent enough to study but does it mean I won't be good enough until I get the HSC? Good enough for what? And who?

'Dad means you could choose from more interesting jobs,' Helen explains as if she's read my mind. 'You're wasted as a clerk.'

'But if Daniel leaves I might get his job. The death claims,' I tell them.

'Humph! Kill you to do that forever,' Mr Belling says, laughing.

Most of the time, if I don't look too deeply at my life, I like it. I've got a job, a flat to live in by myself and nice friends. I go to a church where people are nice to me. All I need to complete the scene is a nice boy to make a home and family of my own with. Sometimes I want it more than ever. Helen says she's sure it will happen and that I just haven't met the right person yet.

Tonight I walk home after church because none of the boys with a car has come. I like walking by myself, quietly humming the hymns we've sung or thinking about the sermon. Footsteps behind me. I turn to see if it's anyone I know. A dark shape moves quickly behind a bush. Must be where they live. No, they're walking again. I walk faster. Footsteps match my pace. Turning again, I see the shape move out of view. Am I imagining it or am I being followed?

I cross the road. Footsteps follow me. I am being followed. Don't be silly. It's just someone going home like you are. I cross back and that's when I know. I am being followed! My heart is beating out of my chest. I'm going to be murdered. Here in my street. Think. Yes, Megan from fellowship lives about here. I rush up to the porch of her house and bang on the door. Come on!

Open up! Bang again. No-one home. Trapped on this porch. Great time to remember Megan's away with her parents. Can't stay here all night. Have to get home. What if he follows me around to my flat? Stay hidden. Trembling on the porch for what seems like an hour doesn't solve the problem. Have to make a run for it.

Go!

At my door I fumble with my key, hoping Prince comes out and looks menacing in the dark. He doesn't. Inside at last. Door slammed shut. Stand in the dark.

Cry. I don't want to be alone. I want a family to come home with. How much longer is it going to take for me to be normal? What else do I have to do to be good enough for nice boys? I pray every day for God to help me be acceptable. I pray again now, fervently. I hate feeling this small and worthless.

'You haven't been married, have you?' I say to Helen, fumbling towards asking her what else I need to do. 'It's just, you're pretty and slim and all but you're not married.'

She looks amused. 'Well, thank you. No, but I'd like to be married.'

'Warren likes you, doesn't he?'

'Yes. We're good friends but I just haven't met the right man to marry.'

'Me either,' I reply.

'There's plenty of time for you!'

'Do you think I will meet someone?'

'Of course you will, with your beautiful face.'

'Sounds like my aunty.

'Aunty ? I thought you didn't have any family except Ken and Kerry.'

'Oh , I've got two aunties who were close friends of my mother. I hardly ever see them. Or my godmother. She's part of their family too. Anyway, Aunty Dot said I'd meet a nice boy to marry

30

because I've got nice teeth and eyes. I grimace to show my teeth and we both laugh. Helen laughs but doesn't take it further. I want to.

'I haven't met any nice boys; well, the fellowship boys are nice but they don't like me . . .'

'Yes they do!' she interrupts.

'No. I mean to go out with.'

'Oh. They're all pairing up, aren't they? They've known each other for so long. Don't worry. You'll meet someone. Bad news about Lance, isn't it?'

'What news?'

'He's going to Vietnam.'

'No!' We sit quietly and then talk about how we'll have to pray that the war ends before he gets there. It's been going for years and people are marching against it but that doesn't seem to make any difference. I want to go to that Menzies person and tell him he can't send Lance. Not gentle, kind Lance. He and Cheryl have plans.

'God will care for him,' Helen declares. 'Keep praying.'

There's a song on the radio called 'Telephone to Jesus' and I think the line will be jammed with my calls all day long as I pray for a boyfriend and for Lance and for Cheryl and for my brother-in-law and Kerry and the babies. I hope Ken doesn't get sent. He hasn't been in the draft yet.

Later, as Helen and I use the same mirror to put our makeup on, Helen gives me a playful nudge.

'Oh, take your lovely face away while I'm doing mine.' I look at her; there's no comparison. She's dainty and pretty and her eyes work without glasses. I'll never be like her. She must mean I look nice, though. I hope I do.

We drive to Jane and Paul's house for dinner. After the meal Helen and Paul will go to the local hospital to do a service there and I'll stay here until church starts. We've done this a few times now and Jane and I are developing a kind of friendship that is made easy by her little girl, Becky. I like listening to Jane talk to

31

Becky. Sometimes she asks me if I remember my childhood.

'Not much,' I tell her and change the subject back to Becky. I don't try to remember what a dreadful child I was. I bury that deep down where no-one can see it.

When Jane talks about herself I wonder why she isn't self-confident. She's tall, slim, creative, funny, married and has Becky. Her sense of humour is the best. Her old car, named Aggy to rhyme with a nickname she has for her mother-in-law, is falling apart. The lining in the roof is held up by a row of nappy pins. 'All part of my emergency kit,' she informs anyone who asks. I often find myself laughing before she's even said some of her favourite phrases.

Becky sees Helen and me at the door before we've rung the bell. 'Arny Ellen! Cake! Arny Ellen! Cake!' she squeals to tell her parents we're here. She'll learn to say our names one day but I hope it won't be soon.

'Hello, you spirds,' Jane smiles as Becky drags us in. It's groovy to call girls 'birds' and Jane plays with words a lot. I'd been grinning with anticipation before she greeted us.

'Dumma Off,' Becky demands.

Helen and I look blank.

'She wants you to read *Drummer Hoff*,' Jane translates. 'I've done it a squillion times today. The whole British army gets a canon ready but Drummer Hoff fires it off.'

'Dumma Off fide id op,' Becky rumbles deeply.

'Any takers? I'm begging you,' Jane laughs, clasping her hands.

'You can, Cake. I've got to sort the music out for the service,' Helen says.

I'm delighted. I sit on the lounge and wait for my little friend to bring her book. I don't know why she loves me but she does and it didn't take more than a visit or two like this one. She is pure joy and she makes me so want babies of my own.

'Bitty Cake.' She smiles as she climbs onto my lap, clutching a battered storybook. She gives me a kiss and repeats, 'Bitty Cake.'

'"Pretty Kate," she's saying. You do look a stunner in blue,' Jane says. 'I'll leave you two to Dumma Off.'

While I read I start to believe that I might really look nice. I read each paragraph and Becky sits waiting to join in. 'Dumma Off fide id op!' she yells, mostly at the right moment.

'Dinner's ready,' Jane calls. 'Come on, you two.' Then louder, 'Paul!'

He comes through as Becky and I stand up. 'Gee, Aunty Cake, you'd be a bit of all right if you weren't so fat.'

Knife stabs my heart. Eyes burn. I dissolve in despair. Why did I ever dare think I'd look nice enough to impress anyone? Why did they all tell me I look nice? Why is he such a pig to tell me the truth just when I was happy and hopeful?

'I have to go,' I blurt at them all. I rush out and run home to my flat, burst in before Prince or Mrs Thomas can get in the way. I sob and sob. I'm fat and ugly and people tell me lies. I'll never be all right and I'll never have a husband or babies. I wash off the makeup that tricked me into thinking I was acceptable, but I can't wash away the void I feel as the nothingness of my future stretches ahead.

Is all the warmth and humour with Jane and Helen real? Or were they just being nice because I'm pathetic? All I feel now is hurt, anger, humiliation, despair. I sit in the darkness remembering the matron at Burnside introducing me to the idea that I am fat and unattractive. I'd been shocked but hadn't cared then because us kids had kept each other feeling acceptable and defiant.

Now though, well, matron had been right all along and she and Paul are the only ones cold enough to tell me the truth. I haven't done anything to get fat or ugly so it's just who I am. I try to fight the tears away by hating Paul more.

Later that night there's a knock on my door. It's Jane.

'Oh, Kate. I'm so sorry about what happened,' she says as she comes in. 'Paul can be such an insensitive pig.'

I don't know what to say. I want her to tell me that what he said isn't true.

'He's just got home and I dragged it out of him. Don't take any notice of him. He tells me I'm too fat too.'

'You! But you're thin! And tall.' And this doesn't match my idea of marriage. Aren't people always kind and complimentary because they love each other?

'Yes, but he tells me I'm too fat. He just can't give a straight out compliment. He has to add a rider. Believe it or not, he meant it as a compliment.'

A compliment! 'I hope he never wants to insult me, then.'

'Are you all right? Will you visit us again?'

'I don't know if . . .' Tears fall.

'Oh, Kate. He really hurt your feelings, didn't he?'

'Just thought I looked nice for once and he said . . .' Sob, sob.

'You do look nice. You always do. You're beautiful, Kate, and not just in your heart. Look, just because Paul says you're something or other, doesn't mean you are.' She puts her arm around my shoulder, gives me a mischievous leer and says, 'Some women, the self included, would give their eye teeth to have your curves!'

We laugh. Jane's humour is irresistible.

'Must go but don't stay away. Come when Paul's not there, if you like. Us girls can have fun without him.'

I'll try to remember what she said. Just because Paul says I'm not all right, it doesn't mean I'm not.

My re-entry into the family is awkward, but Jane's sensitivity and Becky's joyous welcome ease it.

At work, Daniel has decided to leave but his job is given to Bruce. I'm the most senior but girls can't do Daniel's job apparently.

'I wanted that job,' I tell Denise quietly.

'Daniel's? They've never had a girl doing that. It's a senior.'

'I could do it! I help Daniel sometimes,' I tell her. 'I can't see why being a girl matters to what papers you fill in or what documents you ask people for. You only need hands, eyes and a voice

34

and I've got all them. See!' I take them to Bruce's old desk which is now mine. This job soon becomes boring too.

A month later Mr Mansouriani calls me into his office. He hasn't asked me to bring a file.

'How are you going with your work?' he asks.

'Fine thank you.'

'Bruce is leaving and I want you to think about doing that job. We don't usually put girls there but Roy is not ready and you're our most senior clerk. What do you think? Could you manage?'

'Yes,' I tell him instantly.

'We'll get Bruce to train you before he goes. Come and see me if you have any questions that Bruce can't answer. Talk to him and let me know what you decide.'

My decision is made before I talk to Bruce but I go through the motions and tell Mr Mansouriani that I want the job.

'Good,' he responds. 'I think you'll manage. How are you going with the Institute courses?'

'I'm not,' I tell him without thinking.

'But you were doing them, weren't you?'

'It was so boring,' I tell him and watch his face move from surprise to a smile. 'I'm too busy to do them too,' I add.

'Boyfriend keeping you busy?'

'No!' I'm blushing and suddenly anxious. I don't know why. Must be that all the other girls have boyfriends and I don't. Still don't.

Now I'm absorbed by my work. No need to worry about improving my position. My desk is behind Roy's. He congratulates me and says the view behind him has definitely improved. Roy is a chain smoker but I enjoy talking with him because of his lovely Scottish accent. He likes to chat about his kids and his wife, as well as about my interesting files.

'That one's still going, then,' he comments.

'Yeah, I can't get the solicitor to take my call,' I tell him.

'Here,' he grins, taking the phone, 'what's the number?'

He dials and asks for the solicitor by name. Soon he's singing, 'Miss Shayler from Colonial Mutual for you, sir. Please hold and she will be with yoop.' He hands me the phone. I'm laughing so much I can barely speak. I pull myself together to talk to the solicitor and tell him what documents I'm waiting for. He apologises for the delay and promises to send them in tomorrow's mail.

'They can't fob off a man like they can a lassie,' Roy explains. 'Try to sound bold. And older.'

'Bold and old.' It becomes my announcement to Roy that I'm about to take on another solicitor. He laughs but his advice often works. Not always, but I work out another trick for those times.

'I'm sorry. Mr Manson is in a meeting.'

'Then I'll wait, thank you.'

'It may be a while. It would be better if he calls you back.'

'It's all right. I'll wait.'

When I do this, the Mr Mansons are often just coming out of their meetings. Roy swivels his chair around and says, 'Ach, but my Mary would be proud of you, lassie!'

Our boss has told me to teach Roy my job if we get spare time and so I've started doing this. Sometimes, like today, it's a great relief that he can take over.

An elderly man comes to the counter. Verna comes to tell me it's a claim for me to process. I walk to the counter and ask the man how I can help him.

'It's the wife,' he says tearily. 'I don't know what happened. She was alive five minutes before she died!'

'Oh!' is the only word I can manage before I grab his policy and try to look as if I'm inspecting every word of it, while I try to hold back a severe fit of giggles. Too hard. 'Excuse me,' I splutter and walk quickly around the corner where I burst.

'What on earth's happened, lassie?'

'The man at the coun– . . .' I can't finish. I'm crippled with giggles. 'He said his wife . . .'

Roy grins as he asks, 'Is he still there?'

'Yes. Here. Practise.' I shove the file at him.

Roy does the claim and after the poor customer has left I tell him what had made me laugh. 'That's not funny,' he says, chuckling. 'Pull yourself together. Here, have a tissue. Oh, stop it. Go on. Back to your desk. Go!'

My work and my contact with solicitors makes me wonder what's happened about Dad's estate. I ring Ken, who says he hasn't heard anything for a long time. He knows who the solicitor is. I might as well ring and ask how it's going. I don't care about getting any money, because I wouldn't know what to do with it, but it would be good to know what's happening. I'm nervous but I try to be the clerk at work when I ring.

'Mr Louth, my name is Kate Shayler. I understand you are handling my father's estate. Charley Shayler. He died in nineteen sixty-seven. Yes, sixty-seven. My brother and I would like to know what progress you've made.'

'Who are you? Ah yes, the daughter. Well now, let's see. Yes, we have a problem. Your sister has contested the will . . .'

'Kerry? Kerry has contested the will?'

'Kerry. Is that her name?'

I hear pages rustle while I wonder what he's talking about. Kerry hasn't told us she's contested the will.

'Kerry isn't the name, is it?' Mr Louth says, still rustling papers.

'Well, she's the only sister I've got.'

'Zelda,' he says. 'Zelda Martha Bevin. Your sister, isn't she?'

I feel stupid. I'd forgotten about Zelda, our half-sister. We haven't seen or heard from her since Dad's funeral. 'Zelda has contested your father's will,' Mr Louth continues. 'I've been trying to contact you others to get your instructions.'

'We haven't heard anything about this!'

'No. I didn't know your whereabouts.'

'Well, I can give you our addresses but Uncle Jack already knows them,' I tell him. He's making excuses for no action at all. 'What is going to happen now?'

'I suggest you give her what she wants,' he says tersely.

'What does she want?'

'A quarter of the estate. Your father left her nothing so she's made a claim under the Child and Family Maintenance Act.'

'She's not a child! She's forty something!'

'The Child and Family Maintenance Act entitles her to claim,' he says impatiently.

The conversation ends quickly as I get intimidated by my ignorance about Acts and half-sisters. I wonder what to do. Now that I've hung up I think of questions I should have asked. It's different when you're discussing an insurance claim with a solicitor. Feelings don't get in the way like they do when it's your own father's estate.

Next day I ring Mr Louth with my questions ready and waiting.

'I'm sorry, he's in a meeting.'

'Thank you. I'll hold.'

'He may be some time.'

'Thank you. I don't mind holding the line.'

'Oh. Here he is now. Putting you through.'

'I've been wondering why we don't challenge Zelda's contest,' I tell our solicitor.

'Point is, if you take it to court the whole estate will go in costs. You'll finish with nothing. The estate is not extensive.'

'But would we have a chance of winning it?'

'Very little chance at all. Think it over. Let me know,' he says dismissively.

'Wait,' I say loudly. 'Can you send explanations to my brother and sister?'

'I'll put you through to my secretary,' he snaps and is gone.

I tell Roy what's happening.

'She's forty and she's claiming child support! Greedy shite if you ask me. Fight her.'

I tell Ken; he's as angry as I am but he knows more.

'Dad left her out because he said he'd given her enough when he was alive. The only time she ever came to the house was when she wanted a handout. Never just to see how Dad was and

38

say hello. Just when she wanted money.'

'And when he was dying,' I say in her defence.

'Same thing,' Ken says bitterly and I see what he means.

'I remember Aunty Dot telling me ages ago that the house was bought with our mother's lottery winnings. What about that anyway? She wasn't Zelda's mother!' Wish I'd remembered this earlier.

'Yeah, that's right. Does the solicitor know that?'

'Don't know. What will we do?' I ask.

We decide we'd like to discuss it with the solicitor and not just do as he says. Ken thinks the law should protect us, especially as it was really our mother's house.

'Mr Louth is in a meeting,' the receptionist tells me yet again.

Soon the ritual is complete and I'm talking to Mr Louth, telling him we'd like to discuss our matter with him at his office. We want to give him some information, we want to know what Dad's estate consists of and we want to hear the arguments for and against taking it to court and what our arguments would be if we did.

I get an appointment but Ken can't make it. I go by myself at lunchtime and I'm ushered into Mr Louth's gloomy office by an aging woman. He should have been an undertaker! His office is drab, depressing and musty, mouldy smelling. His clothes are drab and dull too, and even the bands that hold his shirt sleeves up are dull, not shiny like Mr Mansouriani's. His thinning hair is slicked back with hair oil. 'Brylcreem. A little dab'll do ya!' He mustn't have heard the bit about just a little dab'll do.

'Have a seat,' he says as if I'm a waste of his time. While he walks around to his old leather chair I look straight ahead. No, he definitely hasn't heard that a little dab'll do ya. There's a large, grimy smudge on the wallpaper behind his chair. He must rest his head there when his feet are up. Daniel would have had a lesser smudge if he'd had a wall behind him.

Everything here has the colour and odour of oldness, even our file, which he's had for nearly four years. He opens it and folds his hands on it.

'Well now, what can I do for you, Miss Shayler?'

I feel like saying, 'Just do something.' But I retreat into my good manners. I ask my first question.

'We want to know what was included in our father's estate.'

'What was included?' he asks indignantly.

I feel intimidated. I'll pretend this is a work file. 'Yes. We'd like to know what our father owned when he died, and we'd like to know the total value of his estate. For a start.' Oh, I hope I don't sound like one of those awful people who come in to the counter and say things like, 'Mum died last week. What's she worth?'

Mr Louth gives me a figure and tells me Dad owned the house, some shares and government bonds.

'And that whole amount would be paid out to solicitors if we took it to court?'

'That is correct,' he says, leaning back and adding to the slick on the wall. I hope he falls off his chair like Bruce did once when he was mucking about in the office.

'But what if we won the case?' I ask, realising Mr Louth has had almost centuries of practice balancing on those two legs of his chair.

'You would not win.'

'But what about the fact that the house was bought with our mother's lottery winnings?'

He looks at me blankly.

'Our mother, not Zelda's mother.'

'I see. Probably immaterial. Joint ownership. Your mother's estate went to your father I take it?'

'I don't know. I was four when she died.'

'Sure it would have.'

'And what about the fact that Dad gave Zelda money all his life. He gave her thousands when she bought a motel in Junee and thousands again when she went bankrupt. Then she bought a milk bar and Dad gave her more.'

'How do you know all this?' He sounds surprised as he lands safely on all four chair legs.

40

FLAT

'Ken told me. He was living with Dad when some of it happened.'

'Is there any documentation? Any record?'

'Not that we know of,' I reply, knowing what he'll say.

'We can't argue on the word of a boy against his sister. There is no documentation. My advice is to settle with this Zelda out of court.'

'But how can that law let her claim it when she's an adult?' Mr and Mrs Jenson had asked me that when I discussed it with them. It seemed like a fair question. 'Isn't that law meant to help the children – not that we're children but we're young? Starting out.'

'The law is intended to support families,' Mr Louth informs me. 'She may be older but she is your father's daughter, his family. She is entitled to a share.'

'But surely that was Dad's decision! What about the fact that Dad decided she'd had her share?'

'She is entitled to contest his decision.'

We decide to settle and within a few months we each get a cheque for two thousand dollars. I bank mine. I don't know what else to do with it. I don't want a secondhand car. I forget about it after I've had a cry over that being all there is left of my father's hard work.

There is more of my father's legacy. His dark, vile side is hidden in my secret place, deep inside so that now it has a dreamlike quality. It's being covered with new experiences and ideas and by my concentrating on his loyalty and humour. His good side.

At church we feel we're too mature to have fellowship in the old way. We'll have Bible studies instead. Glen and Mel, recently married, suggest we come to their place for the studies. I hurry home from the station, get a quick dinner, then hurry down to their place. I'm so hot and thirsty when I arrive.

'Hello, Kate. Glad you could come,' Glen says, ushering me in. 'Would you like some cider? It's pretty hot, isn't it?'

Apple cider. I love that. 'Yes please. That'd be good.'

Most people have arrived by now but I have time for a quick gulp before we pray. The cider tastes sour but it's refreshing. Time to pray. We start with prayers for Lance and Cheryl and soon I'm drifting off in a strange haze.

'Amen,' wakes me and I hear Glen, from far away, suggest we start our study.

I take another gulp of my drink to wake me up. No, it's not as sweet as other apple cider I've had. Just as refreshing though. Glen talks on and other people comment and I feel like I'm not really all here. Have I left my body somewhere else? Is my head struggling to find it? That'd be why I'm struggling to focus.

Terese reads from the Old Testament. I try to concentrate.

'What is circumcision?' I hear my voice ask. Big word must be important.

Is there really complete silence or is it just that my head still isn't attached? Better have another cool sip to wake me up.

I can hear the voices but I can't keep up with what they're saying. Just sit quietly sipping, trying to learn. Better go to the ladies room before supper. It's such an effort to coordinate my parts to stand up. Whoops! Room's tilting. Have to sit down. Try again. Slowly. Slowly tilting.

'Mel, wezza ladeesh?' Tongue won't work properly either.

'Up the hall and turn right.' She smiles. 'Are you all right?'

'Feel weird.'

'Oh! Have you had cider before?'

'Think so. At my pardy.'

'Not apple cider! Cider. Oh gosh. Didn't you know?'

'Know what?'

'It's alcoholic cider. Not apple cider. Oh sorry. Are you all right?'

'Yeth shanks.' No need to panic. I wander up the hall and find myself in the study. I sway around to the right room. I wonder if I'm drunk. People at work have talked about it and so did the girls at the hostel. This must be it but why do they like it? It's awful. Oh hells bells, they talked about technicolour yawns, too! Hope I don't do that!

Mel makes coffee and then someone drives me home. Tonight I learnt that when it comes to cider I have to listen for the 'apple'. I know what cider is and I don't know what circumcision is. Doesn't matter.

It's getting easier for me to ask questions of the people at church, even without cider.

A group of us is walking home one night and Terese, who's at college studying something to do with little kids, starts talking about a discussion they had on whether little kids should see other kids nude.

Suddenly I feel afraid. I don't know why but I want to hide so no-one can see me. Who was that little girl in a memory that just flashed by? She was naked. She's a bad, filthy, unlovable thing in a group of nice little naked children. As quickly as she appeared she's gone but I'm walking along in dark shame while the others are chatting, laughing and relaxed.

Terese says, 'Well, the theorists say it's normal for kids to want to know what other bodies look like. It's just like they want to explore everything they come across. It isn't bad to be interested. It's normal. Wholesome.'

Her words stand alone as if she'd said them directly to me in a vacuum where only the two of us exist. I treasure the words and wrap them in blue velvet. Blue velvet? I had a dress of blue velvet when I was a princess. Haven't thought of that for years. I don't now either. I hide the parcel of words away in my mind without understanding why they are so special. I tell myself that that bad child, whoever she was, might not have been bad after all. I'll try to remember to think about her later. But I don't try. It's too dark where she is. I keep that naked little girl buried in my secret place. Buried with Terese's words, though.

Maybe I could study to be a teacher. Terese says I could and her course sounds interesting. The kids at Sunday school like me and so does Becky. With my inheritance money from Dad maybe I could study. One day.

I make inquiries about HSC courses and I discover that I'm eligible to go to tech. The only thing stopping me is my fear that I might try and fail. What then? I'd have to find a new job and how would I do that? My social worker at Burnside, Miss Molesworth, got me the insurance job but she's dead. She was special and I miss her, but when I make my clothes I remember her; she'd suggested I save up and buy a sewing machine. I remember her too when I wear her beautiful brooch that her mother gave me after the funeral.

Mr Mansouriani has been promoted again and his office is further away. My new boss is an older man called Mr Binns. He says he has a daughter my age and he wonders why I'm wasting my time and my brain as a clerk. He thinks I should study more too. He tells me that if I left here, I'd get a lot of money because I haven't used any of my holidays or taken any sick leave. I could use that to support myself while I study.

'But what if I can't do the work and I have to drop out? I won't have a job. Then I won't have a place to live . . .'

'I'm sure they'd give you a job here,' he assures me.

'I'll think about it,' I tell him.

I'm twenty-two and still haven't got a boyfriend. What if I stay working here forever? Phyllis and Merle are about thirty something and they're both single. Lots of people joke about spinsters and I always imagine it's them. We giggle about their dips in and out of love with various men in the office. At one time Merle even seemed to be in love with one of the older men who proudly carries a photo of a Japanese soldier he says he killed in World War Two in his pocket. He took me aside and showed me once, describing the sound it made when he trod on the body. That war is not over for him yet. Will I go a bit mad too if I stay here too long?

Wouldn't it be wonderful to be in love like Gen and Tom? They haven't been married for long and they've started coming to our church. Gen is small and dark-haired and seems to tuck under her husband's arm snugly, a bit like Becky and her teddy. Tom is tall and muscular with dark hair and a beard. She is quiet. He is noisy. They smile and laugh all the time and they call each other 'darling' and 'my love', as well as silly names that make me giggle. They live near Helen and make friends with her easily. That friendship starts to include me. They don't seem to notice that I'm shy.

'How about coming away camping with us next weekend?' Gen asks. 'There'll be about ten of us, just friends of ours from our past lives. We're going to the Warrumbungles.'

'I'd love to,' I tell her. I don't usually feel comfortable with new people but I like Gen and Tom so much and I like short new experiences where there are no expectations of me. But will I go? What if they decide I'm awful? What if I can't think of anything to say?

'People said you wouldn't because you're shy. Are you shy?'

'Sometimes,' I tell her, feeling my face heat up but also feeling peeved that I'm not allowed to change. That does it. I will go camping. I'll show them.

We drive through the night and camp beside the road for a short sleep, so we'll get an early start next morning. This is as far away as I've ever been, I think. This land is so big and flat! How could there be so many stars? When the jagged range appears on the horizon, I'm in awe. I can't believe I'm here, so far from home.

We meet the others and I feel nervous. They're mostly strong young men and, although Gen and Tom think I'm healthy enough to do walks with them, I begin to wonder. I also hope they'll keep liking me if I get shy out here. For now, though, I love being in this fantastic place where no-one knows I'm shy.

Our days are spent walking and I keep up well until we reach the steep parts and then I can't breathe.

'Lovely view on the left, ladies and gentlemen,' Tom shouts at regular intervals, stopping and pointing at a view that may or may not be lovely. I laugh and feel relieved that I have a chance to catch my breath.

At night we cook and sit chatting around the fire. They all think it's wrong that Australian soldiers are in Vietnam, and they've been to demonstrations. Wait a minute! Aren't demonstrators awful, dirty dropouts with no brains? No. These aren't. As I listen to them I admire their enthusiasm and that they know so much. Lance is over there and he shouldn't be. The government is getting worried by all the demonstrations so maybe they'll bring the troops home soon. There's going to be an election and that might mean a change. Dad always said to vote Labor because they care about the workers. These people are talking about voting by the parties' views about the war. They sound right.

The talk turns to topics I've hardly heard discussed before.

'We can't keep putting our sewage into the sea. We need to value oceans and the life that's in them, not use them as garbage dumps.'

'We can't keep putting rubbish in dumps, though. Dumps leach toxins into the ground water.'

I learn words like biodegradability, sustainability, environment and ecology. I learn to start thinking of the Earth as the planet that's our home, the home of the human race. If we destroy it we'll have no home. Anywhere.

Most of these people are uni students or graduates and I assume they'll think I'm dumb and boring if I talk about my job. They don't seem to when I do, but mostly I don't say much. It doesn't matter. I think I'd like to go to university and learn about all these things as well as the stuff Terese is learning.

We're in a hurry to get home. Tom is speeding. I'm given the job of looking out the back window at regular intervals to see if there are any police cars following. I get drowsy but keep watch as best I can.

'Pull over, driver,' a burly officer calls out from beside his parked car as we approach Dunedoo. 'Can I see your licence, please?'

'Why?' says Tom.

'You were clocked at forty in a thirty-five mile an hour zone, sir. I need to see your licence.'

'You didn't clock me.'

'If you want to challenge me, sir, take it up with the magistrate,' the officer says aggressively. 'Meanwhile, I need to see your licence.'

The paperwork is done and after snide remarks are exchanged between Tom and the officer we set off again. Tom is furious because he reckons the policeman couldn't have clocked him or we'd have seen him. He's just guessing Tom was speeding, to fill his quota. I'm sitting in the back stunned. I didn't know you could answer back to policemen or challenge them! Tom did and he's angry and says he's going to appeal against the fine. It's a sour note to finish a wonderful weekend on but Tom and, to a lesser extent, Gen seem to be getting a kick out of the argument they're about to have with the police.

I tell Mr and Mrs Jenson what a wonderful time we had and they're very pleased that I seem to be getting over being shy. They are very fond of Gen and Tom too and say they think my new friends are doing me a lot of good.

Gen and Tom have a lot to say at Bible study and they read other books too, books that have new ideas that challenge our traditional ways of thinking sometimes. We meet alternately at their flat and mine, now that Glen and Mel have moved away. I often have dinner with Gen and Tom before the others arrive for Bible study. I love being in their company. I don't feel that I have to try to be incredibly good and polite all the time. It turns out I am, anyway, but I don't do it by trying hard.

We laugh a lot and Tom jokes about things us others never talk about.

'Old Mrs Harvey's been perving through the window again.' He grins. Mrs Harvey lives in the flats next door to theirs and she has been picking on them since they moved in. She thinks Tom is a hippy with his beard and all.

47

'Oh, don't tell them what you did!' Gen pleads.

'Don't tell them I took off all my clothes and danced naked for her?'

'And answered the door in your birthday suit when she came to complain about your music!'

'I'm praying for her,' Tom replies. We clutch our aching sides.

It's my turn to have the study at my flat and I don't have enough plates. The two of everything I took from Dad's house won't do. I have enough money to buy a dinner set so I go shopping and choose a plain white setting. I can hardly lift the box. What will I do? Tom agrees to meet me at the bus stop, if I can make it that far, and he carries the set to their place. Mine's too far from the bus stop. We walk slowly up the hill that I remember vaguely from my childhood, before my mother died. Tom is like a giant and I can't believe how strong he is. I feel little walking beside him.

'My gentle giant,' Gen grins as we arrive at their place.

I wish I had one. Big, kind, funny, clever and gentle. Not all husbands are judges like Paul.

Gen always invites people to stay if they arrive at dinnertime, and she cooks meals I've never heard of. Tonight it's beef stroganoff and it feels naughty putting wine in it and drinking some too. Gen gives me recipes all the time and I keep them in a folder with the ones Jane gives me, in case I ever have anyone to cook for. There's steak diane, beef Burgundy, chicken Marengo as well as some for exotic desserts with no names but lots of slices of various chocolate bars in them.

People seem to assume that because I live in a flat by myself I am very modern and at ease in the world. They don't know that I survive by pretending and trying to do what people like Gen or Jane do as hostesses. Apparently I'm convincing when they're here but when they go I'm so relieved that I'm alone and I don't have to keep up the coping act any longer. I don't feel like that with Gen and Tom or Helen but I do with the others.

We all start having dinner together before our Bible studies, and Tom talks one night about having communion as part of our meals. At church we have bread and wine in the communion service and the minister reads what Jesus said: 'Do this, as oft as ye shall drink it, in remembrance of me.' Tom says we can do it as part of our meal like the disciples did. Jesus told them to use their ordinary bread and wine to remember him when they had meals together. The Bible story says that. But can we really have the holy sacrament here in my flat?

We do. We pass a piece of bread around and as we take a piece off we say, 'The body of Christ who died for you. Eat this in remembrance of Him.' I feel very self-conscious saying the words that our rector usually says with great ceremony and dressed in his robes. Next we pass around a glass of wine and say to the person we hand it to, 'The blood of Christ was shed for you. Drink this in remembrance of Him.' No lightning strikes. I feel spiritually more part of this little group, more bound to them by our beliefs, than I do to the church.

Gen and Tom have not only started me thinking about Christian rituals but they've made me think I might be brainy enough to study too.

'You should get your HSC and go to uni. Course you could! You'd breeze through it.' I start getting confident but I'd have to wait until next year to start.

A few weeks later, Tom and Gen have a surprise for us at Bible study.

'The Rev wants to come next week. Apparently he's not a happy chap because we're having communion without him.'

When the Rev, Mr Cooper, arrives at my flat he smiles sweetly and joins us for dinner. He has told Tom that we cannot have communion unless he officiates so we don't have it. After dinner we divide into two study groups because there are so many people here tonight. My only two rooms are in the lounge/kitchen and the bedroom, apart from the bathroom but we can't sit in there. The Reverend Cooper chokes when one study group gathers on my bed, but what can he do?

When we finish our group discussions he begins a sermon about communion. We listen to him but he doesn't listen to us. He has a set of words and ideas that he just keeps saying over and over again.

It's been hard for me to do something that the people in charge of church have said is wrong but when I think for myself, I think the people in charge are wrong. That's a challenge, thinking that people in authority can be wrong. I've always been afraid to even question them. As a child I was told they were always right and if I disagreed, I was wrong.

One night there's an unexpected knock on my door that turns my world upside down. Megan who lives down the street is standing there grim and pale.

'What's wrong?' I ask.

'It's Tom,' she says. 'He died this morning.'

'What?'

'Tom died this morning.'

'No! He can't. He carried my . . . I went there . . . No.'

She's crying. It might be true!

'Mrs Brown rang and asked me to tell you.'

No. There's a mistake. Mrs Brown lives near Gen and Tom.

'Where's Gen?' I ask. She'll tell me it's not true. They'll both be here soon, Gen and the gentle giant and he'll laugh and say it was a mistake or a joke or something.

'I think she's with her parents,' I hear Megan say.

I'm crying, 'He can't be! He can't be.'

'He is, Kate. It's hard to believe it but he is.'

It hurts so much! How can Gen bear it if it's this hard for me? How can she bear it?

There's nothing to do but go to work and come home.

Mrs Brown comes to see me. She's never been here before and I get a fleeting feeling that she's a matron and I'm in trouble.

'I've been thinking so much about you, Kate,' she says gently. 'I've been wondering how you are.'

'All right.'

'You were very close to Gen and Tom,' she says, looking straight into eyes that are beginning to moisten and burn. 'They really brought you out of yourself, didn't they? I was thinking this must be very hard for you.'

I don't hear what else she says. I'm just so grateful that she understands my pain. I'm sobbing and she's holding me and stroking my hair.

'It hurts so much,' I sob.

'I know. I know.' Stroking.

'Why? Why did he have to die?'

'I don't know,' is all she says. Stroking. Sobbing.

'I just don't know why,' she says again.

I'm grateful that she doesn't spout empty, ritual words.

When I calm down, she says, 'You know you are always welcome at our house, don't you? If you get lonely or too sad you just come around. Or ring and we'll come and get you.'

'Thank you.'

'I'm not just saying it. You will call, won't you?'

'I will. Thank you.'

After the angel goes home I cry some more and feel understood and accepted in places I didn't know I was.

But Tom can't be dead and I fantasise about other explanations. Maybe the Russians poisoned and kidnapped him and one day he'll escape and come back. Or maybe our government did it because he protested against their policies, so they are brainwashing him and he'll be allowed back afterwards. Anything seems more possible than that he's gone forever because a vein in his lung burst.

Tom's funeral is a celebration of his life but I feel too shattered to be cheerful. 'The Lord giveth and the Lord taketh away. Blessed be the name of the Lord.' But why is it blessed to take such a gift as Tom away? It's not! Not for us here at the funeral. It's unfair. Did Gen and Tom have too much happiness? God gave them that. They always said so. It's cruel to take him away. From all of us who loved him.

I visit Gen sometimes. We cry or talk or pray but Tom is still completely gone. Sometimes Gen is unbearably sad, sometimes she's angry and sometimes she's vulnerable. Most of all she's lonely for Tom.

We try to have Bible studies again but our hearts are broken, not in it. We stop trying. Some people stop believing. I don't but I just don't understand God. Tom often used to joke about the Lord working in mysterious ways.

The McMahon government topples at the election and I feel as if I helped. The new prime minister is Mr Whitlam and he says he will bring the Australian troops home. Tom would have been so pleased. Lance will be, and Cheryl too.

When he does come home, Lance doesn't want to see anyone but Cheryl. The boy who tried to teach me to drive has gone. In his place is a man who is broken and troubled. Newspapers say the war is over. They are wrong.

GOODBYE AGAIN

Why don't I just leave work and try the HSC? I'll get a job back here if I fail. Gen thinks she might do uni to distract her from her grief and I could go with her if I pass. All I need to do is wait for this year to end, then I'll be ready.

'Hello, Aunt Cake,' Helen's tired voice says on the phone at work. 'Would you be able to babysit for Jane on Saturday morning?'

'Yes. Is anything wrong?'

'Well, maybe. She found a lump and it's not looking good.'

'What lump?'

'In her breast. They sent her for X-rays and now she has to see a specialist.'

I'll ask her later what all that means but I'm looking forward to a morning with Becky. Jane's second baby, Mark, has been born. He is so fat his parents dub him Mao Tse-tung, which Becky translates as Mousy Toong, probably a character from a book in her mind.

Jane will take Mousy with her to the specialist. Paul is away, so I'll babysit.

My plan for a cheerful time with Becky is shattered as she screams desperately when Jane gets in the car with Mousy. What's wrong with her? She's always so glad to see me. What have I done?

'Pick her up and cuddle her,' Jane calls out. 'Haven't left her before.'

I pick her up and she buries her little face into my shoulder where screams subside to little sobs. I blink back tears.

'What will we do 'til Mummy comes back?' I ask, feeling less sure of myself now.

Soon Becky is her cheerful little self again. The time passes slowly and Becky cries when Jane comes back. I'm embarrassed.

'She hasn't cried since you left. I promise!'

'Oh I know. Her cousin does the same when I babysit him. It's what they do when their mothers leave them. Pay back!' She hugs Becky and I notice tears leaking from her eyes. 'You go and find Bunny while I talk to Kate.' We watch her go, then Jane dries her eyes and says, 'Oh sorry. Bad news, I'm afraid. The X-rays show lung cancer as well.'

'Lung cancer! What . . . how . . . what will happen?'

'I have to go into hospital, try some treatments. Oh I don't know. I suddenly feel so old and weary. Let's have some tea. Do you remember the first time your mother left you?'

'No.' I wonder why she's thinking about that when she's had such awful news. I just don't see the connection between what happened to me all those years ago and what could happen to Becky now.

'Can you stay 'til Paul gets home? I need a rest, if you don't mind extending babysitting honours.'

As Becky plays, I remember what we learnt about cancer in the Insurance Institute course: 'bad risk'. Death? Surely not. Not Jane, anyway. She can't. Not with two little kids!

'The aunts', four of us who are friends of Jane from church, take turns of helping out when Jane goes into hospital.

I visit her at lunchtimes but by the time I get there it's time to say goodbye and go back to work.

'Ask to change your hours,' Helen suggests. 'Start early and have an hour for lunch? Or work late?'

'Don't know if I can ask,' I tell her. Don't you have to just work to the set rules? Am I allowed to ask for a favour?

Mr Binns surprises me by letting me work my hours however I like. I visit Jane again. She's calm and hopeful that she'll get well, so I am too. We talk like we always do. She wants to know how work is, if I'm seeing Helen this week and so on.

'I'll have a go now,' I say.

'Give the kids a hug for me and tell them I can't wait to see them on the weekend,' she says. Her eyes are burning and a tear falls. I can't wait for her to get out of hospital and home. I don't know why she's so emotional about the kids. We know she'll be home again soon.

It's my turn to tuck Becky in and read the bedtime story. She picks a wretchedly long one and falls asleep while I'm reading. I lean over to put the book away and Helen whispers from the doorway, 'Kate! What's that lump on your back? It's huge!'

'What lump?' I ask as my life flashes by.

'Stretch your arm out,' she says, turning me around. 'You'd better see a doctor. It's the size of a tennis ball. Does it hurt?'

'Didn't know it was there,' I tell her quickly. I rush to the bathroom and close the door. I can't breathe. I've got cancer and it's going to kill me. I twist around trying to see the lump but the mirror is too high. I don't know any doctors. I'll have to ask Helen about them. But I don't want her to talk about it. Not any more. Not 'til . . . I just don't want to talk about it.

I find the nearest doctor in the phonebook. He is non-committal and refers me to a specialist. I have to wait weeks. For my death sentence? I don't tell anyone about the lump and I don't let anyone stand behind me when I'm filing or stretching. At home there's a huge mirror and I've worked out how to see my back using my compact mirror as well. How could I not know about or feel a lump that big?

'Helen says you've got a lump,' Jane says when I visit her next.

'Yeah,' I reply, wishing Jane didn't know so we didn't have to talk about it and make it real here too.

'It might be nothing. Try not to worry, Cake. You're too young to get anything toiminal.'

'So are you. How's the treatment?'

'Pretty awful. Can you give me a drink? So dry.'

Her hands are blue with bruising. She takes small sips.

'Keep praying,' she begs as I leave.

At church we pray for Jane's recovery and for her family who miss her. I wish Gen and Tom were here so we could talk about what we really think. Mr Cooper's sermons are about healing and God's will. He doesn't see any reason for despair in this case because God has told him that Jane will be healed. He assures us that when people pray believing, God heals. I pray desperately-hoping prayers rather than believing ones but I do try to believe. I don't dare admit that I don't have absolute faith. I could have admitted that at Bible study but not here where everyone else is so sure. Maybe I should stay away like Gen does. I want to be with other people, though.

Meanwhile, there's my lump. The specialist examines it. 'Hmm. Distal to the scapula. How did you find this? Must've been the boyfriend, eh?'

'No,' I reply. Everyone assumes I've got a boyfriend, as if it's as predictable as a nose. I'm a freak. With a lump. The doctor keeps pressing and probing. 'I don't have a boyfriend.'

'I'm sure you do,' he says distractedly. 'Who do you have who could look after you? I notice from your card that your parents have passed away.'

'No-one. I live by myself.' He means who'll look after me while I die of cancer. I'm so frightened.

'Get dressed,' he says, washing his hands. 'Then come and sit down.'

Sit down for the death sentence. Please just say it quickly and let me go.

'Well, first I have to say that I don't think it's a cancer.'

Crying and it isn't a cancer! Stop crying and listen.

'It's too mobile and not firm. We could do a biopsy to be certain but I put the odds at ninety per cent against cancer.'

'What is it, then?' What other horrible threats are there?

'I think it's a lipoma. Your blood has deposited lipids in a kind of tumour instead of distributing them in the usual places. We could remove it or leave it alone.'

'What will happen if we leave it?' I squeak.

'Nothing. It's not dangerous. It may get bigger, though, and that could be a problem.'

I'll be a hunchback spinster! 'I want to get it off.'

'Yes. That's probably the best option,' he says. 'Give it some more thought and let me know.'

I don't need to think about it. I ring the next day and tell his receptionist that I've decided to have the operation.

Mr Binns is concerned and says it's such a relief that the lump is probably not cancer.

Probably not? Ninety per cent, the specialist said. Oh, but what about the other ten per cent: what if it is? I'm frightened again. Those ten points feel more like ninety. But my ten per cent seems almost irrelevant when I think of Jane whose treatment isn't having much effect now. It's so unfair that I get this kind of tumour and Jane, who's got kids who need her so much, has got cancer. I tell God I'll trade places but we both know I don't mean it. I'm ashamed.

'You'll be all right,' Jane says. 'Don't cry, Cake. You'll be fine.' Her dry lips struggle to get the words out. I give her a drink.

'Won't be able to come for a week or so,' I tell her. 'Lucky you. You'll get to sleep through my lunch hour.'

Soon I'm in Marrickville hospital where my dad went before he died. It seems as gloomy as it did then and I'm anxious. As I'm wheeled into theatre, I pray, 'Please don't let it be cancer. Please heal Jane.'

'You're here in the hospital recovery room, dear.' It's Mrs Brown. The angel who pops up when you need her. Reminds me where I am. Reminds me of Jane in another hospital.

'Hello. How's Jane?'

'You've had your operation, Kate, and you're at the hospital.'

'Yes, but how's Jane?' Why doesn't she answer my question?

'Jane's the same and you're in the recovery room. Don't worry, it's just the anaesthetic making you groggy and confused. I'll stay until you wake up properly. How do you feel?'

'Groggy and confused.'

She stays and chats for a while and then she has to go.

The specialist tells me the tumour was definitely not cancer. I cry as he looks at the dressing. 'It was more extensive than I thought, so you'll experience quite a bit of pain. Do you have someone who could look after you for a while?'

I go home and for a day I only feel itchy and sleepy but then the pain sets in. Mrs Jenson takes me to stay with them until I'm better. I sleep a lot. Mrs Jenson helps me wash and keeps me posted about how Jane is. When I'm well enough we go to a prayer meeting. I can feel that something is wrong. More wrong than it was before. The cancer has spread.

Reverend Cooper exhorts us to pray believing. God will heal our sister. We mustn't lose faith now. I try harder to believe what he says.

At last, back to work and to visiting Jane. I'm shocked by how pale and thin she is but she manages a smile and says softly, 'Nice to have Cake again.'

'Nice to be here. How are you?'

I can't hear her answer. I get the water. 'Put your head . . .' she whispers, patting the pillow weakly.

With my head on the pillow I can hear her say, 'Gone to my spleen. Trying to get better but gone . . .'

We cry on the pillow. A nurse comes in but leaves quickly.

'We're praying at church,' I tell her, wanting there to be some hope.

'Me too,' she whispers. 'Rev visits, tells me. What if God wants me to die?'

'But you've got kids.'

'Your mum died.'

The parallels hit me like a ton of bricks, knocking my hope out. I grab at straws.

'No-one was praying for her. And she was old.'

'What was it like for you?'

'Pardon?'

'When she died? What's it like?'

'I don't remember.'

'Don't let the kids forget me.' More tears that make me wish I'd thought more carefully before I'd answered.

'We won't let them forget you.'

'Keep praying.'

I wipe our eyes and say goodbye.

Reverend Cooper organises a prayer vigil. Jane will know that someone in our church is praying for her at every minute of the day and night. 'Keep you faith,' he counsels. 'Our prayers will be answered if we have faith.'

I'm in a horrible, horrible predicament. I believe that God can heal but I don't believe that we can make Him do it. Is that a lack of faith? Don't know but it's real. Am I the only one in the church who doesn't have faith? The one who will cause Jane to die? They've always said that God's will is done for reasons that we sometimes can't fathom. So why do I now have to believe that I can change God's mind about His will?

There is nothing I want more in the world right now. Not babies of my own or a nice man. Nothing more than for Jane to be healthy and at home where she belongs. That is my prayer. I tell God my whole truth.

The next day at the hospital Jane is sleeping and she looks the same. I put my head on her pillow and listen to her breathing. After a few minutes I hear, 'Kate, you came. Thanks.'

'How are you?'

'Sore. Got up in a fit of faith. Collapsed,' she whispers. Tears leak from the corners of her eyes. 'I think God wants me to go.'

'No, Jane,' I weep. *Don't go. Don't leave me.*

I dry our eyes but it's useless.

We lie still until we can talk again.

'Really wanted to get well. Gone to my liver now.' That seems so final, the way she says it. 'You aunts help Paul, won't you? Be there for kids.'

'We'll be there.' *Don't go. Don't leave me.*

Soon she's asleep and I go back to work.

Weary and strained aunts have dinner together. 'I don't think Jane's going to be healed,' someone says.

What an incredible relief it is to be able to tell the truth somewhere!

'It's so bloody unfair, with those little kids,' Gen says bitterly.

We agree. We talk about how we'll keep looking after the kids and making sure they don't forget Jane, the vital person she was before she got so sick.

Reverend Cooper announces that it seems to be the Lord's will to take Jane, and that we should now support her and her family in this very difficult time. *Traitor,* I want to shout. *Traitor!* Why can't you keep praying and make God change his mind? You're the one who said He would!

Jane slips in and out of consciousness and she's moved to a hospice. I can't visit her at lunchtimes there but Helen keeps me up to date. 'She doesn't know you're there anyway, so don't feel bad about not going. Today she was hallucinating about fish swimming around the walls.'

'That's awful!'

'No. It was lovely. She was peaceful. Enjoying it.'

'As long as she's peaceful,' I reply.

Her funeral is sheer misery. I give thanks for her life but how can I just give thanks and not be angry that it's over! Tom's too. How can God do this? How can I keep loving people if they're just going to up and die? No more. Please. No more.

Helen and I do aunty duty together again; we put the kids to bed and start washing up but soon Becky is screaming. Helen goes to her and then I hear banging and shouting. I go to see what's happening.

Becky is standing on the bed, screaming, and Helen is whacking the fireplace with a broom and shouting, 'You bad thing. I'm going to get you. You can't come here. Stay away or I'll get you,' she's demanding. Has a cat come down the chimney or has Helen gone nuts? She comes out and says, 'Cake, put this in the fire, please,' and hands me a bundle of nothing. 'There. It's gone,' she says as she cuddles Becky. 'It can't come back again. We've killed it. Go to sleep now. There there. Go to sleep.'

'What were you doing in there?' I ask when Helen returns to the kitchen.

'She thought a monster was in the fireplace again. I asked a psychologist friend what to do and he said that it's real to Becky so we should treat it as if it's real. So I got the broom and beat it, then you burnt it. If any more come we'll have to beat and burn them too. Okay?'

'Oh. Okay.'

I never have to beat monsters. They stop coming down the chimney. Now we only have to deal with Becky's rages and tears. Mousy likes lots of cuddles and songs but Becky throws things and has tantrums and screams and shouts. Then she breaks down and sobs her heart out. Sometimes I do too.

Working with death claims has a sour taste now but I must keep working, paying the rent, dreaming my dreams, getting ready for my tech year.

I go to the technical college and enrol. Dad's money should keep me going for the year and then I'll see what happens. Gen and I might go to uni. She's confident but I'm not.

'Do you know you're probably entitled to teese?' the enrolment officer asks.

'What's that?'

'T.E.A.S. Tertiary Education Assistance Scheme, a Whitlam government initiative.' She hands me the application. It's the kind of financial support Mr Jenson thought should exist for people like me but it didn't until the Labor government came to power. I fill the form in and post it off.

'I've decided to leave and go to tech,' I tell Mr Binns.

'Good idea.' He smiles. 'We'll miss you, of course, but it's a good idea. Well, you'd better get on with training Roy.'

Roy is keen to get my job and there's not much he doesn't know by now.

'Before you go, there's something you can help me with,' he says. He's grinning and I can't imagine what it could be. He opens his drawer and takes out a packet of cigarettes. He hands them to me.

'I don't smoke!'

'No, well that's it, you see, lassie. I want to stop and I've tried at home but I come here and start again. So if you help, I could stop.'

'Good idea. To stop, I mean.'

'You ever tried?'

'Smoking? Yeah. When we were kids we thought any kind of smoke would do so we rolled paper around a burning stick and breathed it in.' Roy laughs as I explain how I choked for what felt like twenty-four hours. 'Never wanted to do it again. And now with the cancer thing.'

'Damn expensive too. So will you help?'

'Help save you from lung disease? Gladly. 'What do I have to do?' I'm remembering Jane again.

'Keep the fags and only give me one a day.'

'One a day. One cig, not one pack?' He usually smokes a pack and a half.

'One cig. Whatever I do, don't give me any more.'

I put the packet in my desk but he soon swings around. 'What about one in the morning, one after lunch and one before home time?'

'Doesn't sound like stopping.'

'Ah, you're right. All right, one in the morning, one at home time.'

Soon he's saying he wants one now and I'm saying he can't have it. It feels like a game where I'm the mum and he's the bad child who's trying to wheedle another lolly. Soon it changes.

'Come on Kate, I just want one. Give it to me,' he demands aggressively.

'No. You told me not to.'

'Give it to me!'

He's scary! 'You told me not to,' I repeat but I'm losing resolve in the face of his aggression. He stands up and I cringe like I used to at Burnside in the face of anger. I'm embarrassed. 'Here, have them all.' He takes them and is soon gulping smoke and coughing relief. I'm shaken. I try to concentrate on my work.

'Kate, I'm really sorry,' he says. 'Start again.'

'No. You're awful when you want a smoke.'

'Sorry. I know. One more try?'

'You'll get cranky again when I say no.'

'I won't. Not this time. I really mean it,' he insists and pushes the packet across my desk. Unable to keep resisting the pressure, I take them. But after a few refusals he says, 'Oh look, I'm going to get cranky pretty soon. Better give me the damn pack.' He lights up, draws a deep slow breath, then says, 'Oh by the way, they want to know what you want for a goodbye present.'

'Oh I don't know.' But I do. I've thought about it in case someone asks. 'I suppose some wine glasses would be good.'

Denise doesn't see why I want to study. 'Girls don't need to. You'll only get married and leave whatever else you do.'

'Maybe I won't.'

'Isn't your French good enough yet?' she laughs.

'My what?' I ask, puzzled. Sometimes we talk in schoolgirl French but I have no idea what she means right now.

'Your French,' she repeats.

'What French? What are you talking about?'

'Your French boyfriend. Aren't you going to marry him one day?'

'I haven't got a French boyfriend. I don't even know any French people!'

'Your sailor. Heather saw you with him down at Circular Quay.'

Oh I remember! 'Oh, please, no! He wasn't my boyfriend! Oh good grief. He was just some creep who kept grabbing me!'

'Truly? We all thought he must be your boyfriend. Who do you talk to on the phone at lunchtimes, then?'

'A girlfriend. About another friend who was sick in hospital. The one I used to visit. Oh that's revolting to think of that creep as a boyfriend.'

'We thought that's why you're not interested in the boys here.'

Aren't I? I thought none of them was interested in me – and they weren't, because everyone said I had a boyfriend! Oh well, too late now.

I work until the Friday before tech starts. At the end of the day, people from our floor gather outside Mr Mansouriani's office and put a chair for me in the middle of the space where desks have been cleared.

Mr Binns makes a nice speech about what a good worker I've been and how I have always been polite and friendly and how sure he is that I'll do well in my studies. He hands me my present, which I open, trying not to let my hands shake too much.

'Oh, they're lovely,' I say. I wish they were plain glass instead of bubbly glass. Of course I don't say that.

Mr Mansouriani clears his throat and begins his speech. 'Ladies and gentlemen today is both a sad day and a happy one. Certainly it's a happy one for Kate as she leaves us to meet new challenges. But for me it's a very sad day. Kate came to us fresh out of school, a very shy young girl who soon proved to be a willing worker and a polite, charming person. I've had the privilege of seeing her blossom into a beautiful young woman whom anyone would be proud to know. I am certainly proud of the friendship we share . . .'

Friendship! I hadn't realised Mr Mansouriani still cared about me or thought we were friends. He isn't a friend, is he? He's my boss's boss. I feel muddled about the friendship thing.

Now he's wishing me success and happiness and telling me to keep in touch. People clap and call out, 'Speech, speech!' No-one else who's left the company has had to make a speech. Do I really have to just because I've been here for seven years? What should I say?

'I'd just like to thank Mr Binns and Mr Mansouriani for their lovely words and good wishes. And thank you all for the beautiful glasses. Oh, and good luck to Roy as he takes my job.' I know I've made a woefully inadequate response.

The office gradually empties as people say goodbye and go home. Roy promises to give up smoking by the time I come back. If I come back. But if I come back, I can't have his new job.

'Well, Kate Shayler,' Mr Mansouriani says for the last time, 'let's go home.'

He kisses my cheek when we get out of the lift and we say goodbye. 'And don't forget, I'll welcome you back anytime.'

I can't help letting a few tears escape as I walk down Martin Place and head for Wynyard station. I have changed, haven't I?

BROADER HORIZONS

Oh Lord, do I belong here among all this noise and bustle, at tech, where hundreds of students, brainy people, jostle into classrooms chatting and laughing confidently? There are hundreds of us but not a single face I know. I don't keep looking around, looking desperate to find a friend. Wearing weekend clothes instead of a work dress was good but I'd better get some jeans.

Maths is my first class. Our teacher – 'tutor', the church lot say I should call them – is not much older than me. She has a constant smile that makes me confident. She tells us to call her Anne.

'The way I teach this course is to go through it twice during the year.' I'm glad there'll be so much time. 'It might feel as if I'm going too fast but don't worry.' I worry. 'If you don't understand things the first time around, you'll get them the second time. Yeah, you will. I promise. Remember the most important thing, oh, apart from getting assignments in on time, is Don't Worry.' I worry.

As Anne writes on the board, I get more worried. I know what the numbers are but what does that symbol mean? A line with a dot above and a dot below. I know I've seen it before but I can't remember what it means. She's moved on, going too fast already. Don't worry, she said. I'm not worrying, not worrying, not worrying. But should I ring Mr Mansouriani now?

'Shit, Miss,' says a boy at the back. 'I haven't got a clue what you're talkin' about!'

Anne doesn't reprimand him for swearing.

'Good,' she says. 'I need you to let me know if you're stuck. That's the only way I'll know how you're coping. Is anyone else having trouble?'

A few of us put our hands up.

'Bear with me,' she says. 'I'll go over it again but I'll finish it for the others first.' The others seem so young. They must have been at school last year.

Anne does a hands-up survey of where we've all come from and how long it's been since we did any algebra or trigonometry. Trig what? There's a range of people, from those who didn't do well enough in the HSC last year, to people who are changing careers, as well as a couple of older people who want to learn what the youngsters are learning these days.

It's like this in all the classes. Teachers tell us to call them by their first names and they assure us that they want to get us through the HSC as much as we want to get through.

Our English teacher is different. He's young like most of the teachers but he seems mean on the first day when he saunters in, drops his folder on the table, slumps into his chair and slowly crosses his legs.

'Morning,' he mumbles, condescending to look up at us rather than his folders. 'Get down to business, shall we? Anyone who's going to waste my fucking time can get out now.' He narrows his eyes. 'You're not here to enjoy yourselves and I'm not your bloody babysitter. If you work hard I'll support you but just don't think you can come here and do bugger all.' He pauses at last, then adds, 'Questions? Anyone?'

Don't you know any good adjectives? I'd like to ask, but I'm not game. I've never heard so many swear words all at once, except when I was a kid and we whispered all the ones we knew to each other at Burnside.

'Yeah. I've got a question. What's yer name and room number?' It sounds like the same boy who told Anne he wasn't following. This time he sounds insolent, like he's offended, like the rest of us probably feel. Like I do.

'Name's Terry McFadden. Keep that attitude, smart arse, and you'll be out on your ear.' He's controlled, forcing calm, like any moment now he'll call us all smart arses, then explode.

'You keep that up and *you* will be,' Smart Arse replies.

Terry ignores him and goes on with our lesson with his restricted range adjectives and absence of warmth. In other classes we've been made to feel we can come to the staff rooms and ask for help if we're having problems with the work. I don't know if I'd be game to do that even with the nice teachers but I hope I don't ever need help with English. If I do I'll see if someone at church can help. I didn't know there were teachers like Terry or students who talk back to them. It makes me nervous but I stay quiet, watch and listen. At the very least, tech is already interesting.

In the canteen I sit on an empty chair and soon get drawn into a conversation about why we're here and how we're funding our study. Lots of people have part-time jobs in cafes. Should I try to get a waitressing job? I'd be too shy and clumsy. Anyway, I have enough money to get through the year, as long as they stop telling us to buy books. Especially in English. Some people have academic arguments and that's when I wish I was back being a clerk and talking about dress patterns and makeup.

'How's tech?' Helen asks on the weekend.

'I don't know if I've done the right thing. Some subjects are okay. I like geography and economics. The English teacher is a real pain. Doesn't look like he'll be much help. Maths is hard but the teacher says we'll get it the second time around. She keeps saying try to stay with her and don't worry. So far science is bearable but we haven't got to the chemistry or physics strands yet.'

'You can do it, Aunty Cake. You just don't realise how intelligent you are.'

I laugh. 'I hope I can do it. I suppose I'll just keep plodding on and see what happens. It was so embarrassing in maths when I couldn't even remember what the division sign was.'

'How long is it since you met a division sign? Anyway, there are lots of uni students in your group at church who could help. Keep going.'

'Might as well. 'Til the money runs out.'

'What about TEAS? You get that, don't you?'

'Yeah, but it's not enough to live on. I'm using my savings as well and inflation's rocketing up. I hope you're impressed that I know about inflation!'

'Very impressed. Could you fix inflation?'

'Haven't learnt to do that yet. But it's so interesting discussing how political philosophies affect the distribution of wealth. It's how come Mr Whitlam gives me TEAS. I mean, we're living in economics! It's stuff I haven't even thought about before. I've always thought people were rich or poor because they worked hard or they didn't, but it's not like that, is it? There are so many other factors. How hard you work can be irrelevant.' Helen listens as I explore ideas of justice and wealth redistribution and employment statistics and so on. She smiles as she sees my enthusiasm mounting.

'So you like economics, do you?' She grins at last.

'Yeah and it's not only economics! It's physical geography too. Finding out how landforms are made and how long it takes, and it makes you see how insignificant humans are in time and space. Tom wouldn't say that, though, would he? He would have said we can still make enough mess to ruin the planet.'

'And that we matter to God.'

We're quiet for a while. Remembering.

'Any nice men there?' Helen asks.

'Economics! The teacher. Prince absolutely Charming.' I don't say that he's so charming he intimidates me. Why is it always like that? I get so nervous, anxious even, when there's a man about who I'd like to impress. 'There are some nice-looking students too but most of them are school boys or old chaps. The ones my age are all girls.'

As the term progresses our classes get smaller as people drop out. I consider joining them sometimes but at least I'm getting passes on assignments. I have to work hard but I'm enjoying the learning so much.

In English we have to listen to Terry drone on about his favourite rock bands and their controversial lyrics, and he gets angry when he asks a question of someone who doesn't know anything about them. I hold my breath and look at my desk when he's on the prowl. He's scathing of classical music lovers, people he thinks are ordinary, Christians, housewives and marriage. He is especially scathing of Christians.

Today he's baiting us with a filthy lyric about Jesus, and his usual swearing. I don't know what to say. Two girls in the front row tell him to stop.

'Why?' he demands.

'Because it's offensive and, yes, there are Christians out here.'

'Because it's offensive,' he mocks.

'Stop it, Terry!' Gaye says firmly. She knows Terry outside tech and he seems to take notice of her. He stops mocking and says, 'Anyone with a problem had better have the guts to see me after class, then.'

We go on with the lesson and I decide to see him after class. I'm so nervous I don't know if I'll be able to speak but I want to try because I don't think what he's doing is teaching and that's what we're here for. I'm also curious about whether I can do it. It seems safe to test myself here. How will Terry react? Will it make a difference?

'I want to talk to you, please,' I tell him after class.

'About?' He's looking at me down his nose through narrow eyes.

'About your language and how you behaved today.' Blimey, I sound like I should have a handbag over my arm, sensible black lace-up shoes and glasses at the end of my nose.

'Walk with me,' he says. He stops at the corner of the corridor, turns slowly and asks, as if he has the weight of the world on his shoulders, 'What do you want to say?'

'That, for an English teacher, you don't seem to have a very good command of English.'

'Go on,' he grunts.

'Your swearing offends me and so does your attitude to people with religious beliefs. I'm a Christian and you were offensive . . . er . . . to me . . . It seemed like you just wanted to shock us, not to teach us anything, and I don't think you should do that. We come to learn the English syllabus and we want you to teach us.' At last I stop and breathe. Listen to me! Who'd believe it!

'All right,' Terry replies slowly. He seems to be thinking, then he answers. 'I might have got carried away but I just want people to wake up. To make them contribute.'

'The way you did it doesn't make me want to.'

'Thanks for speaking your mind. I admire that you had the guts to do it. I'll try to curb the swearing if it's offensive. Thanks. Have to go to my next class. Thank you.'

At our next class he says that someone had come and talked to him and so he will watch his language. But it's really our fault. We make him want to swear because we don't argue. We just sit like a room full of sponges waiting to soak up what he says.

'You're the teacher, mate,' Smart Arse reminds him.

'So?' Terry asks menacingly.

'So teach us,' a few people say in unison.

'Look. I'm not here to fu–, sorry, to spoon feed you. You're adults. With minds. Think, for Chris– . Think! Use your brains. English is about ideas, arguments.' A few paces, then he bares his teeth, adding, 'Dis-cuss-i-on. That is what I want. I'm not going to stand up here and tell you what to think. You've got to have your own response to texts.'

'Well, I just don't know what Donne is trying to say,' someone contributes.

'Dammit, that's my point! What arrogant bastard says Donne is trying to say anything?'

In the deafening silence I wonder why Donne bothered writing and why we have to study his work if he wasn't trying to say anything. The silence is broken by Erica who expresses my thoughts.

Terry heaves a sigh at the housewife's question. 'Listen everybody. Carefully. Donne was not trying to say anything.' This time he stresses the word 'trying'. 'He has said what he has said. Right! What you have to do is try to understand what he has said. Discuss it. Argue about it, for Chri– . Discussion.'

'If they be two, they are two so
As stiffe twin compasses are two
Thy firmness draws my circle just
And make me end where I begunne.'

Good grief. Can't you just translate it into modern English?

We try to fathom the meaning of the text. Discussion is feeble. We don't know what Donne's on about beyond the literal meaning. I'm struggling but others are too. Terry's bullying doesn't help. It's entertaining when he has to stop himself swearing though.

'Well! You made an impression, didn't you?' Gaye says after class. 'It was you, wasn't it? He can barely speak without interrupting himself. Coming for coffee?'

We go to the canteen with some other people, including Trish who worked with Helen last year in her office. Soon we're grumbling about Terry and his teaching style again.

'He really is a great guy,' Gaye says firmly. 'He's got a brilliant mind.'

'It certainly doesn't show in class,' Trish challenges. 'He's so incredibly rude. And he doesn't teach. He just rants about and humiliates people.'

We all agree with Trish. All except Gaye who keeps defending him. 'He has such a brilliant mind he feels he should be doing something else.'

'Other than wasting his time with us dropouts and morons!' says Michelle who left school early, ran away from home and lived on the streets of Sydney.

'No. Well, oh I don't know,' Gaye says. 'Look, he has his good points too. Doesn't he, Kate?'

'Eh?' None that I know of.

'Well, you've talked to him.'

'Yeah, I did. He listened and he was polite. Then! But I don't reckon I should have needed to. He is rude in class.'

We often leave English feeling like this but as the class gets smaller, Terry's bad days seem to get less frequent. I discuss English with Lisa at home because she loves it. I spend a lot of time in the library when I can.

There are two different buses I can catch to get home but the timetables don't fit my tech hours so I spend a lot of time waiting around Central Station. Trish has a little motor scooter that she uses to get about. Could I get one? Just a little one like Trish's, not like Ken's. They don't cost much or use much petrol, Trish says. I could just afford one if I use Dad's money and I wouldn't have any more bus fares.

'Those little Hondas are rubbish,' Ken says. 'Get something with some grunt. A seven fifty. Something like that.'

'I want to look at your seven fifties,' I tell a salesman.

Is he laughing or just smiling very broadly as he says, 'A seven fifty, eh! Follow me'?

It's ages since Ken gave me a ride on his bike. Standing beside a seven fifty reminds me of standing beside a horse and wondering why they're measured in hands not yards.

'Can I get on?' I ask the salesman.

I must resemble Becky climbing onto her jungle gym. My feet

don't reach the ground when I make it onto the seat. The price tag makes me get off very quickly.

'Thought about something smaller? I suggest a two fifty. You've got power but not the height,' the salesman asks.

We move to the two fifties but again my toes barely reach the ground. The price tag makes me find it quickly.

'That's more like it,' the dealer says.

'No. I can't put my feet down.'

'Why do you want to put your feet down? You'll be riding it, not standing still. Tell you what. I'll let you have it for . . .'

Friends warned me about salesmen's pressure. 'I'll get my brother to look at it before I decide,' I tell him. He keeps trying to talk me into putting a deposit down but I keep walking.

Trish thinks I should get a scooter like hers and she's convincing, but the Jensons think a fifty cc motor is too small. We have the car discussion again.

'A young lady shouldn't be tearing around in city traffic on a scooter,' Mr Jenson says adamantly. But brick walls jump out in front of cars, don't they?

I compromise and buy a Honda ninety, a small step through with a small motor and automatic clutch. Gavin rides it home for me and offers to help me learn to ride.

'Thanks, but a friend from tech's going to teach me.' I'd rather make a fool of myself in front of a girl from tech than a boy from church. Especially a boy who I like but who thinks of me as a good listener, not a girlfriend.

Trish comes for our first lesson, which starts in the backyard. She tells me where all the controls are and what they're for. She makes it sound easy.

'Righto, on you get. Yeah, now. Oh, you silly. It's a step through! You don't have to get on that way. Just step through and sit down. Now turn the key. Yep. Now kick it over. No, of course I don't mean literally.'

The motor starts. 'Oh help! Oh help!'

'Now put it in first. Yeah, one click down. Now give it some

74

throttle. Not too mu– . Oh! Are you all right?' She laughs as I stagger like a drunk wrestling a bull.

Prince, the dog, comes out to watch and pants up my helmet.

'Oh go away,' I tell him. 'I don't need an audience with a breath like yours!'

'Okay. Try again. Get on and this time not too much throttle,' Trish commands.

This time I hold the handlebar tight and give it too much throttle. When the bike starts moving off without me I keep my grip. The bike spins and knocks me over. Trish is killing herself laughing. Prince is dancing about, barking. And now here's Mrs Thomas to see what Prince is getting so excited about.

'Oh, having some lessons, are you?' she says, leaning against the corner of the house.

Oh, being an audience, are you?

'Show me again?' I ask Trish when she can stand up straight.

Soon Prince is prancing around, barking again. Mercifully Mrs Thomas has to take him inside so he won't get hurt.

'Your turn,' Trish says. 'Did you see I didn't give it too much?'

This time the bike wobbles slowly along and I stay on. For a bit longer.

'Better!' Trish shouts, her eyebrows are nearly off the top of her face. 'Get on again.'

She's almost hoarse by the time I get enough courage to speed along at one mile per hour. Then two.

'Oh blimey! Oh blimey, oh blimey. I'm doing it!' Then, 'Oh blimey, oh blimey, oh blimey, the tree!' Well, it's only a shrub and it's not too prickly to land in.

Poor Trish is exhausted and her sides ache but she has to go to work.

'Did you take this long to learn?' I ask her.

'Don't think so,' she laughs. 'But you're getting better. No brick walls! See you in English.'

*

'Off to church, then?' asks my geriatric gaoler with matching dog.

'Yes. Off to church.'

'Not going on your scooter?'

'Not yet. Still walking.'

'Oh, I thought you'd go on your scooter.'

'No. I'm not good enough yet.'

Gavin asks again if I'd like him to give me some lessons. I'd die if he saw me wobbling along and landing in bushes. That does it! I just have to make myself get out on the street and learn.

'Going riding, are you?' Mrs Thomas asks.

'Just having a practice.' Wouldn't you like a long rest? Or a nice, long cup of tea? With Prince?

I start the bike and wobble down the yard into the street. Our street is very wide and it doesn't have much traffic unless the nearby Greek Orthodox church is having a festival. They aren't today, thank goodness. The lady next door comes out to rock her baby in the sunshine. I wave to her but she doesn't recognise me in all my gear. I've got my helmet on and a big yellow coat so I'll be easy to see in traffic.

The first time I fall off I only have an audience of two people and a dog. It seems the number swells by two each time I hit the ground. I can't go to the next street because it's a main road. All right! That's enough. I'm going home. I get on, rev the throttle because I'm so annoyed with myself for not being able to balance.

A miracle! I'm riding. I'm going fast enough to stay up! I can hear people clapping. I keep going right to the end of the street and even manage to stop the more conventional way. Yes! I've done it. Try going back. Yes!

Soon I've become boring to the audience but I'm happily puttering up and down Clyde Street at the awesome speed of fifteen miles an hour. I can't wait to tell Trish. Show her maybe. Will I ride to tech tomorrow?

'You'll have to get some practice in traffic before you go into town!' Mrs Jenson warns me.

'You're not riding it to tech, are you? Into town?' Mr Jenson demands.

'Oh, be careful, won't you?' Mrs Jenson pleads.

Everyone is sure I'm going to be killed or maimed if I use the bike for the purpose I bought it. I don't know whether I'm impressed by their concern or insulted that they think I can't manage. I practise for a few more weeks and study the road rules. Trish says I ought to ride it into town now. She tells me where the free parking spots are around Central, the ones where bikes don't get stolen if you chain them up.

The traffic is smelly and often slow but I love travelling this way. No waiting around for buses and no creepy, groping weirdos to ignore. Just me. My helmet makes a useful footstool and carry bag, though it's a bit heavy and clumsy at times. I can stay in the library and study without worrying about the bus times or I can zip off home and study there.

Soon I'm going to someone's for dinner nearly every night and I'm struggling to keep up with my work.

'All right, *The Dubliners*,' Terry sighs. 'One of Joyce's classics, would you say?'

No-one contributes. We recognise the belligerent tone. He's had a bad weekend. Am I the only one who found *The Dubliners* too depressing to stay home and read past the first few chapters? I look at my desk, not at Terry.

'Anyone?'

I still get anxious when he's angry, when anyone is angry. I cringe inside.

'Dust!' he shouts, slamming his *Dubliners* on the table and beginning to pace. 'How does Joyce use dust as a symbol? Hm? A symbol for what? Hm? Anyone? No-one? Jeezuz Curiste!'

Silence.

'Has anyone read the fucking book?'

'Yes,' some people mumble.

'All right, then.' He sounds as if he's trying to pull himself together. 'Let's look at dust. Remember the scene in the kitchen?

Hm?' He can't do it. He's furious, pacing up the aisle between our desks. Stopping next to mine.

'What have you got? Dust for brains! Christ, say something, someone. Kate?'

I freeze. Can't think. Beside me. Shouting.

'Is there dust on your cupboard?'

'Don't know.'

'Don't know!' he yells. 'You bloody well ought to know.'

He keeps pacing and shouting at me, then at everyone.

It gradually occurs to me that I don't have to put up with this. I can just go home. I pack my bag and walk slowly out. I'm in a peaceful daze. Going home. On my bike.

Halfway there it hits me. I've walked out on a class! Am I allowed to? Will I be able to go back or will I get chucked out of the course? What will happen then? You can't do much without English. I feel tears welling up with anxiety. I've ruined everything. I've been doing well enough and even applied for a teaching scholarship. I've come this far and now I've just thrown it all away.

Calm down and think. Talk it through with friends. Helen and Gen are sharing a flat in Glebe now so I call in and tell them what's happened.

'Good for you,' Helen says. She talks a lot about people treating each other respectfully.

'Yeah! You're right to walk out. He's a teacher. You pay him to teach not bully you,' Gen agrees. 'Do it again if he starts carrying on like that again.'

'So you reckon I can just go back?'

'Course you can go back. Just roll up and sit down like you always do. You might have made him stop and think.'

I make sure I've finished reading *The Dubliners* before the next English class. When Terry comes in, he walks straight to my desk and puts an envelope in front of me. What do I do? Open it now or wait 'til class is finished? It might say, 'Get out and don't come back' or 'You'd better change to someone else's English class. I'm not having you in mine.' He must have intended for me to open it now or he'd have kept it for later.

It's an apology. Terry says it's frustrating having people with ideas who don't express them but it's no excuse for behaving badly.

'What does it say?' people want to know later.

'It's an apology,' I tell them.

'Oh yeah. He did that after you left. Big apology and then a proper lesson. *Dubliners*! God, I don't know what that's on the syllabus for!'

What will I do about the letter? I think the right thing to do is to say that I accept the apology. I have a few tries before I'm satisfied with my reply.

Dear Terry,
Thank you for your apology.
I will try to say what I think but I find it hard to express my ideas out loud. It's harder when you are angry.
I accept your apology.
Sincerely,
Kate.

I go to the phone box down the street to ring and ask Gen and Helen what they think before I give Terry the letter. No-one is home so I hang up. My money doesn't fall through to the refund chute. I put my finger up the chute, hoping that, if my coins are stuck I might be able to dislodge them. No coins. Just a wad of paper. It's hard to pull it out but when I do a flood of coins comes pouring out, spilling onto the floor. When will they stop?

What will I do? I only wanted my coins back but now I've got everybody's. Will I take it all? I shouldn't. It's not mine. But if I don't, someone else will. But what if the person who stuck the paper up there sees me and comes after me? I scoop the money up quickly and shove it in my pockets, then dash home hoping no-one's watching.

Will I go back later? No. The letter will be all right. I can't go back to the phone box tonight. What if the paperstuffer comes back for his money?

I leave the letter on Terry's desk and no more is said. English classes improve and I find myself enjoying them. I enjoy the literature and the ideas and I'm getting less worried when there's no right answer or a single truth. *King Lear* is especially interesting. Why doesn't Cordelia just say what her father wants to hear and make him happy? Would it cost so much to make him happy? Daughters should do that, shouldn't they? But if she does, she won't be telling the truth and she'll be flattering a too proud old man who needs to learn some lessons. But, then again, she shouldn't break his heart.

I hope I never get into a situation where the boundary between right and wrong is so confusing and the consequences so dire. I don't understand, at this stage, that I have been Cordelia. It will be years before I remember, before I confront the confusion again and move on.

Richard II is our drama for the HSC and we start discussing it over lunch.

'Wish we could just sit somewhere and read the whole thing straight through.'

'Yeah. Take parts and just keep reading.'

'The rooms here are all used at night as well as during the day, though. Where could we do it?'

'Come to my place!' I say, as if this is the church group.

To my surprise everyone is keen. I can't back out. I tell them I know someone who's an English teacher, and people say it would be great if he came too.

Harvey is single and lives with his parents. He loves good wine, which he rolls in magazines and hides in his wine rack so his Temperance Union parents think it's just a magazine rack. Being one of the few men still unmarried at church, Harvey, with his gentleness and intelligent conversation was popular with the single women. He became a different kind of popular when he came out about his preference for men. I like Harvey but I've never found him attractive. That means I'm relaxed with him, relaxed enough to ask him to come and read *Richard II* with us. He loves Shakespeare and he's very keen to help out.

I'm nervous about having the students at my flat but I get busy cooking spaghetti and then welcoming them. They want to know why I'm alone and so on but soon we get on to talking about tech. Harvey arrives just after we've started reading.

He starts talking and it becomes obvious that he's brought his two-hour lecture along. I can't make him stop! He allows questions but then he's off again. We're not doing what we planned. No-one seems bothered but me, though. They're listening attentively.

'How long do you reckon it'd take us to read the text through in one go?' someone asks.

'Let's give it a go!' someone else suggests before Harvey can get revved up again.

'Jack can be Richard and . . .'

'Yes. Good idea,' says Harvey. 'Mind you, you'll have a pretty late night! I have a tape of the whole play that you could borrow, Kate, and if you get together again you could listen to it. Anyway, I'd better be off and do my marking.'

'I'm so sorry he talked so much,' I tell them after he leaves.

'No! That was great! I think I know what we're supposed to see in it now.'

'Yeah. I don't agree with him but I think I know what the arguments are.'

'Wish bloody Terry would teach us like that!'

We start reading and the play comes alive. Those of us who don't read parts are as involved as the rest, and I'm sad when someone says, 'Better call it quits, I reckon. I have to be up early for work.'

I relive the night as I fall asleep. I'm so relieved that I don't have to work as well as study! I'm so lucky with Dad's money, my work payout and the TEAS allowance.

*

We've finished the physical geography strand of our course and now we're studying human geography. Why do people live where they do? What structures exist to support them and how these interact?

The roles of schools, churches, clubs and so on fascinate me. Are they means of social control or are they expressions of our culture? What if there were no controls? Would that be worse than too much control? Growing up at Burnside meant rules that controlled every breath we took. Is it really true that other institutions were controlling all the people who didn't grow up in orphanages, the outsiders I thought were doing whatever they liked? Like I do now? Is the church controlling me? I think the church presents me with ideas and I decide whether to live by them or not. I control the controlling with my conscience. But is my conscience controlled? I'm enjoying the arguments even if I am losing control of my brain!

Do I mind that my church wants to control me? I remember Jane's dying time. I mind that one man can claim a monopoly on God. Why does what Reverend Cooper believes carry more weight than what I or Gen or any of the others believe? Why can't we express our beliefs in ways we see as appropriate, without that one man directing and judging?

I keep thinking of a movie I saw recently, *The Shoes of the Fisherman*. Social and economic inequalities in the world are explored and, in the closing scene, the Pope pledges the wealth of the church to feed the poor of the world. Now I'm wondering if my church has wealth stored away in vaults. Jesus would hate that. Do I want to be part of that hoarding, ignoring starving millions all over the world? No. But I love the people at our church.

A card arrived in the letter box the other day. It's a World Vision card. A black and white photo of a black woman dressed in rags holding a baby on her hip while another child leans against her thin legs. On the back is a short story about her. Her name is Rosa. When her brother and husband were butchered, she took her baby and began a long walk to a refugee camp. On the way, abandoned children attached themselves to her and she tried to care for them, although she had nothing to give. Now she might have to watch her baby die because she has absolutely nothing left to give him. Unless she makes it to a feeding station.

The church could feed her and those children if it didn't have to repair stained-glass windows, build new halls, and pay ministers who think they're the only people God talks to. When I get a job I'll send money to World Vision. No, Rosa didn't say she'd help when she found work. She helped with what she had, so I will too. I'll give the little bit I gave to the church to World Vision instead. I start sponsoring a child.

Do I want to lose the lovely people in the church? No! They've been so good to me. They've watched over me, been friends and advisers. I don't reject them but I reject the institution in which we met.

In our human geography class we discuss the role of the church.

'Who'd want to believe in God when all He does is create wars and tell people to hang out in churches?'

'God doesn't create wars. People do.'

'People create wars because they reckon God told them to.'

This discussion wouldn't happen at church and I like listening to the arguments. I join in. 'The church isn't the same thing as God. The church is what people, some people, think God wants them to do. But if they get it wrong, it doesn't follow that God got it wrong. Maybe God doesn't go to church.'

Some people laugh. Some argue that God inspires churches to do what they do. Others argue that there's no such thing as God. I know there is, so that doesn't bother me. And then some say that God is just imagined by weak people who can't make decisions for themselves. No, I don't think that's true. I feel weak much of the time but I make decisions and so do lots of people at church. Maybe weak people are too scared to believe in God.

Richard, our teacher, says quietly to me as the others keep

arguing, 'You sound as if you'd enjoy a chat with Martin. Do you know him? He teaches Geography here. He and his wife have a home church. They think the same as you about churches.'

I don't know what a home church is. What if they are a kooky brainwashing sect or something? Now the backing of a huge institution has value because it provides checks and balances with a tradition of teachings going back nearly two thousand years. I'll think about it for a while. No need to decide straight away. At home I look at the photo of Rosa and decide to go and talk with Martin. That can't do any harm.

Martin is warm and jovial, a bit like Tom, and he's been expecting me. 'Glad to meet you.' He grins. 'Pull up a chair. Richard says you had a fairly lively discussion about churches.'

'We did.'

We talk for a while and what Martin describes is what I've come to think a real church ought to be. It sounds like what we had before Tom died – a meeting of believers who do not have a minister to tell them what to think. They own no buildings but meet in each other's houses and share a meal together, with communion.

'Come along, if you like,' Martin invites, writing his address on a piece of paper. 'No pressure, but if you want to, bring something to share for lunch.'

Martin seems normal and he seems to believe the same things that Christians normally do, except for the structure of the church. I decide to give home church a go, even though it's at Ryde. I bake some scones and strap them to my bike with my Bible.

Martin introduces me to Bel, his wife, and then to their little daughter, who reminds me of Becky when I first met her. The other people there are welcoming. Most are teachers or academics. As I mix with them, I can feel that I've changed. I'm not as shy as I used to be. When I'm asked what I do for a living I say I'm a student and it feels more interesting than saying I'm a clerk. When I tell them I've been an insurance clerk they say I'm brave for doing what I'm doing. I can't see anything brave about it. There is a safety net back in Martin Place.

I don't tell them much about Burnside because I don't want to be a curiosity. I don't want to risk their thinking I'm a lesser being, like people from school used to think of us homes kids.

The meeting is noisy and the people seem normal. They obviously care about each other and are respectful in their arguments. No-one is dictating what they have to believe and they talk about everyday life and this meeting as if they are part of each other. Church is not just for Sundays.

Home church becomes a vital part of my Sundays, and when I go back to my old church at night, it seems like ritual without substance. I still love the singing. Just wish I could see the people without having to do the ritual.

At tech we're in the weeks leading up to the HSC exams before we can believe it. Teachers are piling on the work and telling us what they think we most need to review. We're grumbling about the workload but some of us admit quietly that we're grateful for it, too, because our teachers are really committed to getting us through.

When I open the English exam paper, I'm elated. Well, not at first, but when I calm down and think clearly, I realise that there are questions in each section that I have answered and studied during the year. The questions are just worded differently. I settle into writing a storm of words.

Each exam is like this – I know how to answer the questions. Except in the physics and chemistry papers. I go to those exams knowing I should fail because I just don't understand them. In those courses I've sometimes thought I've grasped a fact but without the blackboard demonstration I'm lost. Physics seems to be a series of formulas for a series of insignificant events. I've learnt as many of them as I can and feel grateful for the fact that it's a multiple choice exam, because I might fluke some right answers. Chemistry has a multiple choice component too, so if my equations don't balance and I change gold into slime, or whatever happens in chemistry, I still might fluke a pass.

The results take ages to come, and when they do I'm almost too frightened to open the envelope. I can still be an insurance clerk if I fail.

I've passed! Well enough to get into Macquarie University! I can't believe it! University! Me! I didn't do well enough to get into Sydney University where Lisa went but, good heavens, there's a university that will accept me. Their standards must be low but I don't care. I'm in! I walk quickly to the phone box and start ringing friends. They're all so proud of me and they ask the burning question: 'What will you do at uni?'

'Don't know. I'm waiting to see if I get a teaching scholarship. I'm praying for a scholarship!' People assume I passionately want to be a teacher. God knows!

God, please let me get the scholarship because you know how I'm so scared of having to find a job. That's what I'll have to do if I have to keep studying without one. I pester Him with this prayer as if He'll give in because I'm pestering. Pestering didn't get Jane healed but this is a smaller thing than life and death.

Inflation has reached record levels and my money has dwindled away. Without a scholarship I'll have to give up or work part time and study part time. And there's no social worker like Miss Molesworth now to help me with job interviews if I don't get the scholarship. What if Miss Molesworth is sitting up in Heaven, playing her harp with Jane and Tom, and they're all pestering the Almighty to give me a scholarship? I tell Gen about this scene I've created in my mind.

'You'll get it,' she smiles. 'you're brainy, kiddo! But Tom will be doing his bit I'm sure.'

'Course you will,' Helen adds. 'And if you don't, you could go back to the Colonial Mutual part time, couldn't you?'

'Maybe, but I'd have to spend so much time and money travelling I wouldn't be able to get to classes or get the assignments done.'

'There are plenty of jobs about. Get one close to uni, in the Union or Co-op Bookshop or something.'

'All the students will be competing for the close ones, though, won't they? Especially in the Students' Union. I wouldn't have a hope if I had to compete with young kids straight from school. And Trish and Gaye and all the others said that part-time study is bliss if you don't want to sleep for the next four years. I need the scholarship. If I don't get one I might have to give up and be a clerk.'

'You can't give up now!'

Soon the answer comes. I am offered a teaching scholarship. I have to agree to teach for three years at whatever school the Department of Education sends me to or I'll have to pay back the money they give me. Three years! What if I'm no good at it?

'Face that further down the track. Just do the uni part for now.' That's the advice all my friends give me. All right. I'll do it! I'm going to university. Me! I can hardly believe it. At home I find my Vocational Guidance Report from school.

'Tertiary study would probably be beyond her capabilities.'

I hope they're wrong.

BRAIN STRAIN

'I'll come too,' Gen says.

'You've decided? For sure? You're already a teacher.'

'Yeah. But I could upgrade. Why not? We planned to get Tom's degree done first and then mine. Might as well get mine now.'

We study the course lists but we get so confused we just laugh and throw our proposed lists away. Enrolment day is coming up, though, so we have to knuckle down and work out what we need to do in fourth year, then work backwards to first year to make sure we have the right prerequisites.

All the course descriptions look like they're written in a foreign language. I need a dictionary but my *Blackies Pocket Dictionary* doesn't help. I have to major in education. I don't know what there is to study about education – don't you just have to know everything about the subject and tell it to the kids? But Terese was learning all that child development stuff. I want to learn that, although somewhere inside I feel frightened of it too. Must be that I'm just not confident.

It's all right that we have to go to lectures and tutorials, whatever they are, but I'm horrified to discover that we have to present oral papers, not just written ones, and lead discussions. Can't we just learn stuff and participate in discussions like we did at tech?

Thousands of people wait in queues that meander slowly past advisers' tables on enrolment day. Some students are laughing and looking confident but some of us are still studying our course lists, trying to convince ourselves that we know what we're doing here. At last I'm sitting at a table while an adviser scans my plan.

'Hm. You don't have enough level two courses. What about some history?'

'I've never done history.'

'Well, all I can see is that you'll have to do history or chemistry to get your credit points. Now there you go again – choking when I mention chemistry. History it is, then? Cheer up! You might enjoy it.'

Four years of my brain space are eventually mapped out. I'll be struggling through a series of courses presented in foreign languages that pretend to be English. Four years! What have I done? Maybe I should ring Mr Mansouriani before they've paid me any of the scholarship.

Gen and I meet up after we're through. We both feel a hundred years older. We play Flanders and Swann records to cheer ourselves up. They were Tom's favourites and now, laughing again and remembering hysterical nights back then are what we need.

'A cup of tea. A cup of tea. Aah! Counting credit points. Now where was I? One thousand, six hundred and ninety two credit points. Or was it nine thousand, six hundred. Um! One, two, three.' Laughing and remembering. We'll be right, we tell each other. Gen will be.

I love riding my bike from Marrickville to Macquarie each day with my books strapped on the back. I don't feel worried until the rain starts bucketing down. Then I have to go slowly and watch out for oil on the road. My backpack keeps my things dry and a waterproof suit keeps me dry. It's not until I skid in oil and slide under a car that I realise the risk I'm taking. Nothing but skin and pride are broken but it would be better if I lived closer to uni.

As I read the 'To Let' list in the estate agent's window, my stomach churns. Each place costs more than my whole scholarship.

Talking with home church people about it, they agree that it would be better, safer, for me to move closer.

'Can't your parents help you out?'

'I don't have any parents.' They ask, so I tell them about my mother dying when I was four and my father's death. They don't know what to say except that I'm brave.

Later Bel says, 'My parents have got a house at Ryde and they're going away for three months. They'll be looking for someone to mind it. Would you consider that? They wouldn't want any rent but you might have to take some phone calls for them. People will know Mum and Dad are away, though, so there probably won't be any. What do you think?'

'Take it,' Gen says without hesitation.

'But I'll have to give up my flat. And what'll I do when Bel's parents come back? Where will I go?'

'Don't worry about it. Something will come up. You could meet someone to share with at uni. Take it!'

I feel sad leaving Clyde Street. An era is ending for me and I'm going into a great unknown. It's scary. I load up my step through and Gen puts the rest in her car.

The Greens' house is big but it's homely. I settle in and resolve to study hard on the sunny front verandah every day when I get home. It's great not having to spend so much time travelling.

Lisa, who is now married to Andy, rings. We haven't seen each other since I started uni and she's dying to know how I'm going. She invites me to dinner.

'I'd love to come,' I tell her. 'But there's so much work! So much reading. I can't believe it.'

She asks what courses I'm doing and sounds as if she knows exactly what's involved in each one.

'It seems like I'd better take up residence in Special Reserve,' I say.

'What's Special Reserve? In the Union?'

'No. It's in the library, where tutors put photocopies of articles on the reading list. You can borrow them but not take them away from the library. Hundreds of people want them at the same time so you spend so long waiting around to get them. And you know what a terrible reader I am. A tent in the wretched library's what I need!'

'Can you photocopy articles and take them home? That's what I used to do.'

'Too expensive. Better for my budget to stay in the library. Can we put dinner off until I get the hang of this? Or could you bring it to the library?'

'Course we can. Put it off, I mean. Ring if I can help with anything. We've probably got some of the books you need.'

Lisa helped me out in maths and English last year. She reckons I'll be right because I don't just want to know what to do. I want to know why as well. She says that if you want to understand why, you have the right kind of mind. She's confident that I'll manage. She doesn't believe I'm a poor reader but I really do need to read some things four times before I understand them.

Gen and I share resources and she calls in so we can study together. Our breaks are regular and we spend a fair bit of time sitting on the verandah in the sun, eating pancakes and warbling away to John Denver tapes. Sometimes we really do study, though, because we can't afford to waste too much time. We're passing so far. Their standards mustn't be as high as I thought if I can get passes. Gen's brainy, so she would pass. But me! I struggle with the volume of work and the ideas. Gen struggles against being told what to think and what to present in her papers.

'If they want us to say what we think, they shouldn't mark us down for saying it!'

I am not good at saying what I think, sometimes because I don't know what I think and sometimes because I don't want to show how dumb I am. I don't contribute enough in tutorials. I'll have to try harder and butt in instead of politely waiting for a gap in the discussion. I'm torn between hiding because I'm shy and butting in because the tutor is watching and marking us on our participation.

'Kate, there's a friend of ours, Virginia, who's leaving her husband and I've told her she can move into Mum and Dad's,' Bel tells me one day.

I feel betrayed. 'When do I have to move?'

'No. You don't have to move! Gosh no! She'll just move into Mum's room.'

I don't want to share with a stranger but this is Bel's friend and it's her parents' house.

'Like a cup of coffee?' I offer a welcoming gesture to Virginia when she arrives. I take out my favourite yellow mugs and make us both a cup.

'Oh heavens! Surely they don't use these!' Virginia exclaims as if I've given her a used paper cup from a rubbish dump.

'No. They're mine.'

'Oh! I prefer a cup and saucer.' She takes out two dainty cups and saucers and pours herself a new coffee.

'I'll keep my mug.' Wish I could keep my solitude.

That night I'm woken from a deep sleep by the phone ringing. It's right outside my door.

'Hello. Is Virginia there?'

It's five in the morning. It happens every morning now and Virginia doesn't hear the phone because it isn't outside her door.

'Why does he ring so early?' I ask, hoping Virginia will take the hint.

'He's on his way to work,' she replies, ignoring it.

'Can't he ring later?'

'No.' End of conversation.

I love the days when I get home first. I can sit wherever I like and spread my books and papers as far as I need to. I can drink yellow mugs of coffee and play Rita Coolidge or Rod Stewart.

Where are my mugs? Gone! She wouldn't chuck them out, would she? No. She just hides them at the back of the cupboard behind the pretty cups and saucers. My coming home ritual now is to find my hidden mug before I make my coffee. When I dry my mug I put it at the front and wait for it to be rejected again. Virginia doesn't give up and I don't either. We don't say anything about it. We just keep playing mug hide, mug seek. I giggle about it on good days.

I always get my assignments in at the last minute. The lecturers and tutors have warned us about applying for extensions, which are for emergencies only and will not be given to people who just don't work hard enough. Well, I'm going to have to get an assignment done for Introduction to Psychology soon. The focus of the course is aggression and we've had to buy some really expensive text books because we'll use them so much. *The Dynamics of Aggression*. How could there be a whole book on getting cranky? Probably written in a language they reckon is English too!

My oral paper is about crowding. Does crowding cause aggressive behaviour? Dunno. It does in me at home. Frustration aggression.

With bundles of photocopied articles, I set myself up in the sun and start reading. Mice? This article is about an experiment where mice are kept in a lab in normal numbers and they behave normally. When lots more mice are put in, the mice behave abnormally, often aggressively. Very interesting. What do mice have to do with humans, though? Make 'em frustrated if they can't keep them out of cupboards! Is that frustration aggression? Be serious, get on with it.

What else is there in the mountain of readings? An article about the Kung of the Kalahari who choose to crowd together when they have a whole desert to spread out in. They rarely sit down anywhere without some part of them touching at least one other person. That'd drive me nuts! The Kung have far fewer

93

biological indicators of stress than anyone else in the world and aggression is rare. This is fascinating and I chuckle that I can now say 'biological indicators of stress'. If Denise or Roy at Colonial Mutual could see me now!

Must get my paper written. I'd be quicker if there was one right answer, one explanation that jumps out and whacks me between the eyes. This interpreting behaviour based on our reading and arguing our case is very tedious. I don't know which side of the argument I agree with. Crowding causes aggression or contributes to it or something else is going on. City life is stressful. Desert life is lonely. No, *can* be stressful. *Can* be lonely. Mustn't get cause and correlation mixed up. I don't know what the answer is!

'Just pick one, pretend you believe it, then argue around it!' mature-aged Judy says. 'They don't care what you really think as long as you argue well. Play the game, Kate. That's what you have to do.'

It feels like a game in which the organisers aren't telling us what the actual rules are. Lisa agrees. 'Say what's expected. Just aim to pass and don't worry about distinctions. And don't try to read everything on the list. Just do enough to get by.' I'll have to experiment to find out how much is enough.

Tutorial discussions often spill over into lunchtime. I feel out of my depth sometimes so I take the role of making them laugh by playing with their words like Jane used to do.

'Frustration aggression, could explain the behaviour of so many people in our prisons,' Rosmary declares.

'And chocolate shops,' I suggest.

I can do it for Psychology and for Education too.

'The teacher leads you to the threshold of your own mind! I love Kahlil Gibran,' Linda says dreamily.

'Lead me to someone else's, please!' I beg. It saves me expressing an opinion, blushing madly and then having to keep arguing to support a view I don't really hold. I still hate being the centre of attention. Gen always knows what to say and she doesn't get embarrassed like I do. The social part of uni hasn't been as hard as

I expected because I practised at tech and Gen is often around too. We sit with a group of mature-age students who got into uni via a special program that Macquarie has. I'd been nine months too young to qualify and these people are impressed that I matriculated. I'm impressed that they've come without a year of study practice at tech.

I feel comfortable with them. Mostly.

Noelene, a vivacious ex-cruise ship stewardess, continues a psychology discussion about homosexuality. 'Well, the way I see it is I've got a hole and you've got something to put in it.'

What? Fancy saying that out loud. In public. To a man. Wish Gen was here for this one! Would she just sit with her mouth hanging open? She'd think of something funny to say or change the subject.

She'd know what to do if Georgie started rubbing her on the thigh and making eyes at her too, apart from move further and further away until she's nearly sitting on Sue's lap. Is Georgie really leering at me the way sleazy men do? I don't sit beside her again.

The mature women often say, 'We all know men are only interested in one thing.' It makes me cringe. I think I agree but why? I haven't even had a boyfriend, so how would I know? None of the boys at church behaved that way. Why does what they say feel right? Don't think about it. Must be just that stinking sailor at Circular Quay and the Burnside boys shouting rude things about my big breasts.

One of the women is studying Freud and Jung and she wants us to tell her our recurring dreams. There are classic symbols that help us to understand them, she says. I've been having recurring dreams lately – a wolf attacks me or I steal clocks. And there's one about my father scaring me but it isn't really a dream. Or is it? I don't want to think about it. I definitely don't want to tell this lot about them. I listen while they talk about their dreams and the symbols, but mine make my brain freeze.

*

Bel's parents will be home soon so I need to start looking for a place to live. I've kept an eye on the local paper and there haven't been any places I can afford. Not by myself and I don't know anyone who wants to share. Virginia has found somewhere else and she didn't invite me or my mugs. Back to the local paper, then.

'It's a lovely bush room,' a nice motherly voice says when I ring the number in an ad. 'When would you like to come and look?' The flat is at Epping and costs thirty dollars per week. I can only just about afford it.

'Oh! You didn't say you're a bikie!' the landlady says crossly when I arrive.

'No. It's just a little step through. A scooter,' I tell her.

'Well, I won't have any of those biker people here,' she warns.

'I don't know any bikies,' I tell her. I don't mention that the uni motorcycle club has invited me to go on rides with them. I probably won't go because I don't think I'd keep up with their big bikes. I'll stick to laughing at their jokes about where I put the rubber bands on mine.

The landlady takes me under some bushes, dodging rain drops, to the back of her house. We must be going to a little granny flat like Mrs Thomas's. 'Here we are, then,' she says, smiling and opening the door.

The room is certainly unique, as it was described in the ad. The main wall is a natural cliff and rain is trickling down it into an open drain that runs along the living room floor.

'It's beautifully cool in summer,' she assures me.

'It's cold just now.'

'You could get a radiator! They don't cost much.'

There's a tiny bathroom which also uses the cliff for a wall. I like that this is so unusual but I'm sure I'll freeze to death. The timber walls aren't sealed against the cliff so I imagine hordes of mozzies and flies in summer and hordes of dollars going on electricity in winter.

How do I tell her I don't want to live in her flat? She'll be offended.

'Can I think about it and let you know?'

'Well, I suppose you could, but if anyone else answers the advertisement, I'll have to show them.'

'Yes. All right.'

'Just tell her you don't want it! You don't owe her anything,' Gen says. It's so obvious when Gen says it. I don't owe her anything, do I! Even if she's nice. I ring and tell her that I don't want the flat. It's hard to do and I'm relieved that she says there's a young man who's interested.

'I'll come over on the weekend and we'll look at some others, if you like,' Gen says.

There is only one flat advertised in this week's local paper that I can afford. Just. Gen and I meet the owner there on Saturday morning.

The house is old and the fresh paint doesn't quite disguise its dilapidated state. It's divided into four flats and we're shown into a side one that consists of a bedroom, kitchen, lounge and bathroom.

'Gaps in the weatherboards,' Gen whispers. 'Must have been the verandah and they've filled it in.'

The owner overhears and, throwing her hands in the air, she remarks, 'Twenty-fiva dolla!'

We hear someone walking about in the next flat, and kids laughing through the walls.

'Walls are thin,' says Gen.

'I'd have to buy a fridge. And a heater,' I say.

Again the owner throws her hands up and sings at us, 'Twenty-fiva dolla!'

'We'll talk it over and let you know this afternoon,' Gen tells her. 'It does have some problems.'

Again the hands go up. 'What ken you expeck . . .'

'For twenty-fiva dolla,' Gen and I join in. The owner looks confused but we smile and repeat that we'll let her know.

'Kate, you can't live in that!'

'I'll have to. There's nothing else on offer and I have to move next weekend.'

'Oh well. What can you expect for twenty-fiva dolla?' Gen repeats what is to become our catch phrase for all of life's little disappointments.

My brother, Ken, visits soon after I've moved in. He's amused by my new life and surroundings.

'How's the student sister?' He grins.

'Pretty good,' I tell him. 'The work's hard, though.'

'Brr. It's cold in here. Where's the heater?'

'Haven't got one.'

'Pretty basic, isn't it?' Then he pulls a bundle out of his bag. 'Here. You get these ready and I'll be back.'

'Get what ready?'

'Open it. Open it.' He flips his hand at the parcel.

He's brought us a huge feast of prawns! 'Get 'em ready. I hate peeling them.' And he's gone.

I peel the prawns and wonder what he's up to. Soon he comes back with a very large box.

'Happy birthday,' he beams.

We huddle over my birthday radiator, eating prawns and chatting.

'Heard from Kerry?' I ask.

'Yeah. She's all right. I'm going up to stay with them next month. I've got holidays owing so I might as well go. Haven't seen them since Mike got back.'

Ken helped Kerry out while Mike was in Vietnam and I think he misses them now that they've moved interstate. He's happy at work and in the boarding house. He doesn't mention a girlfriend so I guess he's a late starter like me. But he's very private and only tells what he wants to tell and I don't feel I should probe. It's not like friends who can say anything to each other. Ken decides what happens between us and I just go along with it. Is that what little sisters do? I don't know but it's what I do. Ken says he thinks he'll study law one day. I hope he does and I hope he turns out to be brainier than me.

Soon I meet Carmel, the woman who lives in the front flat

98

with her two little girls. Carmel is a divorcee whose mum cares for the girls while she does uni. We've never noticed each other there, though. We're doing different degrees.

'It must be hard for you with the kids and study,' I say.

'Yes it is, but I don't aim for top grades. I just do the minimum to get through. I finish this year.'

She inspires me. If she can get through with the pressure she's under, surely I can!

When I see her with her girls it reminds me of how much I miss Becky, Mousy and Jane. It reminds me, too, of how much I want to have children. The feeling increases a hundredfold when I go to Martin and Bel's and see them with their new baby. Every fibre of my body screams for babies. When am I going to meet someone? Maybe I won't. I'm twenty-five already. Bel is as sure as Gen that there's someone out there for me. Where's he hiding then?

I keep telling myself there's someone out there for me, so I can push away the feeling that I'm not good enough, that something is wrong with me. One day I will breastfeed a baby like Bel does and my loving husband will change the nappies and help with the baby burping.

At least uni distracts me from this longing. By the end of first semester I'm struggling less with the workload but still struggling. Perhaps I shouldn't have thought their standards were so low. I've had to ask for an extension for one assignment and, luckily I was able to use the excuse of moving house. I begin reading some second semester texts during the break to try to get ahead but we won't get the full reading lists until next semester starts.

During the break I also realise I need a lounge. In my flat I have a bed and a cupboard, a table and two chairs, and a second-hand fridge. But no lounge, so when people come there's nowhere comfortable to sit. I know a furniture place in Glebe that's cheap and they have a special on, including five dollars delivery anywhere in Sydney. I choose my lounge, imagining that it'll have to last a long time and one day I'll share it with my own family.

'I'll have to be careful now,' I tell Gen. 'Someone'll want to marry me for my lounge!'

It should arrive today, and when I dash home after my morning lectures, I find the delivery truck is already waiting. The men watch me park my bike and take off my helmet.

'Hello. You're early. I said I wouldn't get back from uni before now. Sorry you had to wait.'

'Student, are you? Live here while you study, eh?' the older man asks while they carry the lounge inside. 'Cheap rent?' he asks.

'Yeah. I'm a student.'

He goes outside, back to the truck, and the other man waits in the doorway as I count coins to make up the five dollars.

'Three and a kiss,' he says, moving closer.

'What?'

'Kiss me and you can give me three instead of five.' He leers, showing his stained yellow teeth.

Darkness. Old fear. Revulsion. He's the ugliest little creep I've ever seen. I can't think what to say, though. 'Take the five dollars,' I tell him.

He pockets the money and writes a receipt.

'I'll give it back for a kiss. Proper kiss,' he says, still leering.

What should I say now? Suddenly he grabs me and sticks his putrid tongue in my mouth! I try to push him away. He grabs my breast and growls, 'All the way for nothing.'

Now I'm thinking and acting. I push him hard, backwards. He only just balances at the top of my stairs. Should have pushed him hard enough to make him fall and break his bloody neck! He shrugs his vile little shoulders and walks to the truck.

I slam the door and scrub out my mouth. I wash away my tears over and over again. Why? What did I do? Why does he think it's all right to do that? I can still taste his tongue and feel his hand. I have a shower and scrub my mouth out again. I stop when the phone rings.

'Hi, Kate. Lisa. Coming on Friday night?'

I try to sound calm, take a deep breath.

'Kate? Are you there?'

'Yes. Sorry. I'm here.'

'What's wrong?'

I tell her.

'You should report him!'

'Who to? Oh, the furniture lot. Do you think they'd do anything?'

'Hard to know but they ought to be told what sort of creep they've hired. That's disgusting. Who does he think he is?'

I ring the furniture store and tell them what happened. 'Oh, we've heard other stories like this. It could be time we had a serious talk to him.'

'It could be time you sacked him!' I tell them, surprised by my forceful reply. Wait a minute! He knows where I live, what bike I ride and possibly that I live alone. What if they sack him and he comes and bashes me or something?

The phone rings again. 'Lisa again, Kate. I told Andy what happened and he rang his father. You know he's a retired cop. He reckons you should go to the police and report it.'

'But they won't do anything. Won't they just think I'm a prude or something? Won't they say it was just a kiss and forget it? They don't even take rape seriously. Everybody knows that – there are always stories in the paper.'

'Reg said they're taking assaults on women more seriously these days. They've all been retrained.'

'Assault? I suppose it was, wasn't it. Do you think I should?'

At the police station I'm so embarrassed, both about what happened and about having to tell it to men, even if they are kind. I'm told to write a statement and bring it back. I do. An officer says he'll talk to the company and find out where the alleged offender lives.

'Alleged? Don't you believe me?'

'We have to call him that for now. We'll get a name from the company and then we'll pay him a little visit.'

'Will you?' I ask.

'Of course! You don't have to put up with men shoving their tongues down your throat just because they want to! Or groping you.'

Later the officer calls at my flat and tells me they've been to the man's house and had a talk with him. 'He admitted to doing what you said he'd done but he didn't seem to understand how offensive it is.' He rolls his eyes back in disbelief. 'So, we made it very clear that if he ever comes near you again, we'll do more than just talk to him. I'm a big bloke so it made an impression.' He advises me that taking it further would probably not be worth it. The man was trembling in his boots and seemed to have learnt his lesson. I take his advice but check for strange cars and trucks when I get home. Ken fits a chain to my door. I want to live with a nice man in wedded bliss instead of living alone and being vulnerable. When will it happen?

Well, keep hoping but get back to the studies.

Second semester starts and I accept that there are certain things I just have to do. Work in the library. A lot. Pretend I think certain things and argue accordingly. Get assignments in on time. Stop hoping to meet a nice boy.

Gen and I are doing Introduction to Anthropology. We've just read some articles for the tutorial so we're ready to contribute.

'The top joints of the child's middle fingers are amputated at puberty during the initiation rites.' We watch the film in the lecture theatre and see the child trying not to cry as his family supports him.

'They chop their kids' fingers off. Mutilate them! That's what it is!' Gen declares in the tutorial afterwards. 'It's cruel. It's abuse! Anyone who tells them they have to stop has got my vote! I don't care about all your academic arguments.'

I wish I had strong views and the courage to express them like that. Studying beliefs and practices in other cultures is wonderful and sometimes disturbing. Maybe it's all right for people to cut the children's fingers off in the context of their own culture. The children are cared for by their families and they understand why it happens. It's done to all kids as a status symbol. That's different to any of us doing it. Why should we make judgements about other cultures anyway? Doesn't it mean we think ours is the only right way to live? Will I say that? No. I don't think we're supposed to be thinking that way. I need to pass, so I do the discussion like I think they want us to. And write the essays in the library. And go home and write more essays.

Gen's had enough of uni, so she leaves and gets another teaching job. I wish she'd stay. I'll miss her.

The tutor in anthropology sends a list of questions around the table for us to choose our presentation topic from. By the time it gets to me there are two topics left. I haven't the faintest idea what one means. The other is incest.

Choose the one that makes me feel frozen and small or the one I know nothing about? The safe one. Choose the safe one. No. Why are you here? To be safe or to learn what you need to learn? Do you need to learn about why you feel frozen?

I quickly write my name beside the incest question and feel relieved that at least the date it's to be presented is early on when workload won't have built up. I don't feel comfortable, and I don't probe to remember why.

Lisa has arranged for a group of us to go to the snow for the weekend. Most of us can't ski but it'll be fun just to be there.

'I've got an oral paper due the following Tuesday so I'll have to spend some time on that while we're there,' I tell her.

'Oh. I'll help. What's your topic?'

'Incest.'

'Sorry. Didn't do anything about that that I remember. Well, you just say if you want to stay at the lodge and work.'

When the others go out on Saturday, I stay behind and begin reading, but it's like my brain is lying outside in the snow. Four times through the same article and it still doesn't mean anything. My heart keeps racing. Can't concentrate. I go for a walk, come back and try again. Come on. You have to give the paper in three days' time. I work on an education assignment instead and tell

103

the others I'll have to work again for some of the next morning.

Sunday morning sees me staying in again, surrounded by articles. I select one that I haven't looked at before. Stay calm. Read. It's about a clan who live on islands I haven't heard of. Boys are taken away by their fathers and certain practices are carried out that initiate boys to manhood. I understand this article! My brain is working again. Maybe I could tackle some of the others now and get my arguments together.

After I've read the first paragraph of the next article my brain freezes again and my heart is racing. What on earth is happening to me? I feel small and worthless. It's because I'm so dumb. Stupid. What am I doing at uni, anyway?

By Tuesday, I'm in a daze. I start talking, aware that I have very little to say. I introduce the topic and talk about the paper I understood. Soon the whole group is discussing it and being impressive so they'll get a high mark for participation. I don't have to say much. I fumble through a question and our tutor starts talking. She doesn't stop until she says, 'All right. Who's on next week?'

It's time to go.

'She didn't give you much of a chance, did she?' one classmate remarks on our way out.

'Better not do that when I give mine,' another says. 'You ought to challenge her, tell her off. You couldn't get a word in.'

Should I? I'd feel like a fraud. She actually saved me from a fate worse than death. But they're right in that she didn't wait to see if I had anything worthwhile to say. What if she fails me? I'll have to do the course again. What if I get the same topic?

I ring my tutor and ask her if she's going to give me a pass.

'I hardly think you deserve one,' she scoffs. 'What do you think?'

I think I feel sick. 'It was hard,' I say slowly, then I bolt to the point. 'And I couldn't get a word in.'

'What do you mean? You were presenting the paper. The floor was yours!'

'Yes, but you kept talking.'

'I talked because you clearly didn't have much to say. Had you done the reading?'

'Yes. I had trouble with some.'

'Why didn't you come and see me then?'

'I thought I had to do it myself.'

'That's what we're here for. Look, I don't believe you deserve any better than a very low C if I pass you. You'd better show me that you're worth it by making a hell of a contribution to other tutorials.'

I don't care! Any kind of pass will do. I'll read and understand and talk my head off in other people's discussions as long as I don't have to do incest again.

Oh, what's wrong with me anyway? I feel like I had a dream, a bad dream where my father was dark, threatening and crushing me. That's what it felt like when I tried to prepare that paper too.

Too afraid of the darkness and too confused by my confusion, I stay in a mire that feels safer than darkness.

It goes somewhere inside me after a week or so, after the next tutorial in which the tutor is asked by the presenter to give him a fair go. I must get on with the mountain of work that's piling up.

The end of year is approaching and I'm glad I don't have exams. Assessment is by coursework. I've never got better than a B and I'm disappointed. I don't want A+ or high distinctions, but some As would be good. I want to do the best I can but there's so much work that all I can do is pass. Do I really want to keep doing this?

Tonight I'm meeting the Marrickville crowd, the still single ones, for dinner. I feel very trendy because we're going to a Lebanese restaurant where you sit on cushions on the floor and eat exotic food. When I arrive late everyone is sitting down, talking intently.

'What's happening?'

'Whitlam's gone.'

'Gone? Gone where?'

'He's been sacked.'

'You can't sack a prime minister. What do you mean?'

'The Governor General has sacked him!'

'But . . . how? Why? He can't! Can he?'

'The coalition blocked supply and Whitlam was sacked.'

But we elected Mr Whitlam. How can someone sack him? I feel outraged! Mr Whitlam, whose policies made it possible for me to go to uni, who brought the troops home from Vietnam, who cares about people trapped in the cycle of poverty. How can he get the sack? We all seem to be sad, angry and confused.

'What happens next?' I ask.

'Another election, so we can vote him in again.'

'Well, they say there'll be an election anyway.'

'Stupid, isn't it? We'll have an election and vote him in again, then wonder why he was sacked.'

I feel better about it now. We'll get him back at the election, then he can keep helping disadvantaged people.

'How's uni, Kate?'

'Okay. I'm passing. Don't know if I'll keep doing it.' Having said that, I think I will. Being with these people who, along with their parents, kept encouraging me to improve myself reminds me of being a clerk. I hope I can keep going. I've nearly made it through first year.

'What is the farm you all keep talking about?' I ask Bel after home church one Sunday. 'It doesn't sound like an ordinary farm.'

'Oh, well, friends of ours started it. Gosh, how can I explain? You see, there are two couples who used to be in the church, as in the men were ministers, but they decided they could do more good if they weren't ministers. So they've started this farm where people can go and stay when they have big decisions to make or they're in trouble and need somewhere to sort themselves out. People who need time away from their lives so they can decide what to do. It's called Caloola and it means a place where battles are fought. Battles inside yourself, if you know what I mean.'

'Yeah, I think I know. What do people do there?'

'There's a cottage industry part of it where they make craft things to sell in the shop and there's a sheep farming part. That's what our friends do, the farming part.'

'Who can go there?' I want to know if I can but I don't want to sound desperate.

'Anyone really, just ordinary people at turning points in their lives, with big decisions to make.'

'That's me.'

'How do you mean?'

'Oh, I don't know if I want to keep doing uni, but if I don't, I won't know what to do.'

'You're doing well enough at uni, aren't you?'

'Passing, but I want to do well, not just pass. It's too hard, though. I think I might just be too dumb.'

'Oh, course you're not dumb! You'll be a great teacher. You're great with kids.'

I arrange to go to the farm at the end of semester. Caloola is tucked into a valley south of Canberra and it's surrounded by rugged mountains that cast shadows over the valley quite early in the day. The valley is wide and a creek runs through it. Gums and low scrub cloak the mountains in dark green while pastures seem dry and yellow. Old sheds and houses lean lazily in the relentless sun and dogs bark as I pass.

Bel has told me that the main centre where residents stay is not quite finished so I'm not surprised to see two men working on it when I arrive.

'Can you tell me where Col or Geoff is, please?' I ask them.

'Right here,' one answers. 'You must be Kate. Pleased to meet you. I'm Col and he's not.'

'Geoff,' Geoff says. 'How do you do?'

Neither is what I expected. Both are clean shaven, not hippy commune-looking. One even speaks with a posh English accent.

'Go in and meet Cath, the housekeeper,' he says. 'We'll catch up later.'

'Wow. I didn't know it was going to be this big!' I can't help saying to Cath as I gaze around the huge room. There are doorways off two sides of this massive room.

'It used to be an aircraft hanger,' she says, smiling proudly. 'And the rooms were Snowy Mountains huts, you know, for the workers. That one will be yours. The bathroom's there but remember we don't have water laid on just now, so it's rationed. The loo's up the path past the vegie garden, so watch out for snakes on your way.' She smiles again and says she'll let me settle in before we talk about what my contribution might be. She's got to finish the meal she's preparing.

After I've unpacked I go to meet the other people staying here. They don't seem too weird.

When Cath asks what I'd like to work on I tell her I don't mind. I feel that I can do anything here, as long as it doesn't involve riding horses or eating tripe.

'Everyone takes turns at cooking,' she tells me, 'and cleaning the centre, so I'll let you know when you're on. I know! No-one's too keen on the chooks at the moment – could you take them on?'

'Chooks? All right, but you'll have to show me what to do. I don't know anything about them.'

I thought I knew all about living in a community from my Burnside experience but the very first job I get is one I know nothing at all about. Still, I like the friendly round hens who squawk and chatter constantly and totter up to meet me when I bring the scraps bucket out for them. I help work the vegie garden too. I'm enjoying the work but I wish the water flowed more freely. I'd love to soak my weary self in a full bath instead of the two inches we restrict ourselves to. That's better than taking turns in the same water, though, as some of them do. The alternative is to bathe in the river but I'm not game. You can't tell who or what might amble along. I like my privacy.

Along with daily jobs, we choose between craft work and farm work. Geoff comes in each morning and gets people organised for craft work. I don't mind what I do and soon I'm in the workshop sanding wooden boxes that will be candle holders. Someone has routed a design into the sides of the boxes and I have to sand the splinters off. It soon becomes boring.

'Have you done any candle-making?' Hana asks.

'No. I could learn, though.'

Now I'm setting up moulds and tying wicks. Oh well, I suppose there has to be some repetition. Geoff comes in every now and then, shouts cheerful greetings or instructions, then disappears.

Most of my days are spent like this but I'm saved today by Ernesto who is popular and very charming sometimes. He's created a huge mural that seems to depict seasons and the struggles people face in their lives. Ernesto will be leaving soon and he needs help to finish his mural. I offer because he's using the rug-making technique that Bel taught me a few months ago. I'm given instructions and then Ernesto disappears. Hours later he comes to check my work.

'There's no orange left,' I tell him.

'Use somesing elle,' he shrugs.

'What colour?'

'Oh, you choose,' he says dismissively.

'This part represents heat, you said, but the warm colours are all gone.'

'Maybe he don't mean heat. You decide.'

Me? But you're the artist. What if I choose a colour that means the wrong thing and spoils the concept? The mural is so huge and eye-catching that everyone who comes in sees it, stands gazing and then the interpretation begins. Ernesto seems to pop up out of nowhere to hear the praise and comment on interpretations. He seems arrogant to me, but all the same I don't want to spoil his creation. I leave the part that should be orange for Ernesto to do when he comes back. If he comes back. I work for hours alone. I can think my thoughts and listen to conversations from a distance.

By the time Ernesto is ready to leave the farm, there are still blanks, so I'm forced to decide what colours to use. If he doesn't care, why should I? Bung in some dull green and a bit of purple. The mural is finished. Everyone admires, interprets and photographs it, and congratulates Ernesto on a job well done. Hey, if I don't make it teaching, then I'll be an artist.

When Geoff arrives each morning, his commanding presence means that you can't do anything but listen to him. Col comes in quietly mostly and says hello to people individually. Today he wants to know if anyone will be available to help bring the hay in to the stack.

'I will,' I say, along with several other people.

We go out late in the afternoon when the sun is low. How could a hay bale – a bunch of dry grass – be so heavy? So prickly. So awkward. Col tells us to put gloves on and pair up. After a half hour, the cottage industry is looking more attractive, even if it's setting up moulds for a thousand candles. But Col makes the hay gathering fun as he talks and jokes. Others join in and I'm relieved that we don't pretend the work is easy. Time passes quickly enough.

'Come down to the house and meet Leonie sometime,' Col says to me when we're finished. 'Martin and Bel have told us about you, and Leonie would like to meet you.'

'When will I come?'

'Let's say dinner tomorrow?'

'All right. Thank you.'

Leonie is welcoming and very polite. I'm anxious that they like me. Everyone at home church thinks these two are wonderful. They have a little boy who's talkative and lively and a toddler with a ready smile, and they are easy to be with, although I don't feel relaxed yet. Once I didn't know how to be in families that are close and affectionate like this one, but I've learnt about it through Martin and Bel and that helps me feel more comfortable here.

We talk about the farm and then we talk about why I'm here. I want them to tell me what I should do, but they can't, of course.

They leave me to decide for myself after we talk about my past a bit and my options for the future.

By the time I have to leave the farm I've decided that, as I'm passing all my courses, I might as well go back to uni. It's a direction to take, even though it's not easy – and at least I won't have to do a job interview.

REAL LEARNING

Sometimes I actually enjoy uni now that I'm steaming through second year. It's not easy but it's so interesting. History! Once I understand that what's written is not necessarily the truth, I turn detective, sifting through the evidence to find motives and distortions, telling Solon and Euripides, 'Oh, I see! I know what you're up to.'

Australian history has little to do with dates and names of explorers crossing the Blue Mountains. There are journals, the actual words of explorers, military governors and settlers. There are inventories of supply ships from England and the Pacific Islands.

'Pigs, Genevieve. Pigs!' I tell Gen when she asks what I'm doing for my history assignment. 'I'm looking at the use of salt pork in early white Australia. No, it isn't dull! It's fascinating. I have to find out where ships went to get salt from Pacific islands like Tahiti and what they traded for it and how pig farmers found cabbage tree palms to keep their porkers alive. They kept people and the economy going, you know. They weren't just muckin' about in the sty.' We laugh and Gen says she's glad she doesn't have the pressure of study any more.

The mature-aged students I spent so much time with last year have different timetables this year, so I hardly see them. Most students doing courses in education seem so young. The only one my age is Denis. He's in my history and education tutorials. Today he sits beside me in the Union cafe and begins a conversation about my crash helmet.

'Used to have one when I worked in the bank,' he tells me.

'Your helmet probably didn't go with the kind of bike I've got though. It's only a step through.'

He laughs and says yes, his was bigger. He is gentle, his smile is warm and he is very good-looking. Wish I'd relax, not be so nervous. At least I made him laugh. We talk about the difference between the demands on our thought processes in our working lives and student lives. This is better, we decide before moving on.

'What do you think of the election result?' he asks.

'I can't believe it! How can people vote for Fraser and put him in when we'd already voted for Whitlam?'

'You wonder about us Australians, don't you?'

'And the fact that our elected PM could be dismissed by the Governor General. But yeah, I think the biggest wonder is why people didn't jump up and down say, "No, you can't do that," and put Whitlam back where he belongs.'

'I agree. I don't know anyone who voted for Fraser. How did he get in?'

'I don't know anyone who did either. Not who'll admit to it, anyway.'

Wow. Listen to me. Spouting off about politics. And to a man! When it's time to go I hope this isn't the last time he comes to sit with me. It isn't. He looks for me most lunchtimes.

Later, looking for a table in the Union, a girl from my history tutorial smiles and indicates that she'd like company.

'How are you finding the workload?' I ask her. That's what I've learnt to say and it always works.

'Pretty tough but I guess it'll be easier now.'

'Why? It seems harder at this level,' I reply.

'Just broken up with my boyfriend,' she says, eyes reddening. 'Probably going to have lots of time now.'

'Oh dear. I guess you will. Are you okay?' I hope she is because I won't know what to say if she isn't.

'Thanks, yeah. I'm okay. You're lucky, aren't you?'

'Ah, why?'

'You've got Denis. You're both students.'

'Denis? Have I? We just met at uni.'

'Well, he really likes you a lot. He's just been talking about Kate this and Kate that in a tutorial. You're lucky.'

I'm really out of my depth now. What should I do? Look out for him? Try to accidentally bump into him? What should I talk about? What happens then? My nerves are twanging at the prospects.

Next time he sits with me at lunch I'm unbearably nervous. He chats as comfortably as usual.

'Must be hard getting your assignments done when you work as well,' I say, wishing I could think of something witty or even remotely interesting.

'Oh, it's pretty pressured but Kate keeps everything else together. She's pretty wonderful.'

'Kate!' Reality dawns. 'Oh. Is that your wife?' Stay calm. Don't let the disappointment show as the daydream fades. Married to Kate the Great. Darn! Married men should be tied down and gold bands forced onto their ring fingers. We relax into a friendship that I know is going nowhere but friendship. I hope there's another one like him about who doesn't already have a Kate the Great.

On weekends I keep going to home church and Bel invites me for dinner regularly. She's a bit like Jane, though she doesn't have the delightfully silly humour Jane had. Now that Bel and Martin have two little girls, I can make myself useful as well as just enjoying being there. I look after the kids or help prepare meals.

'You'll make a great teacher, Kate. You get along with kids so easily. You're a natural,' Bel says.

'I hope you're right. The work's pretty solid to get there, though.'

'Stick with it. It'll be worth it.'

I'm learning things, too, as I watch how they all interact and speak to each other. I notice that Bel lets her little one make decisions sometimes instead of just telling her what to do, and she talks to her respectfully and reasons with her. I like that.

'Lucy, remember I asked you to put your toys in the box? Now it's time to do it because dinner's just about ready. Lucy, now, please. Yes, I know you're tired. I am too. No. Daddy can't. He's feeding the baby. I'll help you when I've done this but they are your toys, aren't they?'

'Um, will I help? I don't mean to interfere but if you want, I could help.'

'That would be great. Lucy, Kate is going to help. No, you do it too.'

'Come on. Let's do it together. That's the way.'

Martin feels safer than Paul. He would never launch barbs of criticism like Paul did. He is much more sensitive. I didn't know men got this involved in babies' lives. Once I would have thought that it was sissy for a father to do what Martin does, but when I watch him and consider what we talk about at uni, about gender roles and so on, I can see it's not sissy. It's important. Gives Bel time to peel the skin off the broccoli stalks so they won't be too tough.

How I want to have a family of my own! I can see that being a mother is a huge responsibility, bigger than it is in my daydreams of being in love, my life cloaked in romance and smooth sailing contentment with my perfectly behaved children. Bel and I talk about my hopes and Martin joins in too sometimes. They think I'll meet someone and it's just a matter of time.

'All the guys my age at uni are taken,' I tell them. 'And there aren't any at church, are there?'

'There's no rush, is there? You'll find someone,' Bel says, cradling her baby on her breast. I try to feel confident as every single cell of my body wants what Bel has. And wants to know how to get it.

Today in our education tutorial we're going to discuss maternal deprivation. What is there to discuss? I've read a bit but it seems like making a mountain out of a molehill. When your mother dies you just forget her and get on with your life.

The session begins with a short talk about John Bowlby who pioneered the major work in the field. As they talk I start to feel like a freak. People who are deprived of maternal care can end up with all sorts of psychological irregularities and unmet needs. Am I a psychological mess and I'm blissfully unaware?

There's a video so the lights are turned off. We watch as a little orphaned boy is brought to a playroom by a welfare worker who leaves him. He looks around and starts to play. Next day he arrives and cries. I know him! Where have I seen him? Don't be silly! This is an English film. I feel like sobbing. I want someone to come and rock me and tell me it'll be all right. Stop it! Anyone would be upset by this, wouldn't they? When I look up again the boy is beyond crying. He's in a corner by himself, a rocking, staring foetus. Rocking himself is his only comfort.

The lights come on and people are talking. Some were a little disturbed. Can't listen. Too thick in my head. Thoughts to fathom. Why do I know that boy? Left when my mother died? Don't remember. What about that little girl and the blue velvet dress Terese made me remember? Mightn't be me. Can't think now. Have to go to my next tute. Won't do a paper on maternal deprivation. Plenty of topics to choose from. Get on with getting the degree. Improving myself.

It seems that the role of videos is to disturb in one way or another. Today we watch a documentary about Aboriginal education. I can't imagine what there is to say about it. If you're white you go to school and get taught. If you're black you go to school and get taught.

The documentary challenges my paltry knowledge. Going to school is not so simple. Until very recently, Aboriginal kids could be expelled if they didn't behave like good little white kids. White kids who didn't behave like good little white kids were allowed to stay. Some teachers have different expectations for the two groups, put in different effort for each and thereby fulfil their own prophecies. Some prejudice is less overt. A video tells the story of an Aboriginal boy who complained to his teacher that his knee was sore and he needed to go home. For days he complained but the teacher said he was malingering. He eventually collapsed, was taken to hospital and X-rayed. A rusty nail was found embedded and festering in his knee. He remembered getting a sting while his father was mowing, but because there was just a tiny hole they thought a stone had hit him. The question is, would the teacher have treated him differently if he'd been white?

There's so much I don't know! I thought we were nice to Aborigines but now I'm learning that being patronising can be just as racist as overt vilification. Giving out food and clothes seemed kind but it created dependence and loss of people's ability to live healthily off the land. That seems cruel. Not as cruel as some things I wish I hadn't learned about. Like that horrible thing where English soldiers used Aboriginal babies' heads for footballs while their mothers were tied up and forced to watch. What is Australia? I didn't know such cruelty existed. Well, there was Hitler but he was a one-off, wasn't he? I enjoy learning but I wish there wasn't this kind of thing to learn about. You can't not learn it, though. That wouldn't be learning or truth. When I'm a teacher I'll try to listen to what people want for their children, without prejudice.

Meanwhile, I need to leave these paralysing truths and keep working on the mountain of assignments.

A young man, Duncan, starts coming to home church and, although I don't find him attractive, I enjoy his humour enormously. He describes himself as 'a refugee from the Anglicans'.

Sometimes Duncan and I bump into each other at uni.

'Ah, g'day. Like to have dinner after lectures?' he asks.

Is this a date? I don't want it to be but I might as well accept just for the experience. Forget the leftovers in the fridge.

'Union or bistro?' Duncan asks when I meet him.

'I don't mind. Which do you like?' He knows what he can afford.

'Bistro,' he decides. 'The food's better.'

We order and Duncan asks, 'So what's your story? Strange childhood, I hear.'

Do I want to talk about that over dinner? Oh well, there's not much to say.

'I grew up in a home.' Good. It sounds boring. 'Not much to tell.'

'A home? You mean an institution? You grew up in an institution?'

'Hmm,' mumbles the freak.

'Why did you? Grow up in a home, I mean, not grow up.'

'Because my mother died. I suppose my father couldn't cope. He was old.'

'Really? My father was old too. He died a few years ago. That was a mixed blessing.'

'How? Mixed blessing, not died.'

'He was an odd chap. Very critical and never satisfied, even if we'd done our best. Nothing was good enough. What's yours like?'

'Dead,' I reply before I've thought about it.

'Oh, sorry,' he says, blushing slightly. Then, after a pause, he adds, 'Well, who's supporting you? Er, if you don't mind me asking.'

'I'm on a scholarship.'

'Can't live on that, can you?'

'Barely.'

'Dad left me quite a big inheritance so I'm pretty well set up. Don't know what I'll do with it but it'll keep me going for the rest of my life.'

'Gosh! What do you think you'll do? You're doing Education here, aren't you?'

'Yeah. I've got it invested for now. Might go overseas or something when I'm finished training.'

He talks about his family, his interest in being a missionary teacher, courses and so on. And on. And on. All I have to do is pop a question in every now and then and there are no uncomfortable silences. Duncan got whatever he wanted growing up, except his father's approval.

'We had a huge house at Lindfield. Lots of space for friends to come over.'

'Aha! There's a thing we have in common,' I interrupt. 'I lived in a huge house too.'

'Oh, the institution? Where was it again?'

'Burnside. Big castles. I lived in one castle, then moved to the big girls' one.' I haven't thought of that for years. The phrase 'big girls' sends an anxious shiver through me as my first horrible day there flashes unbidden through my mind. Furious old witch beating a big girl with a scrubbing brush. I was going to be left with that witch.

'That place on Pennant Hills Road?' Duncan interrupts. 'Did you live there? Our house was probably not that big but it was big.'

He talks on and I drift between listening and remembering a witchy woman beating a girl with a brush. Stop. I should be listening to Duncan. 'We'd better work out our shares of the bill,' he's saying, mumble mumble. 'Yours is nineteen dollars.'

Mine? But you invited . . . oh, there's such a lot to learn at uni. Nineteen dollars! Do I have nineteen dollars? Glad as I am that I didn't choose something expensive, I still have to rummage in the bottom of my bag to find the last dollar.

When I'd met Tom and Gen's friends on the camping trip at the Warrumbungles I'd decided to study the environment but the lectures didn't fit into my program. I sit in on some anyway and sometimes I understand what they're about. Sadly, I can't keep it up. I need all the time I have to do the compulsory study. And read and read and read. The Imaginative World of Man requires two novels or plays or books of poetry to be read every week just about. Reading's still not a strong point but it's improving and it matters now. There's an exam for the Imaginative World of Man as well as tutorial assessment.

Tonight I stay in the library late reading from the microfiche screen for a history essay. The little green words blur and I can't focus whatever I do with the focus knob. When I leave it's very dark and it's raining. I rug up in my wet-weather gear and start my trip home, very slowly. It's hard to see as the raindrops on my visor refract the light from approaching headlights. 'Don't look at the lights,' Ken always said. 'Look at the side of the road.' I do. I slow down until the cars pass, then off I go.

Where am I? What are those fluorescent lights and why are they flashing by? I'm lying down. Moving. Being wheeled? I try to sit up. A hand on my shoulder gently pushing.

'You've been in an accident. You're in hospital,' someone tells me, I think. Or is this a dream?

Sleepy. Go away. Why do you have to keep waking me and shining your torch in my eyes?

In the morning a policeman arrives and asks me what happened.

'I don't know. I was going home, then I was here.'

'You were found behind a parked truck. Can you explain that?'

'No.'

'We could be looking at a negligent driving charge here, Miss. You'd better give me more information.'

'Sorry. I don't have any. I don't remember any truck.' And I want to go back to sleep. Go away.

He keeps asking and I keep saying I don't know until at last he gives up and says, 'The truck was caked with mud. Maybe you couldn't see the reflectors in the rain. Could that be it?'

'Could be. I don't remember a truck or reflectors.' I'm really trying to help but my brain must be back at the truck.

'Well, you wouldn't have seen anything but mud. All right. I'll write it up but I may have to come back to see you about it.' He doesn't and it's just as well because my head doesn't work like it used to. My thoughts have to wade through an ooze of thick porridge to make sense and they're not doing very well.

Bel arrives. 'Thank God you are all right,' she says, emphasising each word. 'Come home to us for a few days,' she suggests.

'I'll be all right. I don't want to be a pest.' Live with you? What if you don't like me up that close? The question manages to struggle through to my consciousness.

'Kate, you've got concussion! You can't go home! Of course you won't be a pest. Come on. I've got the car outside. We'd love to have you. Especially Lucy. She can't wait!'

In the car it occurs to me to ask, 'How did you know I was here?'

'You told the lady who found you where we live.'

'I did?'

'Don't you remember? You gave her our phone number and address.'

'Don't remember. How could I have a conversation and not remember?'

'Must be the concussion.'

I drift through a day or two not knowing anything much except that I have to behave well here so they'll still like me. It isn't hard, because I don't seem able to stay awake for long enough to make a bad impression. Unless not staying awake makes a bad impression!

'I think I'm ready to go home, Bel.'

'Are you sure? You can stay longer. It's no trouble.'

At home I feel so relaxed but am still only able to stay awake for half a day at a time. On the day of my exam the Imaginative World of Man is buried under porridge. I go to uni, sit at the table in the exam room and wait for the exam paper. I can't understand a single question. I sit in a daze until the supervisor announces that anyone wishing to leave may do so now. That, I understand.

'Didn't you apply for a post?' Gen asks.

'To lean on?'

'No! You know, a post. Take the exam later. You should have got a post.'

'I didn't know I could. I'll just have to make up the credits next year.'

'Go and see someone first.'

It's no surprise when my request is refused. I didn't contribute much to tutorials and struggled to get the reading done.

'What's the point of applying now?' my tutor scoffs. 'You do that before, not after an exam.'

'I had concussion.'

'Then you should have got someone to do it for you.'

Perhaps I should keep arguing but I've already surprised myself getting this far with the argument. I'm not being a nice polite person. I'm arguing with an authority figure again. Fun, isn't it? When you know there won't be any disastrous consequences. Weird how I always think there will be.

One F and an equal number of Bs and Cs for my second year. I must be getting the hang of study. Won't have to go back to Mr Mansouriani and beg for my job back. Not yet. Maybe never!

I'm going to the farm for the summer holiday. One more baby-sitting night with Becky and Mousy then I'm off. Gen says Paul is probably going to marry Mousy's daycare teacher. I'm glad she's a person who knows about kids and how to care for Jane's properly. Perhaps that's how I'll end up, married to a widower with children. I'm twenty-six and still haven't got a boyfriend. Don't know what's wrong with me. Still got the eyes and teeth and I'm getting over being shy. Are my friends right? Just haven't met the right person yet?

Just as well I'm getting over being shy. We start prac teaching next year and I'm worried about that. We've studied how teachers are supposed to reflect the values of the community. What if I still don't know what they are, like when I left Burnside? Most of the time I think I do but sometimes I find I don't. And what if I get a class full of kids who don't like me? Or a class full of kids with problems like Down's syndrome or ADD or no English! I don't think I've learnt anything practical about dealing with any of the problems we've learnt about. Not yet. Maybe next year. Just go to the farm and get refreshed.

It's so hot and there aren't a lot of people staying just now. Cath the housekeeper is on holidays and three of the four people here in the Main Centre will be leaving in a day or two. That will leave Jim and me. Jim is incredibly attractive so I become incredibly nervous. He's tall and dark and speaks quietly, about the church as family and communities of care where disabled people are equals. He cares about the natural environment too and sees it as a place where people are stewards not owners. Everything about him is impressive. Almost. He's less impressive when he's furiously scratching his arms and asking if I know what to do about lice in the chook house. I do.

This time I spend more time with Leonie and Col at their house nearby and they make me feel like I'm an old friend returning. There's a lot of craft work to be done too to keep the shop supplied but Geoff doesn't spend much time on any of it. Jim spends a lot of time writing and reading, but we share the cooking and cleaning. Because the water is low again, we bathe in the river. I walk a long way up the valley to find a waterhole that gives me a view of approaching sheep. Or people. Wouldn't want Jim to catch me in a private moment.

The sheep need to be dipped and I offer to help. Other farmers in the valley are bringing mobs as well, so it'll be a very full-on day, I'm told. The dust rises easily as the sheep are penned. Dogs bark, sheep run and people like me sneeze a lot and get sore eyes.

'How would you like to work the other end?' Col asks. 'Not as dusty up there.'

He shows me how to use a hairless broom to push the sheep's heads under the water. If their heads don't get done, the whole process will be rendered useless.

'Won't they drown?'

'No. They'll just duck under and up. Part of your job is to make sure they do all come up. Shout straight away if you think one hasn't. Some of the old girls find the water heavy in their wool but you shouldn't have any trouble with this lot. Oh, and if any miss their ducking shout too.'

Soon sheep are belly flopping into the dip and I'm working like a frantic piston, plunging their heads in, trying not to let any of them drown. It is less dusty here. My clothes get damp with water from the dip but it's fun. Sometimes I have to yell, 'Um! Stop. Stop! They're piling up!' when the sheep in the water start getting dive-bombed by the ones coming after them. Belly-flop bombing! I remember us kids at the pool at Burnside and what fun we had. A farmer rushes up, grabs my broom and lifts the top sheep off, then helps the sunken ones out.

By smoko I'm pleased to have a break. The sun dries me and the tea and cake revive us. Back to work. By lunchtime I feel like my arms will drop into the dip at any minute. I'm exhausted and wet. Sheep don't do graceful, splashless dives.

'Better go and have a wash in the river, Kate. There's arsenic in the dip.'

I have time to slosh water over my skin before we start on the next lot. Some of the farmers' wives give me a break in the afternoon.

Everyone is content when we finish, even the sheep who've gone back to grazing.

'Go and have a really good bath in the river now,' Col says. 'We'll be a while here before we bring this lot across.'

Now I have to find a waterhole big enough to sit in and get all the dip off me. What if the farmers come? I have to get on with it because they'll be crossing through my bathroom soon. Here, will this pool do? No. A bit exposed. This one? Not enough water.

This one? No, the first one was better and if I'm quick I'll be out before they come. I undress quickly and creep into the water that's cold despite the summer. I start washing.

Baa. My! Those sheep are early! They must know the escap–, oh no! Hundreds of sheep are coming down the bank. It's not that I mind if sheep see me in my birthday suit but I draw the line at the farmers. I get out quickly grab my clothes and hide behind an inadequate bush. Prickly bush. I try to dress – don't care how – as the sheep and drovers wander by. I don't think any of them saw me. A dog heads in my direction but he gets yelled at to stay behind the sheep. Must learn to be quicker or much less modest.

Next day, 'Well, I leave tomorrow,' Jim says. 'Back to the real world. Here's my address. Stay in touch, won't you?'

I wish he wasn't going but then why would handsome, charming, intelligent him be interested in ordinary me?

'I've enjoyed your company so much, Kate.' His arms go round me. 'I'll miss you and our talks.' He holds me gently. I probably feel like a gum tree I'm so stiff. Everyone hugs everyone here and I decided I'd try to get used to it, to being touched safely. I've made progress but now I'm rigid. I've never felt this way about any other hugger. Wanting so much to be hugged, yet frozen with I don't know what. Couldn't be fear. Not here, but it feels like fear. This hug is taking so long. Does that mean he likes me more than in a sisterly way? I don't want it to stop but I do too. I'm on overload. Suddenly he pulls me very close, squashing my confused face into his chest, then pushes me back, bends his head, kisses me. He goes quickly to his car and gets in. I want to scream, 'Don't go!' as my eyes start to burn and I feel wretched.

This is silly. You hardly know him. Pull yourself together.

'Write to me,' he calls as he drives away. Don't know what to say. It'll probably come to nothing because I'm so ordinary. But that kiss was so . . . so . . . nice. I think. I write to Jim for a year or so but his replies are so far apart, I doubt he is interested. I stop writing.

*

Third year! I've made it to third year! Goodbye Mr Mansouriani. This will be a big year so I start assignments early and read as much as I can. We are sent to schools to watch demonstration lessons. Mrs Arthurs makes it look so easy and the kids are so well behaved. In tutorials we talk about all the kinds of problems we could come up against. Gosh, I hope my first class consists of white Anglo Saxons with normal brains and perfect families. Well, normal families. People with normal families wouldn't have any problems.

Unless they are Kristy who lives in the back flat on the other side of my bedroom wall.

'My mother,' she says, pronouncing 'mother' as if she was talking about a ring worm, 'is coming to stay on the weekend.'

'Won't that be any good?'

'You're joking. She'll nag and nag and shout at me that I should be doing this and that and the other. Nothing I do is ever what she reckons I ought to do. Anyway, I just came to ask a favour.'

'What is it?'

'Well, if she starts yelling at me, will you bang on the wall and pretend she's freaking you out?'

'You want me to bang on the wall?'

'Yeah. And yell a bit too, will you? She'll shut the hell up if she knows someone else can hear her.'

Me? Yell? And surely someone's mother wouldn't be like that!

Kristy's is. I find myself banging on the wall but no-one hears. Kristy is yelling too. Do I stop banging or keep it up? If I bang louder I'll knock the flimsy wall over.

At the clothesline Kristy seethes. 'Did you hear her?'

'Yeah. I banged but you didn't hear.'

'Do it as soon as she starts up again, will you?'

As soon as the yelling starts I bang on the wall and there's silence. I feel so rude. I call out, 'Sorry, but I'm trying to study in here.' I don't hear another sound.

As the semester rolls on it's time to go into some preschools. The Whitlam government had built new preschools in disadvantaged areas so the kids can get a start before they reach school, to catch up with normal kids. Oh no! That means there'll be lots of problems, I suppose.

When the kids come in to start their day, I'm supposed to zoom in and play with them. I don't. I watch. They all seem to know what they're doing and they're glad to be here. Their teacher has told me the purpose of some of the games but I didn't really know what she was on about apart from developing motor skills.

'Eh, you! What your name is?' a little boy says.

I don't know the answer!

'Uh. Mrs Harding, should I say my name is Kate or Miss Shayler?'

'Good question. Children, listen to me, please,' she commands loudly. 'We have a special visitor here today. Larry, look this way, please! This is Miss Shayler. Say good morning to Miss Shayler. Good. Miss Shayler will be spending the morning with us and she'll want you to show her how we do things. Will you help?'

'Eh, gum 'ere Shayler!' my little mate says.

He doesn't talk much but we play car crashes and some other boys join in. It gets noisy and Mrs Harding suggests we play something more quiet. In the glow of the stop light that is my face I get a building game out and we build towers that my original fan loves kicking over.

'Knock it with your hand, then you won't kick anyone,' I suggest.

'Good strategy,' Mrs Harding says, and I hope she means me.

None of these kids or their parents know me but the kids like my company and I like playing. I feel I belong here. Sometimes I can see the educational significance of play, like when they have to build a road to reach a tower, they're doing maths and fine-tuning their coordination. Every piece of equipment has some educational purpose and my job is to help kids play so they get the benefit. Sometimes I can't see any educational value, especially in playing dollies. Sure, they like it, but what's the benefit? I can't see it yet and I dodge playing there.

I go to this centre every week and learn so much. Mrs Harding gives me a glowing report and mentions my improving under-standing of the value of structured play. Back at uni we discuss our experiences and find that most of us enjoyed what we'd done, then we groan about how much work we have to catch up on now. We wonder what will become of us when we do full-time practicums next year.

I still feel uncertain sometimes about who I am and what I'm doing here, but I feel more sure when I get my semester results. I've passed all my courses and caught up on the points I failed last year. Who needs the Imaginative World of Man?

This semester I'll do a primary school prac and I'm worried about that. Older kids. I don't know anyone that age. What are they like and what do you do with them?

'What if they don't do as you say?'

'What if you've got a kid with brain damage?'

'How do we make them understand us when they're ESL? Don't speak English?'

'What if we've been through all the discipline stuff and they still won't do as we say?'

'Look,' our tutor says firmly, 'you've got to stop thinking of a classroom as a combat zone. It isn't them versus us. Most kids, just about all kids, will want to please you if you treat them well. Yes. Truly. They will respect you. Unless of course you earn their disrespect.'

Relief! I'm drowning in it! Now, if only I can find out what to try to teach them.

'And stop thinking of non-English speakers as problems. We'll be looking at the richness of cultural diversity soon and I hope you'll all get to grips with the fact that people from other countries bring a wealth of skills and difference to us. Not problems.'

Not problems. Phew. She could be right. Marrickville had people from other countries and they weren't problems. We got new restaurants and smells and sounds. They were as friendly, sometimes friendlier than people born here. All right. But it must be tricky when the kids don't know English.

'Try to shift your thinking from what they don't know to what they do know. They know other languages. Yes? Other cultures. More useful than they don't know anything?'

Yes.

Study and home church are all I can cope with these days and I haven't seen my Marrickville friends for months. Ken still visits and tells me Kerry's news but I don't have time to write to her much and she doesn't have time to reply. This time Ken tells me he's off to Thailand for a holiday. I can't imagine how he got the courage to go to stay in a different culture. I stay home and keep studying.

'Martin and I have talked about this, Kate, so don't argue,' Bel says one night after dinner. 'You don't get much of an income and we get more than we need, right. So we've decided we'd like to give you something each fortnight. Is that all right with you?'

'You mean like a fortnightly kick in the behind to keep me studying?' I joke to cover my . . . what? Embarrassment? Discomfort? No, it isn't either of those. Shock? Yes, that's it. I'm shocked that they would care enough to make such an offer. To me! People generally guard their money and want as much as they can get, don't they? That's why people encouraged me to do more study. So I'd improve myself, which seemed to mean be able to earn more money. And now here are some friends offering to give me some of theirs.

'We really want to do this,' Bel says. 'It's only money.'

'I don't know what to say!'

'Say yes. It's not a fortune. Just say yes. Come on.' She grins.

'Yes.'

'Yes. And huge big thanks.'

'Good. Huge big thanks to you too. Now we won't mention it again. We'll just do it.'

'Well, I'll pay you ba–'

'You will not! It's a gift. You don't give them back.'

It's hard to accept my friends' gift because it's money but that's what they want me to do. Every fortnight they slip a note into my hand and I say thanks.

I love study. Australian history continues to enthral me as our tutor discusses her research on first-generation white Australians. She brings history and people to life. Luckily, part of the exam for the course is a take-home paper. I'm ready for that. Stay home. Read and write. Done. I should pass this one.

Travelling by bike is part of who I am now and it feels like the bike is part of my body; it lets me drift effortlessly to my destination. The fear of stacking and breaking my spine is still with me and makes me defensive but it doesn't detract from the joy of riding. I don't think I'll ever want to upgrade to a car.

On exam day I set off with plenty of time to get to uni and settle before it begins. Putt putt pu–, oh no! What's wrong? Kick start again and the bike coughs and stops. I'll have to push it to the service station. Okay. Plenty of time.

Workshop man looks up at a steaming, sweaty me, about to collapse, pushing step through uphill towards him.

'Help you?' man asks, wiping hands on dirty rag.

'My bike died,' I puff. 'Can you look at it?'

'Not 'til, let's see. I could do it next Thursday.'

'Oh! Not straight away?'

'Next Thursday. Best I can do.'

'But I'm on my way to an exam!'

'Tell me what happened.'

I do and he asks, 'Have you got petrol?'

Oh! I know what the problem is. And it's not just the empty tank.

Parking isn't a problem at uni and nor is dashing into the exam room with only thirty seconds to spare.

At home I'd decided to do the question about perceptions of the Australian character. The answer is to be written in the form of a letter to a new overseas contact.

Dear Horace, I write.
Forgive my saying so but your name almost describes the start to my day. I resolved to write and answer your question about the

Australian character as described in certain texts, in time to catch the ten o'clock mail. Alas I missed it but let me tell you why, by way of illustrating one of our alleged characteristics – the notion of she'll be right, mate.

I set out on my trusty step through, with plenty of time to spare, knowing I could cope with any challenge your questions presented. Imagine this! My machine, always reliable, coughs, splutters and refuses to go a centimetre further. Of its own accord, that is. Yes, Horace! In order to get your letter done I was forced to push the beast one kilometre, uphill, yes, up, to a service station. I will not humiliate myself by telling you about the over-reliance on the she'll be right ethic that led me to forget to buy petrol. Suffice to say that in order to get this letter in the twelve o'clock mail I had to ignore the dreadful need to go home, have a shower and start all over again.

There, that feels better. Now I can get on with the answer I've prepared.

A few weeks later, I pass my tutor who beams a broad smile at me. 'I'm still laughing about your paper. That was the most original start I've ever come across. What made you think of that?'

'It really happened!' I say and she laughs outright. 'Did I pass?'

'You most certainly did. It was a risky way to start but it worked.'

Phew! One year to go. I'll spend a large part of the holiday at home reading and I'll visit Leonie and Col too. They said I'd be welcome anytime. I don't know why they feel that way but I like their company and I don't suppose they'd say it if they didn't mean it.

I have a lovely time with them and they really do seem to like me. They tell me I'll be right in fourth year as I head back to Sydney.

This year I won't have to catch up any credits. I passed everything last year. Most of my courses this year are in the Faculty of

Education and include more prac teaching but this time it won't be observation. It'll be actual teaching.

My master teacher, Mrs Vella, is young, pretty and enthusiastic. The kids obviously love her. I feel drab and dull and can't imagine what the kids will think when I get up to teach. I've decided to do a science unit with them and we'll study air. I've read lots of resource books about teaching this subject and I'm confident I can find links to all the other curriculum areas.

Each week I get the kids to do an activity and make observations that they record on their charts by writing and drawing pictures. Mrs Vella gives lots of positive feedback and makes suggestions for improvement sometimes. I don't mind her watching me after the first time, because she was so positive and helpful.

My unit culminates in kite-making. I have a simple pattern and Mrs Vella has supplied the tissue, string and balsa wood. The kids are very excited and the room is a mess by the time the kites are finished, ready to take home.

'Let's clean up now,' I say. 'You've got reading next.' I'm pleased that my timing was good. I haven't cut into Mrs Vella's next lesson.

'Would you like to leave the cleaning up 'til later?' Mrs Vella asks the class. 'We're all too excited. We just have to fly kites now!' she whispers to me as she holds up hers. 'Let's not lose the momentum! We'll get some great writing from them later.'

A great teacher would have realised they'd want to fly their kites straight away. She would also have realised, before the class is heading towards the oval, that she doesn't actually know how to fly a kite.

Johnny Stavros is ahead of everyone, holding his kite high above his head. 'Run, Johnny Stavros!' I yell, hoping his podgy little body can run. Johnny runs and his kite lifts as if by magic. What a triumph! Up it goes, ever higher to the sound of 'wow' and 'gees look at that!' My spirit soars at least as high because

I haven't been caught out in my final lesson not knowing what I'm doing.

Soon kids are running all over the oval flying their kites. The inevitable crashes begin. 'We'll have to make a kite clinic,' Mrs Vella says. 'Don't cry, Angela. Look, fix it and try again.'

When I leave the class for the last time, I feel sad. We've all said our thanks and goodbyes and Mrs Vella has given me a great report.

As I walk across the playground the principal stops and says, 'You'll be a hard act to follow!'

'Thank you,' I laugh.

I loved that prac but if I choose to pursue infants teaching I could be sent to a primary class and I don't want that. When the time comes to choose between general primary or early childhood streams, I choose early childhood.

We have lectures and tutorials on all sorts of theoretical issues and structures that I don't find very helpful when it comes to actually being in a classroom. My preschool pracs are fun and I feel this is where I belong.

'Preschool's just babysitting though, isn't it?' says Colin, a gawky, tactless aspiring primary teacher. Us early childhood students huff at him. Some people explain that it's the beginning of learning to be social outside the family and to analyse and explore a stimulating dynamic environment and so on.

Have I trained for four years to have a career that's perceived to be babysitting? It is just as enjoyable but it's so much more! I can see that now and I'm looking forward to it. As long as there aren't any problem kids – I still don't feel that I'm prepared for them.

By the year's end, we're all exhausted and we wish each other well before going our separate ways. I'm a qualified teacher and I need only wait until January to find out where I'll be appointed.

My notice arrives from the Department of Education and I have to look up my street directory to find out where my school is. It's a long way from here but when I get a pay cheque I'll move closer to work. The appointment is to a reserve position. Too many teachers have been trained, so while us bonded people wait for positions to become available, we are reserves who can be used by principals in whatever ways they think best suit their schools' needs. Oh please let the school have a preschool!

I can't wait for Sunday when I can tell my home church people about the appointment. Meanwhile I start ringing other friends to let them know.

I haven't heard from Ken since he went overseas and he hasn't answered my letters. I must make sure I tell him my new address when I get one. Can't wait to tell him that I have a job!

NOTHING'S WRONG

'You're early childhood trained, aren't you?' my imposing boss, Mrs Cornwall, asks.

'Yes,' I squeak. Will I beg her to let me sit in the staff room and cover books or put nice red ticks on worksheets all day?

'Good,' she says. 'We'll put you on preschool for a few weeks. You can work with Hariette. She'll be off in term two so it'll be good if you learn the ropes before she goes.'

Forget the red ticks! Every book in the universe can stay coverless. I almost skip to the preschool. Lots of my peers will be given their own class to bungle about in today but I'll be team teaching, learning as I go. How did I get this lucky?

Hariette is tall and brittle-looking but she welcomes me warmly. Wanda, the teachers' aide, is welcoming too, but obviously too busy to stand about chatting. We spend the day setting up and I'm given enrolment forms to read. These show that the kids come from working-class families, that most families are English speakers, with two parents, and that lots of our kids have older brothers and sisters at the school.

'Yes. They're the ones who settle in easily, so we bring them in first. They help the new families later.'

'They don't all come at once?'

'Goodness no! Can you imagine twenty-five three-year-olds all crying for their mums at once?' I shudder, remember the little orphaned boy screaming and rocking. Little girl. 'We spread the intake over two weeks,' Hariette explains.

The first kids arrive. They know their way around. We play, have snack time, story time and sing and then they all go home. Hariette gets busy with notes and Wanda with cleaning. I help Wanda, then we gulp down our lunch and start again with another lot of confident little brothers and sisters. This is going to be easy! Nice staff, kids who know what to do and no preparation because Hariette wants to do it all.

Two days later the real work begins as kids who have never left their mums before come. Some look anxious, others cry and some scream. I feel like joining them. I remember Jane yelling, 'Pick her up!' Are we allowed to? Little boy rocking. Little girl, alone, sobbing.

Leave that. Watch Wanda. Watch how she comforts them and do the same. Never leave a child crying alone. I know what to do. Between us we get them settled. Some break down during the session and we cuddle and reassure them that their mums will be back soon to take them home. Remember the tutorial about high-quality care avoiding damage to kids' emotions when they leave their mums. I think we're getting it right.

With weekends free of assignments I look for something social to do. Join the bushwalking group I've heard about? It'll be good exercise and I love being in the bush. I pack my backpack and meet a group of people at Cronulla Station. We get a ferry to Bundeena and spend the day walking along the coast in the Royal National Park. How could there be a place this beautiful and unspoiled in our city? Bush beside the sea. Perfect. I'm more shy than I thought I'd be here but my companions are good at conversations about plants, rock formations, the National Parks

Association structure and its role as the National Parks watchdog. I just want to walk, not be a watchdog. I keep listening. There are lawyers, secretaries, accountants, mechanics, a whole range of people all enjoying the bush. When we say goodbye, I know I'll be back again and again. This becomes my favourite weekend pastime and the people a new set of friends.

My first two weeks' teaching is up quickly. My first pay slip arrives and I take a while to work out which column tells me how much I'm getting. Wow! Four hundred and thirty-three dollars. That much! I started with thirty-eight dollars sixty as a clerk ten or so years ago. I'll be able to move to Meadowbank, into the unit Robyn from home church is vacating. It's clean, airy, has a sunny balcony and there's not a single hole in any wall. It's closer to school too.

It's Easter already and during the holiday I can't wait to get back to work. I'll be the teacher in the preschool for a whole term.

'Wanda, who owns these little hammers?' I ask.

'We do but Hariette doesn't use them. They're too noisy.'

'Do we have any wood?'

'Not much. You could ask the parents to bring some if you want more. It is noisy, though.'

'We'll do it out on the verandah. That's what that bench is for, isn't it?'

'Well, yes. The noise is quite deafening, though, even there.'

While I'm waiting for our supply of wood to increase I stick to the more mundane activities that usually happen. Kids are happy and learning. Most of them.

'Gary, don't throw the car, please. You might break the window.' No. You've learnt to make positive statements that tell Gary what to do, not what not to do. 'Gary, keep the car on the floor, please.' On the road. On the bench. On the table. 'Gary. Stop throwing the car!' It's becoming a mantra.

'Uh, Kate, I don't mean to interfere,' Wanda says sheepishly. 'But Hariette sends them to sit by themselves if they don't do as we tell them. To her office door.'

Behaviour modification. Of course! What's the matter with me? This is behaviour mod in the real world. 'Gary, you will have time out if you do it again. Yes, at the office door. All right, Gary. Time out. Yes, I mean it. That's right.'

'Kate, have you forgotten Gary?' Wanda asks. 'He should only be there for four minutes. A minute for each year of his age.'

Whoops! 'Gary, what's the rule about cars? Yes, that's right. Can you do that? Off to play, then. Your time out is finished.' I remember to check with him later to give him positive feedback for compliance.

At last we have enough wood. Soon kids are whacking nails into bits of pine, winding wool around the nails and painting their creations, which they proudly present to their parents.

'Uh, what is it, Viv?'

'A pizza.'

'Of course. A pizza. I should have guessed.'

Parents offer to stay and help and the noise escalates. I've been really sympathetic when kids whack their fingers. Being a good first aider, I tell them to put the finger in the cold water we've got ready in a bucket nearby and I give them a cuddle if they want one.

'Don't sook!' Mrs Fry tells Jeffrey, her son. 'Just suck it and get on with it.' I try her method and kids get over the pain more quickly than when we do it my way. Some still need cuddles and cold water.

I'm learning so much here and a lot of it's from people without degrees.

Wanda is gleeful when the wood runs out. 'It's so quiet here now.' She grins.

When I tell her about suds sculpture, she tries to be enthusiastic. 'One of the students at uni did it. You put Lux flakes in water and beat it. Like in the washing machine. The kids sculpt the suds. It's a great sensory activity. Soft and fragrant.'

She tries to smile and says she'll prepare it. 'How much Lux?'

'Mm. Can't remember.'

We guess and leave the tub on the verandah. By the time the kids get to it the mixture is a slimy, congealed lump.

'Ah yuck. Looks like snot!' Michael says.

'Yeah, let's play with the boogies,' Jason says enthusiastically.

'Wanda, could we have some blue and yellow dye, please.'

'We gunna make it blue boogies?'

'Yep. Blue first, then we'll put in yellow and see what happens.'

After they've all gone home, Wanda's face almost matches the colour of the mixture. 'Miss Shayler, how am I going to clean the, um, stuff in the tub?'

'Er. Let's keep it for a couple of days. I think they'd like to have it again.'

'*They* would,' she replies.

I have a wonderful time at preschool and Wanda warms to the point where I think we're friends. 'Kate Shayler, you're just the kind of person who should be doing this job. But if you ever tell me to make that slimy mess again, I do believe I'll strangle you.'

'Next week?'

'Never!'

I love this job. There's no chance of meeting a nice boy. Well, man is more like it for a twenty-nine-year-old. The only men I meet are the kids' fathers and there are no widowers like Paul was. But I'm enjoying myself so much, I hardly care. Wanda teaches me more practical skills than I learned in all those years at uni. The theories were interesting but this is the real learning time, a time to translate theory to practice. After work, I go home and read my text books and lecture notes. Behaviour modification, sensory perception, fine motor development, hand–eye coordination, parallel play. It's all real now. Alive. I'm alive like I haven't been before.

'Kate, there's a call for you that you'd better take in the office,' Mrs Cornwall says as she steps over a play picnic. 'I'll stay here 'til you get back.'

'Kate Shayler? It's Joy from staffing. You're a reserve there, aren't you? I'm ringing to offer you a position in the new centre on Shortus Road.'

I don't want to leave! 'When would it start?'

'Third term.'

I can't even finish the year here!

'I need to know whether you'll accept.'

'Um, I don't know. When do you need to know?'

'Now. What's the problem? This is a completely new centre. You could set it up however you like. I thought you'd jump at the chance.'

'I thought I'd be at this school for a year. I love it here. This is so unexpected.'

'Look, think it over and ring me first thing tomorrow. We'll need to find someone quickly if you don't accept.'

'It's too good an opportunity to miss!' Wanda says, amazed that I'm even thinking of declining.

'But I love it here, Wanda. I thought I'd be here for the whole year.' My eyes are burning.

'We love having you too, but Hariette's coming back and you'd be shoved from pillar to post for the second half of the year. You'd be mad not to accept that new place!'

At home I ring friends and the consensus is I'd be mad not to accept. I tell Mrs Cornwall I'm accepting and make the phone call.

'Whatcha have to leave for?'

'Don't you like us after all?'

'Can't you tell 'em you wanna stay here? We want you to.'

The appreciation of the parents is humbling and I'm sorry to say goodbye. I've learnt that working-class people are fun, not problems. They're good people doing the best they can on low-paid jobs or pensions.

Best of all, I've learned how good it feels to have done my best for the kids I teach.

*

Everyone is busy when I arrive at my new school. The principal, a cold, stern man, sends me straight to the infants staff room.

Mrs Pontifex, the infants mistress to whom I will be directly responsible, is round, warm and welcoming. 'We haven't had a preschool before but we're really looking forward to it. The parents are very keen. They've been involved since the idea was proposed and the kids have watched the building go up. I haven't had any experience of preschool so I'll have to rely on you to show us how it's done. Any problems, come and see me and I'll help as much as I can of course. Everything is still in boxes down there but you'll have today to set up. Kids start tomorrow.'

One day to set up! Crikey, better stop talking and get on with it. As I'm about to leave, Mrs Pontifex adds, 'Oh, and Mrs Gillespie, the senior consultant, she'll be coming to see you at ten. What's wrong?'

'Oh nothing. There's such a lot to do and I wonder why Mrs Gillespie is coming in the middle of it all.' Don't Department of Education advisors know that I've got to set up in a day. No time to talk. No advice needed yet thanks.

'Yes, I know what you mean. Well, just do your best. We'll talk more later.'

I feel like Bel's daughter, Lucy, under the Christmas tree as I unpack box after box of new equipment. Books, building sets, puzzles, painting easels. There's plenty of shelving and storage and – oh drat! This must be the great Gillespie. She looks like a Burnside matron and I feel smaller. Well, I hope she goes soon.

'Hello, Kate. It's so nice to meet you. Do you like what we've done here?'

'Yes. It's lovely.' Now go away and let me get on with it. Why are you fishing about in your bag?

'Well, we hoped you'd accept the position because you've had the most up-to-date training and you're more mature than most of our new graduates,' she says, tying up her apron. Apron! Rubber gloves next! Good heavens, she's here to help, not lecture or advise and get in the way.

As we work, Mrs Gillespie talks about the preschool program and how it came into being. I know some of this already but she fills in the gaps. The program is statewide and intended to have the same effect as the American Headstart program and the British Nursery School one: to give disadvantaged children a chance to learn so that they know as much as other kids when they all start school.

'Let's break for a cuppa,' she suggests.

'Um, do we have any cups?'

She finds them and brings some cakes out of her bag. I can't believe a senior officer could play a Mary Poppins role like this. Thank goodness she came!

Next day my aide Ella arrives half an hour before the kids. She's friendly and interested in everything. Ella asks what she needs to know and willingly does as I ask her.

The parents arrive with their excited kids. A few tears are shed when the parents leave but the kids settle quickly.

Another incredibly happy period of work begins.

The Education Department doesn't have a preschool curriculum and I'm not sure how far to push the kids' learning towards the kindergarten curriculum. Some kindy teachers feel preschool teachers are an utter pest when they start teaching reading and maths. But I've been taught that I should find out what kids know and build on that according to each kid's ability and interest level. I'd better ask Mrs Pontifex what she expects.

'As long as they're safe, happy and learning, I'm happy,' she begins. 'If they leave there knowing that school is safe and they are valued and respected, well, we can't ask for more. If you can push them academically, it's a bonus but we want them happy and socialised when you hand them over.'

The rest of the year passes quickly and soon I'm teary again. I hate goodbyes. What a send off! I've never had this many Christmas presents! Parents thank Ella and me profusely for a wonderful start to their kids' school lives. I go home loaded up with chocolates, soap and funny little ornaments that I'd never buy myself but that I love anyway.

Our home church has got so big we've decided it's time to split it. We're not sure whether to call it dividing or multiplying. Bel and Martin have moved further north and it takes so long to get there from Meadowbank. The second church is close so I decide to go to that but keep in touch with the others, especially Martin and Bel.

Our first meeting is at a new couple's house. Tom and Tess are cheerful. Tess, a women's counsellor, is outspoken and funny. Tom, an architect, is quiet and warm. Their two little boys are bubbly and vocal. One day I might talk to Tess about the recurring dreams I've been having. The wolf one is getting very scary and the clock one is weird. I might tell her about my father. What he did was foul and I know it wasn't really just a bad dream. But it doesn't have words. How could I talk about it? Remembering tiny bits is bad enough.

Watching Tom and Tess with their kids has the same effect on me as watching other friends. It makes me want a family of my own. Gen has married a lovely bloke called Paddy and she's pregnant now. Will I ever get the chance? I'm twenty-nine. Thirty has always been my age limit for babies. I'll have to extend it. Mothers would always bring their new babies into preschool and give them to me to fuss over. They'd call it practice. I call it torture now. I find things to make me look busy so I don't have to go through it. Hiding doesn't feel like me. I like babies. Wish they didn't hurt.

What's wrong with me? Why don't men like me? Decent men I mean, not gropers. I feel so afraid of all that. It must be to do with my father but I'm too scared to think about it in depth. Newspapers and magazines have had lots of articles about that kind of thing lately. About women who were abused as children having emotional problems when they grow up. Have I got emotional problems? I don't think so. I just get frightened sometimes. And have nightmares. Do you know you've got problems if you've got them? Do I need to see a psychologist and delve into that thing I can't speak about? Maybe.

'Tess, you were a counsellor, weren't you?'

'Yeah. Still am,' she says, looking puzzled.

'Well. Um. You know when I tr– . . . I think there's something wrong with me.'

'You! Funny and clever and gorgeous. I don't think so.'

'Could you find and convince all the single men my age about that, please?' I laugh.

'Oh! Look, you'll meet someone. You're not old.'

'I'm nearly thirty!'

'Oh, that's ancient!' She laughs. 'Don't worry about it.'

'But I do worry and it's because, uh, my, well. It's hard to say it.'

'Say what?' she asks softly.

Too hard. Can't say it.

'Just that I can't meet men and there must be something wrong with me.'

'Kate Shayler, there is absolutely nothing wrong with you.'

Today I go on a bushwalk with the usual crowd.

'Why don't you talk to Claud?' Meg asks as we sit on a rock at Burning Palms.

'What about?'

'I don't know! Just talk. He's really keen on you and you don't respond.'

'Keen on me?'

'Yeah. Haven't you noticed?'

'No.'

Meg sighs. 'It's so hard to be a matchmaker when both parties are shy and one doesn't even see the other's heart on his sleeve. What hope is there? I'll have to keep my day job.'

Is this my chance to at least start something and see what it's like? My mind goes to fast forward and baulks quite soon in our

144

relationship, well before the wedding. I feel anxious. It's just because I haven't had practice. Get on with it. How? Don't know.

After lunch we rest or wander around rock pools. Today I wander and Claud comes with me. After we stumble through a few 'water's warm' and 'nice shell', there doesn't seem to be anything else to say. Now, instead of being a comfortable walking companion in a group of friends, Claud is someone I have to try to impress. And feel wary of without understanding why. Well, do I want walks to be spoilt by trying to be interesting, to be who I'm not? No.

Meg tells me that Claud has given up. He thinks I'm not interested. Oh, who cares! I wasn't interested anyway. If he can't be bothered making a bit more effort to get past my shyness, he's not worth getting upset about. But Claud is nice. But why would he, a clever accountant, be interested in a shy, ordinary, preschool teacher? But. But. But.

I go to Leonie and Col's for a holiday. They live in town now but are building a holiday house in a tiny village near Cooma. We go down to work on it and I love learning about building and tools and family life.

The kids sleep in the attic and they can peep through the knotholes in the floorboards to see what we're up to downstairs. Cleaning up dinner dishes, reading or talking. The holes get a much more interesting role when Col goes upstairs and threads a rope through into the room below. Jack grabs the end of the rope and Col pulls him up to the ceiling, then lets him down a little way so he can swing like Spiderman.

'My turn! My turn!' the girls shout.

Sara giggles so much she has trouble holding on. 'Super Sara!' she shouts as she swings through the dining room.

Now it's little Tina's turn. Up she goes, then a shriek fills the air. 'What's happened?' Col yells.

'You banged my head,' Tina sobs as she tries to hold on.

Col lets her down quickly and she flops to the floor wailing, 'Oooh, you naughty daddy.'

'Oh my little darlin', I'm so, so sorry,' he croons while he rocks her.

Why am I so teary? He's comforting her. She's calming down. It's all right.

Then Col changes the mood to a cheery, 'Pulled my little girl up too fast, did I? You don't weigh much,' and he tickles her. Now she's giggling and agreeing to have another go.

As Tina swings merrily through the air I struggle with tears. I'm just too sentimental, I suppose.

I'm going home in a couple of days and I'd hoped to talk to Leonie and Col about my bad dreams and the thing that's not really a dream. That thing about my father keeps coming into my thoughts, spoiling my days, sending a dark cloud across the sunny times. But what will I say? I'll have to talk, with words. Leonie and Col know a lot about people's problems and they might know what to do or what's wrong with me. What if they don't want to know me when I tell them, though? It's a bad, bad thing I'm going to talk about. What if they tell me to go away, they don't want me around, especially around their kids? They don't seem like that.

'Can we sit down together after the kids have gone to bed, because I want to talk to you.'

'Sure. What about?'

I freeze. Don't do it. See how hard it is! But I want to try to sort it out.

'It's hard to say it.'

'Well, let's leave it 'til after dinner.'

We wash up and I manage not to break anything as enormous tension builds in me. By the time we sit in the lounge room, I'm as brittle as glass. I can't do the small talk that people use to pave the way to heavier issues.

'There was something you wanted to talk to us about wasn't there, Kate?' Leonie asks quietly.

Deep breath, then I blurt out, 'When I was little my father sexually abused me. I'm so ashamed.' I hadn't realised how ashamed I was until this very minute, when I gave the thing words. I can't look at Col or Leonie.

'What?' says Col. See, he's about to send me packing.

'Oh no,' says Leonie. She thinks I'm filth too.

I can hardly breathe as I wait for my marching orders.

'Your father abused you and you feel ashamed?' Col says indignantly.

'Yes.' I'm confused. What's he mean? I'm too confused to listen to Leonie who is talking gently, kindly.

'Yes, what Leonie's saying is so right. I'm just outraged that *you* feel ashamed. You aren't the one who should feel shame! What have you done? Your father ought to be bloody ashamed!'

Oh. He isn't angry with me. He means I shouldn't feel ashamed but my father should. And Leonie's not disgusted with me either.

'Absolutely,' she's saying. 'Kate, can't you see that you were a victim? You were a little kid. You have done nothing to be ashamed of.'

I can't think what to say. I'm so busy processing their reactions. I shouldn't be ashamed! It just keeps replaying in my head without going further. I shouldn't be ashamed!

'Kate, I have to say I'm dumbfounded by this. You seem so together and you should be proud of what you've achieved. Especially with all that behind you.'

'But I feel worthless a lot of the time, when I'm by myself. I think that's what's wrong with me.'

'Kate, there's nothing, nothing wrong with you!'

'Well, I can't get into relationships. With men, I mean. I just get anxious, not romantic. And you know all that stuff that's in the papers about abused children becoming dysfunctional adults.'

'You're not dysfunctional! Look at you. Degree, job, friends. We never would have guessed you had the childhood you did. Lord, the home was bad enough but this too? No! You're a survivor, not a bundle of problems.'

I go to bed still tense but relieved too. They aren't going to reject me. They think I'm normal. What if they talk about it together overnight and change their minds? Please God, don't let them change their minds.

In the morning everything is as it was before I took the biggest step I've ever taken. I'm not a reject. Not to these friends. Just to men who don't know me and never will because I must be ugly or some other thing.

School starts again and I love it as much as before, although I get disturbed by the kids who scream when their mums leave them. Ella and I settle them in and soon they love us and nag their parents from the time they get up to take them to play at preschool.

'Trent loves coming,' Mrs Gould says, 'but what are you letting them throw tea bags at each other for?'

'Tea bags? Good question. What tea ba– oh, bean bags. That must be it. He means bean bags.'

She laughs and says she was a bit surprised.

'Would you like to stay and join in sometimes?'

'Yeah! Can I?'

Soon there's a different parent staying every day to help out or just to watch. Lots of the working parents have jobs in factories and when one brings in little boxes that we turn into a flock of quacking ducks, others start bringing factory waste too.

'See what you can turn this into!' they challenge, and so a game starts to see who can bring the most useful junk and what we can do with it. The families are poor so we try to make things the kids can play with at home. Puppets, dolls, bats and sponge balls and so on.

At school I'm happy and fulfilled. At home I'm getting depressed. I've got to get help. There's a song, 'All My Friends are Getting Married', that is my anthem. I still go bushwalking, but now that I have program preparation to do at home, I can't afford to have two days out on weekends. I can't find anyone to go out with on Saturday nights. My friends are all at home with their kids. These nights at home become a symbol of all that is wrong with me. I'm here, alone, because I'm a reject.

Looking through the walking program, I discover that there's a bush dance on Saturday night. I'll probably know people there from bushwalking. I'll go.

The music reminds me of childhood, in the school playground doing folk dancing on the melting asphalt, looking at the pictures of happy children in the teacher's book, dancing patterns around maypoles or a clover shape.

It doesn't matter that I came alone, because in our group women dance men's parts and vice versa. Instructions are given before the dance starts and then we're off. I haven't laughed solidly for four hours ever before. Bush dancing becomes my Saturday night obsession. When there isn't going to be a dance, I go bush-walking. All this activity hides the fact that I feel dreadfully lonely.

My flat is going to be sold and the owner asks if I'd like to buy it. Heart failure seems imminent when he tells me the price.

'You ought to think about getting your own place,' Gen and Paddy suggest. Helen agrees.

'They don't give loans to single women,' I say.

'Oh yeah. Forgot about that. Have you asked?'

'They offered enough to buy a very large tent.'

Another change of address to tell everyone about. I move to a different block of flats nearer to West Ryde. I ring Aunty Dot and she says, 'It sounds as if you'll be near your relatives.'

'Relatives?' I don't have any, do I? Well, there's Ken, wherever he's gone and not told me, for whatever unfathomable reason, and Kerry who's interstate.

'I'm sure they'd love to see you. You should drop in on them. They're Norma's relatives.'

I'm about to say, 'Who's Norma?' but I remember she was my mother. Will I go and see them? She must mean Uncle Charlie, my mother's brother. Would he and his family want to see me? I've been on the planet for thirty years and we haven't met, so

149

I don't suppose they're all that keen. I'll just go and see where the house is.

It's only a couple of streets away. A charming little weatherboard house that's immaculately painted and the garden is ablaze with azaleas. Will I go in? Just bowl up and say, 'Hello. I'm Norma's daughter?'

A white-haired man is wandering in the garden, cutting dead flowers off. He looks frail. What if I go and say my line? Aunty Dot says how much I look like my mother – he might think I'm a ghost and keel over. Even worse, what if he says, 'Go away. I don't want anything to do with you'? Is that the worst? What if he says, 'Oh, I've waited for this for so long. Come in and be part of your family'? What then? Pressure to be who they expect me to be? Or what if he gets to know me and doesn't like me?

I go home.

I'm missing the ritual of traditional church and, although I still don't like the structure, I decide to go to the local one. I might meet some local people and maybe even a nice man.

'You ride a bike!' a tall chap with a broad grin says after church, boring church. The singing was great, though.

'Step through,' I reply. 'Some people say it's not a real bike.'

'Wouldn't you rather have a car? Bikes are dangerous. I talk from experience.'

His interest makes me nervous so I make sure he thinks I have backup. 'Ah, but my brother taught me defensive riding. The only time I wish I had a car is in winter, when I get to work and I have to pull my frozen hands sideways off the handlebars. I'm thinking of getting a car.'

We chat about what sort I'll get and how I'll learn to drive. Nice chap. Not handsome but a nice chap. Why am I so anxious?

I book a driving lesson and wonder how Lance and Cheryl are. They've moved out of Sydney and I don't hear anything about them now. I hope they are happy.

My driving instructor is about forty.

'I'm really worried about this,' I tell him. 'My last driving lesson ended up in a brick wall.'

'You don't have to worry this time,' he says, patting my thigh. 'I've got controls too.'

Get your hand off me. There isn't much scope for pulling my leg away in here. Am I just a prude? They wouldn't have driving teachers who were sleazy, would they? I'll just try to ignore his hand and concentrate on what he's saying.

When it's my turn to take the wheel, every chiropractor for miles would be rubbing his hands with glee if he could see. Each attempt to change gear lurches us forward and stalls the car. I get more and more agitated and the instructor needs to pat my leg more and more. Will I ever relax and learn this? I'll have to if I want a car. Manuals cost less, so I want a manual, not an automatic.

During my next lesson the lurching makes the instructor need to keep his hand on my thigh. I've had it!

'Would you please take your hand off my leg.'

'Oh. I'm just being reassuring,' he says defensively.

'I don't like it. It is not appropriate.' And it makes me want to hit you with my handbag.

'Oh. Women's libber, are you? All right, I'll try.'

We lurch violently through the lesson. I still don't get it and he seems incapable of keeping his hands to himself for any length of time. Heavens, even my four-year-olds can learn that!

I ring the driving school and tell them I want to change instructors. They say in their advertising that you can do that.

'What's the problem?' the receptionist asks.

'He keeps patting my leg even though I've asked him not to. It makes me nervous and I'm not making progress either.'

'I'm sure he means no harm.'

'I still want to change.'

'All right, we'll send someone else.'

The someone else is an old man called George. He's kind,

reassuring and keeps his hands off me. Reassuring for a few lurches anyway.

'Pull in here,' he says.

I can do that.

'I know you want to learn on a manual but I really think you should learn on an automatic, get your licence, then you can learn manual if you still want to.'

I'm insulted. No! I'm going to learn this. 'One more lesson,' I tell him.

Next time he comes I'm in the middle of doing some school work, and I dash out to the car before I've had time to get agitated.

'All right. Are you going to change to second soon?' George asks.

'Yes.' Zing, zing, zing and we're in second, still cruising!

'Keep your eyes on the road! Yes, that was great. Now try third.'

Smooth!

'Pull in. What's happened to you? That was miraculous!'

Soon I'm doing my driving test, doing a reverse uphill park in the exact spot where George took me to practise yesterday. We get stuck at lights in heavy traffic at Top Ryde where George warned me they take you to test your patience. I wait for three changes of the signals before I go through.

'I got it!' I beam at George.

He congratulates me and says I must bring my car to show him, when I pick it up. I do and he congratulates us both again.

Will I go back to that church? I love the singing and ritual but it's hard not being allowed to discuss or disagree with the minister. I go, for something to do, but decide during the sermon that this will be the last time.

'Where's your helmet?' asks the nice but not handsome man.

'I got a car.'

'Can I have a look at it?'

'You won't be impressed. It's the cheapest one on the market.'

He says lots of good things about my car, which friends have dubbed the Yellow Peril because it's so bright. We chat for a while and discover that we live in the same street and his block of flats is two away from mine.

'Would you like to go to town on Saturday night? We could have dinner and go to the Basement to hear some jazz or something.'

'Oh! All right,' I say before I have time to think. My first date! Thirty years old and I'm going on a real date. There aren't sparks and fireworks but it feels pleasant.

'I'm Gareth, by the way,' he says.

'Kate. Hello.'

Gareth and I start seeing each other regularly, though not every weekend. Sometimes he drops in on his way home and we have dinner together.

'How about I stay the night?' he says as he kisses me goodnight.

My knees turn to jelly when he kisses me but I'm anxious too. 'No,' I tell him. 'I'm not ready for that.' I want a ring and a proposal, don't I?

Oh well, he won't be back. Girls at work and uni always said that if you don't sleep with a man these days he just goes off and finds someone who will. But it doesn't seem like a good enough reason to do it. Especially when you practically freeze with fear like I do.

Gareth doesn't vanish. We keep up our usual contact and I begin to relax with him. I wonder what he does on the weekends when we don't go out.

'I have my kids over.'

'Kids! You've got kids? You're not married, are you?'

'Was. I get the kids every second weekend.'

'Am I going to meet them?'

'I don't know.'

'What are they like?'

He tells me their names and ages and what they're like.

'We could all go out together,' I suggest hopefully.

'No. Sorry, but I just want to keep that side of things separate.'

'Why?' Am I a danger?

'If you really want to know, I don't want their mother to know about you,' he says defensively.

'You are divorced? Aren't you?'

'Been divorced for a year and two months.'

'What's the problem, then? I'm not going to harm them, am I?'

'No, of course not. I just don't want them telling their mother about us. It's none of her business.' He sounds bitter.

The discussion goes around in the same endless circle every time we have it.

I have spare time on weekends when Gareth has his kids. To distract myself from being excluded, I go bushwalking or dancing. Despite the fact that Gareth has this other life, it seems I do have a boyfriend at last. I feel as if I've been admitted into a new club: the acceptably single women's club. I can join conversations in the staff room or with parents now because I can say 'we' not 'I' did such and such.

I look forward to seeing Gareth and I'm surprised to find that it's getting harder to resist his invitations to stay overnight. That's my hormones, but somewhere else, I'm afraid. Something dreadful will be unleashed from the dark inside me. The fear is fuelled by media saturation about sexual abuse. Makes you look at it. Makes you aware and afraid. It's time I worked out why I'm so afraid. Time to look at the dream of the dark father that was a reality, not a dream?

Tess tells me about a counsellor she knows who specialises in treating abused teenagers. His values are the same as ours and she thinks he'd be a good person for me to talk with. She doesn't think I'll need much help because I'm functioning well. I don't know how to explain to her how small and how anxious I feel sometimes with Gareth and his kisses.

As I go into the psychologist's building, I feel as if I'm on stage alone with a spotlight boring down on me and the rest of the world is the audience.

'Sit down, Kate,' Bill says. 'Tess has told me a little about you. You think you might need to do some work on this business with your father.'

'Yes, but, well, I don't really know. I see articles all over the place saying that people who've been abused have all sorts of problems. And there's a man who I want to sleep with, I think, but I'm afraid of something and I don't know what to do.'

'Go back a bit . . .' He asks if I've had any bad times in relationships with men.

'I haven't had any relationships 'til now. Apart from, you know, the, um, abuse one.'

'Oh, I see. How about your boss, then? You get on with him, do you?'

'I hardly have anything to do with him.'

The psychologist deduces that, because I'm a success in my career and socially, the effect of my father's abuse is minimal and I should just get on with my relationship with Gareth.

'So you think I'll be all right if I sleep with him?'

'That's not what I said. You know the Bible says sex outside marriage is wrong.'

A brick wall begins to rise between us, like in a cartoon. Chink, chink, chink. First row. Chink, chink, chink. Second row. I can still see over, though, and talk.

'But if I'm going to unleash problems, I'd rather find them before I have a marriage to ruin.'

'You know what the Christian view is.'

Chink, chink, chink. Third and fourth rows. Chink, chink, chink. Fifth and sixth rows. Can still see over.

'But I want to find out if I'm normal before . . . I can use contraceptives. Isn't that what the Bible's worried about?'

He shakes his head slowly.

Chink, chink, chink. Can't see over. 'We can't discuss it any more, then, can we?'

'Afraid not,' he says.

I walk to the door, sad and confused.

'If you do sleep with him I hope you enjoy it.'

'Pardon?' Haven't you just contradicted yourself?

'It's meant to be enjoyed. I hope you enjoy it, if that's the choice you make.'

I can't sort him out when I'm trying to sort me out.

'Stay,' I tell Gareth.

'Are you sure? I don't mean to pressure you.'

'I want you to.'

Meant to be enjoyed. It is. I must be normal. If Gareth asks me to marry him, what will I say?

Am I moving into the next phase that normal people move into? I'm later than most but I must be in the same world at last. I dearly hope so.

CHALLENGES

Gareth wants to come to Leonie and Col's new farm. I so much want them to like him. I'm nervous. I suppose it's like bringing the boyfriend home to meet mum and dad. Gareth reckons he feels relaxed and when we arrive he sets to helping the kids light a fire for a barbecue. Soon Sara is crying, 'Gareth made the fire go out. We know how to do it, Mummy.' Her parents have taught her good manners so she doesn't say what I know she must be thinking.

'Darling, you kids can light one anytime. Let Gareth do this one. He is our guest.' The kids, unimpressed by my boyfriend's boy scout skills, find something else to do. I, on the other hand, am impressed by his enthusiasm for whatever is happening. He's like a different person down here. More relaxed.

In my thank-you-for-having-us phone call afterwards, Leonie says, 'He's a nice enough bloke, Kate, but he's so uninvolved with your life. He's not really connected with you.'

Uninvolved? I don't understand. We see each other on week-ends and during the week. We'll get closer. Don't we have to give

157

our connection time? I'm more involved with Gareth than I've been with any other man. How should we do 'involved'?

I try to imagine what being married to Gareth would be like. There's a big blank page stretching past his fondness for football, his kids, sex and Rotary. I can't see us being like any of my friends. Well, we aren't them and I haven't lived in a family and none of my friends has married a divorcee.

'Do you think we'd get on if we were married?' I ask him after a few more months.

'No way! Been there, done that.'

His quick, definite answer hurts. 'Well, I haven't and some day I want to.'

'Sorry. Divorce isn't that great, you know.'

'Singleness isn't crash hot either, though, is it?'

He might change. Of course he'd be cynical after a bitter divorce. There's no-one else on the scene so I might as well keep seeing him, keep hoping he'll change his mind.

It's safe wanting to marry Gareth when he doesn't want to marry anyone. I can ignore the nagging doubts and push the anxiety away. Sometimes I talk about marriage and Gareth stops coming as often, but then he's back, saying he's been busy but he missed me. I feel relieved and flattered. We seem closer each time he says he missed me.

Tonight I go to Gareth's for dinner as has become our custom over the last year or so. He doesn't answer the door. Must be late getting home from work. I go back later and he still isn't there. He must have forgotten but it's unlike him.

In the morning I go to his place again and when he doesn't answer I knock on the window. No curtains. The flat is completely empty! I panic. Can't think. Wouldn't move. Has he dumped me?

Don't leave me! Please don't leave me.

I walk home fast, holding back tears until I'm inside. Now they flow. I'm worthless. Stupid. Ugly. Foolish. Lonely. Why has he done this just when I thought we were getting close? What's wrong with me? Why doesn't anyone want me? I'll never get it right. Always be lonely.

Going to school soothes the pain. I'm sad inside but it's so busy here and it's not about me. It's all about the kids' needs. We're getting a lot of Vietnamese boat people's kids now. They drop them off quickly and hurry back to the hostel for English lessons.

The kids are so frightened! They bite and kick and scratch when we try to settle them. Ella and I find that if we leave them to creep about watching us all, they settle more quickly. Then we can start getting near them. It isn't until I'm in the staff room one day that I understand what's happening for these little fighters. Teachers are gathered around a drawing that is the most horrifying thing a child could produce: people with knives, blood gushing from a woman's belly, a baby in the air on the end of a bloody trail, a body on the floor without a head. It's not a floor. It's a deck. The deck of a boat like the ones many of these families came to Australia on. Pirated rusty wrecks. Primary teachers report terrible stories written by older kids with enough English to express themselves that way. They didn't reach us on comfortable ocean liners or jet planes. They've seen more horror than I ever will, I hope. And the adult survivors are so grateful that we welcome their untrusting kids into what we want to be Paradise.

There's a group of seven in the preschool now and they eventually settle down and seem happy enough with us. Although I've made sure I know how to pronounce the kids' names by listening carefully to their parents, they often ignore me.

'Look,' Hung says one day. 'Look.' He takes my hand and pulls me to where he's lined up all his friends.

He walks me along in front of them, touching each one and saying Vietnamese words. He must be counting. At the end of the line he turns back to me and bounces his finger softly up and down on my forehead.

'I don't know what you mean, Hung.'

159

He does the whole performance again and now the line of kids is giggling. Hung taps my forehead again and says, 'Say er.'

'Er,' I say obediently.

Now Hung points to himself and says, 'Hung.' Then to me and says, 'Say er.'

'Oh, names! Hung and Shayler. You're teaching me names.'

Now we go down the line again, reciting the kids' names, me with my best Vietnamese accent that makes them giggle almost to tears. I get Ella to have a lesson with Hung and there's more giggling. He doesn't want to show the local kids what he's doing, though, and he becomes shy of all the attention. But he's pioneered the way for us all to communicate better and, best of all, to be trusting friends. Now we can be more effective teachers.

Soon they're gone. Their parents have found housing and work. I know I'm doing a worthwhile job and I love it, though I miss those kids who leave.

There are so many personalities to deal with here and to help get along together. Boxes help. We change a matching set of them into cows and some kids decide to put theirs on their heads and be cows. Soon we have a herd mooing contentedly on the grass. Luke wants to be a cowboy and drive them with his whip. His manhood is challenged when I suggest he uses a ribbon instead of a skipping rope that'll hurt the cows. He sulks, then joins the herd in disgust. I get teary when I'm laughing these days.

I get teary at home too, but not from laughing. Got to go out more. Stop being alone and miserable. Back to my old fancy-free life. Back to dancing and bushwalking, though it seems my old group has moved on to other things during my Gareth years. I join a bush dance performance group and rehearsals fill up more time. Soon I'm getting out my old sewing machine to make costumes. I buy a bridal gown pattern for my crinolines, and scan op shops to find hats I can turn into bonnets.

'I want frills and pearls and flowers on evening wear,' our director, Isabel, announces. 'And I want teeth!'

Yes, I've got the teeth! Nice teeth. They haven't got me a nice boy but Isabel didn't need to tell me to show them. I'm smiling as soon as the music starts. For most of us a performance brings as much pleasure as a social dance. Being comfortable in my body like this surprises me. I have fun even with an audience watching.

We dance on the Opera House forecourt and in Sydney's Folkloric Festival. Old people's homes like us too. 'It's good to see something lively,' an inmate says as we have tea with them. 'We might be old but we're not dead. Some of the dreary stuff they get for us! Entertainment, they call it!' She makes me hope I won't be alone when I'm old, or end up in a nursing home.

I've been thinking of buying my own place again. It's easier for single women to get loans now and building societies are more forthcoming than banks. I can borrow enough to buy a unit if I go out near Parramatta. It's a bit close to Burnside but I don't have to go there. I find a unit and sign the contract. My own place! I can't believe I'm going to own my own place! The twenty-five-year debt makes my stomach churn but I've got a job so I'll be right. Must start collecting boxes, for packing this time, not for cow-making.

Oh, the relief of a night at home! Nothing to do but watch whatever rubbish is on TV. Have an early night, I think. Then there's a loud knock on my door.

'G'day.' Gareth is grinning enthusiastically on my doorstep.

'What are you doing here?'

'Been in hospital. Glad to see me?'

'What? What happened?' I haven't invited him in. I feel annoyed that he's turned up like this. But he's been in hospital! 'Do you want to come in?'

'That'd be good. I need to sit down.'

'Why? What's wrong?'

'Uh, had most of this muscle ripped off in an accident.' There's a crater where his muscle should be.

'What accident?' I still feel something for him.

'Just an accident. Been in hospital for months. I just got out.'

'Why didn't you tell me? You just disappeared. I didn't know if you were dead or what had happened. I thought you'd dumped me.'

He explains that he'd been too embarrassed to tell me. The accident was such a stupid thing and he didn't want me to know about it. He reluctantly tells me that he lost control of his golf buggy and drove it into a tree. It flipped over and landed on his leg, ripping the muscle away. His brother had packed up his flat and moved his stuff to his place.

We start seeing each other again but it's not the same. It's nice that Gareth missed me and it's nice to be in the club of not exactly single women again. But he shouldn't have had to miss me. He should have told me about the accident. It hurts that he cut me out when I would have wanted to be supportive. He says he's sorry and realises now that that was wrong. He's impressed with my unit and doesn't mind the extra distance from his place.

I love the unit. My unit! I wander around owning walls, corners, cupboards, the sunny balcony. If I want a picture here, I can whack a hook in and no-one can stop me. If I want a trendy pink wall, I can have it! If I want to leave all those boxes in the spare room, I can. And I'll never have to move again, unless I want to.

Gareth tries to be interested in dancing but his absent muscle is a problem. He brings his kids to a dance and the two little ones love it. His eldest is surly, though. She tells me I should cut my hair. I should wear more makeup. The colour of my blouse is wrong. My dancing shoes are frumpy.

'Yeah, but I can dance,' I say, hoping she'll laugh. She doesn't. What she does do is give me a glimpse into what weekends would be like if Gareth and I were married, and a glimpse into my sense of inadequacy in dealing with teenagers.

'I'm buying a house,' Gareth announces one night after dinner.

'Sounds good,' I reply.

'Yeah. I thought I'd like to get married again. Have more kids.'

I keep clearing the table and he starts washing up. Suddenly it dawns on me! I go out to the sink. 'When you said you think you'd like to marry again, did you mean to me or just to someone?'

'To you,' he replies, as if it was obvious.

'Oh.' That's all I can think of to say. The thing I thought I wanted most is just a word away.

My mind is racing. Is it what I really want? Babies! Yes! Oh, yes, I do want that. I've prayed that God would give me the chance. I've begged Him and bargained when I've felt more clucky than I could bear. But babies with the man who disappears when embarrassing things happen? Would I have to disappear like that too? There'd be heaps of embarrassing moments with me and babies, I suppose. I wouldn't really know what to do with them. But Gareth would. He's got kids. What about them? So many questions and Gareth is probably waiting for an answer.

'Let's stay friends for now. I'm not sure what I want any more.'

I need time to explore being with Gareth and this possibility. Do I want to give up teaching, dancing, walking? Is he the sort of bloke who'd give me a break to do them? No. I think he'd expect me to stay tied to the proverbial kitchen sink. He's got all his things – footy, Rotary, work, kids – that he wouldn't want to give up. What about the house he's buying? For us? Where was I when he chose it? If we lived together, all those things would be there all the time. No breaks. They'd be there as hurts and disappointments and he wouldn't want to face them.

Marriage begins to feel like a cage hanging over my head, waiting to drop down and trap me. I had that feeling when Aunty Marj wanted me to go and live with her when I left Burnside: afraid of someone getting to know me up close and rejecting me. Do I want to marry Gareth? That's what I have to think about. Not scary things that I can't face. Things that creep in when I just want to sleep and Gareth isn't tired yet.

But I could have babies! Maybe those other things would work themselves out. What if they didn't? Well, we'd divorce, I suppose, then the babies would just have me. Me! I couldn't do it on my own. I wouldn't know how. I want my babies to have two parents, not half a one or less.

No-one can make this decision for me. I wish there was an authority who'd just say, 'Marry him.' Or, 'I forbid you to marry him.'

The relationship fades away. Gareth stops calling and so do I. I'm more sad than I want to admit. No babies. And I miss having a boyfriend that proves I'm socially acceptable. But I think I made the right decision. I'm thirty-three and it's still not too late to meet someone else and have my babies. I just have to extend my deadline. Again. To thirty five.

School is still wonderful. We have a new principal now and he's a more approachable character. He smiles and waves to our preschoolers as he goes by and they think he's a friend. Today he comes in with a serious face and says, 'Kate, let's go into your office.' Then, 'I don't want to alarm you but I've had a complaint about you.'

Alarmed! Mystified!

'I want to assure you that I don't believe it. I've checked with Mrs Pontifex and she says "no way". We've always had fine comments from parents about this place.'

'What is it? Who said it? What . . .'

'A woman rang and accused you of mistreating kids in your class. Abusing them to be more precise. Now don't worry. We'll get to the bottom of it but I just had to ask you outright, is there anything that I ought to know about?'

'I wouldn't . . . I haven't . . . Nothing has happened! Ask Ella. She's beside me all day, every day. Ask any of the parents who stay. I wouldn't . . .'

'I will, yes. Listen, I don't believe that anything has happened but do you know who'd make these accusations?'

'No! Who?'

'She wasn't willing to give her name, so I told her I wouldn't dignify her claims with an investigation unless she came to see me in person.'

'I can't imagine who!'

'Someone has. I suggest you go about your normal business and come and see me if there's any problem. Be watchful but don't get too worried.'

How can I not worry? It's devastating. Who'd have any reason to make that up? We've always been open about what we do here. We've always got parents joining in. They talk with me and openly question what I do. We've all been so happy here. Haven't we? How could they, whoever it is? She must be hating me behind my back, pretending all is well to my face. How could she? I get suspicious of everyone but they all seem to be their usual happy selves. Now I get angry. She won't even come and talk to me. She's a hypocrite. Which one of you is it? I just can't believe that any of these people would even imagine I'd abuse a child. All I see is goodwill and trust when I look at them. But it's got to be someone!

The boss comes to my room again a few days later.

'Uh? No, mate. Can't play trains just now.' He grins at one of the kids. This time his grin stays put and he says, 'That woman rang back a few minutes ago.'

I'm going to be sick.

'It's not you she's talking about. Sorry. It's Miss Keat. I asked her for the teacher's name and she just said "Keat". So sorry. She's got such a strong accent I could hardly understand her. Kate. Keat.'

I cry.

'Are you all right?'

'Relieved.'

'Yes. Sorry. It was the accent. And when she said little kids, I'm afraid I assumed. Well, I'll have to look into this other now. Seems to be a vendetta, not a real complaint. Anyway, keep this confidential. Miss Keat has a right to privacy too.'

Lately I've been giving Sharna Keat a lift to school because she lives near me with her new boyfriend. A few times I've picked her up she's been floating. Must be love! Half her luck! She's been away for a few days.

'Look, I've got to tell you this,' says Sally, a teacher who lives close to school.

'Not kids blabbing about your undies on the line at show and tell again?'

'Kate, this is serious. You're being followed.'

'What do you mean? Follow the leader?'

'This is serious, Kate. Sharna's been doing drugs. She's not on holidays. She's gone to rehab.'

'You're joking! I thought she was floating around on true love.'

'Listen, the boyfriend got her onto them.'

Sally goes on to explain that Sharna's boyfriend is a dealer and, now that the relationship has soured, he and his people are after Sharna. They want revenge. They're following me to find her and are planning to force me to tell where she is if I don't inadvertently show them.

'Sal, this stuff doesn't happen to me. Anyway, I don't know where she is!'

'I know that, but they don't.'

'I'll go to the police.' They were helpful before.

'They won't do anything until something happens.' Sally knows about that, having been in a violent marriage. 'You can stay with me for a while but that won't help because they know where you work and they know your car.'

I can't drive now without watching the rear vision mirror. I'm afraid to go shopping. I can't stay back at school. I'm a wreck. Should have married Gareth. I'd have someone to look after me. Protect me.

Mrs Pontifex notices that I'm tense and asks with a smile, 'Miss Shayler, you don't seem to be your usual cheerful self. Is there a problem?'

I blurt the whole thing out and she looks stunned.

'Has anyone followed you?'

'I can't tell when I'm driving.'

'Well, try not to worry. I'm sure they'll give up. Sharna isn't even here now.'

'I can't not worry. I don't feel safe, even at home with the door locked!' I squeak.

She realises it's not going to be brushed aside, so she thinks it would be good if I took some leave and went away for a while. She arranges it and gives me the key to her holiday house on the coast.

I pack and drive, too fast, out of Sydney. What if they follow me? I'll be alone in a village with no-one to help me. I pull over and sob. No-one pulls in behind me but I move off quickly. I drive on and eventually lock myself in the little seaside house. I watch out of windows, read for a while, then return to the windows. On the third day I sneak out the back, find a rock and put it in my bag. I go for a short walk with my bag and my rock, listening for footsteps behind me, ready to clobber anyone with my rock. I could almost laugh about that. My walks get longer and I start feeling safe. I have to go back to work.

'Did anything happen while I was away?' I ask Mrs Pontifex.

'Not a thing. You just stop worrying and get back to those lovely kiddies of yours. I've heard they missed you.'

It's nice getting back to those lovely kiddies. Sally says she hasn't heard anything more and that she'll keep me posted.

Something has changed. I've had seven great years here but now I don't feel safe. The people are good people but the threat hangs persistently in the air now. Perhaps it's time I moved on and challenged myself professionally. It's too long since uni for me to go into primary school teaching but I could try a kindergarten class and move along over the years. I apply for a transfer and finish the year watching my back. I start feeling too tired to go out on weekends yet it's depressing being at home. It's deeply sad leaving the families and staff at the end of the year and I try to get excited about the challenge I've set for myself.

I'm transferred to a school in a depressed Housing Commission area that's hemmed in by affluence. I'm not fazed by poverty any more. I hope I get the kindergarten, though.

'I've put you on Year One,' announces the principal. Her perfectly painted fingernails that resemble talons tap on the class list she has in front of her. 'They're a lovely class and I'm sure you'll enjoy them. You haven't taught infants before, have you?'

'No. I've done preschool.'

'Well, come and see me if you have any problems,' she says.

I'll wear a trail to your door.

I just catch one of the other teacher's eyebrows descending to eyes that are popping out of their sockets. What does that mean?

My room is drab and dirty. The walls are speckled with grimy Blu-Tack and myriad bits of masking tape and drawing pins that refuse to let go of paper that's hung there for years. What equipment there is, is old, dirty and mostly broken. Why did I leave my bright, clean, well-equipped preschool?

Some of my thirty-six kids are lively, curious and open. Some would be if they'd been born into different families. About a third know less than the preschoolers I've left behind and a third have emotional problems that affect their behaviour either strangely or badly. Some parents are warm and friendly, some warn me about others, and some are openly hostile.

'I wanna talk to you,' a round, shabby woman demands aggressively as I climb the stairs wearily after bus duty on Friday. 'Why didn't my kid get P.E. today?'

'Hello, Mrs Norward. It was raining today.'

'They always have P.E. on Friday.'

'It was raining so we cancelled it.'

'You pick on my kid one more time and you'll know about it, bitch!'

'Pardon?'

'You heard.'

'And you better leave mine alone, too,' snarls the woman behind her who's smartly dressed but jabbing the air with her finger.

'What's the problem?' I ask. I hope I appear calm, not afraid of the palpable hostility. I force myself to walk slowly towards the staff room door.

'Jakey says you told him to stop talkin'.'

'Yes. I did.'

'He's allowed to talk.'

'Not when we're doing silent reading. Nobody talks then. Not even me.'

'Oh.' I haven't heard 'oh' delivered like a bullet before!

'Is there anything else?' I ask them when I've reached the door.

'What d'ya mean?'

'Do you want to ask me about anything else?'

'Nuh.' She seems confused.

'Well, thanks for your questions. Ask anytime.'

'Sure!' Her sarcasm is nasty.

'I mean it. You won't find out if you don't ask.'

They look befuddled, regain their united strength and add, 'Yer just better not keep pickin' on our kids. That's all.'

I walk into the staff room half expecting a knife in my back. I shut the door. I'm shaking.

'What was that about? A nice chat with my two favourite tarts?' Carol asks.

'Oh, they reckon I pick on their kids.' I'm so relieved to be away from them, I cry and feel foolish and unprofessional.

'Don't let them upset you,' she says. 'They'll keep it up all year if they know they get to you. You should have seen them last year when their kids were new here!'

She sees my red eyes.

'Poor you. You'll learn. Did they see you cry?'

'No,' I say, wiping my eyes. 'I thanked them for talking to me about it,' I add, laughing. I'm laughing at my bravado and then at Carol's face.

'You thanked them!'

'Yeah. They looked a bit confused.' I grin.

'Hey, good move! You might have called their bluff.'

'Hope so. I even told them to ask again if there's a problem.'

'Oh lord! What have you done?' She laughs. 'Seriously, though, you be careful. Watch your back.'

Is that what teaching has become? Trying to achieve the impossible while you're always watching your back? Not feeling safe. Needing a protector, a bodyguard, self-defence classes. A husband?

Another teacher tells me quietly that one of those women spent her first four years locked in a cupboard and was only brought out to be raped. Food was sometimes thrown in to her. The other woman went off the rails when she found that her daughter had been systematically abused by her husband while she was at work. They support each other against the world.

I want to scream. How can I make a difference when the odds are so stacked against these kids? And their mums.

Mrs Norward, the more aggressive of the two women, comes to my room later on.

'Came to say sorry. That was nice how you said that to me about talkin'. I just want the best for me boy, you know.'

'I know. I do too. We need to work together.'

'I do me best but you're the teacher.'

'Yeah, well, we can talk anytime about what I'm teaching. How you can help him.'

I try to make a difference by being respectful, warmhearted and hardworking. Whatever I do is not enough. I try groups based on what kids are capable of, so that I can work intensively with one group while the others do the work I've set them. They go feral when I'm not with them. It's pointless teaching them all together because the below average lot don't get it and the above average ones get bored. And there's Larry. When this seven-year-old comes home from being with the street kids all hell breaks loose. His heroin-dependent mum can't manage her own life, let alone his. Welfare can't keep up with either of them, so how can I? I try with Larry. Each time he comes back I have to convince him again that I'm not the enemy, that I like him and that he can learn. Just when we get it right, he's off again, unable to cope at home.

'Dunno what to write about, Miss,' he tells me when we're doing independent work and I'm circulating. He reminds me of not wanting to write about my life at the home when I was a kid. It was called Composition then. I only passed because I could spell well.

'What do you do when you're away?' I ask him.

'Go to shops and that.'

'And that? What's that? Tell me other words for it.'

'Hang out.'

'What else?'

'Run.'

'Tell me about running.'

'Dunno. We juss run.'

'Why?'

' 'Cause we love it, me an' Mikey. We juss run anywhere 'til we're buggered. One day we ran from the main drag to Cyan Road and back.'

I haven't a clue where that is but that's more words than he's ever said in one conversation. Words about running away from his life.

'That'd be good to write about. That's interesting, Larry. Have a try.'

'How do you spell "when"? Wiv a haitch?'

I wish I could make a difference but sometimes all I want is to shake Larry's mother and tell her she has a child who needs her badly. Why have them if you don't want them? Why keep them tied to your heroin? Why not give them up for adoption or fostering? Why give them life, then give them a life that's so hard? But she's drug dependent. She can't reason. Perhaps she needs a mother too.

If I go to the principal's office for help she's either out or busy. Rumour has it that she's doing a degree and when her door is shut, she's working on an assignment. She sends kids who are sent to her for discipline to sit in my room.

'Your class is so well disciplined, they'll be an example.' She smiles sweetly as she strides away. Fortunately for me teachers don't send kids to her much. What would be the point?

Mrs Sherwood, a mum who helps every day in my class, says to me one day, 'I think I should tell you that Steve is making threats to boys in the toilets.'

'Threats?'

'Yeah. That if they don't suck him, he'll beat them up. Sorry to be so blunt but you've got to do something. All the boys are scared of him and we've talked to them and Steve but he won't stop. Where would a seven-year-old get that stuff!'

Report it. That's what the proper procedure is. Report if you think a child is at risk. The principal thinks it's just a silly boys' joke and dismisses me. When Mrs Sherwood asks how it went, I tell her. I suggest she organises a delegation of parents and reports it too. They do and the matter is passed to Community Services and investigated. Steve has been abused by his big brother and is forced to watch porn that terrifies him. At least we've made that stop but what is the world coming to? I want to go home, curl up and stay there. Rocking.

If the principal won't help, who will? I make an appointment with the school counsellor to ask about a boy who comes every day reeking of stale urine, his hair matted to his smelly head, and money he's got from I don't know where. He brought his grand-mother's jewellery to school to try to buy friends this week. He doesn't seem to be progressing at all in class. The others are, slowly, but I want help with some of them too.

The counsellor listens thoughtfully and mentions some options, most of which have been suggested by other teachers, tried and failed.

'Well, Kate, can you work any harder?'

'No! I spend every night working and weekends as well and it's still not enough.'

'There's your answer.'

'What do you mean?'

'You can't work any harder.'

'But it's not making enough of a difference.'

'You can't fix the world. And it's not what you're paid for. You do your best and they go home. Can you fix their homes? You have to let it go or you'll go under.'

That makes some sense.

'It doesn't feel right just accepting defeat.'

'You don't accept defeat. What you do accept is that you can only do so much. You change what you can when you're teaching. That's all you can do.'

'Every minute, every lesson, there's a problem I don't get to.'

'Let it go.'

Three simple words bring so much relief. Let it go. That's how I'll try to survive the year. Do my best and let the rest go.

'And don't stay home on weekends. You've got to have some fun. It's important that you stay healthy.'

I start going to dances again. Guilt that I have so much work to do undermines the pleasure. What am I doing having this much fun when there's Larry's program to do, in case he's still there on Monday, and Netta's reading, and so much of everything? Dancing feels like it belonged in my distant past when I'd felt happy and young. Now I'm older than most singles here and I wonder how I'd have time for the poor chap if I did meet a man now. Well, I'd make time if he came stamped 'Perfect'. Eliminate the getting-to-know-you business. Just get married, get pregnant and leave work. Leave work. Babies! Bliss! My body clock is doing what everyone else's is but surely it doesn't show. The wives and girlfriends of men at dances clutch their partners fearfully. For goodness sake! I only want to dance with them!

'I was wondering if you'd like to see *We of the Never Never* on Sat'dy night,' Cameron asks. He's been coming to dances for years and I've danced with him but not enjoyed it. He's so stiff and awkward. I'm so surprised that he's asked me out I don't have time to get nervous.

'That would be good.'

'Pick you up at seven. It's at the drive-in.'

The drive-in! Good grief! Oh well, can't say no now. I might as well go for the experience.

By Saturday night all I want to do is sleep. Cameron picks me up at seven and the tyres screech away from the gutter as he hurls the car into the flow of traffic. Maybe he's nervous.

It isn't nerves, though. It's the way he drives! He's a bully on wheels, tailgating anyone who dares stick to the speed limit and dragging off all competitors at the lights. I'm sure I've dented his floor with my braking foot.

'Why are you driving so close?' I ask through clenched teeth when I can't stand it any more.

'The bloody idiot's sittin' on sixty.'

'That's the speed limit.'

'Yeah, but you can get away with eighty here.'

I can't bear it. 'Look,' I say angrily, not quite believing my boldness, 'if you want to take chances like this with your life, go ahead, but don't do it with mine.'

'What?'

'Either drive properly or let me out.'

'I'm driving properly!'

'Well, let me out, then. I'd rather walk. I mean it. Pull over right here. I'll get a bus home.' Do they have buses here?

'All right. I'll be good, Miss.'

He slows down but keeps grumbling about other drivers.

After the first ten minutes of the movie I'm asleep. The sound of motors wakes me. Cameron is surprised when I say I'd rather he didn't come in for coffee.

The following Monday I see him at the dance workshop and he asks me to have every dance with him. It's nice not to have to wait to be asked but he's such a dreadful dancer.

Tuesday night he calls: 'I've just finished work. Can I come over?'

'It's half past nine!'

'I know but I just want to see you for a while.'

'Just for a while.'

He arrives with a huge bunch of roses. I'm overwhelmed. We've only been out once! I make coffee and we sit down to chat.

I know how to keep a conversation going: ask him about himself. He's living with his mother but hates it. She wants to control his life and know all his business. I ask him why he doesn't move out and he says his mother doesn't want him to. She needs him. Anyway, he couldn't afford to rent a place on his own. He talks about his work as a mechanic and his love of racing cars. He talks on and on about his love of racing cars. At last he notices that I'm almost nodding off again.

'You're tired, aren't you? I'd better go.'

'Yes. I am pretty tired.'

'I'd better go then.'

'Yes.'

'Unless you'd like me to stay.'

'What?'

'Would you like me to stay?'

'No thanks!'

'Oh!' He's surprised. 'Can I see you tomorrow?'

'No. I've got too much work to do.' And I don't want to see you.

The next night he rings and invites himself over.

'No, Cameron. I'm too tired and I've got so much work to do. Teaching isn't a job where you just have a night off whenever you feel like it.'

The next night he's at my door with another dozen red roses and a box of chocolates.

'Happy Valentines Day. I love you.' He grins and kisses me.

This is over the top!

'Will you marry me?'

'What?'

'Will you marry me? I love you. Will you marry me?'

'I hardly know you!'

'What would you like to know? Besides that I love you and I want to marry you.'

'There's a lot I want to know. Over time. Not in a recital.'

'Well. I'll just have to keep asking, won't I? Over time.'

I don't think time will make a difference but I should think about it. Shouldn't I? I keep saying I want to meet someone but now there's a man saying he wants to make the big commitment and I'm saying no already. Maybe this is how it's done sometimes. Maybe I'll fall in love with him if he loves me and plans to be persistent. Maybe I'm too fussy and I should broaden my mind. He's going to be around for a while, so I don't have to decide straight away.

Two weeks later: 'Cameron, it's Kate. Haven't heard from you so I thought I'd ring. Are you all right?'

'Yes,' he replies curtly.

'What's wrong?'

'Nothing.'

'It doesn't sound like nothing. What is it?'

'I just don't think we should see each other any more.'

No! Don't leave me. Please don't leave me.

'Why?' I ask, choking back panic and tears that I know are way out of proportion to my feelings for him. I feel small and abandoned. I must be crazy.

'I just don't think we should, that's all.'

Don't leave me. Please don't leave me.

A scene from a dance a few weeks ago flashes into my mind: Cameron talking and laughing with a woman who is new at the dances.

'You're seeing someone else, aren't you?'

'So?'

His mind-your-own-business attitude pulls me up. I feel angry. 'It's Janet, isn't it?'

'Yes.'

'So have you asked her to marry you too?' I ask sarcastically.

To my amazement he replies, 'Not that it's any of your business but, yes, I have.'

Don't leave me! Please, please, don't leave me!

I'm devastated. Abandoned and betrayed. Angry and hurting. I cry for a longer time than my rational self thinks is appropriate.

Gen and I have arranged to meet for a picnic by the river on Saturday.

'Oh Kate, you look dreadful! Have you been sleeping?' she asks, mischievously. She's pleased that I've been going out with someone and more pleased that he proposed.

'He's marrying someone we met at a dance a week ago.'

'No!'

'Yes.'

'Oh Kate, There must be a mistake,' she says. 'Are you sure they're getting married? I mean, who told you? How do you know?'

'He told me himself.'

My friend is speechless.

'I don't know why I'm so upset,' I sob. 'I hardly knew him. That's why I didn't say I'd marry him. Any of the times he asked.'

'Yeah, but you must have loved him or you wouldn't be this upset.'

'I really didn't. I hardly knew him.' Why am I crying like this, then? I must be mad. Seriously mad.

We sit quietly for a while and I compose myself.

'Anyway, I wouldn't marry someone who kisses like a goldfish!' I say, trying to be cheerful.

'Sounds like a lucky escape, kiddo. But I still can't believe it. They've set a date for the wedding?'

'Yes. Six weeks from now.' Crying again.

'You'll get over it. Next time don't fall in love so quickly.'

I give up trying to convince Gen that I hadn't been in love. But I must be mental!

I hate every day at school. I like the kids but the work is impossible. It's a daily grind of failed attempts to help almost forty needy kids.

Then a letter arrives from Wanda.

You've disappointed me, Kate Shayler. You are the exact sort of person who should teach preschoolers! Don't you know that? You saw how those littlies were with you. Whatever possessed you to move? Far be it for me to boss my old boss but here goes – you just get a transfer back to the work God made you for. Or else!

Her letter clarifies what I need to do. I was meant to be a pre-school teacher. I'll apply for a transfer. No, I can't. The deal is we complete three years before we can transfer. Three years! I'd better try that 'let it go' business again. Get out and have fun.

After a few months I go to a weekend folk music festival.

There are musicians playing in every available space and dancers taking advantage of the music. I can join in whatever I like so choose Turkish dancing and try not to trip myself over. I'm laughing again and it's such a relief to be away from my ordinary life.

I sit on the grass to listen to some music. A man comes to sit beside me.

'Hello. I'm Elliott. We met at Chris's fortieth birthday. You were with the dancers, weren't you?'

'Yes. But I've left them. New job. Absolutely exhausting.' We talk for a while about that and I notice that his hands are shaking and his mouth dries up when he talks sometimes. But he seems gentle, intelligent and is quite nice looking. Just as I'm thinking that it would be nice to see him again, he says,

'Would you like to go for a walk in the mountains next Sunday?'

I accept and I'm glad that we have a love of bushwalking in common as well as music and dancing.

We walk along a track and, although dancing has made me fit again, this feels more like a run than a walk. 'Let's have an adventure,' Elliot says and drops down over the edge onto what could be called a track if you were a wallaby. We scramble down to the riverbed and follow it until lunchtime. He shows me where we are on a map and points out the way we'll go next. The close contours are not enticing.

'We'd better step on it. There's a storm coming.'

'Can't go any faster,' I puff.

The storm blows up quickly, cutting off all light in the gully we're in. We press on but before long we can't see a single step in front of us and it's pouring rain. Elliott bangs his head on a rock which we discover is an overhang, so we stumble under it. It's very narrow but if we snuggle up close we don't get much rain on us.

'Doesn't look like it's going to stop,' I say.

'Sorry, but I think we're trapped for the night. What food and clothes have you got?'

'An apple, water in my bottle and a raincoat. Oh, and my towel. It's nearly dry.'

'I've got a piece of cake and an orange. Took my matches out this morning because I didn't think it would rain. I never do that! Oh well, cake and apple for dinner and an orange for breakfast.'

The rain gets heavier and the night gets cold. We hunch over our dinner in the pitch black made by the storm clouds. Sometimes we sleep. We huddle together for warmth and it feels comfortable, though we each keep waking up when the other one tugs at the damp towels, not realising that they aren't nice dry blankets.

Next morning is Monday and I won't make it to school. We're still miles from a phone too. We walk out to the village at Blackheath and I ring the boss. She's been ringing my contact people but no-one could tell her where I was. Now I do.

'I've heard a lot of excuses in my time,' she laughs. I think it's laughing. 'But this one takes the cake! How long 'til you can get here?'

'It's not an excuse. It's true.' You should see the scratches on my legs. Six road maps in one. 'I don't think I can get there 'til lunchtime.'

'You're probably in no fit condition to teach, anyway. Take the day as a sick day and we'll see you tomorrow. If you can find your way here.'

When I get to school everyone thinks we'd been lost. 'No, we knew exactly where we were. It's just that I was slow and a storm blew up . . .'

'Look at your legs!' Carol says. 'There might just be some truth in this tale of maidens in the woods. What did the boss say?'

'Don't think she believed me.'

'It's a good story, anyway. Chivalry, romance. Aah.'

'Were you lost in the jungle, Miss!' Kids think I'm some kind of Jane out there with Tarzan, or a Teenage Mutant Ninja Turtle. Some choose my adventure for their next writing exercise.

Elliott and I keep seeing each other though he isn't impressed with my being constantly tired and having work to do at home. He's an educated, wealthy, nervous man who rarely laughs and definitely does not want children. The initial attraction fades for me in the gloom of my persistent tiredness, his failure to arrive anywhere on time and the constant ledger-keeping he does for all our outings. Well, there's no-one else, so we keep seeing each other.

I'm constantly depressed these days and I have an awful pain in my back from hurling a bag of books into my car the wrong way. Nightmares are more frequent and although I never remember them, they wake me up and it's hard to get back to sleep. I have to do something. I'll apply for a transfer and see what happens.

I take the application to my boss and tell her, 'I don't think I belong in this kind of teaching. I'm good at preschool but this is different.'

'You've had incredible success, especially with reading and writing. Next year you'll find it'll be easier.' After a bit more discussion she signs my application but warns me that it won't be accepted.

As predicted my application is refused because I haven't stayed three years. I know that's the rule but I'm desperate. I get a doctor's certificate and fire off an angry reply in which I tell whoever it is that I'm a person, not a number.

My boss is furious. She's had a call from someone or other about my letter. Now she's raving at me about proper channels and being embarrassed by not knowing about my letter and my not asking for her advice. I tell her I didn't know I needed her advice on letter writing.

An inspector comes to interview me. I feel like a naughty homes girl being called for by the matron to get a thrashing. 'What's really astounding is that you didn't use the support available here.'

'What support?'

'Your principal!'

I lose control. The inspector looks almost as surprised as I am that I'm shouting at her about the principal's closed-door policy, my needy class of forty, my nightmares, tiredness, cold sores and how hard I work to no avail. On and on I go. I think I even spit a bit but I don't care. If this is what it takes to get out of here, I don't care how rude she thinks I am.

When I eventually stop, she says, 'Well, it's obvious you didn't get the support you need but, still, you should have gone through the proper channels.'

'I don't know anything about channels,' I tell her wearily. 'If they're there, they're not working.'

'Yes, I can see that. Leave it with me. I'll see what I can do. Will you make it through to the end of the year?'

'If there's light at the end of the tunnel I will.'

The light shines on a transfer to a preschool further west. A preschool! What I was born to do. I write to Wanda to tell her the good news.

I get teary as I say goodbye and parents thank me for the work I've done with their kids. Larry's mum says a quick thanks and turns away. Steve's mum hugs me and our eyes stay linked a moment longer than others do. Mrs Norward wants to know why I have to go. 'You made Jakey love writin' them stories and he thinks he can read now.'

Perhaps I made a difference but the cost was too high. I'm battered and broken.

I'm going back to preschool. A senior consultant rings to tell me she's had a talk with Mrs Gillespie and they have 'a nice little centre that's had some difficulties' for me. With my experience and skill, they're sure it'll suit me and I'll be good for the centre. Mrs Gillespie with the apron and rubber gloves! I'd forgotten about her. Well, if they're going to ignore my failure this year, I'll try to too, and if I'm half as happy at the new place as I was at the other preschools, I'll be satisfied.

During the holidays I go to the new school to look around. It's further west of Sydney but not too far from home. I get there early and see homeless people rolling up their sleeping gear and moving away. The school is huge compared to the one I've left but it looks cared for and nicely landscaped. I find the preschool and peep through the windows. Gosh, their last day must have been busy. There's a lot of mess in there. Working in a two-unit preschool, side by side with another class, will be interesting.

More than interesting, as it happens.

WHERE I BELONG?

My new teaching colleague is Felicity, a first year out teacher who is cheerful but indignant. She applied to be a primary teacher and gets dumped here in a preschool!

'Mum and Dad say just make the most of it, but I haven't got a clue what I'm doing. Have you done preschool before?' she asks me. 'Do you reckon you could sort of help me out?'

'Of course I will. Just let me know when you want me to. I could loan you an old program or two if you like. Are you right for tomorrow?'

'Yeah, yeah. Alma's got some stuff, I think.'

Alma is Felicity's untrained aide. She lives locally and has worked here for many years. She's large, loud and very funny. And likes to be in control. Of everything. It takes me too long to understand the extensive boundaries of her empire. My career so far has not prepared me for what I'm about to face.

My aide is Maud, a young and surly local woman who tries to be funny and to shock by being as crass as she can be. I'm often not sure what she means until Alma reacts. Maud has done a year here and seems to have a shared agenda with Alma that Felicity and I are excluded from.

We've all met in the general staff room and now it's time to go to the preschool and start work.

'Mm. I don't think I've been welcomed by this many cockroaches before,' I say quietly to Felicity.

'It's filthy!' she exclaims loudly. 'Oh yuck. Look at this!' She quickly drops an indescribable craft glug covered in mouse droppings and chewed up nesting material.

'How did it get this, um, disorganised?' I ask the aides.

'Oh, the last teachers were too busy fighting with each other to bother with cleaning up!' Alma declares proudly. Proudly? 'Weren't they, Maud?'

'Yeah. We got on good but, din we?' Maud replies.

We need to sort out roles. It's unmistakably the aides' job to prepare, clean and store equipment. I'll take it slowly, though, and try to get Maud on-side first. Alma seems to dominate her but she'll be right when we get busy with the kids.

Better look at what needs doing today to get ready for them. This calls for a strong coffee. No, forget the coffee. The kitchen cockroach tribe scurry away off the velvety mould growing on the food that's been left on plates in the sink for a whole summer holiday. There's competition for control everywhere.

Felicity and Alma spend the day in their room, which is divided from ours by a folding door that Maud is endlessly keen on going through. I'm endlessly not keen on asking her to come back. She tries to do the first job cheerfully, but upon discovering that there are ten on her list, her cheer changes to sulking and sulking to resentment. She hasn't finished her holiday.

At lunchtime I get a hint that not only is it my first mistake – expecting Maud to work – but I'm capable of many more.

'What are the people like here?' I ask. 'It looks like a nice suburb. Nice houses, some lovely gardens.'

'Heard about us Westies, have you?' Maud pouts.

'Oh yes, we know about gardens out here,' Alma says. I'm not sure if she's being sarcastic or just joking.

'Well, you do hear about Western Sydney but what I mean is, it looks normal. Nicer than what you hear. I just want to know what the parents hope the preschool will do for their kids.'

'Well, we're working class,' Alma says more gently, 'and there are lots of pensioners, but we want the best for our kids like anyone else does.'

'Yeah. An' we're just as good as them, but!' Maud retorts.

Whatever I say on this subject makes her forehead crease and red blotches appear on her neck and face. Drop it. I look through the enrolment forms and find that there's a range of people, similar to my previous preschool. I'll be right.

The next morning as the kids start arriving, I can see I'll have to work doubly hard to settle them until I sort Maud out. She struts around looking important until the parents have gone, then gets busy slouching on a table, watching me.

'Maud, will you look after Jason. He's crying.'

'Oh yeah,' she replies, suggesting she'll think about it for a while first.

Take it slowly, be friendly, not too bossy. Once we get used to each other she'll understand, then cooperate.

'What do you think about all of us doing a little bit of extra cleaning before lunch each day?' I ask as we sit around the lunch table a few days later. 'There's so much that needs doing.'

'Yeah, we could do that,' Felicity chirps up. 'Knock it over in no time flat. Ugh! Look at this. It's disgusting! Better get it done before we get rabies or something.'

'Well! You might have time for extra work, Kate, but, Felicity, I'm sure you'll find there just isn't time for anything extra at lunchtime,' Alma declares and forces a smile.

'Oh, will I?' Felicity responds looking puzzled.

'Won't have time to scratch yer arse,' Alma replies.

Our next intake means more teary kids and more instructions

to Maud who might or might not help. Be patient. No, leaving kids crying for their mums is just not on! 'Maud, when kids are in our room, your job is to be with them and help settle them in. Comfort them if they're crying.'

'No! That's your job,' she says defiantly, her face turning blotchy. 'You said I have to clean. Remember!'

'It's both of our jobs to settle kids. We never just leave them crying.'

Her attitude doesn't improve but I don't know what to do except keep asking her. Keep on and on asking. And I show her her duty statement, which she slams on the shelf where it stays.

During the hour between morning and afternoon classes, I rush to prepare my room before going to lunch, where conversation is becoming more stilted. I try not to let the cool reception at the lunch table hurt but it does. Am I just not a nice person who is now working with people who can't be bothered pretending? I'll have to try harder to make them like me.

Felicity had been helping with cleaning before lunch but now she prefers a full half hour break, hands that stay clean and the company of Alma who has her under her thumb.

'I'll stay back today,' she whispers sometimes so the others won't hear.

We talk freely when we work back and Felicity uses me as a resource.

'When do your kids play with construction sets and water and home corner? Have you got any of that in your room?' I ask.

'Oh, Alma reckons it's too noisy and messy. Takes forever to pack. We're doing lots of craft, though.'

'Yeah, that's nice. Um, I don't want to interfere but construction is how they develop a lot of their early maths and science concepts. Puzzles too. Home corner helps with social skills, role playing and seeing other people's points of view. Alma's good at craft but it's not her job to do the program. Her job is cleaning, storage and preparing. Then she helps with programs you've set. She's untrained. You're responsible for planning and assessing kids.'

Felicity seems overwhelmed so I give her a copy of the duty statements for the aides. I pay later.

'You reckon Maud and I should clean the kids' toilets at lunchtime, do you, Kate?' Alma demands with a small pretence of civility.

'Well the duty statement for teachers aides does, so, yes, I do.'

'I'm not cleaning any bloody toilets!' she scoffs.

'You won't catch me doing anything with a toilet brush,' Maud sneers. How true! Or a scrubbing brush or even a little pink sponge.

Felicity reddens and stays quiet.

'Maybe we need to go through the duty statements and clarify all of our roles,' I suggest.

'I don't need anyone telling me what my job is, thank you very much, Miss Shayler. I've been here doing this job for many long years and I'm quite aware of what I will and will not do.'

Oh Wanda, where are you! And Ella. Why aren't these two like you? What do I do? Keep being diplomatic? Keep trying to be nice? Keep taking it slowly? I've got to survive three years here.

Each night I go home exhausted and more despondent. It's hard to get to sleep and I wake up feeling as if I only went to sleep two minutes ago. I don't want to go to work and I don't want to stay home alone.

Elliott gets frustrated that all I want to do is sleep and when we go out I want to come home early. He gives me a letter.

Dear Kate,

I think it's time we went our separate ways. I have enjoyed your company so much and you're the first person who's been able to make me laugh. But things have changed. I'm not willing to go out publicly looking like a couple but when we're at home, nothing happens.

We want different things anyway, so there's no point prolonging the agony. I hope you find someone who can fulfil your dream of having a family. You know I don't want that.

187

> *It's just time we both got on with finding the right person for us.*
> *There will always be a special place in my heart for you.*
> *Elliott.*

He's right of course, but I'm bawling my head off.

Don't leave me. Please don't leave me.

I feel so alone and worthless. Everything is going wrong. No-one can make me laugh any more, not even me. I'm trapped with a mortgage and there's no way out unless I want to go backwards and lose my unit.

'Get someone to share,' Gen says.

'There's not enough space in the unit.' And I'm such a misery guts, who'd want to share with me!

'Can you sell it and get a house?'

'No. Couldn't afford it. Only married people get houses and I'm not good enough for that.'

'Oh, course you are. Elliott wasn't right for you, that's all.'

Even home church would be sick of me by now. I wish I hadn't stopped going but how could I keep up the travel every Sunday and spare a whole morning when I had so much work to do? It's harder to remember God when I'm alone. At home church we'd be praying for guidance and sharing ideas and caring.

I ring friends to talk about it but they must be getting sick of me. Wish there was someone with just ears that I could talk at whenever I want to, say the same stuff over and over again. I've never been like this before. Needy and fragile. What's happening to me? Why don't they like me at work?

Driving home I hear a radio program about work relationships that go wrong. It's a ring in show, so I call and begin with, 'I've just changed jobs and my new colleagues don't like me. I've never been disliked at work before and I don't know –'

The radio guest expert interrupts. 'That's a mistake people often make. Why do people have to like us? Has it got anything to do with the job we're employed to do?' He's on a pet subject now and I hang up feeling stupid, desperately hoping no-one recognised my voice.

I suppose it doesn't matter that they don't like me but it's so horrible working in that atmosphere. It hurts. It saps my energy. I just keep trying to be nice.

Tess from home church, the counsellor, used to tell us about getting the women in her workshops to keep journals. They loved journal writing because it clarified their thinking, helped them see their patterns or just offload stress. Julie in home church always kept a journal too and she talked about it as if it was her second best friend, after her husband. Sometimes God spoke to her as she wrote or read over past entries. Bel kept one for a while but ran out of time to do it. (I wonder if she took it up again after the kids started school. I've lost track of them since they moved even further west.)

I buy a green exercise book. Tess's clients bought beautiful books but I want my journal to be inconspicuous in case I ever do share a place. Wouldn't want anyone to notice a beautiful book and open it and find out what a sook I am. Just to be sure I write on the first page, '*This is private. If you are about to read it, please stop.*'

I keep my journal beside the bed and write in it every night. My first real entry is a statement of all the things that are worrying me. I embarrass myself. So many worries! Why would I want to reread this? I write a list of solutions to each of my worries. Talk to the principal and get him to help solve the problems? Remember to smile. Think of the people who love me. Think of the people who say I'm attractive and intelligent. Diet and even more exercise besides my daily swim. Keep going to dances even when tired. Look for a house to buy, then maybe share.

Journals are for recording strengths, triumphs, revelations too. I write a declaration that I'll record those if I ever have any. I'll mark each with an asterisk so I can find them easily to reread later. My journal becomes my friend. Someone to talk it all through with at the end of each day before falling into a deep sleep. Journal writing must free my head of the need for nightmares. I still have the wolf dream sometimes and one about clocks but it's possible for me to sleep through a night now. My stomach only knots up when I get close to school.

'Peter, can I talk with you, please,' I ask the school principal whom I rarely see but who seems to remember me. 'We're having some problems in the preschool and I can't sort them out.'

He groans audibly. 'What's the problem there now?'

Now? 'The aides don't seem to know what their jobs are and the place is, well, it's a disgusting mess.'

'Well, yes, I am aware of that. But you can all clean it up, can't you!'

I feel like the worst dobber. 'That's the trouble. The aides say it's not their job and I can't do it all myself. I've shown them the duty statement . . .'

'The what?'

'Duty statement. Put out by the Department.'

'Better get me a copy of that.' He stands up to dismiss me. Doesn't look like he's going to be much help. Think quickly.

'Will I call Fiona? She might have some ideas,' I suggest.

'Who's Fiona?' he asks.

'The consultant.'

Fiona arrives and starts making all sorts of suggestions that have nothing to do with the problem and that won't work unless the problem is solved. We can't organise parent education workshops unless the general purpose room is emptied of years of rubbish and the finger paint and food, or whatever it is, is scrubbed off the walls. We can't get that done unless the aides know their roles.

'Oh well, do that. You should invite the community nurse . . .' and she's off on another monologue, oblivious.

When the kids arrive for class we're no nearer to a solution. Our consultant follows me into my room and keeps telling me

190

about all her good ideas, while Maud looks impressively busy.

Fiona is my shadow. 'I need to work with Sandy now, Fiona,' I say, but stating the obvious doesn't stop the flow of ideas. Ignoring her and working with Sandy does. Sandy is shy of strangers and we have to move to the quiet area. Damien is trying to climb up Fiona to get on her hip. She thinks it's time to go when she sees what his nose has left on her nice navy skirt.

The other three are getting on and ignoring the dirt and chaos. I spoil the fun. Well, Felicity and I get on when the others aren't there. I must create the problem but I can't solve it. I read books about working in a team. I think I'm doing what they say but things are getting worse. Maud won't even come into our room to set up at all now unless I ask her to. Then she slouches in and around without doing much. Can't she make the effort, just for the kids?

Elliott rings to tell me all about what he's been doing. At last he asks how I am.

'I've decided to buy a house,' I tell him, avoiding the question. 'The building society will give me a loan and the unit's increased its value more than I thought. I can afford western suburbs but I haven't seen anything I like.'

'You ought to look in the Blue Mountains. Houses are really cheap there.'

'I don't want to live that far away! I'm a Sydney person.' Boy, when you want to get rid of someone you really want to get rid of them!

'Look, I'm not busy next Saturday. Let's go up and look at some. Yes, just as friends. I've been thinking about moving there myself.'

There's a house I can afford that has a different bright-coloured carpet in every room. I feel seasick walking around in it. The next house is small and cosy and the best thing is that it has a huge sunny verandah. Can I really own this? Yes! I can.

'Can't stay back today. I'm buying a house,' I tell Felicity after work.

'Oh, where is it?'

'Mountains. Got to go. See you tomorrow.'

'I hear you're buying a house,' Alma says at lunch the next day. 'Sydney not good enough for you, eh?'

'Sydney's not cheap enough for me,' I tell her. At least they can't add snobbery to my list of faults.

'Oh! You'll have to show us pictures. We can help you decorate,' Alma offers with what seems like genuine enthusiasm. Then the trap springs shut: 'There's a house up the street from us that's nice and cheap. Would you like to look at it?'

'Uh, I signed the contract yesterday.'

'All right then!' she snaps and struts out of the room, followed by Maud.

'Round 'ere's not good enough for 'er, is it!' Maud says loudly as they throw their plates in the sink for the night visitors.

I need help. Whatever I say or do is wrong! My teaching, that has been respected, is now being trashed too because it's 'not what they do here'. Alma might be good at craft and Felicity might love all that glitter and glue, but we're not employed to stick things on paper all day. I'll ring Mrs Gillespie. She'll have some advice, being older and more experienced. She's not in this area but she'll suggest ways for me to make the changes. Yes, that's the answer. Mrs Gillespie who knows my reputation.

'Barbara is very ill at the moment; she's off having chemotherapy,' Edna tells me. 'Is there something I can help you with, Kate?'

The problem described, Edna tells me, 'Yes, we've had some problems in that centre. Stick with what you know, Kate.' Edna can't see how stressed and exhausted I am with sticking to what I know. 'Keep doing what you've always done and it'll come good, I'm sure. Rely on your experience.'

I hang up. I'll be dead from stress before it comes good. And, in my experience so far, this situation never existed. Poor Mrs

Gillespie. I hope she gets well but Edna didn't sound hopeful. I wonder if stress can cause cancer. Don't think about it.

Have I changed? Have I become hard to get along with and unable to communicate? Did last year knock it out of me? I didn't think so, but three people don't like me, so it must be me that's the problem.

Maybe Alma was really being friendly when she offered to help decorate my house. I wouldn't want her to, but if she was being friendly, I'll respond accordingly. I take a real estate magazine photo to school. It might help build bridges.

'Huh! Calls that cheap, does she?' Alma smirks as she hands the paper to Maud. Oh, I'm so stupid! Forgot the price was there. Maud doesn't comment. They get up and leave the room.

'Showing us how much better she can do, is she?' Maud's loud voice reverberates against the plate landing on the pile in the sink.

I must be mad. I must be. I should have thought! I don't think I'm better than them. I need help. Should I see a psychologist? That's what mad people do, isn't it? I'm going mad. And I need to learn some coping skills, conflict resolution skills.

I don't want to see a psychologist, a shrink. I've seen a Woody Allen movie where a neurotic middle-aged woman keeps rushing off to her therapist whom she's fallen in love with. She's ridiculous and pitiful. Am I becoming neurotic? I don't want to become ridiculous or pitiful! I can't imagine falling in love with a psychologist and I can't imagine a psychologist falling in love with me. No-one else has, not really. Woody Allen's characters would be based in reality, though, wouldn't they?

What I really want is for someone in charge to come and tell them, 'Kate is an excellent teacher and what she says is right. Stop criticising and do what she says and does.' Back in the real world though, maybe I should talk with the boss again.

Get the move into the house over with first. I've signed a twenty-year mortgage and interest rates are almost thirteen percent! Don't worry. You've got a job. You can do this. Well if not, you can go back to renting. For the rest of your life.

Moving day falls on my thirty-eighth birthday. My present cheers me up: Gen, Paddy and their kids come to help.

'Oh look, Aunty Kate, a glass is broken!' my goddaughter Lizzie says. I feel a little sad because it's one of the set I got when I left the insurance company. 'Never mind,' she adds, 'you've still got one, two, three, four, five left. No. One, two, three, four 'cause this one's cracked. But you've still got four. Just as well no more broke cause then you'd have three and if another one . . .' She does optimistic maths while I wonder if I should go back to being a clerk with very few responsibilities. Or should I have married Gareth?

'This is just so lovely,' Gen says as we flop into chairs at the end of the day. 'You've done well.'

'Yeah. I'm as good as the rest of 'em now,' I say.

'What do you mean? You were always as good as the rest of them.'

How can I explain that owning a house has been something other people did, not me? People who were married. People who'd found someone to love them and make a family with. Not single women who are thirty-eight and alone. They get lovely flats, not lovely houses.

I'm surprised that I feel so lonely when my friends go home. This feels like the end of the earth. Sleep comes easily, though.

I wake in fright. Was that a scream? Listen. Yes. And again! I creep onto my verandah. Another scream drifts up the gully. What can I do? Now it's further away! There's no road there so how could a screaming woman move so quickly? Silence.

I fall asleep again. Wake to the same sound. Will I be all right living here, among strangers, alone? Should I ring the police? Someone else would have by now. I fall asleep again.

Next morning the man we chatted with over the back fence yesterday knocks on my door. He's holding a book.

'Did you hear all that noise last night?' he asks.

'Yes. Sounded like a woman was screaming. But the sound was moving very fast. What was happening?'

'Well, we listened and Pearly reckoned it was a bird. Look at this.'

He shows me a picture and I read beside it 'Barking Owl'.

'Now listen to this,' he says. 'Dah dah dah, here it is. 'Voice: wavering human-like scream.' Our other book says it's also called the murder bird.'

'Good name. I was scared stiff but it didn't make sense. It moved too fast to be a person.'

'If you're ever worried about anything, just pop in. We're both retired, often home.'

He's back a few minutes later.

'Pearly says I should have invited you over for a cuppa. Would you like to come? Say, ten thirty?'

All my neighbours are this friendly. I feel safe and at home. My garden needs work and I have enough energy for that on weekends, but going to Sydney for dances gets harder and harder. Saturday nights at home are spent under a melancholy cloud. I imagine other single people out dancing or on dates, having fun. Saturday nights are proof that I've got problems. It'll be better after I've lived here for a while. People say that in smaller communities it's harder to be lonely.

But work stress sends me spiralling into darkness and I can't get a grip on anything that will lift me out. I pray a lot. It makes me feel better for a while and it's a source of hope. Must find out where the local home church is. Must get nourishment for my soul.

Most of all I need to learn how to resolve the grinding, endless conflict at work. I scan the Teachers' Federation magazine and find ads for psychologists. There's one local practice: *Tony Benton. B.A. Dip. Ed., B.Sc., M.A.. Member, Australian Psychological Society. Member, The Australian Society of Hypnosis*. I cut out the ad and file it in my purse.

'You don't need a psychologist!' Gen declares. After I've told her why I think I do, she says, 'If you decide you really do, make sure it's a good one. Just be careful. Have you been to the doctor?'

'Yes. He sent me to a specialist who did a blood test. Said my immune system was struggling and gave me some pills. He didn't fix my head though.'

Weeks pass and the clipping stays in my purse. Nothing has changed at work despite two terms of trying. There's only one term to go and I just can't let the year end and a new one begin with this cloud. I wouldn't survive two more years of it. I find the clipping and call the Psychological Society. They confirm that Benton is a member. I call the Hypnosis Society and they confirm his membership too. All right, he mustn't be shonky if he belongs to two professional organisations.

I ring to make an appointment. Tony Benton's voice sounds kind. His fee doesn't. I almost choke. Still, he thinks he'll be able to help me, and the health fund gives a partial rebate, so there'll still be enough left in the coffers to pay the mortgage.

Going to a psychologist is an admission that I'm hopeless. They can add that to my list of faults at work if they haven't got it already. But as I drive to my appointment I become more buoyant. Soon I'll know what to do.

WHO AM I?

The door to Tony Benton's office opens before I reach it.

'Kate? You found it all right? Come in, come in,' says a large man who looks a little older than me. He shuts the door and I wish he hadn't. Stirrings from somewhere. 'Have a seat,' he says. He settles into his chair and writes my name on a pad. I watch him. Lord! No worries about falling in love with my psychologist! He's a bit shabby and his hands are white and puffy, as if they need to do some hard work outside. He writes down my address and phone number, date of birth and work details. He asks who my next of kin is.

'I'll give you Genevieve and Patrick's details. They're friends.'

'Why not next of kin?'

'My sister lives interstate and I don't know where my brother is.'

'All right.' He writes down their address and phone number. 'Now, you said on the phone that you're having some problems at work. Tell me about that.'

I tell him.

197

'I see. What about kids and parents?'

'It's fine with the kids and most of the parents but my aide is trying to turn them against me.' Good heavens! I sound paranoid.

'How do you know she's doing that?'

'I've seen her. I know she's talking to parents about me because of the way they look at me while they're talking and stop suddenly when I come near them.'

It feels so good to tell someone the whole thing, someone who is objective, who hasn't heard it all before and who will probably say, 'Well, what you need to do is . . .'

I conclude with, 'I want to learn how to get them on-side and make it all work the way it should. I want them to stop talking about me and talk to me instead. I want it to stop hurting.' I suddenly realise that sums it up. I want to stop hurting.

I wait for my instructions. What can I learn to fix it?

'All right. Tell me about your life, away from school.'

'Why? I just want to get the school thing fixed up.'

'Yes, we'll get to that, but I need to see the wider view. All right?'

'Well, I live by myself but I've got lots of good friends. When I get home from school I've got no energy left so I don't go out much.' Now let's get on with the school solution.

'What about weekends?' he asks.

'Washing, ironing, housework, school work, sleeping.' Boring! He waits. So do I.

'What about your social life?'

'I really just want to get the school thing –'

'The wider view of the person,' he interrupts. 'It gives me an idea of who you are, likes and dislikes, that kind of thing. Influences, support.'

'Oh, all right.' Anything for a quiet life, as Jane used to say. 'Well, when I lived in Sydney I danced every weekend or did bushwalks. I have lots of friends and support there. But since I moved here, I don't have enough energy to get myself to dances or walks. Most things up here are family oriented and I'm not a family.' It sounds pathetic! Well, I'm here trying to do something about it, if this guy would just get on with it.

'What about friends? Who are your closest friends?'

'What does that have to do with sorting out my school problems?'

'I need to know how you handle other relationships. What support you have.'

That makes sense. 'As I said, I have very good friends. But they live so far from here.'

I tell him about Leonie and Col at the farm, Gen and Paddy and some of the dancing lot. He says that the long-term ones show I'm capable of committing to and maintaining friendships.

'You haven't mentioned a boyfriend,' he observes.

Boyfriend! What's that got to do with the school problem? Wants to understand the wider view. 'There isn't one.'

'Has there been?'

'Yes. And now there isn't.'

'When was the last one?'

'It ended a few months ago. We're still friends, sort of. We see each other sometimes.'

'I see. And have you been married?'

'No.' Now it's your turn to ask, What's the matter with you?

'That's unusual for someone your age,' he says and waits.

Yep, there it is. Disguised, but it's That Question. What am I supposed to say? That I don't know what's wrong with me but I wish I did, so I could fix that too?

'You've had boyfriends but never married.'

'Yes.' The silence gets too long. 'Well, what am I supposed to say next?'

'You could tell me more. It would broaden my understanding if you said more about these relationships, how they went.'

'So you could tell me what's wrong with me?'

'Do you think there's something wrong with you?'

'I don't know,' I reply, feeling guilty about my sarcasm. He's trying to help, isn't he? 'I wonder sometimes. Otherwise I would have got married, I suppose. But I just want to fix up the problem at work now, not talk about boyfriends.' I really do want to know what's wrong with me, but until I sort out school, I won't have any energy for boyfriends anyway.

'When you wonder what's wrong with you, what sort of things do you wonder about?'

'Oh, all sorts of things. Mostly I think I'm not slender and gorgeous, not attractive enough. I'm shy too. Of men. I suppose.'

He asks about my height, weight and general health. I tell him about the recent diagnosis that my immune system isn't functioning well and my T-cell count is low.

'Ah huh,' he responds with surprising enthusiasm. 'That tells me a lot about your emotional state.'

'It's a physical condition, not an emotional state!'

'I believe that the two are connected. You see, if you spend a lot of energy suppressing emotional problems it will have an impact on your physical wellbeing, especially your immune system. There's a whole field of study on the subject. It's called psychoimmunology. Are you on medication?'

'Only a prescribed one, Acyclavir, to suppress the cold sore virus so my immune system can build up again.' It sounds interesting and his knowledge is impressive, but I just want to get work sorted out.

'What about general health, energy, exercise regime?'

I tell him I'm healthy but tired. I swim a kilometre every school day and have done for years. Lately, though it's been too hard.

'A kilometre? Yes. Well. I like swimming too,' he says. Now, tell me about your family.'

'Look, we are going to get to the school stuff, aren't we?'

He says he needs to know this because it will help him understand the influences that have shaped me.

Chocolate, fruit, vegies, pasta, pâté and then there's swimming, dancing . . .

'I've told you about my sister and brother. Our parents are dead.' So you see, that's irrelevant. They don't influence me.

Wait a minute. Our parents? Where did that come from. I've never grouped us like that. Our parents? *Our*?

'When did your parents die?'

'My mother when I was four. My father when I was seventeen.' See! Ages ago. Not relevant.

'Oh, I'm so sorry. That's a tragedy,' he says gently.

Why? I'm all right, aren't I? Why are my eyes burning? I'm sniffling.

I feel small and irrelevant. And frustrated that we're not . . .

'Why are you crying?' he asks.

'Because I want you to help me with work and you're just asking about all this other stuff.' Must be that. What else could it be?

'This is important,' he says quietly. 'Your tears tell me that. Think about why you're upset.'

Is he right? Couldn't be. I never even think about my parents. Parents? Mine? While I wonder, he fires off another question.

'How did you feel when your mother died?'

'I don't remember but I don't feel anything now. It's over. Has been for ages.'

'Has it?'

'Yes,' I say, determined to get away from this.

'I want you to think about the way you speak.'

'What's wrong with the way I speak?' Blimey, what's happening? Isn't the problem I came with enough?

'It's not wrong. I just want you to listen to yourself and think about the voice you use.'

'I don't know what you mean,' I reply crossly, confused.

'It's a very small voice.'

'My voice has always been quiet. It's an asset. Kids know I won't shout at them.' *So there!*

'I didn't say it's a quiet voice. I said it's a small voice, a childlike voice.'

'Well, I can't help my voice. I was born with it.' This is ridiculous! I wipe my eyes and add, 'What's the point of you telling me my voice is not okay? There's nowhere to go.'

'Nowhere to go?'

'Yes. My voice is what I communicate with, isn't it? I need to feel confident using it or how am I supposed to communicate?' You twit!

'All right. We'll leave it. But I want you to think about what I said later. Let's move on. Have you been to your mother's grave?'

'No.' What on earth would I want to do that for?

'Do you know where it is?'

'No.' Now ask me if I care.

'I think it's important for you to say goodbye to your mother as an adult. Think about going. I could go with you if you wanted me to.'

Why would I want to go anywhere with you, let alone to a grave? 'I'm not interested in going to the grave. I just want to learn some skills –'

'Yes, for school, but think about the grave visit. And remember my offer. Now, what happened to you and your brother and sister after your mum died?'

'Then we'll get to the school problem?'

'Yes. But tell me what happened after your mother died.'

'The wider view. Right. Well, Ken – that's my brother – and I got put in Burnside Homes and Ke– . . .'

I'm crying. Why? All this is so old I've almost forgotten it! I take a breath to make myself stop but it turns into a bovine snort. Embarrassing! Can't stop. He hands me the tissue box.

'Can you go on with your story now?'

'Don't know why I'm crying. All that was ages ago. Kerry was too little to come with us so sh– . . .' Crying again.

'Look, Kate,' he says gently, 'your crying over this should tell you something.'

Yeah, not to go near the past. To get on with the now, with what I came here for.

'I think my tears mean I'm frustrated because I can't get help with what I came here for,' I sputter angrily. 'I might as well go if we're just going to go on and on about the past.'

'Your background matters, Kate. Any psychologist you go to will ask you about it. It tells us where your patterns originated, where your development might have been arrested and so on. It does matter. Everybody's family matters.'

'I don't have a family.'

'You did, though.'

My family has sat in my head without disturbing me for all these years. Why drag it out now? Oh, all right, the patterns and influences. It makes some sense.

Tony Benton waits for a moment, then – sure that he's convinced me, I suppose – he says, 'So, your mother died when you were four and you were put in a home. Right? What was that like?'

'I hardly remember it.'

'Right,' he says slowly.

Great, at last he can see that there's nothing there to talk about!

'Did you cry?' he asks suddenly.

'I don't know. I suppose I did.'

'But you don't remember.'

'No. I don't remember anything much.'

'What do you remember?'

'Only that I might have been put in a room 'til I stopped crying.'

'Might have been?'

'There's a little girl I remember but I'm not sure it's me.'

'And could that little girl stop crying?'

'I don't know.'

'You're crying now.'

I can't help it. I feel exposed.

'I think they didn't let you cry and that you have never grieved properly over your loss.'

I'm about to ask what this has to do with anything and how the hell he would know, when he fires off another question.

'What about your father?'

'What about him?'

'What did he do when your mother died?'

'I told you. He put us in the home. He was old and he couldn't manage. But he kept visiting us.'

'He abandoned you.'

'He did not! He kept visiting for twelve years and I went to live with him when I left. Then he died.'

'Oh dear,' he says sympathetically. The sympathy feels discrepant coming from the bully Tony Benton. And it's twenty years too late. 'How did you feel when he died?'

'Sad. Relieved.' Damn! Why did I say that? We'll never get to the school stuff now.

'Relieved? He'd been unwell, had he?'

'No. He'd been abusive.' Now shut up about this and get on with my school stuff. I'm teary again.

'Oh dear,' Benton says again. He sits quietly while I cry. I don't like him watching me. I force myself to stop.

'Have you done any work on that, the abuse?' he wants to know.

'Not much. I saw a psychologist ages ago and he thought I was coping well with my life so I didn't need to do anything. I only saw him once.' So drop it.

'All right. Now I'm going to ask you some rather intimate questions. You see, when a child suffers a trauma, she can get stuck at that stage of development. I can imagine from what you've said that that might be the case with you, so I need to ask questions about your sexual behaviour. All right?'

'No, it's not all right! Look, I came here for help with a specific problem, not to talk about any of this. If we're not ever going to get to that, I might as well go home now. What on earth does my sex life have to do with school? It's none of your business.'

'I want you to think about why you are so defensive about this.'

'That's easy! Because it's private. It's got nothing to do with why I came here.' I stand up to leave. Well look at me! First time I've walked out on anyone!

'Oh, hasn't it?' Benton demands.

'I just want to find out how to manage the situation at work. I need you, or someone, to teach me some conflict resolution skills or something. If you can't, I'll go somewhere else. I can cope with the rest of my stuff.'

'But you're not coping.'

'I'm not coping at work! The rest of my life is all right. Work is the problem.' I'm surprised that I'm talking so aggressively. I never talk like this. What's happening to me?

'I am a trained psychologist,' he states, failing to conceal a frown. 'I wouldn't tell you how to teach. If you want me to help you, you'll have to trust me, trust that I know what I'm doing. Can you do that?'

'No. Oh, I don't know.' Is he right? He's the expert. The professional.

'You came here because you want professional help.'

'I do want professional help but I don't seem to be getting it.'

'Look,' he says patiently, 'any trained psychologist will take down your history and that's what I'm trying to do. You have an agenda and we'll get to that. But first, I need to understand your history.'

It seems to be more than taking down my history but maybe that's how they're trained to do it, to probe.

'If you do decide to go on, I'll need to see you for an extended period.'

Oh no! Years of therapy? I'm not that crazy, am I? A trained psychologist thinks I'm a thirty-eight-year series of problems. How will I manage financially if I need years of therapy? With this weirdo or another one? No. I'm not mad. I don't need that.

'I just want a trained psychologist to help me with relationships at work. That's all,' I blurt out. 'But you're not listening to me. You just keep dragging up the past, delving into stuff that's over and not hearing what I've come here for. I just need help with the problems at work.'

He sighs deeply, leans back and folds his hands on his chest.

'My training and my experience tell me that there are certain indications in adults that suggest issues from childhood need to be resolved using the adult cognition. I have listened to you. All right? And I've made certain observations based on my professional knowledge. You came here presenting as a happy enough person with some work issues. When I talk with you I see that there is more to it. A lot more. Who we are today, really are, deep inside, is the product of our childhood to a great extent. Remember what I said about patterns? You've told me about a very troubled childhood.'

'No,' I interrupt. 'I've told you about a childhood. Bits of it. It doesn't bother me. I can live with it. It's the present that's troubled and you're not helping.'

'And you're not listening,' he says, gently again, leaning slightly forward.

That tiny movement sends fear through me like lightning. I don't know why. He's done absolutely nothing to suggest that he'd do anything bad. There isn't time to think about it now. I'm trying to listen.

'You can't have had the kind of childhood you've told me about, even if you've just told me bits of it, without being affected adversely by it. You lost your mother when you really needed her. Your father abandoned you when he was all you had, then he betrayed your trust and abused you. You have a lot of grieving to do, starting, I suspect, with the death of your mother.'

I'm crying again. This is too big. I feel so muddled, like a child being scolded.

'Did you cry when your mummy died?' he suddenly asks again.

'How would I know?'

'How did you feel when your father left you at the home?'

'I don't remember!' What is he doing? Bullying? More tears.

'Kate, all these things upset you. Why do you think that is?'

'It's not them that upset me. It's you not getting to the reason I came. I'm going.' I pick up my bag.

'All right. We can look at the work problem but at some point you're going to have to face the childhood issues and work on them. I believe they're stopping you reaching your full potential. Right?'

'I just want to get help with school and if you can't do that, I'll go. Maybe I need to look at childhood but this is not the time. I can't deal with more than school just now.' Listen to me! This is assertiveness I suppose. Tess used to talk about that when she told us about her counselling work. Tess knew I wasn't crazy. Knew I was okay.

'All right. But true peace doesn't come from hiding. Now, let's look at the work situation. Who's the most highly qualified?'

'I am.'

'Why?'

'Because I have a degree and ten years' experience. The other teacher is first year out and the aides have no training.'

'Has anyone ever questioned your competence in any school you've worked at?'

'No. Well, I used to get questions because I invite people to question me. They haven't questioned my competence, though. They like what I do once they understand.' I sit down.

'Exactly! So what you need to do is be assertive and let the other staff know you are the boss.'

'I'm not the boss. It's an equal status thing with me and the other teacher. The school principal is the boss.'

'But you are the one with experience so you have to show them that you're in charge.'

Oh, what's the use? I'm not in charge. Not in any sense of the word.

'Do you prepare properly?'

'Yes! You can't teach well unless you're prepared properly.'

'And your aide?'

'We go through the day book each morning so she knows what's expected, then she ignores it.'

'Then you just have to make sure she does what you tell her and make sure she knows why.'

'How? That's the problem. I tell her and she ignores the bits she doesn't want to do.'

'Have you thought about leaving her notes?'

207

'I leave my whole program out for her. We go through it together. I haven't got time to write special notes for her. She ignores what I write as it is.'

'Have you discussed it with your boss?'

'Yes. He said I should tell her again and not to worry because she's a casual and they'll soon appoint a permanent person for her position. But there's a chance they'll appoint her, so I have to work something out.'

'Well, the boss is obviously not going to be much help, so you'll have to practise being assertive with this woman.'

We seem to be going around in circles.

'I try to be but it doesn't work. I must be doing it wrong. When I'm being assertive, the back stabbing starts and the work still doesn't get done.'

'Hm. We could certainly work on some of that. I think what we need to do is some ego-strengthening work. You don't seem to be aware of your strengths . . .'

'Strengths?' I interrupt. 'What strengths? That's the trouble; I'm not strong.'

'You have enormous strength! You don't see that? To have survived your childhood and achieved what you've achieved takes great strength. You're educated, independent and you have your own home. Look, women's liberation is only just teaching women that they can do half of what you've already achieved with very little support. You had a disempowering childhood but you kept going.'

Well, what alternative did I have? Oh, but is that me? A strong survivor? No-one's said that before. Not like that. But it's all for nothing if I'm just a mess. And I have no-one to share any of it with. I feel an inkling of pride, then fear. Pride goes before a fall. Are all Christians this afraid of pride?

He's still talking about ego strengthening. It sounds reasonable but he really is stuck on my childhood. Here he goes again. Surely he's noticed my childhood is over?

At last he's looking at his watch.

'Time's nearly up for today. Is Tuesday all right for next week? There's quite a bit of work to be done and I think I can help you. We could do some work on grieving and anger. Some work on the abuse, too.'

'Well, you can, but I just want someone to work on the school issues. I won't need another appointment.'

'You don't want to come back?'

'I don't think so.'

'Oh! Well, think about it. As I said to you before, any psychologist will ask about your past and give you the same advice I've given you.'

'I feel worse now than I did before.' I thought I was just a person with a work problem but now I'm a hopeless, mangled wreck.

'I have given you a lot to think about. Look, there's still a bit of time left. I suggest we try some relaxation hypnosis.'

'Why?'

'I want you to leave feeling relaxed and at peace with what I've given you to think about. Would you like to try it?'

Better than going home traumatised, I suppose. He is a member of that hypnosis group and it might help. Might even be interesting.

'Good. Sit down and get yourself comfortable. Right? Lean back. Get really comfortable.'

I lean back a little.

'Lean right back in the chair,' he says, leaning forward.

Suddenly I'm bolt upright. That small move forward sent lightning through me again!

'What's the matter?'

'I'm frightened,' my small voice says.

'I see,' he says. 'Can you tell me what it is about me that's frightening?'

'Don't know. Leaning back, closing my eyes when you . . . when you. I feel . . .' I never force kids to lie down or close their eyes if they feel vulnerable. That's it! Vulnerable. 'I feel vulnerable.

I suppose because you're a man who I don't feel right about.'

'I assure you that you will be completely in control at all times, and if you want to stop at any point, we can.'

'It's not that. It's you. I can't lean back. Can't . . .'

'You don't feel you can trust me?'

'No. Sorry.'

'No? It's all right. Think about this. I have many feminine attributes as well as male ones.'

You do? What the blazes does that have to do with anything?

'Think about it. You know you're afraid of my maleness but I suspect you have issues with females as well. You've been in several positions where more powerful people have forced their will on you and you've built resistance.'

All I need, desperately, is for him to tell me, to swear on a stack of Bibles, that he won't touch me. At all. The male/female stuff is blah blah.

'. . . resistance can build up around the psyche and the cognitive functions . . .'

Good grief, why would he touch me? I am crazy. I'm nuts. I need a psychologist.

'. . . just listen, sitting up with your eyes open if you prefer. I'll say what I usually say to patients under hypnosis, and you can just stay where your are and keep you eyes open.'

Now he sounds warm and caring. If I listen, it might help.

'All right,' I tell him.

'Good. Now try to put all other thoughts out of your mind and concentrate on my voice. Maybe you could just look at one spot while you listen . . .'

I'm just too sensitive. Listen to him. Concentrate.

'. . . you'll come to recognise your strengths . . . feel at peace . . .'

He finishes after what seems like an eternity then he asks, 'How was that? Feeling better?'

'Yes, more relaxed, I think.'

'Good. Next time we could work more with hypnosis. It's an area I'm very skilled in.' He looks proud.

'I still don't know if I want to come back.'

Now he looks shocked. He says I should think about every-thing he's said because he's sure I'll see some truth in it. I can ring and let him know what I decide.

I pay and leave. As I walk away I feel exhausted. Shutting myself in my car is utter bliss. I close my eyes and feel the peace of my own company. No-one yakking on about childhood and asking irrelevant questions. Just me. I can't wait to get home. I'll be able to blob and not think about anything. No-one there with judgements or questions or expectations. Sweet hot porridge for dinner and cry my head off.

I start crying before I get there. Oh well, why wait? Nearly there. Can still see. A bit. I park under the car port, sit in this tiny dark room and think, try to be honest with myself about whether there could be any truth in what Benton said. After all, my tears were quite out of the blue. Maybe there's something in it. And that word he used, 'disempowering', that rang true. Sounds like it feels at work.

Headlights flash in my rear view mirror and my friends Glenda and Michael are walking in, smiling and waving with little Megan, their daughter. I want to turn the car around and keep driving until the petrol runs out. I really need to be alone.

'Hello! You're home late,' Glenda exclaims as she thrusts Megan towards me.

'Yeah. I'm exhausted. Been at a really heavy, um, meeting.'

We walk inside and Michael tells me they need to get some things from my garage. We were all friends in Sydney, before these two got together and married and now that they've moved here too, I've let them store their spare belongings in the garage until their new house is ready. Although I think I'm being rude, I don't offer them a drink. I go to my room to compose myself.

When I come back out, they leave Megan with me. Glenda knows how much I've wanted children and thinks sharing Megan with me will appease my maternal urges. Not make me feel patro-nised and trivialise my deepest regret.

Megan loves my spinning wheel so we sit beside it and she laughs as the wheel spins at the command of her little fingers. She soon learns that the spokes hurt if she puts her finger too close, so she holds them just close enough to feel a soft tap tap. She giggles and is mesmerised. This little person has no expectations of me except that I sit with her and watch the wheel turn. I start to unwind.

Glenda comes in. 'Oh, she'll hurt her fingers, Kate!' She pulls her Megan away and looks scornful. Megan squirms.

'She won't, Glenda. She's worked it out. She's having fun.'

Glenda is not convinced. She sits Megan on the lounge with a book, then goes back outside to help Michael. Megan and I go back to the spinning wheel.

'Here come Mummy and Daddy,' I tell her at last. I scoop her up and we meet them at the door. Soon they're packing themselves into the car and going home. I explain that I'm too exhausted to be a hostess. They think it's just work.

Alone inside, I try to go over the events of the evening but Glenda's loaning me Megan keeps demanding centre stage. Sure, I'm sad that I don't have children but I'm not a pathetic maiden aunt, am I? Now I feel guilty because I know Glenda's intentions are good. But I need to finish the good cry I started in the car and now I can't. I spill all my thoughts into my journal instead.

In the pool next morning I try to remember what Benton said about how I should behave at work. We talked in circles. You're the boss, so tell her what to do. I tell her and she doesn't do it. I keep swimming my laps and imagine telling Maud more forcefully than my usual polite requests. That would be like an open declaration of war, an escalation, not a resolution.

My stomach knots up as I drive from the pool to school. I set up and Maud eventually arrives, strolls into the adjoining class and starts talking.

'Maud, come in and help set up our room, please,' I say, trying to sound assertive while my heart is racing.

She looks surprised. 'All right. I'm coming.'

Five minutes later she still hasn't come.

'Maud, come in here now, please.'

Without a word she comes in and thumps paint pots into their stands. Her face is red and blotchy, a sure sign that she's furious, in case slamming the paint pots wasn't enough to let me know.

So much for assertiveness. It's just the same again and again. I go to the principal, again.

'She's up to all that again, is she?' Peter says.

'Yes, and I can't fix it.'

'Can't you just tell her?' he says, irritably.

'I can and I do. It just doesn't have any effect coming from me. Well, it does. It makes her worse. I think you should tell her that if she won't do the work, she can't have the job.'

'I've heard that they'll be appointing someone permanent soon. It can wait, can't it?'

'No. It can't. And what if they appoint her!'

'Mm. What's her number on the list?'

'I don't know, but even if she's at the top they just can't give the job to her. She hasn't got what it takes to do it.'

'I could ring them and see how it's going, I suppose.'

I tell him all over again what the problem is and he starts to look bored.

'Yes. All right. Leave it with me.'

I leave it with him, with no confidence that he'll achieve anything but more bad feeling. I'm glad I told him what's going on, though. He might have some influence over who gets the permanent appointment.

Elliott rings to say he'll be up on the weekend to look for a property to buy. He'd like to stay at my place so that he can spend the weekend looking.

'All right,' I tell him. 'I'll probably be as exhausted as usual. How was your week away, in a word?'

'All right,' he replies. 'But . . .'

I should have stressed 'in a word'. Elliott gives me every detail of the trip down.

'Hey,' I interrupt. 'This is an STD call, so how about you leave the detail 'til you're here on the weekend.'

'Well, if that's all you care about, your blasted phone bill, I'll hang up then.' He isn't used to my being anything but endlessly giving and interested.

'It's your bill. You rang me. I'm just really tired. You can tell me all the detail on the weekend.'

'Goodbye,' he says crankily and hangs up.

I cry. Stress all week and now stress with him too. At least I don't feel like I have to be nice and polite when Elliott's inconsiderate any more. But I hate the tension. I wonder why he wants to move up here. Is he going to try to rekindle the dead relationship? I hope not. Friendship is hard enough just now.

In bed I write up my journal. I've missed a few days and it takes a while. I pour out all my stress. I see patterns. All the same stresses. No answers. I write feverishly about my meeting with Tony Benton again. I try to be honest in my analysis of what he said but I just get angry about his dismissal of my agenda in favour of his own. I write the feelings out of my system so I'll be able to sleep.

Elliott and I go to the properties he's interested in and he finds things wrong with all but one. He loves the waratah-dotted acres and log cabin house. He wants it badly. The owner rings when we get home and tells him some other people are willing to pay the full price. He's very disappointed but tries to be philosophical. I wonder what would happen if we lived closer to each other. I wonder too why someone so wealthy would let his dream, rather than some of his money, go.

Holidays soon! I'm going to Leonie and Col's for the second week. I've been going there for fourteen years now. Those friends make it my spiritual and emotional home.

At the farm I relax and try to believe what my wonderful friends say about me being wonderful.

I tell them about my visit to Tony Benton and they're worried.

'We don't think much of those jokers. We've heard more about damage they do than help they've given,' Col says. 'You don't need something like that.'

'I need something. I can't keep feeling this hopeless.'

'You always find good solutions to problems Kate,' Leonie says. 'Good, balanced solutions. You don't need a psychologist. Think carefully before you see that Benton again.'

'I will, Leonie, but I feel like I'm going mental at work. Not with the kids. Just the staff.'

'Kate, you're the sanest person I know,' my friend insists. 'You don't need a psychologist. You just need to realise how fantastic you are. You would if you had people around you who told you you're a champion.'

'I don't know who I am.'

'You're Kate. Wonderful, warm and grounded Kate. We love you.'

'No-one else does.' She knows I mean men. I'm talking about still being single. Again.

'Well, if they're too witless to know quality when they meet it, it's their loss. The right person will turn up, and if they don't, you'll be okay. Just don't sell yourself short.'

She's seen me sell myself short for the want of someone better. The Better Than Nothing syndrome. I've read books about how settling for BTN can grind your self-respect down and distract you from finding the Best. Do those writers really understand the sheer loneliness of going home stressed to an empty house day after day, having to make the decision to pick up the phone and intrude on someone else's happy family just to have a chat, or get reassurance that the work thing is no more your fault than it was last time you rang them?

I feel like I'm living in an endless cycle of needing. Needing and hoping for a person who will make me their number one and care and be there for me when I need them. Instead, I have to be totally responsible for every single detail in my life, with no-one on tap to share the load. And there's the stigma too, of being this age and single. Even if I do look ten years younger than I am, it's still unusual to be single at that age. There are clubs you can't be in. The couples' club is wide and exclusive. The mothers' club huge, with unique kinds of stories – birthing stories, first tooth stories, toilet training and getting Dad to do the nappies. My club is small and silent.

Here at the farm we've been planting trees and we sit down after the last ones are in. I tell Leonie how sick I am of having to be strong and coping with everything alone.

'You can ring us anytime!' she says, apparently surprised that I need to hear that again.

'But then it's an event. I mean, I have to intrude on what you're doing.' It's hard to explain that it needs to be ordinary and immediate sometimes.

We walk down the hill towards home as the sun spreads golden rays across the vast sky. By the time we can see the house, the sky is blazing red and gold. All we can say is, 'Oh look!' The timeless power and magnificence of that sky are deeply calming.

Tonight I write about God and the sky and these treasured friendships in my journal. I mark the entry with an asterisk and add that I need to find a place near home where I can watch sunsets when I'm troubled.

Meanwhile, I have to go home and decide whether to see Tony Benton again.

A BREEZE

I come home feeling valued and more calm, as I always do. I spend time in my garden where I can be sure of the company of neighbours. Today I provide entertainment for them.

Joan has brought some violets to exchange for orchids from my clump. We plant the violets and just as we're standing there admiring our work, a strange creaking sound begins. My bottle-brush is slowly leaning over! I put my hand out to stop it and we laugh at the futility of it. The tired old tree comes to rest across the road.

'Powerful violets, Joan!'

'Goodness me! Better not bring you any more!'

After we've stopped laughing enough to talk, I ask the gathering audience if anyone has a chainsaw. No-one has. I have to do something. Haven't got time to ponder the feeling of aloneness I get from having to ask for help. What can I do? Who can I call? Elliott? One day away. Anyone else?

Then, from nowhere, a team of men arrives in a truck,

chainsaws whirr and soon they've loaded pieces of tree into the truck and it's all gone!

'We were havin' smoko down there at the pump. Couldn't leave a lady with that now, could we. Just don't tell the boss.'

'What will I give them, to thank them?' I ask a neighbour.

'Thanks, love, but we're not allowed to take money. Nuh, not even for beer! Could get the sack if the boss found out.'

After the men leave and the audience disperses, Joan recommends I try watering the violets again.

'That was so nice of those men wasn't it. And handy. Elliott, you know, who you met, has a chainsaw but he's a – oh, Joan! Whoops! I'm so sorry!' The nozzle has popped off the hose and my elderly neighbour is drenched.

'Don't worry, dear,' she shivers. 'I'll go and change. No don't worry.' She turns as she reaches her gate and waves happily.

Inside, alone, I try to hold on to the good cheer as the sun goes down. It's as futile as trying to stop a tree falling over. Here comes the inevitable Saturday-night cloud. There should be some kind of emotional garden stake to make the good cheer stay put, to stop the loneliness. It's warm having people around who think I'm worthy of friendship but they go home. Is gardening the only way I can get company at home?

Should I think about advertising for someone to share the house? It feels so desperate.

I need to think about what Tony Benton said and stop pushing it away. It's time to decide whether I do need to work on those other issues, not just school.

The main thing he said, I think, is to grieve for the loss of my mother. I take down a picture of her from a shelf in my linen cupboard. It's the black and white photo Aunty Dot gave me years ago. I look intensely at the face, into the eyes. No connection. No recognition. No grief. Nothing. Well, of course there isn't! Being only four when she died, I hardly knew her and she hasn't been around for most of my life. Do I need to grieve her passing? I honestly don't think so. I put the photo on the mantelpiece in case I remember anything later.

Do I need to visit her grave? It would be interesting to see it, I suppose, but that's all. I vaguely remember Dad taking us there when we were small but the memory is very dim. All right. Why did Benton say I should visit it? To say goodbye as an adult. Do I need to? No, I don't.

My voice. What about my voice? It's small, childlike, he said. Well, who can help their voice? Am I supposed to go off for voice workshopping to make it big? I don't want to change it. It's an asset at school. Paying attention to it would just get in the way of communication, the purpose of speaking.

What else was there? Oh yes. Stuck in a childhood stage of development because of my childhood traumas. 'Fixated' was the word, I think. He used my choice of profession to illustrate his point. That had hurt but it troubled me too. What if it's true? Why had I chosen this profession? Because I wanted to work with people less powerful or to make a safe childhood for myself? Or because I was offered a scholarship that I took because children like me and I like them? Well, I'm good at what I do. Kids benefit. When I tried something a bit different it didn't work. Now I'm back doing what I'm made for. Does it matter why I chose it? Not to me. So what do I do with Benton's fixation idea? Nothing. I love working with kids. My problem is all the other stuff that happens at work.

Sexual behaviour. What about that? As far as my experience goes, I'm normal. I don't move in circles where it's discussed but I give sexual behaviour an 'irrelevant' rating too.

What about the resistance I've built around myself to prevent people getting close, forming deep emotional attachments? Well, would I have long-term friendships if that was true? We can talk about all kinds of things, including deep personal issues, in the relationships I have with friends. No, I don't accept that I resist people's closeness. Well, maybe with men. Do I resist getting close to them? Is that why I've never accepted a proposal? Were the reasons I found just excuses? There might be some resistance but why then do I get so anxious when they go? What about what Leonie and Col said about Gareth and me, that there was no connection between us? That's the same thing as deep attachment, isn't it? There would be a legacy from having been abused by my father, wouldn't there? If I think deep down that all men are like him, I would resist them. But I don't think they are, do I?

Elliott. What about him? Until recently I've tried so hard to get on with him. No, wait. Tried so hard to be who he wants me to be. Yes, that's it! That's what I'd been doing! For the first time I see I've always done that, tried to be who I think men want me to be, as if who I am isn't good enough. Why haven't I just been myself and if that didn't suit, goodbye men? How could I have a deep emotional connection when I'm trying to be someone else?

This seems important and I wonder if it's connected with the ego strengthening that Benton was talking about. Maybe I need that. Leonie says I don't realise who I am. Maybe I need to work on how I perceive myself so I'll feel strong and confident. That would help at work too, I think. I'd be able to stop it affecting me or be able to fight back. But I don't want to fight! I just want to be likeable and I want them to stop hurting my feelings.

What if I got sorted out, work was fine and I got happy, met Mr Right and achieved my dream? Forty is my absolute limit for having kids, and that's really stretching it.

Perhaps I do need help. From someone. I'm thirty-eight, battered, single and, as much as I hate to admit it, lonely. I have lots of friends but I'm lonely. Is that what Benton means, that if I worked things through I'd be able to form a deep attachment and rid myself of the loneliness?

Although I've disagreed with most of his assertions, I conclude that I need help. But more than anything, the school problem has to be resolved first. Is Tony Benton the person to help me?

'I'm a trained psychologist. I can help you,' he'd said.

Am I just being pig-headed, closed to criticism? Am I questioning his competence because I am afraid of something? He said that whoever I see for help will ask the same questions and draw the same conclusions he did, because of their training. Would they? I don't know.

I'll just try harder to be more assertive at work. I'm not confident that it'll make any difference. Maybe I should just be bitchy to bitchy people. No, I read about the difference between assertiveness and aggression in the holidays. Aggression wouldn't help. And I'd feel horrid.

Deciding whether to see Tony Benton again. That's what I'm doing. Well, I know that if he insists on wasting my time and money on talking about my mother and so on, I won't go back. But I might as well see what we can achieve in terms of the problems at work and if nothing happens, I can stop going.

My mortgage repayments are higher now as the interest rate is thirteen and a half percent. The papers are predicting more rises too, so if I have to pay for therapy as well, I'll be struggling. What would my future be like not even owning a house to belong in? I don't know this self I'm becoming. The old Kate might have been a bit self-conscious but she was happy and energetic, thought there'd be time for babies when she met the right man and never had to deal with nastiness at work. The old Kate had never got into a position of having to pick up the phone to try to dictate terms under which she would continue seeing a psychologist who might be a bully.

'Hello, Mr Benton? It's Kate Shayler.'

'Please, call me Tony. Yes, hello, Kate. I recognised your voice.'

Try to ignore the barb. 'I'm ringing to talk about the possibility of another appointment.'

'When would you like to come? I'll just get the diary.'

'No. Don't get it.' But he's gone.

'I wasn't sure if you'd call again,' he puffs when he returns.

'I'm not ringing to make an appointment necessarily,' I tell him. 'I want to talk about what will happen if I do.'

'Yes?'

'I want to know if you're willing to just deal with the stuff I say I want to work on.'

'What do you mean?'

'I mean I want to deal with my work problem.'

'We can do that,' he says, as if it's obvious.

'You said that before, but you didn't help me with work. You just kept loading me up with other stuff. It was pretty savage –'

'Savage?' he interrupts.

'Yes. You threw the whole book at me and made me feel like I had nothing going for me at all. You were playing God, deciding what I should work on and not listening to what I wanted to do and I just think that if I'm paying for your help you should help with what I want help with and not what you think should be done.' Phew. A breath at last. I wonder if I made any sense.

'I don't believe I was savage,' he says defensively. Then he changes tack. 'You feel I was playing God, do you?'

'Yes. I do. And I felt absolutely mangled when I got home.'

'But we did a relaxation.'

'Yes, but it didn't just dissolve all the other things you talked about. I still took it all home. It was still disturbing. I'm not just a book of problems. So, if that's the way you see me do things, I don't want to come back.'

'I don't see it that way, Kate. I saw, in what you said, how you presented, what my training alerts me to as being possible areas of concern. I'm obliged to mention them.'

'All at once? Regardless of how that makes the person feel?'

'Look, perhaps I was a little heavy-handed but when I see certain things I have to mention them.'

'Why?'

'Because I might be able to help.'

'What if I don't want help?'

'Yes, all right. We can deal with the work issues.'

'So if I see you again we'll deal with my work problem and leave the rest until I decide I'm ready?'

'Well, yes, as far as it's possible to isolate the issues, we could work that way. As I told you, any other psychologist worth his salt would ask you the same questions. It's what we're trained to do. If you want to come back I can assure you that I'll try to be more sensitive to what you want to work on. All right? I won't play God, as you call it. That's not the way I work. We'll take it slowly and work through your issues gradually.'

Long-term therapy. I'm not overjoyed but I don't believe it will take that long to sort out how to deal with the work situation, and I don't need to delve into anything about my mother. My father, possibly, but not my mother.

All right. I'll try to trust him. He's a professional who reckons he can help me.

'Now, let's see. When would you like to come? Any day better than the others?'

'Tuesdays are good for me.'

'Tuesdays. Yes, good for me too. How about the fifth? At, what, about four thirty?'

'Yes, that's all right.'

I'm pleased with myself for standing my ground. I'm not altogether sure Benton will come up with the answers but at least I won't have to go through the life story questions again and I can stop seeing him if he doesn't help. Meanwhile, Tuesdays will be sort-myself-out days.

Back to school with the usual knots. Peter meets me in the corridor.

'Hello, Kate. Had a nice break?'

'Yes thanks. Did you?'

'Good. Yes. It was fine. Oh, tell Maud to come up and see me when she's got a minute, will you,' he adds before disappearing into his office.

Hopefully he would have spoken to her about her work last term, so this might be to tell her that someone permanent has been appointed to her position. Please God, don't let it be her.

'Maud, Peter wants to speak to you today, when you have a minute,' I say.

'What about?' she asks, looking at her watch anxiously.

'Not sure, but we have to set up now so you'll have to go at lunchtime or after school.'

Her telltale blotches emerge as she slams cups on a tray.

The kids arrive happy and confident for their final preschool term. They've been itching to come back and their parents are mostly glad to hand them over. That's one of the satisfying things about the profession I've chosen – helping little people leave their mothers for a short time, grow independent and confident, knowing they'll be safe and able to cope until their mums come back. Even Maud is glad to see them.

At lunchtime she marches off to Peter's office. She returns blotchy, stands with her hands on her hips, blocking my way.

'Did you talk to Peter about me?' she demands.

'Yes, I did. Last term,' I tell her, trying to sound calm. 'We had problems.' So much for Peter having spoken to her last term.

Her nostrils flare, again, and she just about spits at me, 'He's told me I'm not allowed to talk to parents or anyone except him about work.'

'Good! That's how it should be.' I hope I sound assertive.

She spins around and marches off to tell the others.

The mood is icy at the lunch table and Maud stays furious during the afternoon. I struggle to be a cheerful teacher.

After school she plants herself in front of me again. 'So you went to Peter last term, did ya?'

'Yes, I did.' Her aggression, clenched fists on her hips, makes me afraid. I'm afraid of anger in anyone. I walk away slowly, not breathing, feeling like a coward.

'Well,' she seethes behind me. 'He takes his time getting down to business. He'd better be up there now. I've got a fucking mouthful to give him!'

I go home. No-one to tell how frightened I was. Am. No-one to tell me I'll be all right. In my journal I write about being afraid and being so tired of having to cope with everything by myself.

Next morning I see Peter as I'm signing on. 'Good grief, Kate

Shayler,' he says under his breath. 'I see what you mean about that Maud. She's a real case, that one!'

Maybe he understands at last.

It's Tuesday, time for my appointment with Tony Benton. I go nervously. Am I wasting my time? My money?

'Hello, Kate. Come in.'

He follows me in, shutting the door behind him. 'I was glad you rang,' he says. 'I thought you would. I need you to tell me how what I say affects you. It's another tool I use . . .'

Is he making out that my getting upset and then ringing him is just what he planned? Why would he do that? Heavens, maybe I'm paranoid as well as all the rest. Or just dumb.

'Is there anything else you'd like to say to me?'

'There are a few things. The main one is just that I don't want you playing God or bullying me to talk about things I don't want to talk about.'

'Maybe you need to talk about them.'

'You're doing it again! I'm sorry, but you are!'

'There's no need to apologise. Nothing you say to me in this room will offend me. I want you to tell me how you're feeling.'

It wasn't an apology. And your feelings aren't my concern. 'Maybe I do need to talk about childhood sometime, but not now. I'll do it when I'm ready. Right now all I need is to find ways of dealing with school. Conflict resolution or whatever.'

'I won't force you, all right? I'm only trying to help you see how your past is linked to your present. Your future too, for that matter. But all right. What else did you want to say?'

'You said I need long-term work but I won't be able to afford it. I've got a mortgage.'

'Mm. I know what you mean. Let's just see how much we can get done. You could always have a break and come back again when you can afford to do more work. I could give you skills to practise if you can't keep coming. We'll work something out.

I think we could achieve quite a lot in, say, ten weeks, especially if we use hypnosis.'

Skills. At last! Teach me skills. That's what I want. I don't believe we could fix all the problems he reckons I've got even if we had a decade, let alone ten, hypnosis or not.

'Mm. All right. There's just one other thing that worries me, but it's, um, embarrassing.'

He waits.

'It's just that I've read stories and seen movies where neurotic middle-aged women fall in love with their psychologists and dash off to the shrink at the least little worry. I'm worried about that.'

'The shrink, eh!'

'Oh, sorry. That's probably offensive.'

'It's not a term I'm fond of. What in particular worries you? The dashing off to the psychologist or the falling in love?'

'Both. But mostly the falling in love.'

'Do you think there's any chance of that?' he asks, looking down his nose. Good grief! Is he posing?

'No,' I tell him.

'And why is that?' He looks surprised and sounds like he's working on appearing disinterested.

'Because, um, I don't, er, you're not, um. There isn't any attraction.'

'Mm. Well, it can happen because of the nature of therapy, you see. It's perfectly normal for a patient to develop strong positive feelings like love for a therapist as they work together. Or it can go the other way and the feelings can be negative. It's nothing to be afraid of. It's an important tool we can use. It's important that you tell me how you feel towards me as we go along.'

'Well, I don't want any of that. I just want the school stuff sorted out.'

'Would it bother you to develop strong feelings for me?'

'Of course it would! The love ones, anyway.' I hope he doesn't notice the grin I try to suppress. I've virtually said I wouldn't mind if I developed strong feelings of hatred for him.

'And why is that?'

'Because it's not appropriate! I'm here to get help about school. Feelings for you have nothing to do with it.'

'Look, it really isn't something to worry about. It's called transference and it can happen as people share intimate details with each other. If it does happen here, I can use it, manipulate it, to work through your issues, with your father, for example.'

This is crazy. I won't be sharing intimate details.

'I assure you that I am professional. I know how to manage transference. Look, by the time we finish, it'll be resolved, if it happens, and you'll come to think of me just as someone you did business with once.'

'I don't want it to happen at all.' Manipulating emotions seems sick, morally wrong. Oh, but then he's a professional and proud of it. Maybe it's what they all do.

'Let's move on. We may not even use that technique.'

'Move on' means a summary of how we're going to achieve some ego strengthening, so I will be more aware of the true nature of my struggles and successes. He suggests I look into doing more study. Yeah, great. I need more pressure! Then he tells me we'll work on some conflict resolution skills to help me at school and do some work on grieving.

'You agreed to respect my wishes and now you're starting on about grieving again!'

He rambles on about anger in adults sometimes being the result of early bereavement.

'I'm not angry!'

He recites some of my assertions about the people at work.

'Yes, I'm angry with them!' I reply. 'Legitimately angry. With them, not my mother. They don't do their work. They misinterpret whatever I say and do. They make it all so horrible. Yes, I'm angry. With them.'

He talks on and on, giving me his words of wisdom to think about. I say I will, because maybe then we'll get to the resolving-the-problem part. He's been a teacher, himself, he says, so he knows what it's like. Questioning authority is healthy, especially for someone with my upbringing. He did, became disillusioned and left teaching. Now he's saying he thinks my traumatic childhood is contributing to the problems I've had in my career.

'I haven't had problems in my career. It's just this year. I left my old school after seven happy years because I didn't feel safe there any more. Maybe I made a mistake changing to a primary school position. I was out of my depth there and now I'm in a disaster zone. What does any of that have to do with my childhood? Nothing. It's just all unfortunate circumstances. I love preschool teaching and that's what I want to do.'

He insists that grieving for my mother and moving on would have let me develop normal modes of coping. I insist that the current problems are as much about the people I work with as my lack of skills. He says we can certainly work on those skills. Some assertiveness would be good for helping me demand that I be treated respectfully.

I agree. When can we start?

'How has it been at work since I saw you last?'

'I tried to be assertive and I told the boss about the problem.'

'Yes. Good. What did he do?'

'He spoke to Maud and made her so furious I thought she was going to attack me. But at least he knows what she's like now.'

'Is he keeping her on?'

'He reckons he has to. It's such a process to sack anyone. They'll appoint someone permanent soon, though.'

'Oh, you don't need to work for ineffective little people like that!'

I'm surprised that he expresses a harsh judgement like that but I suppose he's being supportive of me. All the same I wish I didn't feel flattered. 'But I need a job. I'll have to keep trying to be assertive.'

'How did it go?'

'She did what I asked, but I was so tense.'

'Why?'

'I don't know. I think, well, it's because the others shut me out when I upset Maud. And she's scary when she flexes her muscles too. I thought she'd deck me!'

He grins. He doesn't understand that I believe my fear is justified. 'Well, we've made progress then, haven't we?'

'I suppose so, but I shouldn't feel so anxious about it, should I? I should be able to just do it and forget it.'

'Keep doing it and you will. Practise you see. You're the boss. She knows that. You know what you really ought to think about?'

'No.' Tell me. Quickly. Self-defence classes? Body building. Hiring a bodyguard? Boxing gloves?

'Lecturing. You don't want to have to keep dealing with these small-minded people. You don't need them. Not when you have all that experience and knowledge.'

'I can't be a lecturer!' Flattered again. Disappointed that I'm flattered again.

'Why not? There are people lecturing with much less experience than you've got,' he says. 'Those people who've spent their whole careers in universities know far less than you do about the real world. It'd do them good to have you telling them a thing or two.'

His plans for my career seem to be as much about a grudge he has as improving my position. But I haven't been acknowledged like this before, by an objective person, professionally. I like it. I want more. But that's pathetic!

'What qualifications do you need for lecturing?' I ask.

'Masters, I think. Have you got that?'

'No. Just a B.A.'

'Right. You should think seriously about doing your Masters. You'd breeze through it.'

'I struggled through my B.A.'

'But you didn't know then what you know now, did you? Right? Get your Masters, then get out of that system. It's too demoralising working with little megalomaniacs climbing ladders at your expense.'

I want to hear the affirming parts of this but I want to keep thinking the megalomaniacs are doing their best for the kids too. Mrs Pontifex was certainly no megalomaniac but I have to admit Benton might be right about some others. I wish I felt as confident about my ability to breeze through a Masters degree as he does.

'All right, so we've talked about work and looked at some solutions for you to think about. Right? Now I'd like you to go back to your memories of childhood. I know you're not keen but think about this: if we draw out the memories and your feelings about them, it will help you understand what's happening to you in the world now. It will help you understand your past and then you'll be free of it. Free to achieve your potential. You'll be energised, more able to move on.'

I can imagine being free of worry. But, 'I can't imagine being free of my past, because I don't feel tied to it. It's over.'

He doesn't think so. He says my conscious memories are only small snippets and he thinks they're screen memories, memories that protect me from the trauma hidden behind them.

'I should leave them there then, if they're protecting me, shouldn't I?'

'You could. Or we could use my hypnosis skills to tease out the memory, then use your adult cognition to process what's there and let it go. It's stored with childhood perceptions, childhood understanding of it. All right? It will always stop you achieving what you can until you face it and move on. It takes a lot of energy to keep memories suppressed. It's documented in professional journals, all this. Suppressed memories can express themselves in physical or mental illness too. A low T-cell count can be an indication, as we've discussed before.'

He seems obsessed with his hypnosis ability but his explanation makes sense. 'Oh, I suppose you know what you're doing.'

'Thank you,' he smiles. 'All right. You said you don't remember much about your mother's death.'

'I don't remember anything about it.'

'Tell me about the closest time to that that you remember.'

'I remember a little girl standing in a cold room, crying. But I don't know if it's me.'

'All right. Now I want you to relax and then we'll try to get you closer to that little girl.'

'It mightn't even be me, though.'

'We'll see. Just relax, breathe deeply and try to focus on her, get closer.'

He sits quietly. I have to imagine going close. But I can't see her. I can only feel something that might rob me of my breath. I try going close but how can I when I can't see her? I know she's standing there. She's scary, makes me apprehensive.

'What are you thinking?' Benton asks quietly.

'I don't know if I'm doing this right. I mean, I can't see her. I just know she's there and she's more like . . . feeling.'

'Good. What's the feeling?'

'Frightened. She's sad. She's really upset. Angry.' In that instant I know the child is me. I have always known, somewhere inside. Deep inside. I knew all those years ago when Terese talked about the innate innocence of children. I had wrapped her words in blue velvet and hidden them away like treasure. Will they lend me courage now? 'It's me. She's me,' my small voice says.

Remembering and owning this feels as if there's been a curtain across the memory of my childhood. Now the window has opened slightly and a breeze is shifting the curtain, letting me see behind it. Just a little. The breeze stops. The curtain falls still and the rest of my childhood is hidden again. Until the next breeze.

'So tell me about the feeling,' he says gently, firmly.

'I just did.'

'She is angry. She is frightened,' he says emphasising 'she'.

'She is!'

'Would "I" be more appropriate?'

I am frightened? I am sad? I am fighting to stay adult.

' "I" would be all right if I was still that child, but she's not me. She was, but I'm not that now! I'm an adult. It's who I was, not am.' I'm getting confused because I seem to disbelieve what I'm saying. I feel small and afraid and I'm getting angry.

He waits. I try saying what he wants.

'I'm angry. I'm sad. I feel silly.'

He ignores the feeling silly and continues on his way. 'All right. Go back to her. What is she angry about? Take your time. Be with her. Feel the feelings.'

I stand with her. What's happening? I feel. Her feelings. Someone starts to cry. Me or the child. I don't know who.

'What is she angry about?'

'They put her in the room. She just wants her mummy.'

'She?'

'She.' I don't want to be that scary child. I'm not. Not any more. 'I don't see what it has to do with now.' He probably thinks I'm incredibly dumb.

'How would Miss Shayler feel if she saw someone treat a child that way?'

'Outraged. I do see it at work. Sort of.'

'Yes. But stay with the child you were. What would you do?'

'Get her out and give her a cuddle. Reassure her.'

'They didn't do that for you, did they?'

'No.'

'What does Miss Shayler think about it now?'

'I suppose Miss Shayler might feel angry at the women who put her there.' But I can't feel it. Can I?

'All right. Think more about that when you go home. It's a very important memory. Think about it and see where it takes you.'

It's odd to have permission to say bad things about the matrons at Burnside who must have sent me to that room. It's as if someone has spoken to me in a different language that I might understand if I try hard. I've never done it before, not to the matrons, not as an adult. I've hardly ever thought about them and I've never compared my professional self with them. But the parallels are obvious now and intriguing. More to think about.

'Do you remember anything else?' Benton's voice interrupts.

'I remember having a recurring dream, well, nightmare. I used to have it regularly. Still do sometimes. Recurring dreams are supposed to mean something, aren't they?' I'm glad to be getting away from that little girl. I want to know what this dream means because even the memory of having it disturbs me.

'Yes, they can reveal our subconscious. Would you like to tell me the dream?'

'I dreamt that I was in a room with no doors. There was a wolf outside snarling. I knew he would come in and rip me apart. Then I woke up.'

'How old are you?'

'Thirty-eight.' What's that got to do with anything?

He smiles benevolently. 'How old are you in the dream?'

'Oh! Um. I don't know. Little. Maybe four or five. The room was in the home I was in at Burnside. Do you know what it means?'

'Do you?'

'I suppose it might mean that life was scary.'

'The dream has lots of classical symbols in it that apply in cultures all over the world. Do you know about this?'

'No. I remember people at uni talking about it but it seemed like magic or creative writing or something.'

He tells me a muddle of things, like doors and windows represent female sexuality, walls male sexuality, but he doesn't say what wolves represent. I wish he'd just tell me what the dream means. Instead, he wants me to think about it and work out the meaning myself. I like that he thinks I'm intelligent enough to do it, but aren't I paying him to help me, not give me endless things to think about at home?

I tell him about more hints of memories but they are so vague – legs swinging while I sit in a huge chair listening to a clock ticking, watching a beetle try to climb out of a bottle. I leave the one that hurts most, the one where I'm beating my cringing little sister up, 'til last. I leave the one that terrifies me completely alone. Thick voice mumbling, 'Oh, Katie, Katie.' I can't speak it. It's foul.

'Let's look at the sister one. She's older? No, younger. Right.' He starts talking about sibling rivalry but I have to interrupt.

'But Kerry was no more a sister to me growing up than any of the other girls in the home.'

He says that all the basics were set when we lived in the Shayler family. The what? Oh, I lived in a family once, didn't I? This is the first time I've been aware, known that I did, like everyone else. It doesn't fit the me I know. The homes kid. But Shaylers! Us all in a family together! Strange. Nice. Scarily forgotten.

Benton is still delivering his sibling rivalry lecture and I catch the odd sentence. '. . . undifferentiated sexuality . . . sexual motives . . . competing . . .' He certainly has a lot to say about sexuality. Is he showing off about his knowledge by using all that jargon? Showing me he knows about early childhood too, I think. He burbles on about the child's need to be socialised into appropriate modes of sexual expression. I have to interrupt again.

'Sorry, but I just don't see children as sexual beings with sexual motives.'

He argues against that and goes on to say that when people break taboos with children, those children's socialisation is interrupted and physical sensations of pleasure become associated with shame and secrecy.

Pleasure! What pleasure? Fear is all I remember. Listen to him. Try to be objective and learn.

But my heart is racing. I wish he'd say 'when people abuse children' or 'when people rape children', instead of wishy-washy 'break taboos'.

'. . . possible that on one level you enjoyed the sexual . . .'

'What?' I'm furious. Is this man completely mad? Warped? This is disgusting! What am I doing here?

No, hang on. He's had the training. I haven't. I should at least listen to him.

'You haven't heard this theory before? Everyone is born with an inbuilt potential to reproduce. That's the way the species survives. We all have to learn to express our sexuality in acceptable ways very early in our lives. Some people infringe our taboos and do bad things . . .'

I become too angry and confused to listen. His theory seems to put blame for abuse onto the child who hasn't learnt social conventions yet! It's utter garbage. Was I a seductive little girl who made her father do what he did? Absolutely not. I'm even sickened by the possibility. And there's what we learn in Child Protection Program training – it's always the adult's responsibility to protect the child, not take advantage. Benton couldn't have meant what I thought he did. I'm so dumb! Calm down. Remember he's a professional.

'I think that's enough for today,' I hear him say at last.

'I think so too.'

'You think about what I've said,' he tells me, holding my gaze a moment longer than is comfortable. 'We'll talk more next time.'

'I won't be thinking of that stuff about children seducing adults. It's dangerous. It blames the victim.'

'No it doesn't,' he says softly. 'Of course adults must protect children. Always.' After a short silence he says, 'You have a lot of stress just now. I think it would be good for you to learn some relaxation techniques.'

'Good idea.'

'I'd like to try hypnosis again.'

I remind him that I couldn't do what he wanted last time. I tell him that since then I've seen a hypnotist on television who made people behave like chickens just by clicking his fingers.

'Let's just see how you go. If you're uncomfortable at any time, we can stop. You will always be in control.'

'But those people on stage were out of control.'

'Those performers do a lot to discredit the profession. What they do has nothing to do with the way therapists use hypnosis. There's no magic and I assure you that you have the power to stop it at any time. Right?'

I want to believe him, to learn to relax.

'I'd like you to try it. As I've said, it's a technique I'm especially skilled in, but it does require trust. People say it makes them feel as if they've had a night of perfect sleep. It's deep relaxation that lasts well after you leave. We could possibly use it as a shortcut to resolving some of your memories too. What do you think? Will you trust me?'

'I'll try.' He did say I can stop it if I want to, didn't he?

'All right. I want you to get comfortable. Arms beside you, lean back in the chair.'

So far, so good.

'Now take off your glasses and close your eyes.'

No! Too vulnerable. Frightened, down inside. Tears roll out. Failing again.

'All right. That's all right. We can do it with your eyes open.'

'No, I just don't want to do it. I can't.' I'm breathing too fast. Why?

'All right. It's all right. We'll try something else. Do you like music?'

'What kind of music?' When I'm sad I like silence. When I'm happy I like the blues. When I'm peaceful I like harmony and folk songs.

'Classical. Brahms? Chopin?'

'I don't know much about classics. Why?'

'I use music to relax, so I wonder if you might like to try that. What we'll do is sit quietly and concentrate on the music. Leave our troubles and tensions behind for a while. Will you try it?'

'All right.'

He puts a cassette on and I try to concentrate on the music. I'm much too self-conscious after having spent the best part of the last hour with him measuring and evaluating my reactions. Is he doing it now? I steal a glance at him. His eyes are shut. I stare at nothing, listening, relaxing, forgetting.

'How was that?' Benton asks when the music stops.

'Relaxing.'

'Do you have any music at home?'

'Not classical.'

'I'll make a copy of this for you if you like.'

He copies the tape while I write out a cheque.

'You've got a lot to think about when you leave. Remember it's important to not just recall past events but to remember your feelings. Let me know how you go next time. Tuesday again?'

We still haven't resolved the work problem but he reckons I have to keep practising assertiveness. Do I need to keep coming here then? He was patient and sensitive when I couldn't do hypnosis, so he might not be the bully I thought he was. He respects me and my achievements and it is good to tell an objective person all the work stuff. Maybe I should keep coming. Remembering that I once lived in a family bowled me over, made me feel more normal, like other people. What if there's more of the good stuff to come too?

At home I take out my journal. I'll write what I remember, even if it's vague. In one column I write the memories, in the other, the feelings.

Standing in a cold room.	*Angry, frightened, lonely.*
Beating Kerry up.	*Angry, ashamed, confused, self-loathing.*
Father greeting staff with kiss.	*Embarrassed.*
Father saying that thing.	*Frightened. Can't explore.*

I feel so angry with my father that now I can't call him 'Dad', even in my thoughts. He doesn't deserve it. He's my father, not the other. But I'm always caught in this dilemma: if I own the anger and the loathing, it feels like I'm biting the hand that fed me. He worked until he was seventy something to keep us housed and fed and cared for. Is it all right to bite the hand that feeds you? What if the hand did other things that leave it deserving to be bitten? If I don't bite it, will I ever be normal?

Will I write down the memory I can't speak about? It's important. Try. Can't. The words would be too vile.

I read down the feelings column. I had a lot of anger. What do I do about it now? I don't think I need to do anything. It's interesting but over.

What about that other stuff Benton said about child sexuality? Unbelievable! I write out my confusion in my journal.

I'm afraid to look at that theory. Why? Because I'm afraid that if it's true it will mean there was no childish, innocent affection between me and my father. It spoils the wholesome part of the memory of him. Worse is that it spoils me. It means I was never a wholesome little girl. But that's not how it was! There was real love as well as the other. What about that memory that I can't speak? That isn't a manipulating child. It's a terrified child. You are wrong, Tony Benton.

I'm supposed to think about what that nightmare means too. I get stuck. I need to know about the wolf, not all that stupid stuff about walls being penises or whatever it was. After lots of thinking, I'm no closer to understanding.

I need a rest from all this. Must organise my house warming. Too tired. Dinner, television and sleep.

Next day I ring Macquarie and Sydney Universities and ask them to send information about their Master of Education programs. I don't believe I'm bright enough but there's no harm in looking at the courses. I'll be able to tell Tony Benton that I have done something to contribute to my ego strengthening.

I wander in my garden on Saturday afternoon. I love owning this place, well, me and the building society. Twenty years to go before I really own it. The melancholy cloud drifts over. Twenty more years of work before I can . . . oh, don't think about it. But wretched Saturday night falls and I'm at home while everyone else is out having fun. At least if I do a Masters I'll have assignments to struggle with on Saturday nights next year. An excuse to have to stay home and not be able to go out.

After work on Monday the building society's logo looms in the letter box. I'm anxious before I've even opened the envelope. It isn't wasted anxiety. Interest rates, they regret to say, are going up again. Fourteen percent! How am I going to keep . . .

All right. Take charge. It's no use just getting in a panic. Do something about it. Paint the spare room so it's ready for a boarder.

As the paint dries I write an ad for the local paper. I don't really want a boarder who I don't know, but I don't know anyone who wants to board. I imagine possibilities. One friend who shared a house with a group of people ended up married to one of them. That would be nice. But what if I get someone like that then the relationship goes bad? I'd have to ask him to leave. What if I got someone horrible and had to ask them to leave? What if they wouldn't go? What if they were a murderer or rapist or thief or something? Well, my neighbours are all supportive. I think they'd help me if I got into strife. Do I have the right to ask them? No.

'How will I know if they're the right person?' I ask Leonie.

'You're a good judge of character. I think you'll know. But you could write some questions you want to ask and go through them, I suppose.' That's what Gen said too. And they both remind me that if I don't feel comfortable with someone, I don't have to accept them. It's so obvious when they say it but I hadn't thought of that. I write some questions but I don't really know what I'm doing. Maybe I could just trust my judgement.

I take my ad to the newspaper office and finish painting. I've got my questions ready but what if the only person who answers the ad is odd and the interest rate keeps going up like newspapers are predicting? Well, I'll just deal with it when it happens. Try not to get anxious in the meantime.

Next morning I remember a recurring dream I had again during the night. I'm glad it's only puzzling, not frightening. I write it in my journal.

I sneak about my father's house when no-one else is there. I'm greedily grasping all the clocks and hiding them away so no-one else can get them. I, and only I, must have them all. The clocks are ones that really were in my father's house.

I thought I'd cracked the meaning of this one when I had it a few months ago. I thought it was about my wanting time to stop so I would not be too old to have a baby. That can't be the meaning, though, because I had the dream again last night. You don't have them again, once you understand their meaning. Perhaps Tony Benton can help me work it out.

WHO THE WOLF IS

My ad is in the paper. The phone rings.
'Gudday, love. Shounds young. Got the paper a room f . . . godda room 'ave ya f . . . incher madey.'

'Pardon?'

'Shed, ya godda room in the paper.'

'Uh. No. Sorry, it's gone. Bye.' What have I done? Is that how it's going to be? One drunk who makes the room vanish and that's it! I hope no-one else rings. I'll just have to manage without a boarder.

When the phone rings again I'm tempted not to answer.

'Hello. I read your ad in the paper,' a confident male voice says. 'I'd like to ask about the room and arrangements, if you don't mind. Is this a convenient time?' His name is Harry, he's a student and his current place is too noisy. He can afford the rent, prefers to cook his own meals and will go to Sydney most weekends. We arrange for him to come and look but I want to drag him in and glue his feet to the floor just because he's sober. Should I wait for a woman to call? And miss out on a perfectly decent male?

241

I tell the neighbours what's going on and they say I should call on them if there's a problem.

Harry arrives and after a tour says, 'This is ideal! Can I move in next weekend?'

'Yes,' I reply, trying not to sound desperate. 'As long as your references check out.'

Have I done the right thing? Why am I so nervous? I'm looking forward to Tuesday when I can talk it through with Benton. No, I'm supposed to call him Tony and he'll call me Kate. It's like having a friend to report to regularly without interrupting their dinner or bathing of the kids. Except he's not a friend. He gets paid.

I arrive at his office and no-one answers my knock. I check my diary. Yes, Tuesday. I feel annoyed. I need to talk, and I seem to need it more now that he's not here.

He drives in just as I'm leaving. 'Sorry I'm late. Held up at a meeting. Wait here and I'll be with you in a tick.' He goes inside but soon he's back asking, 'How've you been? Have you been waiting long?'

'No, not long.'

He unpacks his brief case and sets himself up while he says, 'So, tell me about your week.'

At last! I tell him about work. I'm still being ostracised and I still feel anxious when I challenge the others. I'm a wreck at the end of each day. I missed a swim because I woke up with no energy. But I managed not to buy into Maud's sulking as if it was my responsibility. That felt good.

He talks again about the school he worked in and left in disgust because it was such a political hotbed. He seems to think that his way – resigning – is really the only solution for me. Leave, study and do lecturing.

'I've checked it out and I can't afford to do full-time study. Sydney and Macquarie are sending their information. Don't know how I'll find the energy for it after work, though.'

'Good. Good. You'll love study. And you'll be mixing with

242

better people. Not like that small-minded lot you're with now.'

Better people? Don't be flattered. Be Kate who believes in equality. You're not better just because you're a student! You're the same but studying. Well, you open your mind but you're still human like everyone else.

'I think I've found a boarder too. He's moving in on the weekend.'

'How do you think you'll go with a strange man living in your house?' he asks.

'I'm really nervous but he seemed well mannered and everything. He said all the right things and he has good references. I'm nervous but I think I would be with anyone.'

'Well, if it doesn't work out, you can always ask him to leave.'

Tony settles back in his chair. 'Right, let's move on. Last week we looked at some memories, didn't we? What would you think about exploring the memory of your father today? Would you like to talk about that?' he asks quietly.

Let the breeze lift the curtain softly. For a breath or two? '"Like" isn't exactly the right word. Oh, I suppose I should if I'm ever going to work through it.'

'Good. We'll take it slowly. All right? Start with telling me what you remember.'

'Not much. Oh, do you mean about being abused or in general?'

'Just start where you're comfortable. Don't worry if what you remember seems small.'

'Well, my Da– . . . father was funny and he used to come with a string bag of cakes and Minties. He had big leathery hands and he'd play games with us, let us be kids, I suppose. I was taught to be proud of him because he only missed one visiting day in the twelve years I was there in Burnside. He worked 'til he was seventy something so he could pay our way and not make us charity cases. He was a fine English gentleman.' Which seems like an utterly ridiculous thing to say here.

'That's what they taught you to think. But how did you feel about him?'

'I loved him.' My eyes are burning because I loved him. This is the first time I've told anyone.

'You loved him and he betrayed you,' Tony says gently.

'Yes. I hate him!' I sob. 'But I don't want to hate him. He was good and loyal too.'

'Can you tell me when the thing that makes you hate him began?'

'I don't remember . . . um . . . I was small. This is hard. I've never put it in words before. Well, hardly any of it.'

'Just take your time. It's important to give it adult expression, then you can be free of the childhood emotions.'

'I can't remember much . . . um . . . he . . . he was on me . . . I can't. I can't say the words.' I'm trying to force them out but I'm too frightened to go anywhere near it. More things might happen. Bad things. They'd just be words but I'm still frightened. I want to shut the window so the curtain can't drift.

'Do you know the words?'

'Think so.'

'But you can't say them?'

'No.' My voice is very small.

'All right. It's all right.' He waits for me to be calm. 'Did you ever talk to your father about it?'

'No!' I can't imagine anything more disgusting! To say it would make it more real and more vile.

'You never asked him why or told him how it made you feel?'

'No!'

'What about Kerry? Have you talked to her?'

'No. I don't know if it happened to her. I hardly know her, really. We're not like other sisters, ones in normal families. We're not close.'

'It might have happened to her, though.'

'I don't know. And I don't want to ask her, because if it didn't, well, you know. She's entitled to her illusions. She had such a terrible time at Burnside and whatever else my father was, he was the only person who loved us. I wouldn't want to spoil that for her.'

'You both loved him?'

'Yes. I suppose so. I did.' Tears again.

'You needed him and loved him and he betrayed you.'

He asks gently what effect that might have had on my adult relationships. That's too hard. I try to take control. 'I don't want to talk about this.'

'You haven't talked to Kerry about it at all?'

'No.'

'Could you?'

'I just wouldn't,' I say emphatically. 'What if it didn't happen to her? I'd spoil her illusions.'

'Maybe she needs to know the truth.'

'It would just be my truth. Hers might be different. I don't have the right to disillusion her with my stuff.'

'I think she can't talk about it either until you do. If you made an approach, told the truth, you could support one another.'

'It wouldn't be worth the risk.'

'Well, you think about it.'

He starts talking about breaking the incest taboo again and the child's confusion about sensations of pleasure . . . My blood boils again.

'There was no pleasure! It was just fear.'

He waits. I want to get far, far away from this. It's sick.

'Look, at Burnside, anything related to my body was either bad or painful. Pleasure had nothing to do with anything.'

'Tell me about that.'

'Oh, they told me I was too fat and boys wouldn't like me. I got teased about being a four eyes and boys teased me endlessly about my big breasts.'

'What was that? Four eyes? Oh, wearing glasses.'

'Yes. And boys don't make passes at girls who wear glasses.'

'Don't they?'

'Not if you're fat too! No, I suppose they do. They have.'

'And the boys teased you?'

'Yeah, the boys were horrible, but the staff were just as bad, in effect.' The window opens, the curtain shifts and I tell him about my first bra, how I was told to wear it when I was ten. I didn't know what it was or that anyone else had one. I'm self-conscious talking about this to him but I want to make my point. The matron ripped my blouse open to see if I was wearing the wretched thing or just lying again. When she discovered the lie, she screamed abuse at me, telling me how ugly I was.

I look at Tony and he's shaking his head slowly, saying, 'You just don't do that to a kid.'

I have a strong positive feeling about him when I see that reaction.

'What's the earliest memory you have of body things, as you call them?' he asks.

'It's only vague but I remember telling some other kids . . . um, things.'

'What things did you tell them?' He's smiling slightly, as if I might have told them that I've got a belly button.

I start the story away from its epicentre. 'Well, I had a special friend called Kevin and I used to get in his bed when I was frightened.'

'How old were you?'

'Four or five. In the little kids' home. One night, after we'd been bathed, we were waiting for the matron to put our pyjamas on and we were talking about our bodies and nipples . . .' I'm talking fast, getting anxious. What's happening?

Wind is gusting through and the curtain is lifting. Too high?

'Go on,' Tony says.

I struggle with the words. 'Well, I told the others that if . . . that if . . . Can't say it.'

Close the window!

'You can't say what you told them?'

'No. I can't say it. We were just looking . . .' Oh, shut the window! Cover the scene. Crying.

'You know the words but you can't say them.'

'Yes.' I feel very small. And foolishly big. My hand hurts where my fingernails are digging in. 'They told Kevin and all the others . . .' Can't finish.

He waits while I compose myself.

'Why do you think you're having trouble saying the words? What are you feeling?'

'It's scary. Rude. Feels like something bad will happen if I say a rude thing.'

'What happened when you said the words back then, when you kids were just looking?'

'All hell broke loose. I was beaten and shrieked at and the others were told not to play with me or I'd make them filthy too.' I'm sobbing again.

No-one loves me and I'm bad and I make other people bad.

'Bad things happen when you talk about your body,' Tony says gently. 'Bad things will not happen here. You are safe.'

I'm never safe!

I'm bawling my head off as if I am bad and always was.

'I can help you be free of all this pain,' Tony says. 'You'll be a woman who can start to express her latent sexuality fully.'

What? I'll be a what! I'm not a wom– . . . what's happening? Of course I am. But it feels dangerous being a woman.

I pull the window firmly shut and struggle back to my adult self where my adult sexuality is latent because it's alone. I can't express it fully in a vacuum. This is too much. Now I'm crying because I'm a woman and because I'm alone. And not good enough.

'I don't want to tackle anything else right now. I've got too much already.'

'All right. We can leave that for another time. Right?'

'All right,' I agree slowly, disappointed in my lack of strength. 'Suppose I'll have to do it sometime.'

'You do need to think about who was at fault in that scenario. Was it little Kate Shayler or someone else? Think about how the carers dealt with it. Think about how you would deal with a disclosure like that yourself, as a teacher.'

Anger! I'd report it, of course! I want to whack the matrons: Mrs Henderson for betraying me, for treating me so unfairly, for not protecting me; and Miss Thurland, for shouting and scaring me; and Mrs Grable too, for shouting with Miss Thurland and smacking me. Angry tears fall.

'Tell me what that was about,' says Tony.

'Oh, I feel so angry with those matrons. Don't want to keep talking about this.'

'We can leave it until you're ready. All right?'

'All right.'

'Perhaps we could move on to when your mother died. All right?'

'I don't remember that.' Feels safe, though. Nothing about her behind the curtain.

'We talked about grieving, being free of pain from the past.'

It feels like a lucky dip. Peep behind the curtain, pull out a memory and, if I'm lucky, I'll win a bag of freedom. But the questions feel important. Tony thinks they are and he's trained. I can't just keep saying I can't or don't want to. I have to help myself.

'What happened to your mother?'

'She died of a heart attack when she was forty-seven,' I parrot without feeling. 'She had us late.'

'What's your earliest memory of that time?'

'There's nothing about my mother. I don't remember her.' I hope he won't get cross with me for all my negatives. 'Standing by myself in the dining room, crying, is my earliest memory of anything.'

'How old were you?'

'Four.'

'How long were you left there?'

'Don't know.'

'Did someone come and get you?'

'I don't remember.'

'Who did you want to come?'

I shrug. 'Someone. Anyone. Kenny.'

'Your mother?'

'Don't think so. She was dead. They told me, I think.'

'You think more about that. In a quiet moment just go back and think about who you wanted. All right?'

I shrug again. 'All right.'

'What do you do at preschool when four-year-olds cry because they want their mummies?'

'Cuddle them. Tell them their mum will be back.' I'm crying again. No-one cuddled me. I'm embarrassed at feeling sorry for my little self. Tony sits quietly for a while.

'Did the carers let you cry? Talk about your mum? Did they comfort you?'

'No. They shut me in the room and told me to stop,' I say as the curtain drifts up and the memory fills out. 'I had to stay there 'til I stopped. I must have wanted my Da– . . . father.'

'So they shut you in a room and told you to stop crying, when you'd just lost your parents.'

'It's so wrong!' Nearly choking on the words. Half expecting a bolt of lightning to strike me for criticising the matrons.

'All societies have rituals for grieving because people need to grieve. Right? We need to process our pain and move on. You never did that for your mother.' Then he adds softly, 'Kids need to grieve too.'

That makes sense. But now as an adult I don't feel sad about it. It's just when I go back. It seems to go round and round like a slow spin cycle. Remember, be sad, come back, it's all right, remember, be sad, come back . . .

Tony interrupts the cycle and says, 'Look, we'll have to stop now, but think about this during the week.'

We do a relaxation exercise, me sitting up straight again with my eyes closed. I go home with a head that's overflowing. I have to write it all out in my journal.

Why did I get such a jolt when he said I'm a woman? Weird. If he'd said 'lady' it wouldn't have felt dangerous. Is it dangerous being a woman? It's not like being a lady, with manners that control and limit behaviour. Being a woman is about having this body, this dangerous body. There are no limits and you're vulnerable. Have to be on your guard all the time.

But I don't feel vulnerable in relationships, do I? Yes. But that's only when they end, like with Gareth and Cameron. I cried like a baby! All right, but what's that got to do with sexuality? I'm afraid of being dumped. Lots of people are, aren't they, and it's not about sex or latent sexuality. So, what do I do about it? Beats me! Think. Think. Tony said to think about it all. Um. Um. Good grief, being dumped by Cameron was the luckiest escape I've ever had!

Saturday. Elliott is coming up to stay overnight. I'm glad Harry will think I have a man about, even if he does sleep in the study. When Elliott arrives for dinner, Harry has still not come. Maybe I got the day wrong. Elliott had better go house hunting by himself tomorrow and I'll stay home for Harry.

He doesn't arrive and doesn't ring. I feel offended but relieved. As long as the building society's logo doesn't appear in the letter box, I'll be right. Just.

Friends from Sydney, Diedre and Simon, call in and while Simon takes their baby for a walk, Diedre and I talk, as we'd done after dancing in Sydney.

'Don't get me wrong. Being a mother is great but, oh Kate, me ole bod takes so long to catch up with how it was before the birth. I'm bloody knackered!' She's laughing but she does look more tired than I've seen her look before.

'I still want one. Or six.'

'I know, but look, you have to be on duty twenty-four hours a day and I never really understood what that meant until I had Lily! Simon didn't either. We're a pair of aging zombies.' She laughs again.

'I wanna be an aging zombie!' More laughter. It's so good to laugh! And then we talk, about my work and Diedre's. I tell her I've been seeing a psychologist, and she isn't concerned, as long as it's helping.

'I don't know if it is or not, really. The problem at work goes on and on. I move forward in tiny steps but now he's got me doing all this stuff about childhood. I thought I was okay about all that but he thinks I need to work on it.'

Simon, with Lily sleeping on his shoulder, comes back. I wish they'd had a ten-hour walk.

'Get the house warming invites out soon, won't you?' Diedre says as they leave. I feel sad now about being so far away from my old life. Never mind. Things will change. Harry, or someone, will relieve the financial worries and I'll keep working on my stuff with Tony. Meanwhile, I'd better plan the house warming for the beginning of the holidays. First, ring Harry.

'Oh sorry,' he says. 'I should have rung. I'm having a problem with breaking the lease here. I'll have to get back to you in a few weeks.'

Freedom for a few weeks. Good.

The building society's logo in the letter box is as welcome as a funnel-web on the tooth brush. Interest rates are going up to fourteen and a quarter percent. Come on, Harry, get here with your board. The landlady's getting desperate. Anxious. Miserable.

The following Saturday I drag myself out of bed and go to the supermarket. Avoiding the chocolate aisle, searching for a magic slimming potion, I almost run over Tony with my trolley.

'What are you doing here? Oh, you're allowed out sometimes, are you?' I babble.

'Well, even a psychologist has to eat. What do you mean "allowed out"?'

'It's just what kids say when they meet teachers out of school. It's become a joke. With my friends.' I'm blushing brightly. 'I was just surprised to see you. Here.' My babble peters out.

'Why?'

Feels like the Inquisition.

'It's just strange seeing someone who you tell your deepest secrets to out here doing something as mundane as shopping.'

'Your secrets are safe. Even in the biscuits aisle.' He grins. 'Well, must get going. See you soon.'

Thank goodness he's gone. There's not much to talk about in the grocery aisle. The price of eggs doesn't fit. Nor do my childhood or school problems. They're Tuesday things.

Meanwhile at school, Maud decides to ignore her duty to move around and talk to kids while we're outside. She prefers the chair on the verandah.

'You don't need a chair, Maud. You'll be walking around talking with kids.'

'I don't do playground duty,' she spits.

'None of us do. We have outside play time. Put the chair away, please.'

Oh, a compromise. She puts the chair away and stands on the verandah. I'm shaking and teary and furious. I can't cope. Maybe when Fiona, our consultant, comes she'll talk about this stuff. I've asked her to.

No, she only visits Peter this time. She must have imparted another of her fabulous ideas, because now Peter's telling us we have to let kids and their parents into our rooms to play before school starts.

'It'll be good for them to spend time together,' he says.

'They live together!' I exclaim. 'And we need to set up. Besides, we are not legally allowed to start our teaching role until nine o'clock.'

Felicity's support is feeble. Alma and Maud are fuming but quiet.

'Oh, don't be ridiculous, Miss Shayler,' Peter spits. He knows what he wants and that is that.

Now, before each class, our rooms are turned to chaos and we need to clean up before we can start orderly teaching sessions. Even Alma, always keen to impress Peter, is wilting.

Thank goodness tomorrow is Tuesday and I can talk about it

all with Tony. I don't know what we'll do in therapy this week. It seems rather bitsy. Not much continuity. It's my fault. I can't do some things Tony thinks I should, and I seem to be too dumb to think things through and sort out what to do with what I've thought about. It feels like I can't let a breeze blow the curtain and let me see my childhood clearly. I'll try harder so Tony can help me. Fix me.

'How have you been?' he asks warmly.

As I tell him about school, he inserts, 'You did well!' and, 'That was good,' and 'Of course. Of course.'

His unreserved praise and understanding keeps me talking, makes me feel respected. I'm telling an objective person what I did and his judgement is that I did well.

'How did it feel this time?'

'Mixed. I like that I challenged Peter, but it's still hard, especially afterwards.'

'It'll get easier as you build a stronger sense of yourself and your achievements.'

'I want it all to just go away. I'm so tired of it.' Teary about my weakness.

'You've made a good start. You've done well to stand up to all of them. Did you practise the relaxation techniques?'

'Sometimes, but I fall asleep. Or forget. I'm just so tired all the time.'

'You can't get the benefit if you don't do the work.'

Please don't get cranky. Please don't think I'm a lazy, bad thing!

'We've talked before about psychoimmunology studies, haven't we? How low energy levels, low T-cell counts too, can be psychological in origin? Right? Suppressing traumatic memories can put incredible strain on those systems.'

He sits quietly and waits. I don't know what for.

'Have you ever looked into your relationship with your father?

253

Below the surface? I think it might be time to explore those memories.'

Oh no. Hold the curtain shut.

But imagine if I got fixed, met a nice man. I could leave work and find something less stressful. Keeping my house wouldn't matter so much or be so hard. Fancy hoping to be rescued by a knight in shining armour at my age! Back to my father.

'No. I haven't thought much about my father or the abuse. Well, I saw someone, just once, years ago. I told you about that.'

'Did you? Tell me again. Sorry, I can't recall.'

I tell him and add, 'But we had a religious difference and couldn't move forward. Anyway, he thought I was okay. I wasn't having problems with the men in my life, men at work and church. I hadn't been in a relationship before; I hadn't done anything to test how my father might have affected me, I suppose.'

'Hm. What was the specific issue that stopped you going further with that psychologist?'

'Well, he was a Christian. That's why I went to him. I thought it was important to work it out with someone whose values were the same as mine.'

'I can assure you that my moral standards are as high as yours,' Tony interrupts. I don't know why he is so defensive. 'I'm not religious but I believe in doing good for people and honesty and so on. What exactly was the problem with the psychologist?'

Now that he has given a potted version of what he thinks a Christian might want to hear, I can answer. 'Well, I'd just met someone, my first relationship, and I felt concerned about sleeping with him but I wanted to too. I didn't know what I'd be getting into – I'd read articles about problems abused children can have when they grow up. I wanted to talk with the psychologist about all that. To see what he thought. But he just said it's wrong.'

'What did you want him to say?'

'Nothing in particular. For him to tell me whether he thought I'd be all right. I wanted him to tell me what to look out for and what to do if anything felt, you know, um, threatening or something.'

'And what was his opinion?'

'Just that it was wrong. It was like a brick wall went up, like in a cartoon, chink, chink, chink. He thought I'd be fine but that it was morally wrong, against Christian teachings. No discussion. But as I was leaving he said he hoped I'd enjoy it if I did sleep with Gareth.'

'And did you?'

'Enjoy it or sleep with him?'

'Both.'

'Yes, I slept with him. I thought that because I was thirty, not young and innocent, it would be all right. AIDS wasn't about then and we knew about contraception. I was curious too. Wanted to find out if I'd be all right.'

'And did you enjoy it?'

Chink chink chink.

'It's private!'

'If we're going to talk about your father and work on relation-ships, we're going to have to talk about some very intimate things.'

'Very intimate things are private and, anyway, they're not all of what relationships are about.' I'm getting angry. Anxious.

'All right. Let's move on. Would you like to tell me about the relationship with, er, Gareth, was it?'

'The relationship. Yes.'

I tell him.

'How do you feel about it all now?'

'I think it was a good decision to end it. Mostly. But when I'm . . .' Chin twitches. Tears begin. 'When I'm lonely, I wish I'd married him. At least I'd have someone. And kids.'

'Maybe it wasn't a match made in Heaven.'

'But he wasn't a bad person or anything. And he wanted a new family. So I would have had babies.' Sobbing. Hadn't expected exposure of this pain.

'You would like to have kids?'

'Mm.' I wipe my eyes, try to stop my tears with humour. 'I was the cluckiest person in the universe. Thought these wretched bosoms were more than just crumb catchers.' Whoops! Wish I hadn't said that.

Tony chuckles, doesn't take it up. He's looking at my card, saying, 'It isn't too late, is it? How old are you? Oh, I see. Still, people your age can have babies.'

'Maybe, but I can't even get myself married.'

'Would you have to? Some people don't think you need to marry to have a child.'

'I think babies should have two parents, especially if one of them is me.'

'Why do you say that?'

'Oh, I don't know if I know how to be a parent. If I turned out to be hopeless at it, the poor baby wouldn't have anyone else if I wasn't married.'

'Why would you be hopeless? You teach little kids all day!'

'Yeah, but I give them back at three o'clock. And I've read that people who weren't parented properly don't necessarily know how to be parents. It wouldn't be fair on a baby to just have me.'

'Hm, it would be a challenge doing it on your own.'

'Anyway, my friend Diedre had a baby at this age and she said your body never recovers. You just have to accept that you'll always be tired and stressed. I'll die if I add more stress to my life.'

'Die! Why die?' he asks, surprised.

'Like my mother. Bad heart genes. Then where would the baby be?' Crying.

I feel foolish sobbing in front of Tony yet again. But it's surprisingly comforting too, to cry when I need to and not be told everything will be all right. It won't be. Not for me having babies. Maybe not for a partner either. I'm still not thin and I'll never be gorgeous and I've got all the other problems too. Ones I have hardly begun to work on.

'I would have been a bloody good mother,' I declare, faking defiance at my fate.

'You would have been a wonderful mum.'

Tony's given me the ultimate compliment! I sit with it. I'm getting more positive feelings for Tony, whether I want them or not. They're okay. They're just 'like' not 'love'. Aren't they?

'You're seeing someone now, aren't you?'

'No, just an ex-boyfriend sometimes. We're just friends.'

'Why is that?'

'It just didn't work out. Ran out of steam. The attraction wore off and it wasn't worth trying to be who he wanted me to be any more.'

'There was something that wore off. For how long?'

'About six months I think but then it became a habit sort of relationship. Better than no-one.'

'You could ask him to come here and we'll see if we can sort it out.'

'No! I mean, he wouldn't come and I wouldn't want him to. I don't want a permanent relationship with him.'

'Tell me about the relationship.'

I tell him and finish with, 'So I stopped trying.'

'Trying what?'

'To make him like me enough to marry. To be who he wanted me to be. But I hadn't realised I'd been doing that while I was seeing him. It wasn't all his fault. But he didn't put much effort into making it nice or romantic.' I feel silly talking about romance. It doesn't seem to suit a person like me.

'Sex was no good with him?'

'Not especially.' Oh Lord, that again.

'There, that wasn't so hard to tell, was it? Was it good with the other man?'

Chink, chink, chink.

Why do you always bring it down to bloody sex? What about all the other stuff in relationships? Surely that's just as important.

'It was good, if you must know. And private,' I say quietly. 'And I just don't see the point of talking about it. It was fine.'

'All right. All right. We'll move on. You have a lot of stress right now. Let's look at options for changing your circumstances.'

'I have no options. I'm trapped with a mortgage.'

'You could leave work and do something less stressful,' he suggests. 'What about lecturing or tutoring?'

We talk it through again and get the same result. He thinks I could. I don't consider it because I can't afford to stop work and study full time. Part time study seems too exhausting. I nearly nod off just thinking about it. His next question brings me back with a jolt.

'I'm wondering if you could talk about your father now. Have you remembered any more about him?'

'Yes. Some.'

'All right. Will you tell me what you've remembered?'

Ease the window up slowly. Curtain only just shifting.

'Well, as I said before, he was always turning up with a string bag of goodies when we were little,' I say, knowing I'm repeating myself but struggling with that window. 'He brought Minties, you know, the boxes with jokes on them? He made sure we knew what the joke was and had a laugh. He was the only person we laughed with by then.' Good grief. I'm getting teary talking about the happy times. 'We sat on his lap and he sang to us and clapped our hands on his and measured them. He was so . . . good.' Crying. Ambivalent about that window. 'Can we leave this? Do it next time or something?'

'If you like. But if you can give this adult expression you can be free of the pain.'

Open the window. Just a little more. Don't be afraid. You can slam it shut if you want to.

'Well, um . . . the earliest thing is the scary stuff. It's just a small memory, when he was . . . he . . .'

Curtain drifting. Can't say the words.

'All right. How old were you?'

'Four or five. I could only see the side of the bed. Not the top.'
Heart beating faster. Curtain drifting up in the breeze.

'The bed where it happened?'

'I suppose it must be. In his bedroom.' I'm frightened, like
there's a demon waiting to stick knives in me. Heart beating too
fast. Try to see something less threatening behind the curtain. 'He
only missed one visit in the twelve years I lived there.'

'Can you go back a bit? Tell me more about the bedroom.'

Back to the demon! Quick, slam the window shut. Heart
racing again. Breathing hard.

'I can't.' Voice squeaking.

'I know it's difficult but will you try?'

Crying. Screaming inside. Big breath.

'If you can go back, face those memories, you'll be free of
the pain.'

He wants to open the window right up! No! 'Everything about
him seems like pain now. Not just his death.'

'When did he die?'

'Nineteen sixty-seven, when I was seventeen.'

'And that was painful.'

'Mm. I was heartbroken because I thought the only person
who loved me, who would ever love me, was dead. It was so
lonely.' Crying. 'He was good and bad. Both. He did love us.
Women's rights people seem to say abusers are completely bad,
but they aren't. Well Da – . . . my father wasn't, not completely.'

'All right. It's all right. Thank you for sharing that very sad part
of your life with me.' He waits a while, then says, 'We'll leave it
for today. All right?' His habit of ending sentences with a gentle
'all right?' is becoming a trigger that calms me, makes me feel
I have some control. 'During the week, I want you to think about
talking about your more difficult memories, giving them adult
expression. Verbalising those events that happened when you
were in the pre-verbal stage. You need to process them as an adult
and not just keep them as childhood pain. All right?'

'Mm.'

'Have we talked about age regression hypnosis?'

'Don't know.' I'm busy locking the window.

'Look, we'll leave that today, I think. How about we do a relaxation exercise?'

He invites me to feel relaxation moving through my feet, into my legs, all the way up until my eyes feel like they are floating. I walk beside a stream, calm and peaceful before he calls me back to where I've been sitting all along.

As I leave he gives me a tape he's made for me of the script he uses in relaxation. He wants me to use it at home as well. I'm grateful but I leave feeling confused about how therapy or counselling or whatever it is is going. I'm ashamed that I couldn't just talk about stuff and get it over with. How am I going to progress if I just wimp out every time it gets a bit challenging? Tony is kind and patient. How does he do it? I'm feeling much more positive about him now. He's caring when he pushes me to try difficult things. He's doing it because he wants to help. Because he cares. He said I might develop strong positive feelings for him. Are my feelings strong? No. They're just positive. Quite positive. But they are not love. Are they?

Later, in my journal I record that I don't want the feelings for him to be strong. I just want therapy. Falling in love would be futile. It wouldn't be reciprocated and couldn't go anywhere. Except, of course, that Tony said he could use the feelings to help me. That would make things so complicated, and they're complicated enough already with all the bits I'm trying to deal with. And I don't want to be a silly frustrated spinster in love with her therapist. I'll keep resisting if I think the feelings are getting stronger. Keep them out of the way. It's odd that I found him physically unattractive when I met him. Now, if I imagine being held – no stop. It is not appropriate.

Therapy feels piecemeal but there are rewards. Like coming to understand that I'm still a worthwhile professional who might be intelligent enough to do a Masters degree. And getting more assertive at work, though I still have a long way to go with that.

Talking about Gareth and Elliott confirmed that I'd made good decisions about them. Tony's comment that I present myself well and look fine gives me confidence. I rarely hear affirming comments like those, except from friends, who are biased. And it's so good to have someone to talk to, an objective person to debrief with every week, to help me offload the top layers of stress. Maybe talking about childhood, although it makes me anxious, might let me see things about the past that would be rewarding too. It's nice to remember the fun things with Da– . . . my father.

A downside of therapy, apart from the window and confusion about feelings, is the money. If Harry ever turns up, that will take the pressure off. Maybe I could go to Tony fortnightly. Sessions come up so quickly, before I've had time to think things through. Am I now just trying to find excuses for not doing what he says? I have to admit that's a big part of it.

By Saturday night I'm too tired to drive to Sydney for the dance I'd planned to go to. I ring Geoff, an old dancing friend, to tell him I won't be coming. He'll miss me, he says, but is looking forward to the house warming and wishes I'd set a date for it.

'I'll have it in the school hols,' I tell him. 'Can't do it during term. I'm too knackered.'

I stay home. Lonely. Lonelier when I think of all those people down there dancing. I try to relax by listening to Tony's tape. It starts off well but I drift off, come back. '. . . you will feel calm but even if.' What does that mean? Press rewind. Listen again. '. . . you will feel calm but even if. When you need to hear . . .' That's not a sentence. Oh well, listen and hope the voice calms me.

I fall asleep easily. I'm walking down a sunny path at Nanna's house, relaxed and happy. Suddenly the wolf leaps at my throat and the world turns black. The wolf's teeth hold me and we struggle to kill and not be killed. Our eyes meet, up very close, and in those dark pools I see love and deep, deep sorrow. I hate the wolf and love him in the same moment. Love makes me feel loathing for what fear and hatred are making me do. I'm holding his jaws and tearing his beautiful head apart. His blood oozes down my hands. I sob and keep tearing.

I wake terrified, profoundly sad.

I know who the wolf is.

I have to think about my father clearly and honestly. I have to pull the curtain away and look, not just peep.

Not now. Need to relax and sleep. Remember Nanna and the blue velvet dress. I was a princess then.

In the pool on Monday morning I don't do all my laps. I'm tired and I'll have to face the chaos in my room again.

Today there's a surprise for me at lunchtime. Alma admits that she's wilting under the strain of early entry of parents and kids into our classrooms, and grumbles about the chaos.

'I'm going to tell Peter I can't keep doing it,' I tell them all. 'Can I tell him you all feel the same?'

'Sure,' Alma says. The others agree.

Peter appears next morning to see if what I've told him is true. He asks Felicity and Alma what they think and they tell him. He agrees that we can stop.

I feel I've won but why did it have to come down to a contest? Because Peter can't admit there are things he doesn't know and because he has no respect for my experience and knowledge, the capability that Tony has taught me to be proud of. I wish he could teach Peter.

When the *Blue Mountains Gazette* arrives I scan the Public Notices for something local that will get me out on weekends. I need to laugh again and be social. There are ads for various kinds of dancing. Balkan. I like that style of group dancing and I wouldn't need a partner. They'll probably be women but that's all right. I ring but there's no answer. Will I try the ballroom dancing one on the off-chance that there'll be a spare man or two floating about? Might as well. Might be better than staying home.

'We have an instruction session first and then a social dance.

Yes, there'll be plenty of people. You'll find a partner,' Walter, the organiser, tells me.

In the hall there are two women in their sixties and an elderly man. I introduce myself.

'Oh good. You came,' the man says. 'I'm Walter. Sit down and we'll start in a few moments.'

The two ladies dance together so I can watch them and then Walter asks me to dance. He talks the steps through as we go. Soon I'm enjoying a jazz waltz and not making too many mistakes, though Walter tells me I'm too stiff and I need to relax into it. When the dance ends there are still only the four of us.

Now it's time for Nancy to have a turn with Walter. Mary is too tired to dance again so we sit and watch. Four more ladies arrive and they dance with each other when it's not their turn with Walter the Tireless. Next I try to learn the foxtrot with one of the ladies but we decide that watching Walter and his partner might be more helpful.

'And now let's break for supper,' Walter suggests.

I'm glad. Now I can leave.

'Thank you, Walter. I'll be off now.'

'You can't go yet!' he declares as if I've offended him to the core. 'You have to stay for the social dance. You can't just come for lessons.'

'Oh! Well, uh, I didn't know that.'

He moves around so that he blocks the doorway! 'Just have some supper and then we'll start the dance.'

I don't know what to say to make escape possible.

'He does like us all to stay for the whole night,' Mary says, smiling sweetly. 'He's such a wonderful man!'

'We need a few more wonderful men, though, don't we?' I smile back.

'Oh, it would be good. But we do all right,' she says.

So this is it apparently. A social dance with one man to share himself around the now ten or so ladies. I have to think of an escape clause. What would Gen or Diedre do?

'Walter, I'm sorry, but I really have to go.'

'No. You come for the whole night,' he insists.

'Sorry, but I told the babysitter I'd be home by ten,' I blurt out and walk out quickly, trying not to giggle before I'm in the car.

So much for ballroom dancing.

Elliott rings next morning and says he tried to ring me last night.

'I went dancing. Ballroom,' I tell him, deliberately not offering more. I want to see if he cares about my possibly meeting someone else.

'Oh. Well anyway, I've been thinking – you know how we used to talk about going to the Kimberley? I just wondered if you're still interested.'

'When?' I have longed to go to the Red Centre and beyond since Miss Driver, a matron at Burnside and later at the hostel I lived in, showed us her slides. I had never imagined anything as beautiful but here is my chance to see it. Red earth, vast blue sky and that rock!

'Next year. Mid year would be best, when the days aren't too hot.'

'I'd love to go! Who'll be going?'

'Just you and me at the moment. Some others might decide later. Anyway, think about it and let me know. Just wanted to put the idea in your head for now.'

The idea sits happily in my head until I remember I'm supposed to be doing my degree and growing a bigger ego next year. And what if Elliott's mountaineering friends come? I'll be expected to match their stamina! But if it's just the two of us, it might be nice, as long as Elliott remembers I'm a lady, not a man. Or a woman.

REAL CARING

Saturday-morning bliss. Brewed coffee on the verandah, mist swirling gently in the gully. Reading the paper. What? The government wants to encourage women to keep working until they are sixty-five rather than sixty. Bliss fades. Sixty-five! Hells bells! I'll be flat out making it to fifty-five at the rate I'm going. Time to turn to the Masters information. If I have to work for twenty-seven more years, I've got to get out of teaching. But I like teaching. It's all the other nonsense that spoils it.

Reading through the course list, feeling inadequate. You need a postgraduate degree to sort out your postgraduate courses. I ring Gen and we chuckle over memories of trying to sort out our undergraduate courses.

'Pancakes, honey and lemon juice,' she reminds me.

'Ah, we were slim and gorgeous then,' I reply.

'You're fine,' she asserts. 'Just get out and have some fun.'

'Back to Walter's harem! Can't. Got to get my school program done,' I tell her. 'Then sort my uni courses.'

'Then get out there after they're done. Did the boarder move in?'

'No. I don't think he's going to either so I've put the ad in again.'

'I'm so relieved! Paddy and I talked about it and we were worried about a strange man moving in.'

'He wasn't strange. He seemed quite nice.'

'Yeah, but if he turned out not to be what he seemed, well, you're a long way away. Don't get a man in next time. Please. Get a woman.'

'Well, I have to get someone. It was going to be nice to have another person around not to mention the board money helping to pay the mortgage.'

'You've got to go out more. Yeah, I know it's all families out there but there must be something.'

'There's a singles party on every Saturday.'

'Oh no! No. Kate. You are not that desperate. Come to us for the weekend. Play with your godchildren, clean our windows, flea the cat. Anything but that!'

'Now now, Gen. You know very well Prince Charming might be there waiting just for me. Oh, I'll probably chicken out and not go, but honestly, that seems to be all there is for singles here, apart from staying home or going to movies by yourself.'

'Get a woman boarder. We'll all feel safer and you can go to things together.'

'Ducky! A pair of old ducks creaking along to wild parties. Or bridge nights perhaps?'

But she's right. I would feel safer with a woman boarder and I should get out and have some fun. I work hard on my program and fall asleep. I wake up too late to go anywhere. Oh well, I will brace myself and try the singles party next Saturday. Wish I was looking forward to it rather than feeling like it's a punishment.

Friends in Sydney gave me the name of a person to contact for home churches here. But I don't feel I have much to offer right now; I'll ring when I'm more sorted out. God's here anyway, not just at church. I just need to remember to pray. Help me to know how to change what I do at work so they'll come to like me. Help me be brave enough to do what needs to be done in therapy. Help me to be who You want me to be.

Therapy. Where is it going? Tony says to notice what I'm feeling as stressful things happen, but at work my head is so full of work that noticing anything else is impossible. I think that's what he said. I'll try to write down what we do in therapy more thoroughly, straight after each session instead of the next day. I'm looking forward to seeing Tony more than I'd like to be these days. Must try to sort out my muddle of feelings for him.

As I drive to my session I debate whether or not to talk about those feelings with him. He said earlier that I should so we can use them, and that they'd resolve by the end of therapy. But why let them develop if they're going to be over anyway? I don't want to talk about the feelings; I'm embarrassed and confused about them. Tony would be pleased if I did do it, though. That'd be good.

Good grief. Now I'm looking for his approval!

I won't tell him. It'll get in the way of the important stuff. Surely it's normal to want approval from the person who's leading you into scary new territory and helping you reconstruct your view of yourself.

'Good to see you,' he says warmly as he opens the door and lets me in.

'Good to see you too.'

He's keen to know how my plans for study are going and he's not so pleased when I talk about the possibility of taking long service leave to travel with Elliott instead.

'But you don't want a relationship with this man. It's important for you to get your Masters. Get on with your life.'

But I want friends and Elliott is that. Can't I have men who are just friends?

Tony offers to give me the names of people in the faculty to contact about enrolment at uni. I don't know why I need them. We just turned up with thousands of others for our undergraduate enrolment, so I suppose it'll be the same this time. Tony is just trying to be helpful. He seems to be showing off a bit about his membership in the postgrad club too. I wonder if I'll feel that proud when my degree is done.

'And work? How has that been?' he asks.

'The usual but at least we don't have that stupid chaos every morning. I'm just so tired of it all.'

'It must be hard for you without family support. Most people can call on someone.'

'I can call on friends.' I want to defend my friends. It's not for want of invitations to ring them that I sit at home feeling lonely. 'Leonie and Col, Gen and Paddy, Diedre and the others. They all say to ring anytime.'

'Not the same, though, is it?'

'I don't know. Don't know what it's like having a family on tap. Is it different to friendships?'

'It's different,' he says.

'Well, I can't get a family, so I just have to cope.' Burning eyes again.

'I'm here for you. I'll help you,' Tony says quietly and deliberately. 'All right?'

'Wish someone out there would say that. A man, for example,' I say, trying to lighten up.

'You just never know who you're going to meet next year. You'll meet a lot of people, maybe a special man worthy of you. But I'm here for you in the meantime.'

'Thanks. But, well, that's not real, though. Not what I meant.'

'What do you mean it's not real?'

'Well, it's constructed. A Tuesday thing. A business deal that will be over when we finish. I mean, it's not a real relationship like the ones that happen out there. I meant I wish a real one would happen. Out there.'

'You think this is not real caring?' he asks with a frown.

'Yes,' I say slowly. I might have offended him. Better explain. 'Well, it can't be real. I mean, if you had to really care about your patients, you'd sort of run out of caring, wouldn't you? We'd all

268

just be taking and you'd always be giving and you'd get too drained or however you express it.'

'Look,' he says assertively. 'This is real. I care about you very much. It's not something I switch on and off like a light. It is real.' He is offended. 'And no, I don't run out of caring, as you put it,' he says more gently. 'I get a lot back from patients who give too, who share their lives, make gains, move ahead. That's very satisfying. I do other things to look after myself too, but what happens here is real.'

I don't know what to say. How can my coming, grumbling and crying give him anything? Well, I give him money but he has to listen, advise, probe, encourage. How could it be more than a Tuesday thing that he forgets about when I go home? I want his caring for me to be real, though. I wish I didn't feel that way, but I do. And I hope my progress gives him something back.

He's talking about transference again. Feelings of closeness develop as people share. I mustn't resist the feelings that arise, because it will stop us working through the issues. I need to trust him and go with my feelings, talk about them and work them through. It's good that I said what I did, because it shows him more about the relationship that's developing between us.

'So, you're not offended?'

'Nothing you say here will offend me. You don't have to worry about my feelings. You just have to remember to tell me what feelings are developing, so we can work with them. All right?'

'All right.' I take a deep breath and say very quickly, 'Then I should tell you that I, um, like you a lot and I want your approval.'

'Thank you for sharing that,' he says, smiling oddly. I don't know what the smile means. It doesn't seem to match the words. 'That's good. Anything else?'

'I want your caring to be real, not just a Tuesday thing. I want to matter to you, but I'm not comfortable with it.'

'You do matter to me. I admire and respect what you've done, what you've been through and how you're managing these very difficult tasks.'

I want to cry again at the reality of being cared for by someone who I've been an absolute sook in front of, who knows how stupid and inadequate I feel and who knows some of my dark secrets. He knows more about me than any of my friends do but he still cares. It's comforting. Affirming. Makes me feel close to him. Is that love? I don't know.

'It doesn't feel comfortable.'

'How does it feel?'

'Sort of . . . embarrassing.'

'There is nothing to be embarrassed about. These feelings are quite normal. I'm glad you told me. I think you're beginning to trust me.'

'I think I am.'

'All right. I've been thinking during the week about how so many of your childhood memories are small glimpses. Have we talked about age regression hypnosis?'

'I think so. You've talked about hypnosis a few times.'

'Age regression hypnosis uses a similar technique but it's not the same. Using age regression hypnosis I would take you into a deeper trance and guide you back to your childhood. You'll experience being the child . . .'

He keeps talking but my heart starts racing. I hear words like 'hypnotisability', 'abreaction', 'directing'. Fear churns in my stomach. He's trying to pull that window right open and I'm trying to hold it shut.

Be sensible, Kate. Let it open a tiny bit. Just a tiny bit.

Concentrate on what he's saying. 'So we could try that as a way of speeding up the process.'

'When you made me remember that little girl before, it was terrible.'

'Yes, there will be some pain but you are stronger now. You'll use your adult cognition to process the memory. I think it's what you need to do to be free of ambiguous relationships and able to express your full potential.'

'That part sounds good.'

'Think about it. We don't have to do it today. If we decide to take that route, you'll need to try to recall as much detail as you can so that I can use it in hypnosis. All right? Good. Now, you've told me you remember some of your childhood. Tell me about that?'

'About my father?'

'Yes, all right,' he says quietly. 'Tell me more about your dad.'

Don't call him that!

Hard to talk about him when I'm feeling so angry with him. Start somewhere easy. Peep behind the curtain. Sneak up on the horrible stuff. 'His hands were huge and leathery. Um. He was old. His back was bent. His hair was white, white and wiry. He liked jokes. The matrons said he was good and had nice English manners.'

'You didn't think so, though?'

'When we stayed at Burnside for his visits, he did. He was charming. It was only when we were at home that he was . . . bad.'

'He stole your childhood.'

'Yes.' I think that was meant to jolt but it doesn't. I've read about the stolen childhoods of Aboriginal people but I'm numb to the words when they're applied to me.

'You told me you went to live with him when you left Burnside. Is that right?'

'Yes.'

'How was that?'

'Dreadful. He tried to abuse me again.'

'Tried to?'

'Yes, but I was big and strong and I could push him away. He was small and frail by then. I'd lie in bed at night listening for his footsteps and praying that I'd remembered to lock the door, then praying that he didn't have a key, then praying that he'd go away.'

Tony waits.

'Sometimes he called me to come and open the door and say goodnight. "Properly", he called it. That's when I pushed him.'

271

'I see. A good strategy.'

'But I felt so guilty being horrible to him. And ashamed. I was always frightened of being alone with him but I felt sad that he was so frail and old and lonely. I had to make him happy. Keep him alive. I was very mixed up.' Crying. Feeling ashamed. Worthless.

'You felt guilty?'

'Yes. Ashamed.'

Tony waits, then asks, 'Can you see what's wrong here?'

'What?'

'You have to stop your father abusing you. You feel guilt and shame.'

'Oh, I know. I've talked about the shame thing with Leonie and Col and they made me see it's inappropriate. But I was talking about back then, when it happened. I was so confused. That's all I remember about my feelings. Confusion and shame. Fear too. Wish I'd had friends like I've got now.'

'They sound like special people.'

'They are. I'm lucky that way. Burnside always told us we were lucky to have our father. They told us he was so good and we should be proud of him. They said we were his reason for living. So I thought I had to make him want to live.'

I wonder about what would have happened if I'd found the words to tell on him. Then it dawns on me, 'I thought he'd die if I upset him.'

'When did he die?'

'Soon after I left home, left him.' Grief at his passing makes me cry. And grief about his life too.

'How old was he?'

'Seventy-eight.'

'He was seventy-eight! Was it your fault he died?'

It hits me like a ton of bricks: I've always thought, deep inside, that my leaving home made him die. I remember Kerry shouting it at me after the funeral when we were both grieving. I've always known in my head that he died because he was old, but somewhere else I've known he died because I was such a cruel disappointment to him.

'Kate, was it your fault?'

'No.' Tears of utter relief roll out.

'You've done well,' Tony tells me gently.

The session ends and I go home intending to keep my promise to write up what happened in therapy straight away.

What if I get free of my childhood pain? I only feel the pain if I think about it, so if I don't think about . . . no. Tony knows what he's doing, what I need to do. So, what if I get free? Can't imagine it. What if I become someone I don't know? I know who I am like this. It isn't easy but I'm coping. Aren't I? What if I get free but I'm so unattractive nobody wants to know me anyway? What if I meet someone but I'm just no good at relationships anyway? There'll be no hope then. At least now there's hope. Hang on, though. What if I met someone and it did work out! What then, eh? What if I just go to sleep now.

I fall asleep but wake up when something opens the window where my childhood hides. I've had a glimpse behind the curtain and now I'm conscious of two memories. How could I have forgotten them so completely? They disturb me. Wish Tony was here so I could tell him. I should write them down. Right now. Write now. Okay, where's the pen.

How could I have forgotten these things so thoroughly? There are two and I used to know them. They hurt and I'm so angry I don't know if I can bear it.

I can't write them. It'd make it too real and harder to forget. Can't write words. Anyway, I'd die if anyone ever read them.

What if the words dissolve the curtain and those terrible, disgusting things are completely exposed? I need that curtain.

Disappointed in myself. I'm hopeless. Wish I could talk to Tony but it's midnight. Better try to sleep. Too angry to sleep. Angry at my father for what he made that little girl do. She didn't know she was allowed to say 'no' to him. No. I didn't know I was allowed to say 'no'. For hours the curtain drifts away and back. Wish Tony was here so I could tell him. Tell him next time. Must get to sleep. Wish I didn't need him so much. Wish I didn't feel so positive about him.

It's Saturday. I must have got to sleep. Time to get out and have some fun, as Gen said. Put all that away and get out. Go to the singles party no matter what. I ring the number in their ad.

'Yes, it's open to anyone. It starts at eight and you're expected to arrive on time. If you come later than eight thirty you won't be let in, and you have to stay until at least ten thirty.'

Drat. No getting there fashionably late and no escaping early if it's not my cup of tea. Oh well, they can't make me stay.

I've had a note beside the phone for weeks reminding me to ring the cemetery to find out where my mother's grave is. I do it quickly and get the address as if I've just asked the location of the eggs in a supermarket. I leave the note beside the phone and start ironing something to wear to the party before soaking in a hot bath and getting ready to go.

I arrive at the house at eight thirty on the dot. The door is opened by a rotund man who sweeps his arm gallantly as he says, 'A new woman. Do come in.'

The room might have wallpaper but you'd never know. It's lined with men whose purpose seems to be to inspect and mentally label each woman who walks in, possibly so they'll not bother with some of us later. I walk to the table to pay, cursing my inability to think of a witty comment to let them know how offensive that is. Their smutty leers are so indiscreet and repulsive. Why do they think it's okay to do it? Will I make it to ten thirty or will they issue me with a nun's habit and send me home right now? I'll take the habit! Or are the real men out the back?

No, all the women who've run the gauntlet are out here. One welcomes me and does the introductions. At least I've learnt how to join in conversations: recipes, divorce, what's right and wrong with one-night stands and what's happened in the daytime soapies. When they talk about kids I join in using the ones I teach as examples. For their childbirth stories I stay quiet. Can't pretend to be in that club.

At last we're called outside for the barbecue. The noise level rises as the men join in and then it drops again as people sit in little groups to eat. I sit with a lady who, when she hears that I'm a teacher, wants me to solve all the problems she's having with her children on access visits with their father. I don't mind telling her what I think, but when we're still on the same topic after desert, I've had enough. I'm not as good at this as I thought I'd be. It's only ten o'clock.

'Hello, darlin'. Where've you been all night?' a nice-looking drunk asks as I walk through to get my bag.

'Excuse me. I want to get my bag.'

'Whatcha wancha bag for?' His breath is enough to put me over the legal limit.

'I'm going home.'

'Can I come?'

I keep walking.

'I'm going now,' I tell the hostess. 'I've got a longer drive home than I realised. Thanks for having me.'

'Going!' says the man who let me in. 'You can't go yet.'

'I'm going. Thanks for having me.'

'Oh, you haven't been had already, have you?'

I give him my icy glare.

'Oh. Well, you have to stay 'til ten thirty. That's the deal.'

'Look, I'm really tired. I've got a long way to drive and I'm going.'

'You agreed to stay 'til ten thirty. Everybody does. That's when things really hot up,' he adds with a wink.

Do I have to spell it out? This is not my idea of a good night. I'm bored stiff, barely able to stay awake and repelled by tiny, one-track minds.

'Stay for coffee at least,' the hostess says.

I don't want to offend her so I stay for coffee. As soon as I see a chance I leave without saying anything to anybody except, 'Excuse me,' to the man who's still propped in the doorway, refusing to move, forcing people to squeeze past him. Some women obviously don't mind. I'm a freak, a prude and I don't mind if that's how they see me. Saturday nights at home alone are looking brighter.

Sunday with Gen's family is wholesome. We laugh about my Saturday night adventure but Gen is concerned too. I shouldn't take such risks.

'You don't need a social club,' Gen says.

'So I found. Well, better go home and see if that door-holder-upper is ringing to take me away from it all. Or will I just get ready for school?'

Maud has Mondayitis again. She sits on a table.

'Maud, I need you outside, thanks. You're on sandpit today.'

'I'm not paid to play in the sand!'

'You're paid to settle kids in to play. Come outside, please.'

'I'm paid to assist you with preparing things. And you can't deny it. I went to Peter after your little whinge and that's what he said.' Nostrils flair. Blotchy semaphore stays on the table.

'Then you're both wrong,' I tell Maud quietly. 'You're paid for six hours' work. Come outside.'

Blotchy, fuming semaphore goes to the sandpit.

'About this morning,' Maud says after school, 'I shouldn't have said that.' She's red and contrite.

'No. You shouldn't have.'

'Yeah, well, can we talk about it?'

'We have talked about it. Nothing changes.' She doesn't speak. 'You've read your duty statement, haven't you?'

'Yeah.'

'So you know what you're paid for?'

'Yeah.'

'Good. That's all I want you to do. If you don't, I'll just have to whinge to Peter again.'

She looks stunned.

'I've got things to do now. I'm going home. Goodbye.'

I stayed calm! Didn't crumble. Once I would have.

Tuesday tomorrow. I'd better try to get ready. Let the curtain drift and find words for the ugliness behind it.

My father. Anger boils my blood again. I'm trying not to hate him. Christians aren't supposed to hate people. But what about those dark violations? Didn't he earn some hatred? But I want to balance it with love. He deserved that too. Didn't he?

It's just as well I don't have a boarder. I can sob when I want to. Some people I know have been to counselling where they have to talk to pillows, pretending they are people they need to say, or shout things to. The cushions on my lounge halfheartedly put their hands up as volunteers but I feel too silly talking to them. Hands down. And thanks anyway. How am I going to get to sleep with this seething through me? Write it in my journal.

My bloody father. You wasted thirty-eight years of my life. You loved me! Just as well you didn't hate me. What would you have done then! Heaven help me for having loved you, you bastard.

Can't see. Dry my eyes. Blow nose. Ask myself who this lady is who writes words like bastard for her father.

I hate you just now. Hear that? I hate you. I could have been normal, had babies and a family if you hadn't made me so scared. I hate you for taking that away from me. Hate you for making me hate you. Why couldn't you have just loved me like a normal father and left me to be a normal person?

Dry my eyes. Blow nose.

Well, I'm taking control now. I'm not letting you take the rest of my life. I'm going to do that thing with Tony tomorrow and get free of what you left me with.

Tony. Wish I didn't need him and feel so fond of him. I don't like it and I don't like spending so much energy resisting the feelings. What's the use of going along with them and letting them be love? He wouldn't love me back. I'm so damaged and plain. No use playing around with love feelings just in therapy.

I date the entry. November already. Another month gone and the end of the year not far away. Just as well I've accepted I won't have children. Don't have to notice months and years passing. Can't fool myself for long. I notice and I cry. At last I sleep.

Tony welcomes me in with his arm around my shoulder. I feel small this close to him but I like the protected feeling it gives me. I wish I didn't. I'm getting confused and anxious. Oh, don't be silly! He's just showing he cares, confirming what he said about his caring being real.

'How's your week been?' he asks.

'Interesting. School feels safer.' I talk about that and end with, 'I didn't do my usual be nice if Maud's being nice. I just stayed cool.'

'Good. You're getting stronger.'

Suddenly I'm wilting. 'I'm sick of having to cope with everything and be responsible for every little thing that happens around me and keep on coping. I'm tired of it all. It's too much to . . . Sorry,' I say. Take a deep breath.

'There's no need to be sorry. You don't have to be strong here. If you want to be small, you can.'

The relief of being given permission not to be strong is huge. I cry.

'That's it. Let it all out,' Tony says gently, then he sits quietly waiting.

I pull myself together. Fancy having a tantrum at my age!

'You are strong,' Tony says quietly and firmly. 'You've got a lot to cope with just now but you are strong.'

'At work I'm strong. Sometimes. But at home I'm . . . depressed.' Chin crinkles, eyes burn. 'I just don't feel strong.'

'You are strong. All right? You've achieved by yourself what the women's lib people have only just started talking about,' he reminds me.

Warmed by approval.

'I rang the cemetery during the week. I got an address for my mother's grave,' I tell him, avoiding the big stuff behind the curtain. 'I might go in the holidays.'

'That's great. Do you want me to go with you?'

'No. No thanks. I'll be right.' The suggestion still seems odd but less so.

'I once had a very moving experience at a grave and you may well do the same. Think about whether you might need support and ring me if you change your mind. All right?'

'All right. Thanks.'

He talks again about the importance of grieving and I still can't see the need when I don't feel anything at all for my mother.

'Did you think about age regression hypnosis?'

'Yes,' I say hesitantly. 'I'd like to try it, to get free, but I'm scared. You want me to tell you the memories, don't you?'

'It would be useful. I could use those to guide you when you're in the hypnotic trance.'

'I know what you said about stopping at any time and all that but I'm frightened too. Don't want more pain.'

'Think about this. Grief and fear are different things. All right?'

'Yes.' So?

We both wait.

'Well, I believe that you might confuse the two. When you remember trauma, you cry. You think it's fear and you back away. You block it. What if it's grief you're feeling, not fear?'

'Grieving isn't easier than fearing.'

'Grieving can be a release,' he tells me. Fear makes me hide and suppress memory instead of dealing with it and letting it go. Both need to be dealt with, of course, but differently. Maybe it's grief I feel, not fear, in which case I need to do the grieving, release it and move on.

Wow! That makes sense. Is it fear or grief that stops me pulling back the curtain, flinging the window open, looking closely? Fear.

'All right?'

'I think so.'

'Will you tell me the memories you've had?'

'All right.'

He waits.

'It's hard.'

He waits.

I take a deep breath. This is it. 'He said it was . . . was . . . He said it was . . .' Can't squeeze the words out. Squeeze the breath out.

'Take your time. He said it was?'

'It was . . . He said it was . . .' Breathe. Can't breathe. 'Saidit's-calledJock.' Said fast. Isn't really said. Curtain still there. Closed.

'I see. He said that . . .'

No! Don't say it! Don't.

He doesn't. He waits.

Heart's pounding. Said words. Foul words. Fast, but said.

'Thank you for telling me that. I know it was hard for you. You did well. We can build on this.'

No! Don't build on it! Hide it away again behind the . . .

Have to move on. Free of fear.

'Can you tell me the other memory?'

'I told you the easier one. The next one is . . . so . . . awful.' Squeaking, little words. Words behind the curtain. Far away.

'Just take your time. This is important.'

'Well, I remember him saying . . . saying . . . I can't say it.'

Waiting. Curtain shifting.

'The voice said "Oh . . ." It said "Oh . . ." Tears burning. Deep breath. Blow out the words, "Oh, Katie, Katie."'

'Whose voice was it?'

'Father's.' Vile words. Loathsome. Go back behind the curtain.

'It's all right. You've done well.'

Pull the curtain shut. Make it heavy brocade. No-one must ever say those words. People do but they mustn't say them to me. Ever.

Waiting. Curtain settling. Breathing slowing. Coming back to Kate. Big Kate. Shaken by little words.

I sneak a look at my watch. Oh no! There's still lots of my hour left.

'Thank you. You've shared some very important memories today and we can use them to get you moving forward, get you free from that pain and fear. You've seen that nothing bad happens when you talk about these things, haven't you?'

'Mm. But it's so . . . hard.'

'I won't pretend it isn't hard work, but I think you're ready, strong enough. All right?'

I agree and he tells me about the process he'll use. He has to check out my hypnotisability and he describes a test he'll do.

'I'll just lift my arm?'

'Yes. It won't be voluntary. It'll just happen when I suggest it. People describe it as floating. It shows me that you're in a trance, an altered state of consciousness, and ready for the next stage. Remember you can stop it at any time. All right?'

'All right.' Might as well get it over with.

'Good. That's good. Now get comfortable. Lean back. All right?'

Once I couldn't do this. Progress!

'If you're wearing anything tight you should loosen it. Your watch? Belt? Shoes?'

'They're okay.'

'Glasses off. Oh, you look quite different without them.'

'You look different without them too. You're a blur.' This time joking doesn't quite work to relieve my tension.

Tony chuckles. 'Have you thought about contact lenses?'

'You sound like the person ages ago who told me I look almost human without my specs.'

'No. You look fine either way. I meant for the convenience. And there are some theorists who argue that glasses are a barrier between you and other people.'

'Yeah, I've heard that but I think it's nonsense. I feel me in glasses. I was born with them so they don't bother me.' I settle myself.

'Let's move on. All right?'

'Yes.'

He goes through the same things we've done in relaxation before but all the 'what ifs' start creeping into my head. What if it's too horrible? What if I can't cope when there's no curtain to hide . . . ?

'Put all other thoughts out of your mind and concentrate on my voice.'

He can see into my head! I concentrate on his voice. I feel the relaxation move up each leg from my feet, up each arm from my fingers, across my body into my diaphragm, and into my face. I stay relaxed, listening, listening. Wandering beside a cool mountain stream, feet glide easily over the rich green moss and rocks. Listen to birds, to leaves gently stirring high above. Completely free of all worries, keep wandering without getting tired. Drifting along, Tony talking about being able to face whatever happens calmly and maturely. All right, but I'm just going to keep wandering . . .

' . . . your arm will float up . . .'

I know this bit. Nothing is happening.

'Kate, focus on my voice. Your arm will float up.'

No floating.

'Focus on my voice, Kate.'

I am. I am.

' . . . and now your arm will float up off the chair . . .'

My arm stays put.

'Your arm will float up, up . . .'

He sounds angry. I'm worried. Confused. Am I supposed to lift my arm? Isn't it supposed to go up without my doing anything? I'm agitated because he's angry. What will happen if my arm won't do what he tells it? I'm frightened. What did he say to do if I wanted to stop?

'It's all right. Just relax. Relax. Breathe deeply. Concentrate on my voice. You are in control.'

Safe again. I'm in control.

Concentrate on breathing, relaxing the muscles in my legs and so on and on to the muscles in my face. '. . . now feel your arm float up . . .'

I don't want him to be angry again but my arm stays flopped on the chair beside me.

'Kate, feel your arm float up . . .'

It's not floating. My arm's not floating. What if I just lift it? He won't be angry then. I lift my arm just a millimetre. It's floating! I'm not doing it! It's floating by itself, as if I gave it permission and up it went!

'Good. Put your arm slowly down now and concentrate on my voice . . . counting back now. Three. Starting to wake. Two. Waking more. And, one. Wide awake now. Open your eyes. Breathe deeply.'

It's too much of an effort to open my eyes.

'All right? How was that?'

'This is like trying to talk through custard now. I have to force my eyes open. It's hard to come back. That was so calming.' I feel stupid about the anger thing. I don't mention it. Of course this gentle man wouldn't have been angry with me.

'Not too scary?'

'No. Comfortable. Been to perfect and back. The arm thing was interesting. It was like it floated but I had to let it, like giving it permission or something before it could.'

He tells me we'll do this first next time, then move on to age regression. He'll take me deeper into trance, back to childhood and see if we can expand on memories and then he'll help me reprocess them as an adult, not as a fearful child. It'll be quicker than taking months or years.

Relaxation fades as he talks. Pressure from demons behind the ragged curtain.

'I do need to get it done quickly,' I tell him. 'I can't afford to do this for much longer.' I can hear the flatness in my voice.

'Yes. Let's do what we can and you can come back anytime and take up where we leave off.'

As I rummage for my cheque book, he drops a bombshell.

'Oh, by the way, I'll be away in December. A business trip overseas. Just so you know.'

No. Don't go. Don't leave me!

My stomach churns and I try to fight the rising panic. What if I'm in the middle of a horrible time when he goes? Who'll look after me?

Please, please don't leave me.

I feel mangled. Should I tell him?

'I'll miss you. Miss your support.'

'You'll be fine. It's just for a couple of weeks and then we can get together again.'

At home I keep struggling with the panic. I keep telling myself I will be fine. I'm getting stronger, coping with work and I can ring friends and lean on them, as they've told me to do so often. I will be fine. Especially if I can master the age regression thing before he goes.

At least I look forward to school sometimes these days.

Mrs Blackmore, one of the mums, comes into the staff room at lunchtime beaming.

'Hey, Miss Shayler. Just wanted to tell ya that thing really works what you told me to do. I just tell 'im we're not goin' to school yet and I don't discuss it. It works. He stops naggin'. Oh, not always, but he's gettin' the idea.'

'Good for you, Mrs Blackmore,' I tell her, resisting the urge to jump up and hug her for acknowledging my advice in front of the others.

'Yeah, I didn't know what to do 'til you told me. So thanks, okay. I'm the boss, aren't I, mate?'

I smile. Tony has often told me I need to notice how much I know. This time I do. Mrs Blackmore is just one of the parents who comes to me for advice, and it comes automatically to me to give it. But when I take notice today, I see that I do know a lot about children and I do help parents even though I'm not one myself.

It's exhausting staying this confident. I wish I had someone here at home who would keep telling me I'm all right. Tell me they care and tell me they'll look after me. Crying again. Lonely again. Depressed.

Elliott rings when I get home. We chat for a while, then he says, 'By the way, I'll be away for a week or so. Going north to look for land.'

No! Don't go! Don't leave me!

'Not looking around here any more?' I ask, fighting the ridiculous feelings.

'No. There's nothing up there that feels like a dream come true. Might as well try the north coast. My mate George says it's cheap, warm, all that sort of thing.'

Elliot's going north will make no difference at all to the friendship we have. Why do I do that panic thing? One day I'll work that out too. Tony will help. In the meantime, I'll try not to think about him going on his business trip either.

SITTING TOGETHER

The room I've been slowly cleaning out at school is almost done. When Fiona sees it, she is filled with ideas about how it can be used.

'You could have workshops here for parents, on things like holiday activities, to keep kids' learning on track.'

'Will you run them?' Alma asks sarcastically. Sometimes she's valuable.

'Oh! No,' Fiona responds quickly. 'One of you teachers could.'

'When?' we ask in unison.

'You could have them at lunchtime.'

Yes, well.

Mothers and kids on holidays. It gets me wondering about my mother again. I've felt a tiny connection with her since I've remembered going to look at her clothes and her watch in the bedroom after she died. But when I look at her photo now there's still no recognition. I should go to the cemetery soon, it might be interesting. Maybe I'll go next weekend.

She's buried in the Field of Mars. I remember my father saying that and I remember two little kids skipping happily about between towering gum trees. Ken and me at the grave? Feels like it. If everything behind that curtain was going to feel like those skipping kids, I'd rip it wide open and feast on memories. Skipping happily around a cemetery is bizarre but the memory feels so light. Carefree. Optimistic.

Ken was a schoolboy when our mother died. I'd love to know where he is so that I could pick his brains about what he remembers of us as a family. I guess it's his choice to stay out of touch but I don't understand why he'd want to. We got on all right, I thought.

I've had the clock dream a lot lately. More often than usual. I'll talk with Tony about it on Tuesday. Meanwhile, I try not to get anxious about age regression. It's only memories, not real things happening. It feels daft, out here in the real world, to be so afraid and anxious about them.

As the day draws closer I start drifting, unfocused. I have to write notes to myself and lean heavily on the calendar. I can't concentrate, haven't written a program for work. I'm bluffing along on experience.

My head is clogged and I go to the doctor who diagnoses flu. I drift through some days off work. Sleeping, curtain lifting and falling, revealing bits of my childhood: being lifted into the big bath, running through a bindii patch, eating porridge, fine toothcombs, bras like they don't make any more and balls of hard horse manure. Awful memories too. Push them away. Get to the good ones. Nanna's baked dinners. Blue velvet dress. Roger, her dog. That skinny little kid who came out with us sometimes.

Tuesday at last. Tony and I talk about school, then I take control.

'You know how we talked about recurring dreams a while ago? Well, there's another one I've had a lot recently. Can I tell you about it?' On the right side of the curtain. 'This one isn't scary. It's just puzzling. It's in my father's house. I'm the only one there and I'm sneaking about, collecting all the clocks.'

'The clocks?'

'Yes. I'm greedy for them. I can't let anyone else get them and even though I'm loaded up with clocks, I keep taking more. They're ones we really had but they're in multiples. What are they? Are clocks one of those classic symbols?'

'What do you think they are?'

'Time, I suppose. I want to stop time passing. But that seems so obvious. I don't need a recurring dream to tell me that.'

Tony sits quietly. I'm uncomfortable so I add, 'I'm not frightened in the dream. Just eager to get the clocks.'

'Where were the clocks? The real ones.'

'One was on the dresser in the dining room. One was on the dressing t– oh, I remember. One was on my mother's dressing table! Oh, I remember! It was like a little temple or Parthenon. Orange, with columns.'

'And it was in the bedroom?'

'Yes,' I say slowly, recognising movement in the curtain. 'I used to go to the bedroom to look at my mother's things after she died.'

'Go on. What did you see?'

'I saw her wardrobe and glory box. I loved her things, especially her clock on the dressing table. It's the main clock I keep stealing.'

'This is the room where the abuse happened, isn't it?'

'Mm. What's it about? Do you know?'

'It could be a lot of things but see what you think of this. You're alone in the house. You don't want anyone else to have the clocks. The clock saw what your father was doing. You take the clocks so no-one else will know what they know.'

It feels right. I don't want anyone else to know what he did in that room.

Tony talks about the dream. The clock is like a screen memory that's come into my consciousness at a useful time. He tells me about a classic case where a woman kept dreaming about a huge tree. In therapy she looked more closely at the tree and she remembered being raped regularly by a family member. Each time it happened she focused on the tree. 'Dissociated', he calls it. I think he's saying that the tree became a screen memory for her and that the clock may have a similar function for me.

'It's an important dream,' he says gravely. 'I'm sure it will be helpful when we work with age regression. Right.'

My attempt to stay on the safe side of the curtain has opened the window, anyway.

Tony describes the process he'll use again and reassures me I can stop at any time. 'We need to find something in the bedroom scenario that's less threatening and I'm thinking about the clock.'

'The clock feels safe.'

He's enthusiastic to get started, I think, to put his plan into action. He enjoys working with hypnosis and he knows he's good at it.

'All right. We'll use the clock. We'll get you to focus on that, then move outwards. Are you ready to start?'

'Yes,' a small voice replies.

'What else do you remember about the room?'

The curtain shifts.

'Walking about looking at the furniture. The wardrobe, the dressing table, my mother's glory box.' Hard to breathe. Heart racing. 'I don't know if I can go back there.'

'You are strong enough to face the pain. Remember you can stop at any time. Just raise your hand. All right? I'll know if you're getting too stressed. Remember we've talked about that? I'll be watching for the signs. All right?'

'All right.' Get it over with. Open the window.

Soon I'm wandering along beside the mountain stream, relaxed, no stress at all. Arm floats up, then down.

'Go into the house and tell me what you can see.' Tony's voice seems far away but I know where I am and what's happening.

I can ignore his instructions or I can focus on his voice and go to the house. He's helping and I trust him. I go to the house.

'Big sideboard. Vases with emus' eggs. The clock's on the dresser. Dog statues.'

'Tell me what the clock is like.'

'Brown. Bridge shape. Numbers all round. Holes for winding it up.'

'Where is the clock?'

'On the dresser.'

'In the bedroom?'

'Lounge room.'

'All right. Go to the bedroom door now. Take your time. Don't go in. Just to the door.'

Drifting up the hall, heart beating fast. Waiting at the door. Listening for darkness.

'Are you at the door?'

'Yes.'

'All right. Go in. It's all right. You're safe. Nothing will happen. Just walk in. Are you inside the room?'

'Yes.'

'Good. What can you see?'

'Mummy's necklaces. Her watch. Some little drawers. The joining thing where the mirror joins on.'

I can hear my child voice as if I'm both speaker and observer. In myself and out too, seeing minute details. The hinge that holds the mirror makes me anxious. Breathing fast.

'All right. It's all right. Nothing will hurt you.'

I can hear Tony's voice here and not here. He can't see that hinge on the mirror.

'Now walk around the room and tell me what you see. Don't see anything upsetting. What can you see?'

'Mummy's glory box. It's got a heart on it.' I open the box and smell mothballs, not Mummy.

'What else?'

'Wardrobe.' Face in her clothes. Wanting the smell of her.

Wanting her. She might be here somewhere. Mummy's clothes. Mummy's smell.

'All right. Now go to the clock. You'll be all right. Go to the clock and tell me what you see.'

'Orange with steps and all the num–' A noise.

'What is it? What's upsetting you?'

No words. Find some words. 'A noise,' I whimper.

'There's a noise? What noise is it?'

'Bad.'

'Is someone else in the room?' Tony asks.

Don't let him be here!

'Who else is in the room?'

'Someone.'

'Who is it?'

'He's making noises.'

'Who is making noises?'

'No!'

'Turn around. Have a look.'

'Daddy.'

'What is Daddy doing?'

'Making noises. Holding something. Awful noises.'

'What is he doing?'

'Looking at me. No! Don't.'

'What is Daddy doing?'

'Telling me to come close.' Thick voice. Not Daddy's. 'No! Don't want to go clo– . . . no . . .' Heart pounding. Where's Mummy? Come and get me.

'Go closer. You will be all right this time.'

'No.' Small whimper. 'Want Mummy.'

'Where are your daddy's pants?' Tony's big voice.

Have to find Mummy. Frightened. Want Mummy! Come and get me!

'Where are your father's pants?' Tony's thick voice demands again. Thick urgent voice. 'Tell me where his pants are.' Thick, dark demands.

Who cares about pants! Can't you see? Terror flinging me against walls, onto the bed. Need my mummy. Please! Where are you? Come and get me. Please! Fear whirling me around and around the room on the end of a terror rope.

'Mummy!' I scream. 'Mummy! Want Mummy!'

Can't breathe. Something's crushing me. 'Mummy!' Try to scream. Dark noises say she's gone, can't come back. Crushing breath out of me.

'All right. You're all right, Kate. Focus on my voice.'

'Where's Mummy?' Don't let him, Mummy! Make him stop!

'Kate, listen to my voice. You are all right. Focus on my voice. Breathe deeply.'

Focus. Tony's voice. Not thick now. Quick. Get me out. Walk down path . . . Can't walk. Have to run. Breathe deeply, calmly. All over. Let go of . . . Must breathe. Water. Stream. Breathe. Stream. Water. Breathe deeply. Relax. Nothing can hurt me here. Deeply. Breathe. Breathe.

'Counting you back now. Three . . .'

When I come back into Tony's room I can't speak. I remember so clearly exactly where I've been. Not just looking behind the curtain but going through it to the darkest place. Screaming there. I keep my eyes closed and wonder how can it be that I've never remembered missing my mother so much or needing her so desperately. Nor had I remembered how utterly terrified I was of my dark father. I knew I was scared but that was sheer terror. I'll never go back there. Never. I'm struggling to get back to Tony's office and stay there. I slowly open my eyes and fix the office scene over the bedroom one. Or try to.

'Would you tell me about what happened?' Tony asks.

His voice is normal now. It had been dark, I'm sure. Now he's smiling gently, looking deeply caring.

When I try to put it all into words, it's as if my vocabulary has shrunk. I'm scanning my mind for adult resources to tell about the child.

'It was terrible,' I say. 'It was so real and I feel like I've just been there.' I tell him what happened. I tell him that I didn't know I'd ever needed my mother so desperately. 'I knew she could stop the . . . the badness. So I think she must have been . . . um . . . good. Um, sort of . . . powerful.' I'm clumsy with mother talk.

'Loving? Constant? Reliable? Faithful? Trustworthy?'

'Yes. All of the above.'

We sit quietly with this new dimension to my mother. I try to turn my back on the darkness but I can't push it away. It's so real I have to sob about my father's vile betrayal. All the lost years and wasted time, all the deceit and terrible darkness around me, the child.

Tony waits for the tide to ebb. I don't try to force it.

'That was a very important memory for you. You did well. Now you need to process it as an adult, notice how it affects you and take control. Use that ego strength and adult cognition we've talked about.'

His jargon seems out of place here where I'm struggling for any words at all. But I think I know what he means and I hope I can do it. Now that I know about the terror, I want desperately to be free of it. Not sure what mental gyrations I'll have to do to process it all but that might become clear at home when I feel normal again.

'I'm very impressed with today's events,' Tony says. 'I'll be interested to know how you get on. Tuesday next week? No. Right, you're changing to fortnightly, aren't you? Well, let me know if you need to come earlier. What we've done today is so very important.' He checks that I'm feeling all right, relaxed and ready to go home.

At home, exhausted, I have hot sweet porridge for dinner and go to bed. I write in my journal. I've never felt terror like that with any other man, so I don't know what it could teach me about how I function now. The real importance for me seems to be about me and my mother. I understand now that the reason I went into my parents' bedroom was to search for her. I was four and didn't understand what 'dead' meant. I went to see if she'd come back. Her smells and her things were the next best thing to having her, a way of being with her and warding off the vast loneliness she left me in. My father betrayed me at the time I needed her most. And him. I loathe him.

My thoughts drift around what it is to be a child. I remember little Lucy, Bel's daughter. I remember Becky before Jane died. Becky after, briefly. For a child, life is simple. You don't question that your parents will be there if things get tough. Or fun or exciting or confusing. You just take safety and love for granted. And so you should. I was a child like that once. I must have been, mustn't I? A child without fear. Can you call it childhood if you're always afraid, if you're aware of dangers that kids shouldn't know about? When the one and only person you should be able to trust becomes the biggest danger, is that childhood? What's it like to be the other kind of child? The one without fear. I'll never know. My father took that away. Forever.

I hate him. I pour venom onto the pages of my journal.

I'm sobbing and it feels wholesome to let it all out. I can't stop. I should stop, shouldn't I? Eventually I do.

So that's what looking at my father honestly, with adult cognition, comes to, is it? Hating him. But I don't only hate him. I love him too. Shouldn't the adult view be unambiguous? Well, I can't just delete one of them. They'll have to sit side by side. Love and hatred. There's grief about that. Grief is what I'm supposed to feel for my mother. Not my father. Grief.

Can I handle going to the cemetery? I can. It has nothing to do with my father and I have almost no feelings about my mother being buried there. It'll just be interesting.

On the first weekend of the school holidays I go. I'm surprised to find that the Field of Mars is so ugly. Where are the trees and the fairies and colours I thought I remembered? Preoccupied with the ugliness of this place and finding numbers on the graves, I'm not ready for the bright gold letters of my father's name glaring at me.

Oh no. Not you! I didn't come here for you. What you did was . . . Go away.

Anger boils. I want to kick the bloody gravestone over. How dare he defile my mother's grave. She's a saint. How dare his gold letters shout false saintliness to the world.

Where's my mother?

Where's Mummy? I find myself asking. Where's Mummy? I want my mummy.

As the child struggles with the adult, tears roll out and I fumble to find the tissues I brought, just in case.

Oh where's Mummy? Someone tell me where she is.

I feel weak. I sit on the grave and look for my mother's name. Yes, there it is, below the gold one. Norma Shayler's name is here but her gold has worn away.

Beloved mother of Kenneth 6, Katherine 4 and Kerry 2.

The child who is me sits sniffling. Stares at her mother's name so near her own.

Right. I stand up. It's time to go. I've been to the grave, seen my mother's name on it. Now it's time to go home. It's silly just sitting here crying.

But the child is bound to the name on the grave, no matter how dull it's become. She demands that we stay.

I have to sit down again. The child becomes restless. She draws my eyes back to the gold and the anger.

I'll deal with you another time. Stay out of my way. I'm thinking about Mummy. The word, just the word Mummy sets up a flood of tears again. Another handful of tissues.

Mummy. Mummy. Oh, Mummy.

Where is this coming from? This is not me. I don't have a mother. I'm thirty-eight years old and I do not need . . . Pull yourself together. This is not how grown women behave. It's embarrassing.

'Oh, but I miss you so much, Mummy. Come back.'

Time passes with alternate sobbing and trying not to. Finding out and telling Mummy how much I miss her. 'I still need you. I still need you to love me and tell me who I am.' I sit with my need for her. I feel the new awareness that comes from the lonely knowledge that I've never known love, whole love, since my mother died and took hers away. I can see clearly now that some friendships I've pursued have been out of a longing for my mother. She's who has been missing. I've been searching for love like hers that made me whole and perfect.

'You knew me.'

I sit talking with her, remembering and feeling loved. My tears are gentle now. I was loved wholly and I was good. I loved wholly too. That makes me feel powerful. Cry, remember and cry again. Let the pain and the joy come.

Eventually it's time to go. Time to say goodbye. Afraid to leave the one who knows me. I try.

'Goodbye M– . . .'

No. Can't do it yet. More tears flow. I look at my watch. I've been here for four hours! I try the last goodbye again but it still gets stuck.

'I'll be all right, you know,' I tell my mother. I try to feel what being all right will be like but it's too early for that.

I breathe deeply.

I am thirty-eight. I am not a child. I will be all right. It will be hard and lonely sometimes but you loved me. I am lovable. I'll take that with me and I'll be all right.

Another deep, smooth breath. The child is quiet. I, the woman, stand up.

I begin, 'Goodbye . . .' Eyes wander too far up the headstone and see the obscene gold of my father's name.

'I'll deal with you later. I was good but you weren't. Not always. But today is too big for darkness. I will not let it in.'

I let my eyes drop to the dull name.

'Goodbye, Mummy. I'll be all right.'

I drive home in a euphoric daze. Sometimes I grin like a fool and say, 'Hey, my mummy loved me!' I want to tell the people who pull up beside me at the lights. I want to stop at the houses of each of my friends and tell them too. Not just that she loved me but that I loved her too. That I loved with a pure and wholesome love. 'Hey, I loved my mummy too!' I want to shout.

As I approach home, I start wishing she could see my house and my kids at school and meet my friends. But she's never coming back. The finality of her death clouts me and I'm sobbing again. I need to pull over. I can't see.

At home I take down the picture of my mother and stare at her. Into her eyes. I still don't remember the face but now I place the love and the longing for her in the frame. I tell her again how much I wish she could come back. I cry with her face pressed to my heart. I will be all right. I loved and was loved by my mother.

I want to ring Tony. I can't ring him at home can I? He said I could, but it doesn't feel right to interrupt his family life. I wonder what they're like, the wife and kids he mentions sometimes, all at home together. Oh forget it. I'm too tired to call, anyway. I fall asleep exhausted, my photo of my mother on her glory box that sits beside my bed. Her glory box that I've had with me all these years. Like the photo, it is truly mine now.

Have I started a new kind of life now that I know I was lovable, now that I understand that my mother won't be back? Now that the nameless search has a name and is over? Will I be stronger? Lighter? Will I find love and give it too, in full measure?

A few days later Tony rings to say he's prepared the consent form to get my file from Burnside. In the tumult of emotions I'd been feeling, I'd forgotten about the file. We'd talked about how people get a sense of self from family stories and records. In my case I could get it from the records kept at Burnside. I'll need to sign a consent for my file to be released to Tony. Great! I can tell him about the enhancement of my sense of self at the cemetery. Tell him today instead of waiting for my next session. I want to tell him I'm grateful that he sent me there too.

I sign the form quickly. How much time can I have? This isn't a session.

'You won't believe what I did yesterday,' I say.

'Tell me what you did yesterday.' He smiles benevolently.

'Went to the cemetery.'

'That's good.' He says it as if I've told him I bought a pair of grey socks!

'I remembered my mother, that she loved me.' It feels silly saying this to an actual person, especially when they're so stunningly uninterested. 'She was, um, she could have fixed anything!' Now I feel sillier. My mum the mechanic.

He starts talking about the child's view of the mother as omnipotent. He says that people who grow up with parents learn that this is not the case, that parents are sometimes weak and fallible. I'll come to see my mother more realistically. Well, he can say what he likes. My mother feels omnipotent and I'm going to relish that thought, not dump it.

'You needed to go. It'll give you closure,' he says.

'It doesn't feel like closure. It feels like a beginning. New knowledge and confidence. More like hello than goodbye. Mostly.'

'The thing is, you said goodbye as an adult. I'm not telling you to forget her. Just to understand that she's gone.'

But I don't want her to be! I'll have to miss her. I don't want her to be gone just when I've found her again! I just want to sit with her for . . . ages.

'I feel low when I think about her being gone forever. It's lonelier when you understand what you haven't got any more. I just want this euphoria to last.'

'Look, you're going to have feelings of dysphoria,' he says. Impatiently? Standing up. 'You have to put those feelings aside.'

'Dis what?' I ask, standing too.

'Dysphoria. The opposite of euphoria. Right? Put the dysphoria aside. Don't let it control you. The euphoria will settle too, into an adult view of yourself and your mum.'

He's ushering me out already.

'Anyway, I want to thank you for suggesting that I go. To the grave. You were right about that,' I say as I walk to the door.

'Glad to help,' he says. 'See you next time. We might know something about your file by then.'

His reaction to the most important thing that's ever happened to me is so disappointing. I thought he'd do cartwheels of happiness. Must be because he's so busy.

The photo of my mother keeps drawing me to it. 'You used to be just Norma Nobody Shayler. Not now. I had you for a mummy.' Just as well I don't have a boarder. I can ask the photo, 'Are you my mother?' like in the Dr Seuss book we love at preschool. I grin the answer, 'You're not a cat or a dog or cow. You're a bird and you're my mother.' Good grief, your daughter's a bit of a twit. Doesn't matter. It's fun and who'll know!

Then into my reverie sneaks, 'You're never coming back. I'm on my own.' I feel more alone than I ever have as the finality of her death hits home thirty-four years late. It feels like I'll never be loved again. Put it aside, Tony said.

All right. I'll go for a bushwalk to distract myself. I search for tiny terrestrial orchids that appear sometimes; they're exquisite and I'm trying to learn their names. I watch tadpoles in pools and listen to birds that I can't see and to the waterfall. I feel calm here in the bush. As I walk down the path to my house I see a familiar car approaching. It stops beside me at my gate.

'Oh, hello, Tony. Thought I knew the car. What are you doing here?'

'Hello! So this is where you live? I'm just on my way home from a patient up there.'

'You make house calls?'

'In emergencies. Someone has problems and couldn't get away so I saw her at home. So this is your place.'

'Yep. This is it.'

Instead of going, he waits as if he expects to be invited in. 'Would you like to come in?'

It feels like there's no more to say to Tony in my house than there was in the supermarket. Show him my mother's photo! Better than standing about wondering what to say. He follows me up the hall to the bedroom where I pick up the photo. I feel awkward having him in the bedroom but he doesn't seem to notice which room it is. He studies the photo while I hope he approves of my mum. She's not beautiful or even good-looking. When I first got the photo I was disappointed that my mum wasn't beautiful but I see beauty differently now, for my mother anyway.

At last Tony says, 'Mm. She looks robust. Jovial but intense. It's hard to read her.'

I replace the photo and start walking down the hall surprised by what he sees in my mother's face.

'Who are these?' Tony asks on the way to the lounge room.

'That's us three. Ken, Kerry and me. We don't know when it was taken but an aunty, sort of aunty, gave it to me years ago.'

Now Tony studies this photo. He doesn't speak.

'What are you thinking?' The silence is uncomfortable.

'I'm not thinking,' he replies. 'I'm trying to get a feeling.'

'Oh. Well, what are you feeling?'

'There's no anguish in it. You all look bemused. I think it was taken before your mum died.'

'That's interesting. I thought it was taken after, because we look confused, puzzled. You don't think there's any distress?'

'Hard to say, but no. I don't think so.'

I show him the rest of the house. He picks up my guitar that I leave beside the lounge and plays some chords. They sound like discords to me but I'm no expert. He looks at me and I think I'm supposed to be impressed. 'What's that?' I ask.

'Just something my band used to play.'

'Band?'

'Oh yeah! I had a band once. Rock and roll.' He grins and strums more chords. 'Legend in my own mind, I was,' he laughs. I don't like his music and can't think of anything polite to say.

I wish he'd go. Now he's playing something classical, watching me again as if he wants to impress!

'Lovely,' I say, wishing I wasn't a musical ignoramus.

'What do you play?'

'Bush music. Badly,' I tell him, hoping that will curb his interest.

'Hm. Well. Better be going. You're all right after your cemetery visit then?'

'Yes thanks. Oh, sometimes. I get really sad sometimes too though.'

'That's the dysphoria. Push it away. But you know I'm there for you if you need me. You only have to ring. Right?'

He goes and I'm left wishing I didn't feel so fond of him. Wish he wasn't an out of-bounds married man too. Why would a talented, intelligent person like him be interested in someone as ordinary as me, anyway? And he knows all my secrets and failings and fears. Should I talk to him about this? Probably. It's nice that he cares. Sometimes he seems like a substitute mother giving care, advice, guidance. That's what mothers do, don't they?

I keep trying to push away the thought of missing my mother and the loneliness it evokes. Before my visit to the grave, Tony said I needed to grieve. I can't do it all in a day, can I? When Tom and Jane died all those years ago, I grieved for months and months. I still cry about each of them sometimes. This is about my own mother now. Surely I can't do it in a day. Tony must have been too busy when he said push it away. He said once that I need to express my grief in adult language. Well, all I come up with when I try is, 'I loved you' and 'I miss you so much'. It doesn't diminish the grief. It evokes the deepest loneliness and the hottest tears.

Thank God it's still holidays. I go to the farm for the second week. I can't wait to tell Leonie and Col what I've done. They're still sure I don't need a psychologist. When I tell them about the cemetery visit they're interested but they don't do cartwheels of joy either. Must be the way I tell it. I wish I could express better how vital it is to remember and to know my mother loved me.

The holiday is over too soon and as I drive home I get teary. Saying goodbye has always been hard but this time I want to sob. The sense of calm and belonging is overtaken by impending loneliness. And gloomy thoughts of Maud and the others.

Righto. What I need to do is to harness some strength from my mother's loving me. Be positive and use the power. I'm exhausted just making the plan. The kinds of women I work with are like slaps in the face compared to the kind of woman my mother was. Must have been. Well, I'll just try to stay strong and positive, feeling whole and worthy of respect.

Back at school and Maud's constant challenges wear me down. Why bother caring about getting the job done properly? Just leave her to it. But I do care. I want to make childhood the best it can be for these kids while I've got them.

Lunchtime. Try to be strong and friendly. 'How was your holiday, Alma?'

'Fabulous! Up at the Gold Coast. We swam every day and hung around the trough every night. How was yours, Kate?'

'Great. I went to the farm and the cemetery.'

'Cemetery, eh! Party down, girl!' Alma replies.

'Nobody died, did they?' Felicity interrupts.

'No. Just my mother.'

Her eyes pop.

'Oh, sorry. It was ages ago. I went to see where she was buried.'

'Ages ago? How old were you?' Alma asks. Is she really interested?

'Four.'

'Shit! Four years old? What happened to you?'

'I went to a home.'

'Like an orphanage?'

302

'Yes. Burnside.'

'Oh, I know that place. The castles. You grew up in them?'

'That's the place.'

'Must have been rough.'

That she should have any empathy at all stuns me. 'It was rough sometimes. Oh! Time to get back to work.' And I'm relieved. I don't want to be treated like a curiosity here. Not any more than I already am.

'Oh, Kate, you're such a stickler for rules,' Alma groans comically.

'I know. I'm a homes kid.'

My home now is getting harder to hold on to as there's another hike in interest rates. How will I manage? I'll just have to get a boarder. In this state? Stressed. Depressed. Drowning in an emotion morass and unable to pull myself up and out of it?

Can't wait for my next appointment with Tony. A fortnight is too long. He said to call in if I need to but when I do he isn't there.

You promised you'd be here if I needed you. You said you were here for me. I cry and feel weak and dependent.

Try to do what he said, to recognise the dysphoria and push it away. Try. Try harder. How? I spiral down, having no-one. My mother will never be here and I have to manage every single thing by myself. Too hard. Wish my number was up. It's worse now because once there was someone. Now there's no-one. Further to fall. This is what knowing my mother will never come back is like. Do it by yourself. Your whole life, completely by yourself, on and on.

Well, that's how it is. You can't change it and your number doesn't seem to be up, so you have to cope. There's no knight in shining armour coming to the rescue. No omnipotent, champion mother. Have to hope that somewhere down the track things might get better. Someone might turn up and love me wholly.

Can't ring Tony. Couldn't bear the disappointment if he's not there or if he just tells me to pull myself out of it. Can't ring the farm or Gen and Paddy and tell them yet again.

Stay busy. Don't just sit around worrying. Do something. Put another ad in the paper. If you get a boarder, find ways of stressing out quietly.

Blow it! Gen mightn't mind if I ring her yet again.

'I'm really missing my mum. Feeling desperate for a mate too. And babies and all that.'

Some of the mums at school have two or three children by different fathers. Almost as soon as one man leaves, they find another.

'How come some of them find men so easily and I can't even find one?' I ask Gen.

'But would you want the ones some of them find!'

'Good point. But I can't even find one of any sort of sperm donor to trick into a baby.'

'Oh, Kate! You wouldn't.'

'No, I know I wouldn't. But sometimes! Just find a desperado . . . No, you're right. I wouldn't and I couldn't but you know how clucky I am. Still am.'

'I know. You still might.'

I need something nice to do this weekend. A distraction. I'm getting too introspective. There's a one-day medieval history course on. That'll do.

As usual I'm drawn to the older women. I know what it is now. Looking for Mummy. A well-known, older spinster is doing the course. I'd like to talk with her but I'm intimidated by her fame. What will I say to her after hello? 'How's your empire coming along?' 'Seen any nice Rolls Royces lately?'

At morning tea she's near the tea urn looking uncomfortably alone. 'Tea's mighty strong,' she offers as I arrive.

'I'm a coffee person. I hope it's mighty strong,' I reply.

She talks. I listen. My ears prick up when she asks, 'Do you know what the most important thing I learnt at school was?'

'No.' Give me words of wisdom. Right now.

'Latin,' she declares.

'Oh!' I feel cheated. I wanted something soul sustaining! 'I thought you were going to quote an ancient philosopher's wisdom.'

'No. Latin. If you read Latin, a whole other world is open to you. Including the philosophers.'

Couldn't you paraphrase a gem or two?

I need to stop looking for my mother, who probably didn't know Latin. I remind myself that I'm an adult and I can draw on my adequate cognitive resources to look after myself. Even without Latin.

At the end of the day, most people have to dash off to family commitments. I envy them. They envy me my freedom. I don't have to dash off. I can do what I like.

As night falls, my freedom sneaks up and overwhelms me. I plunge into a deep pool of anger – my mother left me to be betrayed by her husband. How could she love someone who'd do what her husband, my father, did? He betrayed her too. Was she desperate to marry him? My gene pool is looking rather unattractive. There's no hope! No, Kerry is married and has kids. It could happen for me. Oh, who am I trying to fool?

Trying to get out of the downward spiral feels like swimming against a tide of tar. I'm a zombie in tar. I go through the motions at work but feel nothing. I come home and stare at the walls. Sunset is the worst time. Beautiful sky. Cool darkness. Cold loneliness.

Elliott comes to stay for a few days on his way north again. I tell him about my visit to the cemetery.

'Oh. That's, um, interesting. Glad it was helpful. Did I tell you about the house in the rainforest?' He's excited about two properties he's found. That's what he wants to think about. Rainforest, not cemetery. Where's his taste! I'm disappointed that I still feel anxious about him going to live so far away.

Felicity and Alma are being friendlier now that they've seen what support I have from parents. Maud sometimes pretends she likes me too. It's not particularly uplifting to be included. In fact, I don't feel anything but flat, unable to connect with anything or anybody.

Proof that I'm a zombie comes in the form of a letter saying that if I don't pay the water bill immediately, supply will be cut off. How could I just forget to pay it? It's been on my list for weeks. Every little thing has to be done by me. I'm hopeless.

No, I'm not! I'm sad. All right, I'm supposed to give my sadness adult expression. Here goes. The woman who gave birth to me had strong positive feelings for me and I reciprocated. Feel better? No. But my mummy loved me and she died and I miss her.

When should I let myself feel the sadness and when should I push it away? It just keeps on coming. Should it take so long? Is it just that I haven't learnt to translate the whole thing into the stuff of daily living yet, to reinterpret who I am?

Try to focus on what Tony says are my impressive achievements. Where have they got me? Alone. No-one to share any of it with. I'm just small and sad and needy. I wish Tony was here to convince me that I'm all right, that I'll be all right. Thank goodness it's Tuesday tomorrow.

Soon I'm unburdening, telling Tony how easy it is for me to become miserable, grieving for my mother.

'Just remember these are the childhood feelings,' he says almost dismissively. 'The child you were is not the adult you are today.'

'You told me when I first started seeing you that I needed to grieve and feel the feelings. How much is enough? It just keeps coming. Should I squash it all the time? Isn't that just suppressing it all over again?'

'You needed to grieve. Yes. Acknowledge the sadness, grieve for the child you were, but move on. There's no point in wallowing in it.'

Wallowing! I'm offended, hurt. He knows I often feel fat and ugly. 'A poor body image', he calls it. To use the word 'wallowing' is so insensitive! Hippos wallow. I shrink back to smallness and fear. What am I afraid of? Is he going to be repelled and send me away?

No! Don't leave me!

I cry. 'I don't know how to stop the sadness.' I try to stop the tears. Tony's judgement feels harsh. 'Sorry.'

'There's no need to be sorry. Look, I'll put it this way. Life dishes up some pretty awful stuff to lots of people. You got more than your share but you don't have to keep eating shit sandwiches!'

Who is this! Tony doesn't speak like this. Crudely. He's had enough of me. No wonder.

'You need to think about this. You are entitled to happiness, like anyone else. You don't have to keep punishing yourself. Right?'

I'm not punishing myself, am I? I'm grieving. Aren't I? I don't know what I'm doing. I want Tony to tell me that everything will be fine and he will be here for me, like he used to say. I don't want him to be annoyed with me and push me away.

Please don't leave me.

I hate this needing him. Needing to matter. Feeling lonely when he rejects me. I'm supposed to talk with him about the feelings I have for him. Will I? I'll feel so stupid. He'll think I'm more stupid than he does already. When I'm not here, when he's not in this mood, I've thought I might love him. Surely I don't! He isn't nice-looking and in this mood he's awful. But I need him and want his approval and it hurts when he's cold and critical. I want him to love me.

Oh, for goodness sake, isn't it just dependence? Does dependence feel like love? I don't know. I'm so confused. There's not enough room in my brain to sort this out.

I force myself to look at him. I'm surprised that he looks so tired and haggard – that's why he's being crass and cold.

I'm so selfish, didn't even notice. I'm sorry now and anxious that he might tell me to go away and come back another time, when he has the energy for someone like me.

'You look weary,' I say.

'Yeah. It's been a pretty busy week trying to manage the business and family and getting ready for the trip. Looking for new rooms too.'

'Are you moving?'

Don't leave me!

The fact that his trip is coming up soon is bad enough but he's not coming back here!

'Just to a new place in the town. There's lots of work to be done to get it ready.'

You're coming back. Thank goodness.

'I'll let you know the address. Anyway,' he straightens up in his chair, 'how have you been?'

'Like I just said. Sad.'

'Oh, sorry,' Tony says. 'I'm just not myself today. Of course, you just said. Sorry. Well, look, you have to recognise the essential tragedy of the loss of your mother and move on. Use your adult strengths to go forward, not back.'

'I try,' I tell him. Perhaps if I tell him about the positive times, he'll see that I am trying, not just moaning.

'I felt really strong and powerful at the cemetery, remembering about my mother loving me. I still smile for hours and I want to tell everyone about it.'

'Good. That's good.'

It's no use pretending. I need his help.

'But it doesn't last. I just go back down to missing her all the time. I need you to help me,' I cry.

'I'm here,' he says quietly, like the old Tony.

I have to talk about the feelings. If he's going away, I have to sort them out, resolve them, not feel this agitated for the weeks he's gone. 'You know early on, you said I should tell you about my feelings for you?'

308

'Yes. Do you have something to tell me?'

'Yes. Well, they . . . The feelings . . . I feel . . . uh. I've come to really like being with you and I um . . . I don't know how to say it.'

'Just say what you feel.' Quietly, gently.

I take a deep breath and say, cautiously, 'I've become very fond of you. You're a good egg.' I hold my breath. What now?

'Why was that so hard to say?'

'I don't know. It's embarrassing. Doesn't seem right.'

'Why is that?'

'Because it might be love. I don't . . . It isn't right.' And I want you to just spirit them away. Vaporise them so I can think straight again.

He talks about transference again. People develop strong feelings, positive or negative, when they share important or intimate events, such as they do in therapy. Such as we have done. It's perfectly normal that I should develop feelings for him. It's a trick of nature to make people out there in society want to be together and perpetuate the species. In therapy, where the transference reaction can be manipulated, people are sometimes really responding to an idealised or despised person from their past. In my case it could be my father.

'No! I'm well and truly in touch with the despised version of him just now and it isn't anything like you. The idealised one doesn't exist any more. '

'Consider this, then. You might be responding to the idealised mother. I'm a man but it doesn't mean it can't be that. I've been told I have some feminine qualities . . .'

He talks and I think. What he's saying is essentially silly. Why does it have to be an idealised anyone I'm responding to? Why isn't it just Tony?

'I think I'm just responding to you,' I tell him. 'It feels like I love you. Or whatever you call it. The positive feelings.'

He says it is all right to call the feelings love and they're nothing to be ashamed of or embarrassed about. He says he has developed strong positive feelings for me, too. That's called a counter transference.

For me! Surely not! I've fantasised about that and seen him beaming approval at me each day when I come home from work, kissing me, holding me, telling me I'm clever, beautiful, attractive, his number-one person. But I did that knowing it would never happen. His positive feelings for me are confusing. What does he do with them?

'What should I do with these feelings?' I ask, wanting there to be some limits, some shape to it all.

'Just let them happen, talk them through with me.'

'But you won't be here. You're going away.'

'I won't abandon you. I will be back.'

Abandon me? Odd thing to say but thank goodness he will be back. These feelings are strong and I can't walk about with them unresolved. Talking about them, owning them, seems to intensify them. Tony still respecting me does too.

'We can use these feelings to help you,' he says. 'And they will resolve.' He emphasises 'will'. Feels like I'm being acknowledged but pushed away. Being pushed away and it hurts. I get anxious and start breathing too fast. Calm down! You're not going to fall apart. You're just confused. Tony is saying come close in one breath and go away in the next. What's the point? 'When you're studying next year you'll meet lots of people like me. Trust me. And when the transference happens, you'll know what it is and not fall in love until that's resolved itself. You'll have an advantage.'

'I will?'

'Mm. Most people don't know about this. They think it's love in the early stage and then the transference resolves and there's nothing left. You won't make that mistake.'

I can't imagine meeting anyone to make the mistake with but if I do, I hope I don't feel this dependent on them.

'Let's move on,' Tony suggests. 'What would you like to do today? Talk more about your father?'

'I just seem to go round in circles with that. I hate him because he betrayed me and I suppose I still love him because he was loyal. There's not much point in going over it again, is there?'

'Probably not. You have a good sense now of what the relationship with him was. Best to focus on the positive aspects of it rather than dwelling on the abuse.'

The abuse, the betrayal, doesn't feel resolved, though. What about the legacy of it? 'I don't know how it affects me in relationships, but I can't fathom that 'til I'm in one, can I? Not unless you can tell me what to look out for. If I ever do get into a relationship.'

'Wait and see,' he says, smiling.

'I've had some memories about the time after my mother died, when we were put in Burnside. I've been remembering some awful stuff.'

'Would you like to talk about it?'

'Yes. I think so.'

'All right. We can do that.'

'Well, I had a friend called Kevin. I used to get in his bed when I was frightened of the monsters under my bed. I think I loved him, you know, as kids do with special friends.'

'That's nice. That's good.'

'The matrons didn't think so. They caught us and ranted and raved and said I was making Kevin bad. They stopped us being friends. I was so lonely after that. Being friends with me made people bad.'

'Mm. They didn't do that well, did they?'

'It was just after the other thing happened with the kids waiting to be dressed, that I tried to tell you about before.' The curtain is wafting up but I can't find the words again.

'Can you tell me now?'

'It's one of those hard-to-say-it things.' We wait a while, then I try again. 'Some of us were waiting for the matron to dress us for bed after we'd been bathed. All of a sudden I was in dreadful trouble. Not the others. Just me. I said something bad. I didn't know it was bad but there was anger all around me. They said I was filth.' Can only just get the last word out. Chin quivers.

'Oh dear. What did you say?'

'That . . . It's hard to say it. Like before, with my father.'

'You're stronger now. Take your time. You know nothing will happen if you say the words.'

'True.' Rip back the curtain, stare, then shut it. A deep breath, then I blurt out quickly, 'I told them if someone rubbed his penis on your nipple, stuff would come out of you.' Said quickly, but Tony heard.

'Where did you get that information?'

Shut the curtain! Talk about it and the window will get jammed open. Then it dawns on me that what I'd said back then was about what my father did to me! It's about why he crushed the breath out of me. I was talking about ejaculation! I hadn't realised that's what it was until now. Shut the curtain, but I'll still know. The matrons knew!

'If one of the kids in your class said that, what would you think?'

'I'd wonder how they'd got the information. I'd report it.'

'Not scream and shout at them and call them filth?'

My adult self is about to say 'of course not', then I think of little Kate. 'They should have gone for my father, not me!' I'm crying and going on, 'They told the others to stay away from me because I was so bad. Contaminate them.'

Tony waits.

'They said I took my filth to Kevin's bed! What kind of minds did they have? I just wanted to be near someone so the monsters wouldn't get me.' Sobbing subsides. Noisy nose-blowing. 'I can't believe I've never understood what I was talking about 'til now. My father made all that trouble and I got stuck with it.'

'He did,' Tony says sombrely. 'And the matrons?'

'The matrons? They should have understood that a four-year-old shouldn't know that stuff. They freaked out about me getting into Kevin's bed but they didn't do anything about my father. They just stopped me having friends. Made me lonely. So lonely.' Drying my eyes again.

'You probably didn't get much in the way of warmth or affection as a child. You would have got it wherever you could. Did any of the matrons show affection?'

'No. Oh well, Mum Perry later. She changed to a more humane person just before I left. I knew she liked me. But when I was younger, from four years old to about fourteen, there was no affection. Two years of it just wasn't enough.'

'Why didn't you get affection?'

'Because I was bad, I suppose. They told me I was, all the time.'

'Were you bad?'

'I believed I was because they told me I was.'

'Were you?'

'No. I wasn't. I was good, normal. Sort of.'

'It'll be such a help to get your records. We'll have a bit more information to work on.'

What if there's something about how naughty I was in it? No! I wasn't naughty. I was good.

'Well, we'll be winding up soon,' Tony is saying. 'I'll be overseas for a while but we'll look into it when I get back, if we haven't got it before I go.'

No! Don't leave me!

Try to be adult. 'Where are you going?'

'My partner, Vlad, and I are going to Europe to do some research and networking. We're tendering for a big contract locally but we need some information from overseas before we make the submission.'

'Well, I hope it goes well. I'll miss you.'

'And I'll miss you too. It cuts both ways.'

'Thanks,' I say. 'I wish you weren't going just yet. I've got too much going on in here,' I tell him, tapping my head. 'Don't know how to process it all, the memories and feelings, without you.'

'Your task is to use your strength, the same strength and determination you've used to get you this far, to move on.'

Go forth, Kate Shayler, and teach nuclear physics!

'None of that felt strong, though. I just drifted along and did it. There were always safety nets. This stuff seems so heavy and complicated. It's going into the unknown.'

'It's important stuff, as you call it. Now you need to see the objective truth of your achievements and use your strengths to do the processing.'

'And what do I do about the feelings for you?'

'I'll be in touch when I get back. Let's see how you go. We can get together then if you want to. Work on some resolution, if you need to.'

I won't see him for more than a month. Good for the budget but not for the psyche.

'I feel like a dependent child or something.'

'You'll be fine. And you can ring before I go if you need to. All right?'

Not all right. *Don't leave me!*

As we say goodbye, I get teary, anxious. I walk away quickly so he won't see.

At home I try to crush the panic of feeling alone and mangled. I try to imagine not needing to pay for a supporter. What would I be like if my mother had lived? I wish she was here. When I need her. Gen can call her mum anytime but she's not dependent. Would I be? Would I still be like a dependent child? I don't know. I only know my mother as a child knows a mother, not as an adult. My friends seem to be friends with their mothers. They're equals. People my age don't have champions. People my age manage by themselves. No. That's not right either. They get support from their partners.

A letter from Sydney University confirms that I've been recommended for candidature in the Masters course. Why do I think

I'm smart enough to do a higher degree? If I was, I'd be able to sort myself out, wouldn't I? I might as well go with the plan and see what happens. What have I got to lose? If I fail, I won't be surprised. If I succeed, I'll be pleased. Well, stunned. I review my course work sequence and feel vulnerable.

I'm interrupted by a knock on the door.

Joan has brought some bulbs from her garden. 'I brought them yesterday but you were out.'

Without thinking, I tell her I'd been to counselling.

'Oh, you're having some difficulties, are you, dear?' she asks kindly and without a trace of criticism.

'Yes. Sorry. Didn't mean to burden you, Joan. I'm just trying to work through some childhood stuff.' I've already told her about my mother having died when I was young and she seems to have taken me under her wing, as older women tend to do. I am practising being an adult now, not looking for a mother. I am Joan's equal. I'll share with her as an equal, then. I tell her about the visit to the grave and she can see the relevance straight away.

'Sometimes I feel sad and unloved and sometimes I'm elated because I was loved by my mother.'

'Yes, I see.'

'A nice thing is that I didn't know I was capable of loving either, until I went to the grave and remembered. It's a special thing to know I can love like that.'

'Haven't you ever loved anyone? Apart from your mum.'

Her frank question surprises me. But the honest answer stuns me.

'No.'

'Never?'

'No. I've had crushes and been attracted, you know, hormones, but I haven't loved anybody, not as an equal, not being myself.'

Joan needs to know that's not the case. 'What about your friend, what's his name? Elliott.'

315

'Oh, I don't love Elliott. I thought I did once but it wore off or something. He definitely doesn't want children and I definitely do. Or did. I like him. I don't love him.' After a while I add, 'I don't think any man has loved me either. Not really.'

'Oh my dear, I find that hard to believe.'

Saying that I haven't loved anyone as an equal shocks me but I think it's true. All my loving has been out of need or curiosity or trying to join the ranks of women worthy of men's attention, not mutual respect and valuing. Not connecting as adults. Now I love Tony but that isn't real. Sort of.

Joan goes home and soon I'm crying again because I have to advertise for company and pay for support. Because I haven't loved anyone freely since my mother died. Because I love Tony but it's not real. Because I'm frightened that I will always be alone and crying. Because I am nobody's number-one person.

SHARING

Elliott rings to invite me to an exhibition of slides of Australia's wilderness. He has some exciting news that he'll tell me when he's here.

Almost as soon as we've hung up, the phone rings again.

'Hello. My name is James. I'm calling about your ad in the paper for a room to let.'

Drat, a man. We each ask and answer questions, then make a time for him to come on Saturday. I'm pleased Elliott will be here again.

Elliott can't wait to tell me his news. 'They've accepted my offer on that house. The one with all the wildlife, birds and wallabies and so on. Honestly, it's a dream come true! Aaah. So in six weeks I'll be off.'

Don't leave me.

The exhibition is in a huge church building. To our surprise the official opening includes prayers for sick and troubled members and praise to the God whose creation we are about to witness in the slides.

'Gawd, didn't know it was going to be one of these!' Elliott hisses. In the congregation there's moaning, arm-waving and lots of shouting, 'Hallelujah!' and 'Praise the Lord!' I'm uncomfortable too but the caring these people have for each other stirs my longing to be part of a church. My faith has changed but it's still there and it needs like-minded people to remind me to make it part of everyday life. I must find that home church I've been told about.

James, who arrives on time next morning, is polite, neat and totally devoid of humour. He likes the room, the house and the location. His engagement has just been called off so he is moving out and hopes to save and build a place of his own. He has a day job and a night one too.

'Thanks for coming, James. I think it could work well. I'll check your references and let you know. Yes, this week.'

Elliott and I think James is harmless, especially as far as side-splitting laughter is concerned. He'll be good to share with because I'll hardly ever see him. 'I'm glad you were here,' I tell Elliott.

'Oh, were you?'

'Yes. I'd have felt vulnerable having a strange man come in and think I'm alone.'

'But you are. Ah, you mean he knows you've got a muscle man on call.' He grins.

'Something like that.'

'You could call me but I'll be a long way away, won't I?'

Don't go. Don't leave me.

Wish I could talk to Tony. I'm a mess and it's worse because I'm worried that I'm so dependent on him. Still, he's the professional. He'll know what to do about it. Will I ring him? No. See if you can do this yourself. Rely on your strengths and stop blubbering like a baby. Get to sleep. Work tomorrow.

What a lovely surprise! Maud is sick. Gwen, the casual who replaces her, is warm and as enthusiastic about work as she is about her makeup – bright pink lipstick and bright, multicoloured eyeshadow that intrigues and attracts even the shyest kids.

'What do you want me to do first off?' she asks cheerily.

I tell her, then ask, 'Is your name down for a permanent job?' It would be so good to work with someone who likes kids and working.

'No. I don't want full-time work,' Gwen replies. 'These casual days are enough with my kids still at school. Call me anytime Maud gets sick.'

I wish there were such a thing as flu germ spray. I'd put in a bulk order.

Maud is well again.

'When's that rainbow lady coming back?' Daniel asks.

'I don't know, Daniel. It'd be good if it was soon, wouldn't it?'

As the day of Tony's departure gets closer I get more and more anxious. Anxious about my feelings for him, anxious about James who's moving in, anxious about school and my father and depression and being alone forever and not loving. Anxious about being so anxious.

'Tony, it's Kate. I need to make another appointment.'

'Oh, all right,' he says tersely. 'I can fit you in tomorrow at four.'

'All right.'

'At four. See you then. Bye.' And he hangs up quickly.

He hates me for needing him! I cry. I shouldn't have rung. Yes, I should. I need help. But now he despises me.

This is mad. I have got to get this sorted out before he goes. I can't keep feeling like I'm a sheet about to go through the wringer.

I drive to Tony's office thinking it's a mistake. He hates me and he's going to tell me off.

'Come in. Come in,' he says with his usual caring voice. 'How are you?'

'Anxious. And sad,' I tell him. 'Depressed and I can't stop crying. Then I can't feel anything else. What's happening to me?'

'As I've said to you before, you've got to expect times of dysphoria. They're the result of a profound experience. But you'll learn to put it aside.'

'I don't just mean the dysphoria thing. I mean my feelings for you. I'm mangled and anxious about you going away. Everything else seems harder to cope with.'

'Tell me about the feelings.'

'They're like I told you last time. Dependence, love, need. Only it felt like you were pushing me away too, and I couldn't cope without you but you couldn't see that. Then when I rang you for this appointment you were so abrupt it sounded like you were pushing me away, sick of me because I need you. I'm so confused I can't think straight.' I'm so embarrassed saying all this.

'We've talked about transference neurosis, haven't we?'

'No!' Neurosis? I'm neurotic, a Woody Allen character after all! Being called neurotic makes me more anxious.

'We've talked about it before. Transference. You don't remember?'

'Yes, transference, but not neurosis.'

'Transference. Transference neurosis.'

Anxious about being so dumb!

'We've talked about the bond between people who share deep experiences,' Tony continues. 'It may last a couple of months, then it resolves. You feel certain things for me and they are reciprocated. All right? I've become very fond of you. You're a lovely, attractive, intelligent woman and I feel very close to you. All right? It's real. From the heart. It's not a game or a trick. It is real.'

'But it's so . . . so . . . false. I mean, what do you do about it?'

'It is real. The feelings of love are real and there's no need to worry or be anxious about it. I'm trained to keep it in a professional perspective and not let it get out of control. Right?'

320

'But it makes me dependent. Anxious. Can't manage without you and you're going away.' And I'm crying again.

'I know, but I know how to stop the dependence getting out of control. Look, we'll work through all this when I get back if you need to, but my prediction is that you'll feel much less strongly by then.'

'Can't imagine this just dissolving.'

'I assure you it will resolve and I can help you with that if you need my help,' he says gently, calmly.

'I don't like love. Not like this is. In fact, you know, well, can I tell you something disturbing? My neighbour asked me if I've ever loved anybody, a man, and when I was honest, I had to say no, I hadn't. That's dreadful, isn't it?'

'Well, no. Let's look at it. Think about the inhibitors that get in the way of a proper transference happening for you. You react to men the way you reacted to your father when you were a child. All the inhibitions that that relationship created operate in relationships now. All right?'

'I don't know.' I want to please him by saying I understand, but I can't say it. I loved my father when I was a child. I was afraid of him and I loved him. I can't see how that translates to the present day. 'How do I change and be like normal people?'

'You're making progress with the work we're doing here. Next time you meet someone you'll be different.'

'Well, I'd better feel differently about you by the time I do. And much less dependent. This is weird.'

'Don't worry. We'll work through it.'

'Wish there was a quick fix. But I suppose we just plug on when you get back and I'll go bankrupt getting sane. The boarder is coming, so I might be able to afford more work then. As long as the building society cooperates with interest rates.'

'We'll see. But we've covered the basic aims of therapy . . .'

Covered the basics! Tony keeps talking but I'm not listening. How can he think we're finished? I wasn't a neurotic mess like this when we started. Is he just saying that because I told him

I might not be able to afford more work for a while? Surely therapy shouldn't leave a person feeling dependent and in love with their therapist. I should feel as if we've finished, shouldn't I? Resolved feelings about my father. Realistic view of my mother. Truly strong at work. And if I mee–

'All right?'

'Mm? Oh, I don't feel like we've covered everything. I feel as if we've started lots of things but they haven't come together yet. They're not finished. My health fund rebate is all I see as finished. I need you to show me how to pull all the bits together and change how I do things.'

'Well, of course we can do more later, at any time. But for now the task is to use the skills you've learnt to move ahead, into the next phase of your life. Right?'

Don't leave me! Please, please don't leave me!

'Look, let's do some deep hypnosis work on ego strength and relaxation.'

'Good idea.' I have progressed.

'Would you like to lie down?'

'No!' Maybe I haven't progressed.

Disappointed in myself, I sit in the chair and listen to Tony's voice. I feel relaxation move down my arms and soon I'm wandering along a stream then Tony is counting me back to the office.

'It's always hard to come back,' I tell him.

'That's good. Well, let's see how you're going when I get back. I'll give you a call.'

I don't feel as anxious about his going now. 'Before you go, I want to tell you that I'm very grateful for your help with all this. Especially going to my mother's grave and remembering her.'

'Thank you.' He smiles and hesitates as if he's savouring my thanks. Then he adds, 'I've enjoyed helping. It's been good for me too.'

I can't imagine why.

'Our next step will be to get your file and use that to expand

322

your knowledge of yourself. I'll be in touch when I get back.'

'All right. Hope your trip goes well.'

'Oh. How about you take this and read it?' he suggests, handing me a book from his shelf. 'It'll get you in the mood for your study and get you thinking. It's a classic. You know about the Bowlby study, don't you? Maternal deprivation and so on?'

The book is called *Attachment and Loss*. I'd prefer a Mickey Mouse comic but I accept the book and tell myself I'll read it.

Driving home, getting worried. No! I won't think about him being away. If I do, though, I'll keep reminding myself that I will be able to cope. I am strong. I'll replay the words over and over in my head. I wish the love would go away. He said he'll miss me. He loves me. Someone who knows all about my deepest, darkest secrets loves me! Imagine . . . No, stop! Back to reality. It's not real, even if he says it is. It isn't for keeps. He has a wife and kids. I just have to wait for the feelings to resolve.

All right. What do I need to do or how do I need to think so that I'll keep progressing? Tony says it will happen more quickly when I'm doing ego-strengthening study. That's not 'til next year. What 'til then? If only I could bottle that feeling of power I had at the cemetery. I'd take a swig every time loneliness or depression or insecurity threaten.

What about those inhibitions Tony said stop normal transference happening? Elliott. Am I, was I afraid of him? No. Gareth? No. Cameron? No. See. There's nothing there to get me moving forward. Do I have to wait for the next man who I meet and experiment on him?

Oh, someone tell me what to do! I want my mummy. She probably wouldn't know either. She was a late starter too. I wonder why. I'll never know.

Tony said, 'Next time you meet a man you won't make the same mistakes you've made in the past.' What was the mistake with Gareth? Curiosity about whether I was too damaged to have a normal sexual relationship. Had that tricked me into thinking I was in love? Maybe, but I think it was more that I got love and sex confused. Movies and magazines encourage that confusion, if you don't watch out. What about Cameron? Nothing happened for me with him except that weird thing when he dumped me. I never felt close to him. No transference. Nothing until the sheer panic when he dumped me. What was that about? Haven't even got to that panic thing with Tony yet. How can he think we could call it finished? No, he said we could do more later. Back to the point. Elliott. Was that a transference reaction? Maybe for me. Not for him. He can take or leave me. No counter transference. Well, where is all this going, anyway? Don't know.

I try not to notice the date today but no amount of trying helps. It's the day Tony and Vlad leave for their trip. Keep telling myself I'll be all right. At least I won't be alone tonight. It's Gen's father's seventieth birthday party. Gen's parents have always treated me warmly and I like that they welcome me as family and obviously care. This time, surrounded by the big family, I feel calmer, less like a poor relation. I would have been part of a family like this if my mother had survived. I'd have had a normal family. I'm not a lesser being. I had a family once.

'How are your uni plans going?' Gen asks. She thinks I'll breeze through.

'I've sorted out two years' worth and then I hope I'll do a thesis. Won't have to go in to uni every week then. But Elliott's invited me to go to the Kimberley next year so I might take second semester off and use some long service leave.'

'Oh, Kate! Don't. Get your degree.'

'It's only one semester.'

'You're wasting your time with Elliott! He's got no commitment to you. He's just using you.'

'Using me? Oh, we're using each other, I suppose. I wouldn't get to see that country at all if it weren't for Elliott. We're going as friends, that's all. Just friends.'

'Take a bus trip when you finish your degree. How are you going to meet anyone when you keep seeing him?'

'I'll think about it, Mum,' I tell Gen. We call each other 'Mum' when we're giving advice.

As I drive home I think about my mum. Specifically about her heart. Not the one she loved me with but the physical one that gave up when she was forty-seven. I've got nine years to go. What? Nine years until what? Good heavens! I realise now that I've always thought I'd die at forty-seven because my mother did. It hasn't been a conscious thought. Just something I've known. But I don't want to die at forty-seven! I must be stark raving bonkers. I don't have to die. I might not. I'm healthy and strong. Just have to cut down on stress. I drive home forcing myself to be calm but soon I'm feverishly planning strategies to stay healthy and alive beyond the next nine years.

Aerobics. They have that at the local gym. I join a night class and find it's fun. Stops me thinking about Tony being away. Until I wake at night from my new recurring dream.

My face is inches from my mother's orange clock. I'm watching it, intrigued. I move it aside and there behind it is the brown clock, leering menacingly. I wake up terrified. Got to tell Tony. Got to hear him tell me the clock can't hurt me. Whatever the clock is. What is it? Cache of my secrets? But I know that now so I don't need a new dream to show me that. A terror clock behind a lovely clock. A screen behind a screen? Surely memories aren't like onions that burn your eyes with every layer you pull off.

There's the locker dream too. How many times now have I tried to bundle all my stuff out of my Burnside locker and into my suitcase on the day I'm leaving? The locker is always full and I don't know what is mine or whether I'm really coming or going. I don't know where I live. The real locker at Burnside was a thirty-centimetre cube and all I owned was kept in it. We stole from each other and hid our treasures right at the back. Is that what it's about somehow, or is the locker a symbol?

Symbol for what? I haven't a clue.

Should start that book Tony loaned me. I do but I can't concentrate. Do it later. In the holidays at the farm.

At uni the enrolment queue is much longer than I imagined it would be. So much for Tony's insinuation that Masters students are a small elite group. There are hundreds of us winding our way around like sheep in yards, waiting to get processed. I take my course program to the table and hand it to the professor, who smiles, scans and checks my plan, then hands it back. 'Well, you know who you are and where you're going!'

'Sometimes anyway,' I mumble as I join the next queue. I have come a long way since Tony suggested I do another degree. Most of the time I'm less fragile, stronger, more in control or at least more confident that I'll get control. As I meander slowly along in the queue, I look at the other students, especially the men's left-hand ring fingers, testing Tony's assertion that I'll meet Mr Right here. The prospects look grim. Most students are women and the few men have rings on the target finger. Where do single men go? It's one of life's great mysteries. Are they all hiding in a secret men's university, secret men's bushwalking clubs or music societies or dance groups?

James has moved in and I hardly see him. Tonight I'm in a deep sleep but I'm woken by banging on the front door. James might answer it. 'Kate, are you awake?' he yells from outside. I get up and just as I arrive to let him in, he opens the door.

'The key doesn't work,' he declares.

'You're in!'

'Couldn't get it to turn.'

'I'll look in the morning. Goodnight.'

More words than we've had for two or three days. I get a new key cut and leave it with a note. The key and note are gone when I get home from work. If only all my life were this simple! Leave a note, problem solved.

At school we're getting ready for the end of year celebrations. Kids are enjoying making presents for their families and decorating our room. We've finished enrolling next year's lot and I'm already looking forward to teaching them. If only I could sort Maud out permanently.

'I'm hoping to hear today or tomorrow who'll be appointed for next year,' Peter tells me. 'Let's hope it's not Maud.'

'If it is, I won't be back,' I reply.

Do I mean it? Probably not. But I want to make a stand against the irresponsible employment of someone so obviously unsuitable for the job. I'll wait and see what happens. I could probably get a job somewhere else but I'd have to take a sizeable drop in salary. James's board money won't pay the mortgage.

We don't hear of a replacement for Maud before the end of the year. I go on holidays hoping it will be sorted out by the time we come back.

I ring the home church. The man who answers, Phil, listens while I tell him my Sydney contacts. We have some mutual friends. He gives me the information I ask for but I find myself resisting committing myself to go to it. I have nothing to offer. I'd be a taker, not a sharer. I tell Phil I'll be in touch again after my holiday.

Next I go shopping. I saw an idea for Christmas parcels of homemade biscuits and I'm going to give these to the neighbours. Tony too. It'll be an excuse to see him and tell him the transference thing is not abating.

Spending the morning cooking, I remember Aunty Dot telling me that my mother loved baking and that she'd been a professional cake decorator for a while. I'll learn decorating one day. Wish my mother could teach me.

I'm getting gloomy again, feeling lonely. Wanting to ring Tony. He'd be back by now but he hasn't contacted me like he said he would. It hurts. I suppose he's busy. Wish he could permanently stop this sadness sneaking up, instead of my always having to hide from it by keeping busy. I make a mental tally of my friends, starting as usual with the close ones and working my way out to the edges of friendship circles. I shouldn't feel lonely but the depth of that feeling is getting scary, sapping my energy, always there like a cat ready to pounce.

'Been baking?' James, back from his day job, interrupts.

'Yes. Christmas presents,' I tell him.

'Mind if I make tea?'

While he makes his usual cup of tea and toast with vegemite, he suggests how I should wrap the biscuits and what I should tie them with.

'That's all sorted out. By the way, I'm having a house warming at the end of January. An all-day thing, so I hope you don't mind. You're welcome to join in if you want to.'

'No, that doesn't bother me. Who's coming?'

'Friends from Sydney mostly, where I used to live. School, church, dancing and music friends.'

'Sounds good.' He suggests I should do this, that and the other on the day. Thank goodness he and his ideas are off to work again.

I package the biscuits, make cards, and set them out in a basket. They look pretty good! Classy and festive. Perhaps I inherited some artistic talent from my mother. The neighbours seem pleased as I deliver the gifts. Only Tony's to go. What if he thinks it's silly or inappropriate? What if he doesn't like them? What if? What if? What if? Surrounded by calories and what ifs, I decide to just do it. He's told me so many times to express my feelings, so I will.

On the card I write, *Dear Tony, Happy Christmas and thanks.* What next? *Love, Kate? From Kate? Kate?*

Do the vacuuming, then decide.

It's okay to call it love and not be ashamed or embarrassed. If that's what I feel, that's what I have to say. '*Love from Kate.*' I write it on the card. My heart sinks because he still hasn't rung. If he doesn't soon, I'll ring him, I suppose.

I go for a walk. With every step loneliness seems to be

magnified. I wish it was time to go to the farm. In the street I can see people's decorations and sometimes their trees in the front window. I have a wreath on my door but what's the use of a tree? I'll be at the farm, anyway. James can have one if he likes. No, he doesn't condone the commercial exploitation of his Christian values. Thank goodness for my treasured friends at the farm! We'll have a tree with presents, as well as prayers, singing and reading of the Christmas story.

Back at home the phone rings. 'G'day Kate. Tony here.'

'Oh hello. How was your trip?' How soon can I see you?

'Good. It was good. Very productive. We made some important contacts and now we can get our submission together. We've been flat out on it, as a matter of fact.'

'I'm glad you're back.'

'Thanks. Look, I've got your file from the home here, so drop in sometime and pick it up. All right?'

'When?'

'Oh, anytime. I'll be here. All right?'

He still cares. The doubts I've been harbouring are erased. It's my insecurity that's the problem, not him.

'This afternoon? Will you be there?'

'Yes. That will be fine.'

I'll take the biscuits, tell him about the clock dream and get the file. Then I'll ask two very specific questions: What can I do to resolve the love? And how can I stop the loneliness? Stop it, not hide from it. Perhaps I won't be able to ask, though. This isn't a session. It's just-a pick-up-the-file meeting.

It'll be interesting to see the file too. It might be scary, though. What if there's something in it about the darkness and my fil– . . . what I said that day and . . . I forget so easily that I wasn't bad or filthy.

When I knock on Tony's door I'm less confident about bringing the gift. I feel quaint and silly but I can't hide it now.

'What's this?' he smiles as I hand it to him. 'For me? Did you make these for me?' He places the parcel carefully on his table and looks at it for a while. I'm embarrassed because he thinks I baked just for him. 'I'm really touched. Thank you.'

Now I feel appreciated. Relieved.

'Well now, the Burnside file.' He takes an envelope from his drawer and puts it on his table. I don't want a polite introduction to it. I want to snatch it and rip it open, see if there's anything about Kevin, about the matrons knowing about my father. But Tony clasps his hands on it and explains, 'I've read it through and I don't think there's anything in it that would trouble you too much. There'll be some sobering moments but you will know what to do with them. All right?'

'All right. Gosh, it looks so thin!'

'There's not a lot but it'll be interesting for you. Remember we talked about ego strengthening. This will give you a picture of the child you were, where you came from.' His serious face melts to a smile and he adds, 'The worst thing is you Shayler kids nearly didn't get into the homes because you had bad eyesight!' He slides the envelope across the table adding, 'Take it home and read it when you've got a quiet moment. Just take it slowly and use your strengths to process what you find.'

It feels light. I squeeze it, hoping it's thicker than it looks. 'I write more than this in a year for every single kid I teach! This is all there is for twelve years!'

'They've blocked out some parts, too, because they think those are not your business,' he says with a grin, standing up to see me to the door!

'It's in my file and it's not my business?' I say, staying seated.

'It's about your brother and sister. They have to maintain their privacy.'

I remember how my sister and I fought as girls. 'What if it's too horrible?'

'I'm sure you'll cope.' He's standing beside the chair now so I gather my bag and my questions.

'I'm off to the farm this week. I'll ring when I get back. With the boarder I might be able to afford more work.'

'Good. How is it going with the boarder?'

'Oh, all right. His favourite thing is to give me a sermon on toast every afternoon. But I don't see much of him. I need his money, though. More therapy. Sort out my feelings and . . . stuff.' How embarrassing that all this great mind can come up with is 'stuff'! 'I mean, like the depression and anxiety and feeling like . . .'

'If you like, we can do more work, but wait 'til you're studying and see how you are then.'

Don't leave me.

'I can't stop crying sometimes, getting depressed.' Chin quivers.

'When you're studying, you'll be right. You'll be mixing with interesting people, learning more and you'll be more aware of your strengths.'

I can't make him understand how utterly miserable I get. How lonely I feel despite friendships. How can study change that? Keeping busy isn't the answer. It's just hiding. Stop ushering me out and let me ask the big question.

'Can you tell me . . . um . . . well . . . I still have these feelings for you. They didn't go away when you were overseas. I want to know how to make them go. I mean, you said they'd resolve, but they haven't. They're getting worse.'

'If you still have those feelings when you get back from the farm, I'll be very surprised. All right?'

'I won't,' I reply. 'Be surprised, I mean.'

'We'll see.'

'Well. Have a happy Christmas,' I say, standing at last.

'You too, love,' he says gently. He puts his arm around me as we walk to the door.

Love! He called me love. Meaningless. Forget it.

A whirlwind is messing around in my head as I leave. It must be meaningless. I shouldn't take any notice, shouldn't wish it had meant something. It's a therapeutic tool that will resolve to nothing. He's married too. Forget it.

Meanwhile, I'll have a look at my ego-strengthening file.

The first page is a polite covering letter from the Aftercare Worker offering help if I need it. The offer evokes a sense of foreboding, as if an old bag of a matron will be watching, ready to punish me if I get the responses to my file wrong. My distrust of current Burnside staff surprises me. It'd be a whole new staff by now. Aftercare Worker. Is that a position that had to be created because other homes kids had problems fitting in out here too? I don't know any others. I haven't met a single one since I left. Not that it's something you'd tell anyone or want anyone to know.

Under the covering letter is a form so familiar to me from my insurance clerking days. Certificate of Death. But this time my mother's name is on it. It slams into my chest, ruptures my heart. The never of never seeing her again is amplified a million times. I'm sobbing.

Mummy, Mummy, Mummy. Where are you? Come back!

I try to stop crying. To be an adult. But I'm not. I'm the child again and I want my mummy. Curled up like a baby, wanting Mummy.

Have to stop. Contact strong and capable adult. Mummy loved me, knew I was perfect. Perfect is lovable. I'm all right. Will be all right. Won't I? If I can ever stop crying. Missing her so badly. Feeling so lonely.

Can't read any more. Don't want to know the unlovable child I was. No, the unlovable child I became after I got lost, when the whole, perfect child waited inside herself for her mother to come back. While the self she came to know best was loathsome filth.

Put the file away. It's not ego strengthening. It's depressing. Work in the garden. Try not to think. Eventually curiosity draws me back.

Norma Shayler died on the twenty-second of November. Exactly thirty-four years and one month ago! How could it hurt so much after thirty-four years and one month?

There are our names, Ken's, Kerry's and mine. A temporary

family on a death certificate. And a gravestone. Wipe the tears away and turn the page.

A report from Mr Bolton, whoever he is, about our family is next. There we are together at our address in a little house. Like normal people. The Smiths, Joneses and Shaylers. Mr Bolton thinks it's important to record that our father was earning seventeen pounds a week as a plumber and he owned the house.

His age is such that it is out of the question for him to care for the children much longer. He shows such depression at the loss of his wife that it is not out of the bounds of possibility that he may not long survive her.

I need tissues to get to the end of that paragraph, confronted with new pain. My father's. Have I ever understood that he was grieving? Dying of grief?

Oh, I'm sorry, Dad. I'm so, so sorry. I didn't know.

Crying for the old man who's lost his wife and can't go on. He's sitting in the kitchen weeping, stopping himself, going through the motions for three bewildered children who won't let him forget for a minute.

I remember an old blue book of my father's with a piece of paper hidden in it. He'd written on it but had forbidden me to read it. I did later and I kept it when he died. The secret words were about me asking if Mummy would ever come back. He'd written that Jesus is the only one who's ever come back. I remember a little pink card with bobby pins slid onto it. I found that after our father died and I've kept it too. An adult had written, '*Happy Mother's Day, Mummy, from Katherine.*' It had made me cry before I'd started any of this. We must have done normal family things once, before our family fell apart. Our daddy fell apart. Our father, I mean.

But he had us. Didn't that help? He still had her in her children. People who lose spouses get comfort from their children, don't they? They do in movies. Weren't we enough?

A TUESDAY THING

Remembering what my father turned into, his darkness and destruction, I get angry. Furious. No excuses, Dad. Ever. Why did you do it? Why? You were all we had left!

Stop reading. Too much energy. Pace, steaming with anger and hurt and confusion. Who is this person I'm becoming? Go back to the file. Get it over with.

Mr Bolton reports that there are no relatives who can help us. Our thirty-seven-year-old half-sister, Zelda, has little contact with us and she's only mentioned because she's our next of kin. Her ex-husband, Jack, has remained friends with our father and so his details are recorded too.

Uncle Jack! I remember him. I haven't seen him since my father died. He bought a farm somewhere I think. Uncle Jack with his taxi that drove us around the triangle of poppies near a road close to Burnside. 'Around the poppies,' and I knew another goodbye to my father would have to be said soon. We'd been to Nanna's. Nanna!

Crying for Nanna.

Our father took us to her place on visiting days. Red peanut lollies from shopkeeper on the way from Wiley Park station. A packet of ballerina lollies for Nanna. Nanna in her pinny waiting, smiling, at the door. Roger, her dog, who we adored! Baked dinners! Ice-cream and blowfly topping. If only everything behind the curtain was like this.

Crying softly, remembering Nanna. Nanna's love. Nanna's dog. Their deaths. When will I have cried enough?

Is there something here I can read out without crying?

Why does Mr Bolton say we had no relatives who could help? We did. The aunties who visited at Burnside, Aunty Dot and Aunty Marj. Well they weren't real relatives but they were close friends of my mother. So was my godmother who I don't remember seeing more than once or twice. Our father used to tell us that we had no relatives in Australia then one day some women who said they were our aunties started coming to Burnside. They took other kids out on visiting days but we met them

334

too. When I left Burnside I saw them sometimes and Aunty Dot told me she wanted to take Kerry and me after our mother died but our father didn't want to separate us. He must have told Mr Bolton there was no-one.

The Children. There's a paragraph about us. I have a photo of the three of us and friends say we were gorgeous. I want to read the paragraph about us being gorgeous.

I was not altogether impressed with these . . .

Stupid, stupid man.

After tears, curiosity.

I was not altogether impressed with these but it is very difficult to form any judgement on them for they show obvious signs of upset at the loss of the mother. They may be a little spoiled as they gave me that impression when I called to see them.

The floodgates open.

Mummy's gone somewhere and no-one wants us. When's she coming back?

I throw the file angrily on the table and pace like a fire-breathing dragon. I have to, to stop myself exploding. I wish I hadn't read any of that stuff.

Upset! Bolton said we were 'upset'. At the loss of our mother! Who was that fool who describes it as 'upset'? Try 'traumatised'! Is that in your vocab? We were, I was, I am, much more upset than upset. And it's thirty four-years later!

I snatch the bloody file and read Bolton's last paragraph to finish him off.

In view of the difficulty Shayler is finding in securing help in his emergency he asked that the case be treated as an urgent one and that we admit the children before Christmas, if possible.

Freeze.

Don't think. Stay numb.

Wander. Repack the Christmas presents for Col and Leonie and the kids.

Admit the children before Christmas.

Don't think.

Going to Gen and Paddy's for dinner. I wrap the presents for my gorgeous godchildren, whom I would give my life to if their parents died. As I drive to Sydney I concentrate on the radio and the traffic that seems more frenetic than it was six months ago when I drove in it without this tension. I don't mind the congestion, noise, speed, aggression. It all helps to stop me thinking about anything else.

We have a happy night and I'm pleased that the kids love their presents. I never used to compare friends' families with what mine might have been like, but now I do. My family might have been like this one. Mother, father, three kids. Three loved and wanted kids.

'Tony got my file from Burnside,' I tell Gen and Paddy as we wash up.

'Oh good. Does it say anything? I'd love to read it,' says Gen.

'There's not much of it but it's so depressing. I don't know why anyone'd want to see it. My mother's death certificate made me bawl my head off and that was at the front.'

'Well it would, wouldn't it? You haven't seen it before.'

'Tony thought it wouldn't,' I reply shakily.

'Oh, of course it would!'

'I get sad about my mother's,' Paddy says.

'Do you? Still? After all these years.'

'Yeah, still.'

'That's encouraging. Oh! Sorry. I just mean maybe I'm not nuts then.'

'Now listen Kate.' He grins. 'It's quite possible we both are. You're a reformed homes kids and I'm a reformed Catholic.' We laugh but I wonder why Tony thought I wouldn't be distressed.

Soon it's time for me to thank my friends for the offer of a bed for the night and drive home.

'Thanks, but I'm going to the farm in the morning.'

A farm welcome includes hugs from everyone and keeping presents hidden under a rug in my car while my bag is whisked away to a new shearers' hut that Leonie and Col have built across the garden from the house. It's fresh and cosy. And mine! Well, for now anyway.

When I go to bed I decide to tackle my file again. Not the best bedtime story available but Leonie and Col want to look at it before I go home. They're as keen as Gen and Paddy. I'm lucky I have friends who are so concerned and interested in my childhood and my life now.

Death certificate lump in my throat. I'm able to read more of it now. My grandmother's name was Mary. Mary! My middle name. Wow! Mother's mother. Grandmother! Named after my grandmother. Family expanding, at least on paper. My father hadn't been able to remember where my 'Mary' had come from when I asked him.

My mother's father – mother's father equals grandfather – my grandfather's name was Frederick Eli, an engine-room attendant. Eli! The name reminds me of my favourite Bible story as a child. Samuel, the child sent to live with Eli, the old priest. Samuel found God, not Eli, calling him in the night. I didn't know why I loved the story. Maybe I felt like Samuel, alienated from his family. Maybe I wanted an Eli to guide me.

When I was young God spoke to me in the night across the universe, inside me. He said, 'I am with you,' and made me belong. Wish I'd remember that more, feel it again. When I go home, I'll join the home church and spend time with people who do remember.

I flip through the type-written pages of the file and see some ragged handwriting. It's my own anxious teenage script. I close the file and turn off the light. I'm afraid of sleep tonight but I don't like being awake and thinking either. Awake and crying. Thank God the hut I stay in is away from the house.

The next day I hand my file over to Col, although I haven't read half of it. When he puts the file on his desk to read later, I want to grab it back and read some more, but there's work to be done. As we walk out to the paddock I wonder what having a grandmother would be like. The farm kids have two who they love to bits. Nanna! I had Nanna. Perhaps I know.

We pull out and bag saffron thistle, trying to control it without chemicals. Leonie and I talk while the kids are not around, but just as I broach the subject of therapy and the issues it's brought to the surface, an exultant little voice calls, 'Hi there, Mum and Kate. Bet you didn't know I could catch up so quick!' Tina beams her usual smile and swings her skipping rope.

The conversation changes and we wander home. We watch the sky turn gold as the sun sets. It reminds me of what seems a lifetime ago when I'd just met Gareth and was full of hope that I'd have a husband and children and live happily ever after. If only this glorious, golden sky was a promise and not just a glorious golden sky.

The night before I'm due to leave the farm, Leonie and Col make sure there's time for us to sit down together after the kids are in bed. This is a custom I treasure. If there hasn't been time to talk about something, there'll always be this chance.

Col hands the file back and says, 'That's really something. There's so much in it. Heart-wrenching stuff, some of it. Well, most of it.'

'You think so?' It's not just me overreacting?

'Oh, the scene with your father warming his hands on the stove. And those letters you wrote as a teenager. That's powerful stuff.'

'It is? I haven't read the letters yet.'

'It's not so much the words. It's what's behind them.'

'We had no idea you'd been through all that,' Leonie says solemnly.

'I don't remember a lot of it. It was grim sometimes, I think, especially when the social worker went and carked it right when I needed her.' Tears are threatening.

'What happened to her?'

'Don't know. I think she must have had a heart attack or something but she wasn't very old. That was the worst time. I got suicidal then. That's when I wrote the letters, I think.'

'You're such a champion. You've been through all that and you've still got such a great sense of humour and you're so sane! It never ceases to amaze me and now even more so.'

While I wish I felt sane, Col concurs.

'M'dear, I couldn't have put it better myself. Have you written any of your story yet?'

They've both been telling me for years that I should. 'Ah, the trials and tribulations of a Burnside Childhood. Chapter one, the tale of the holy Sunday afternoon toilet paper folding! No, I haven't. Who'd want to know? Except you? Ewes?'

We laugh and they tell me lots of people would want to know. But Leonie and Col are biased. They love me.

It's time to go home but it doesn't feel like home this time. James, harmless but so annoying, will be there but not companionable.

I manage to dodge him as I unpack my farm bag and repack for Gulgong. I'm going to the music festival there. I'll see old friends, invite them to my house warming and get some dancing done.

Use up time. Avoid a paper teenager in the file.

When I get back home I write to Aunty Dot and tell her I've been thinking a lot about Mum. I like using the word, especially to Aunty Dot who remembers the relationship. We usually exchange Christmas cards with brief news, Aunty Dot's handwriting becoming shakier every year. But brief news isn't enough this year. She was my mother's close friend and I need her to tell me every detail she remembers. Aunty Marj and my godmother could do that too. I invite them all to come up and see my house. I'm sure they'll be pleased that I've got one and it would be nice to see them.

They don't reply to my invitation but I'll go and see them all one day.

I really should read more of my file. No use putting it off. Aftercare Worker, death certificate, unimpressive children. Uh, a social worker's report of nineteen sixty-three. Thirteen I was then.

Miss Molesworth must have written it. Mary Molesworth, who I loved, who I needed and who died. It seems so long ago but it still makes me sad. I still sometimes wear her brooch, the memento her mother gave me after the funeral. The brooch is lovely and I like that I have a reminder of the light she brought to my troubled teenage years.

Miss Molesworth has written a summary of our family, the dates of our admission and reasons we were sent to Burnside. She says my father has been most responsible over the years in visiting and in paying his fees. He is very much aware of his children's feelings.

Yes. That's the Dad we were taught to love and be proud of. That's the Dad who makes me feel so guilty when I hate him. There's not even a hint of darkness in this report. He hid it so well and left me, the child, with the consequences. Was he aware of my feelings!

The children spent the Christmas vacation with their father and he is adamant that he does not want them to go to strangers.

Strangers! Stranger danger. What a joke! Research shows that children are in more danger from people known to their families than from strangers. We've been told that in Child Protection Program training at school and I'm living proof of it.

Move on before it gets too dark.

A letter to my father from Burnside.

One of our social workers would like to have a talk with you when you visit on Saturday, 19th September. Please ring and let us know what time is convenient.

Both girls have German measles and are in our hospital, though they are not very sick. They will probably be home when you visit.

Nineteen sixty-four. Fourteen. I remember German measles! Well, I remember being in the hospital, lazing in the sun on a banana chair, dozing like we were never allowed to at home. Garden of Eden and the chorus of a thousand magpies singing in the gum trees.

Another social worker's report. This might say what they talked to him about. Heart beats a little faster. Did they know now and confront him?

22.3.65. Katherine is unable to work out a plan to join the Parramatta fellowship unless Christine goes with her. With a lot of help she was able to talk about her shyness and difficulty approaching strangers. I suggested she tends to wait until people come ninety-nine percent of the way to her. We talked about how people get to know each other. She could accept this intellectually but her anxiety around new and strange experiences is too great to let her make an adjustment.

Heart racing. Told I had to go to fellowship by myself. Cripplingly shy. Anxious. That social worker, Mrs Nordstrom, with an accent I could almost understand, said it would be good for me. Me, expected to have conversations! Mrs Nordstrom thought I knew what she was talking about, while I wondered what whatever it was had to do with me. She was the only person in the world who called me Katherine.

Mr Ross is not in favour of Christine joining Katherine and the two going together.

Oh yeah. Old Ross wouldn't let Christine come. She wanted to go but I didn't; she wasn't allowed to and I was forced. Terrified of all those outsiders gawking at me, feeling superior. Looking superior. Being superior?

I talked with Miss Porter from the school and she is quite willing to call for Katherine. She and her fiancé are the fellowship leaders and she assures me there is a group of friendly girls Katherine's age who would make a newcomer welcome.

Disaster as drab, shy me tries to talk to prissy, confident outsiders who turn their backs. Pain? Details later. Keep reading.

At fifteen I was called to the social worker's office again. She wanted to hear what my goals were, because I'd soon be leaving. She was impressed that I had gaols. Unimpressive child has impressive goals! Mrs Nordstrom didn't know that I got the goals from the school careers adviser. I simply regurgitated what she'd said. Girls like me would probably marry and leave work to have a family, so a career like bank clerk or public servant would suffice. I had very little idea what adult women did but I didn't care, because I was going to meet a nice boy and so on.

Except, *Kate is a rather plump girl with glasses and acne but she has a pleasant personality.*

The genesis of 'poor body image', as Tony calls it. It hurts as much now as it did then. When they first told me that I was the wrong shape I was shocked. I'd never thought it mattered until then. Us girls had compared our dimensions and praised the big ones because we were strong and tough. Skinny girls at high school skited about bikinis but I didn't want such a rude outfit anyway. The staff taught me to despise my dimensions and there were diets and pills that convinced me I was ugly. And the reason I should lose weight, they said, was so I'd look nicer. Nicer for whom? Well, boys, of course! Mrs Nordstrom managed to find one redeeming feature. I think she meant I was polite. The aunties at least added teeth and eyes to the list of my redeeming features. How can I recover from twenty years of telling myself that from the chin down I'm not all right?

I resist the urge to look in the mirror. What is in my head is what I need to deal with, not what's over there in the mirror. But this has been one of the most persistent clouds over my adult life. I'm never good enough because I'm the wrong shape. Maybe Gareth, Elliott, and even Cameron had poor eyesight or poor judgement. Tony said I'm attractive but he must have meant what he sees beyond the external shape.

Tony. He thought I wouldn't be too upset by any of this. I must be weak or stupid or something. As well as upset.

There's a note now saying that the social worker was curious about my hobbies. Hobbies! A luxury allowed only in the last year I was there. Prior to that we'd worked like slaves in our 'free time'. I nominated swimming as my main hobby and knitting next. Unimpressive hobbies of unimpressive girl. Well, I could have knitted a swimming cossie while swimming.

Hmm. Must be time to stop reading for a while.

It's raining and the wallpaper in the bathroom is starting to curl up at the edges. I was always going to take it off, so maybe now is the time. How easily will it come off? I rip and half a sheet lets go. Easy. Next please. Oh, not so easy and now the bathroom looks dreadful. I have to finish the job now – can't leave it like this for James or the house warming. Ripping paper off is therapeutic!

A man from home church rings to invite me for dinner with his family. 'Thea and I thought it might be nice for you to get to know some of us before you come to church. And vice versa,' he explains.

I know I'm being checked out, so I'll be honest about my reservations, what I believe in and how I feel.

Brian and Thea have two little boys who are delightfully mis-chievous and who smooth my passage into conversation. I peep during grace and see little Owen peeping at me. We grin and close our eyes. During dinner I discover that Brian is a teacher and he understands how it must be working with untrained people. Thea is an artist but she has been a teacher too.

'Lots of us teachers in the church,' Brian says.

'Where does your family live, Kate?' Thea asks.

'Um. I don't have any.'

'How do you mean? What happened?'

'Uh, I don't know if I should say with the short people present.' This is the first time I've been in this position. Other friends knew my story before their kids were born.

'Oh, right. Later. Where did you start your teaching . . .'

After dinner, when the short people are giggling in their bedroom, we exchange stories. I give a very brief version of mine, to avoid an emotional trial and end with, 'So I don't feel I have a lot to give just now. I make a mean loaf of bread, though!'

'Great! We'll take the bread!' Thea laughs.

'I'm not sure how you feel about having someone who's got a psychologist working on them either,' I add.

'Gosh, no wonder you have,' says Brian. 'Everyone needs help sometimes. We all have various levels of needing and giving at different times, don't you think so, love?'

'Oh, absolutely. There are other people in our church who've had counselling and we don't think they're crazy. Don't worry about it.'

'Well, I'll see you on Sunday.'

Wish I could see Tony. I need to get all this childhood trauma into some shape and perspective. To give it limits and work out how it affects me now. And I need to tell him that I still feel this way about him. I can't ring. I'm too embarrassed to still need him when he thinks I should be moving on. I'll keep trying to keep being an adult.

I'll tackle the file – The File – again. Social worker's notes, continued:

I tried to point out to Kate that her father's age and feeble health could make it most difficult for him to care for three teenagers.

344

Kate listened intently to all the drawbacks I described but she probably has very little concept of the real difficulties.

I'd hated the social worker then. She was telling me my father, my ticket to family bliss, was going to die. For twelve years I'd watched other kids leave in triumph to go and live in families. At last it was my turn and she was trying to spoil it. Telling me I needed to think about alternatives. I saw none. My father was the only person I belonged with. He hadn't abused me since my periods had started at age ten. He was where I belonged but Miss Molesworth was willing him to die before I got there. Got home. I didn't know how right she was or how much I'd come to love her. I just cried and cried at the thought that I might not have a family after all. Might not have a father. I'm crying now.

I skip through the next few pages to get to my letters but my father's name catches my eye.

Mr Shayler was sitting in the kitchen beside the stove with the hotplate on to warm his hands.

Crying for my old father who felt the cold so badly through his tissue-thin skin. How poor was he if he couldn't afford a radiator? Why was he poor? Because his wage went to pay our Burnside fees? His were the hands that fed us and now they were freezing because we took it all from him.

I'm sorry, Dad. Sorry we took it all. Sorry you were cold. And poor. And lonely. I'm so sorry.

He accepts that he will have to retire soon but he is a very proud old man and doesn't want charity or handouts. He has made some halfhearted inquiries about the old age pension but doesn't know how he'll manage as his income will be halved . . . I explained the benefits he would be entitled to.

He was seventy-five and too proud to stop work and get a pension! Poor, cold, frail, proud.

Can't bear any more of this. It doesn't help me feel strong and confident. It drags me down.

Bathroom wallpaper therapy can distract me for a time. It's been curling up again in the damp so I can strip more off, ready for painting.

'Oh, hello. I was about to have a shower,' James says as he walks by.

'All right. I'll stop.'

'You should hire a steamer. Be much quicker,' Mr Knowall suggests.

'Your shower will be the steamer,' I tell him. And you should shut up or offer to help. Don't be bitchy, Kate. He's under no obligation. Can't he just offer out of human kindness or something!

Soon he's off again and mindless wallpaper ripping lets me wonder about those teenage letters.

I find my tortured handwriting in the file, and as I read I'm instantly plunged into teenage despair. Such despair! Hopelessness. Wanted to die.

He made me want to die. Fumbled through a job I didn't understand all day, then went home to loneliness and fighting him off at night. No friends. No skills. No way out. No nice boy to the rescue. And then no Miss Molesworth.

Read the rest and be done with it.

The letters say polite things, as I'd been taught.

Thank you for writing to me. When I feel lonely I read your letter and I feel a little bit better. I miss my friends at Burnside so much and I cry sometimes. I wish I was living there and not here.

Then say, politely, that I need help.

I'm very worried about Dad. It upsets me to see him so frail. Do you know if I can get someone to look after him while I'm at work?

A lonely cage. There had to be a key.

And where am I now, this capable adult? In a lonely cage without a key.

Another mental list of my friends. Shouldn't feel lonely. Sit here howling.

I want my mummy.

For the next few days I don't look at the file. It feels toxic. But I can't stop thinking about it.

Our father didn't want to keep us. He wanted us to go. Gave us up willingly. My heart starts racing as I think about the date he left us at Burnside. But he tried to make up for it. He didn't just dump us and forget us. He kept visiting for twelve years. He was a sad man but not with us. He must have been when he was at home alone, before Ken went to live with him. So alone. If he felt the loss of his Norma like I feel it now, he must have sat alone and howled too.

The phone rings. Quick blow of my nose, then grab the phone before they hang up. Hope it's Tony.

'It's Gen. Listen, can we bring the kids to the house warming?'

'Yeah, course you can!'

'You're crying.'

'No. I've stopped.'

'What's wrong? Are you all right?'

'Oh, just thinking about my ego-strengthening Burnside file.'

'What about it? What's in it?'

'Letters I wrote a couple of years before I met you and Tom. Reports from when we were put in Burnside. That kind of thing. We went there on the twenty-fourth of December. He didn't want us for . . . Christmas.' 'Christmas' only just makes its way out.

'Oh, Kate! Couldn't he have kept you for just one more day? Oh, I suppose he didn't feel very much like Christmas, though, did he? Still, couldn't he have pretended for you kids!'

'There's a report that says they didn't think he'd live through his grief.' Now it's 'grief' that squeaks out.

'Don't read any more. Honestly. Why keep doing this to yourself, Kate? Put it away and have some fun.'

'Tony says it will be good for me to see where I've come from.'

'Yeah, but does he know what it's doing to you? When do you see him next?'

'Haven't got an appointment. Can't afford it for a while.'

'You get one. Hang the expense. You can't go on like this. Ring him. Kate? Ring him and go and see him.'

'Yes, Mum.'

'You will, won't you?'

'Oh, I feel so stupid. He thinks I should have, you know, well, he called them sobering moments, but it feels like sobering life, not just moments. I think I'm going batty. I'm not supposed to react this way.'

'I'm going to hang up and you ring him. See you soon. I'll ring you.'

I ring Tony's number but hang up before he can answer. I'm supposed to be coping as an adult, not ringing like a needy child. It would be good to talk with him because I miss him, but I have to get the feelings resolved and I have to be an adult and cope. Just have to try harder and not use Tony as a crutch.

Painting the bathroom takes up time but doesn't stop me feeling. Likewise, the gym.

Fill the emptiness of having been unwanted with more information. Pick up the file. Read on. It can't get any worse.

A woman rang from Marrickville, being a neighbour of Mr Shayler, seeking information regarding admission of his three children.

So that's how it happened! A neighbour helped our father find a place for us to go. I wonder who she was. I'll have to keep wondering because I'll never know now.

The official application for Ken and me to go to Burnside is here. Kerry was only two years old, too young to come with us. She was sent to Ashfield babies' home.

Ken and I were admitted to Burnside on the twenty-third of December, nineteen fifty-four. Is that why Christmas every year is such an emotional challenge for me, why I always struggle hard to feel as festive as other people do? Didn't we discuss this kind of thing at uni? Kinaesthetic memory or something like that, where the body remembers traumas and patterns that perhaps the consciousness doesn't. I'll think about it, read about it, later. Now, I'll keep reading the wretched file.

I expect to find short notes about little me and my progress but there are none. Next is the nineteen sixty-three social worker's report, then a letter dated sixty-four. Nine years of my life are missing.

Where is my childhood? Where are the notes about when I started preschool, how I progressed, when I started school, learnt to read, count, spell, moved to the big girls' home, got swimming awards, my period starting, the bra and the diet tablets?

Wretched file. Only shows that nobody wanted me after my mother died. Nobody's child, then. A nothing.

I feel empty, worthless. I don't care about the teenager I was. I know her. I remember. This file is supposed to tell me things I didn't know. To strengthen my ego, not slay it! Well, I suppose I didn't know how little I was wanted as a motherless child. I've learnt that, but you'd hardly call it strengthening, Tony!

AS FRIENDS

Whatever I do, it feels as if the neediest kid at preschool is watching, wanting attention. But this isn't preschool and what keeps demanding attention is that wretched file. Back to the letters in which I'd tried to find words to say that there was more about my father that worried me than just his health. I'd failed. I was afraid of my father, afraid that he'd die and leave me a nobody with nowhere to belong. The letters are embarrassing now as I remember how I'd tried to get Burnside to take me back. How desperately needy I was! Unable to cope without an adult telling me what to do.

I need to talk to Tony.

No-one answers when I ring. I'm relieved. I'm forced to work this through myself, as an adult. How? Don't know.

I do what I can to get my spiritual life on track again by going to the home church. But there I feel pressure to do children's activities because that's what I'm good at. It starts to feel like work. I'll keep going, though, and see what happens. Families. They are all families. I'm the only single person.

I'll get fit and healthy at aerobics before school starts too.

'You might meet Tarzan there!' Gen laughs.

'Me Jane,' I grunt. 'Nah. I don't like men obsessed with their bodies, skipping about in bits of singlet, muscles hanging out. Give me a nice bearded bushwalking dag any day. Or a Morris man with flowers in his hat!'

'You never know,' my would-be matchmaker says.

'Tarzan is very unlikely to find me attractive.'

'His loss. Now what can we bring to the house warming?'

I'd better start thinking about the house warming and get myself organised. Should I invite Tony and his wife? Don't be silly. Why would they want to come? They might, though.

At last Tony answers his phone. He sounds busy but asks how I am.

'Distressed by my file. I want to make an appointment.'

'Oh, you don't, do you?'

Don't leave me!

Confused, hurt, rejected.

'Well, yes.'

'Look, things are really flat out just now. Come down and we'll chat over coffee. All right?'

It's not all right but it will have to do.

The new office smells of paint. It's formal and comfortable. Tony shows off his new desk, custom made by a patient who couldn't afford to pay a debt. He makes coffee and we sit down to talk.

'I've been reading my Burnside file and it makes me depressed, all the letters and even the death certificate at the front.' I have to stop talking to stop myself crying. 'It's supposed to be ego strengthening but all it's doing is making me feel more miserable, reminding me of stuff I'd forgotten.'

'I told you there was some sobering material there. Read it and move on. You'll be right when school goes back and you start studying. You just need to keep busy.'

He's dismissing me! This isn't how my therapist behaves.

351

I want an appointment to do some proper work, not to be told to keep busy. But he should know. He's the professional.

'Look, I've had an idea. What do you do at nights?'

'Nothing much. There isn't anything local, if you don't like pubs or clubs.'

'All right. Look, Vlad, my partner and I are starting a walking group for local people. You should think about joining in.'

'Who'd be in it?'

'It's just starting but local doctors are supporting it as an exercise program. We'll get referrals from them. There'd be about ten or so. Let's see. There'd be Vlad, my wife Amanda and me, a few neighbours, then there's a few people who doctors have referred. We'll build it up but that's about it for now.'

It sounds like a good idea and I'd be meeting local people.

'You think about it and if you want to come, be at our place at eight o'clock on Tuesday night.'

'Night?'

'Yes. Most people work during the day so nights are best. Cooler too. Why? Is there a problem?'

I might get a chance to talk with Tony as we walk. Or maybe he's right and the feelings will fade. Surely they will if he's with his wife. Maybe I'll gradually process the young Kate file too.

When I arrive for my first walk, only Vlad, Amanda and Tony are there and we set off straight away, Tony assuring me that others will be along next time. Amanda and I make small talk while Tony and Vlad talk business. I wouldn't mind if we walked faster but Tony grumbles when Amanda speeds up. I walk with him for a while but it's uncomfortable making small talk when the big issues are waiting.

Next time I turn up for walking, Amanda is waiting and she tells me Tony is busy at work.

'What about the others?'

'Others? What others?'

'Tony said there'd be about ten people doing this.'

'Oh! I don't know about that but it's just us tonight. How are you going with Tony?'

'All right,' I reply, hoping she'll consider the subject closed.

'Tony said you've had a hard life.'

'Mm.' I'm offended that my therapy has become her business. I walk faster so we won't have enough breath to talk. Amanda keeps up easily. Have to get the conversation off me.

'Do you have a job?' I ask.

'Not yet. I've been studying but I'm through now, so I'm looking.'

Safety at last! We chat about child development theories and practices and career paths. Amanda's knowledge is impressive.

We reach my car at last. 'Well, goodnight,' I say.

'Goodnight and thanks. See you next time.'

I hope there'll be a big group. A hundred or so, who don't know about my seeing Tony, would be good.

Tony is the only other person walking this time. We start talking but the context is wrong. I want to discuss my file, my feelings, how to resolve them and so on, not gardens and house styles.

'I need to make an appointment before I go home,' I tell him. 'Do you?'

'Yes. I'm still confused with feelings for you and . . .'

'You'll be right,' he interrupts. 'Just wait 'til uni starts.'

'It's not just the feelings. It's that file. It really upsets me.'

'Yeah, but you'll be right. What have you got on 'til school goes back?'

'The house warming on Saturday. I don't suppose you'd want to but I wondered if you and Amanda would like to come.' I imagine he'll say no because Amanda had mentioned to me last week that their marriage is in trouble. They probably don't go anywhere together just now.

'We'd love to come,' Tony says. 'What time?'

Soon we're back to small talk and I still don't have an appointment. Out here Tony doesn't seem like the same person he is in his office where the strong feelings of caring are real and not just a Tuesday thing. Well, I'll just have to trust what he says about keeping busy and I'll try harder to just, well, get over the file.

More small talk fills some of the silence as we keep walking. Tony talks about his degrees and his new office and the contract he and Vlad have signed. I wish he'd walk faster. I'm glad to get to my car when we finish.

He rings the following week to say our next walk will have to be later than the usual eight o'clock start. I don't go to bed until late in the holidays, so that's fine. I guess the others don't mind either. He's waiting in the street by himself and I'm surprised that he's the only one again. We start walking straight away. Small talk again and I'm not as uncomfortable this time. I'm just bored because we seem to be dawdling. I wish the doctors would start sending other people to join the group.

'Thanks for the walk,' I say as I unlock my car door. I turn as I'm saying it and he moves forward to kiss me on the mouth! I turn my cheek to him but I'm confused. What's he doing?

'See you soon,' he says warmly as I get in my car.

Why did he do that? What does it mean? I wish he hadn't. It's confusing. It's not what we do.

Oh, don't be stupid. It's Tony, your therapist, who wouldn't do anything unprofessional. Must stop letting my fantasies get twisted into the reality of genuine caring and a strong transference reaction. I'm such a twit!

The phone rings a lot now as friends accept the invitation to my house warming. Lots of people are coming and I find myself getting more excited than I thought I would. I'd better get busy preparing. My friend Sandra is staying over, so she'll help.

Sandra and I met when I was in my late teens, though she's a bit older so she wasn't in my fellowship group. She's a teacher too but in the far west, so this time together is a rare treat. We talk about how the teaching role is changing. Once we were just expected to teach but now we're supposed to be cleaners, decorators, stocktakers, gardeners, social workers, family therapists, child psychologists and so on and on and on. I tell her about the trouble I've had communicating with Peter and the arguments I have with him.

'It's different arguing with men, isn't it?' she says. 'They argue to win, whereas us women argue to find a solution. Fred does that all the time.'

'Oh. I didn't know you two argued.'

'Yeah, well, marriage isn't all it's made out to be. It's so constant and Fred is so, how do I put it? Oh well, he can't help it, the poor pet.'

'Sounds like Peter. Except the pet bit. He's the centre of the known universe and the rest of us just fit in around him. He doesn't know that there are so many things he doesn't know.'

'That's my Fred!'

'Really? Are you happy enough?' Please say yes.

'Oh yes! There are lots and lots of good times, but it is hard work sometimes. I just get sick of it.'

James interrupts as he pops in for vegemite toast and tea.

'Bad news for you, Kate,' he says. 'A friend has just lost his job. I'm afraid I'll be moving in with him to help out with his mortgage.'

What about my mortgage?

I dash up to the newspaper office with my ad again. Now I have to focus on the house warming preparations. Meanwhile, I imagine the peace of being home with no possibility of James popping up with a sermon on toast. It'll be bliss.

House warming day is sunny but the ground is still muddy from all the rain so the house and verandah are crammed with cheer. Friends from teaching, dancing and even from church back when I'd been a troubled teenager come. Some neighbours drop in and Tony and Amanda do too. Friends who've never met do now and I have a wonderful, exhausting day dancing and playing music like in the days before I left Sydney. Gen and Paddy stay after dinner to help wash up after everyone else has gone.

'Did you enjoy the day?' I ask.

'Wonderful. You know some lovely people.'

'Indeed I do. Some stay and help wash up too! Did you meet Tony?'

'Yeah. He's nice but, I hope you don't mind me saying this, you watch out for him.'

'What do you mean?'

'We sat with him and, Amanda, is it? He spent the whole time saying how wonderful and clever and gorgeous you are!'

'Yeah, but he's just my therapist.' I wish I didn't feel so flattered all the same. I don't tell Gen about my feelings for Tony. 'He has to say that, you know, for ego-strengthening kinds of things.'

'Not in front of his wife, he doesn't! You watch him.'

'We've talked about it in therapy. It's called transference. You get close but then it wears off. It's at the wearing off stage now, he says. Amanda would know about it, the transference thing. She's a psychologist's wife, after all.'

Next walk night Amanda and I are the only starters again.

'You've got a lot friends, haven't you?' she comments when I ask if she enjoyed the house warming.

'Yeah. I have. Friends, not family.'

'You're really lucky having so many people who care about you.'

'I am. I know, but I'd really like to have a family like you've got too. Husband, kids. The lot.'

'You've had a lot to cope with, haven't you? But then you've got your freedom.'

I can't believe I've walked straight into the danger area. Amanda envies my singleness. She thinks marriage has a lot of drawbacks.

'Well, I might be daft but I'd still like to give it a go,' I tell her.

'Are you seeing anyone?'

'No. It's so hard to meet single blokes here. They're all hiding and the ones who aren't hiding are taken.'

We keep walking for a while then Amanda says, 'I know just the man for you! He lives in Sydney but he's got a car. He's a lovely person. Gentle and intelligent. Not bad-looking either.'

'How do you know him?'

'He knew Tony at uni. I'll get him to ring him.'

It's tempting and, let's face it, Amanda knows a good man when she sees one. The trouble is, what might have been normal interest on my part is dampened and confused by my feelings for Tony. Even if they are going to resolve.

When we finish the walk Amanda invites me in for coffee. Tony is home and she tells him she thinks he should get Darren and me together. So soon? I feel silly, like a desperate spinster, but if Tony agrees to get us together, I'll go along with it. It might help me get over my feelings for him.

Tony says he might. Amanda pressures him, and when he doesn't relent, she enlists my support. 'Come on, Kate. You tell him!'

'Um. He might be good for me?' Good heavens! What am I doing?

'Maybe,' Tony grins. Does he know how stupid I feel?

'Oh, come on, Tony.' Amanda tells him. 'You know he's a lovely man. Cut the bullshit and ring him.'

'I can't go organising my patients' social lives!' he says, picking up his pocket book. He's joking. He's organised social walks for us patients and others. Well, maybe Darren won't be in and I can just scoot off home and relax. Alone.

Soon Tony is talking to Darren and he signals us to leave the room. Later he comes out and doesn't say anything about it. Maybe Darren isn't interested.

'Well?' Amanda asks.

'Well, what?' Tony frowns.

'Well, what about Darren?'

'I didn't organise anything. He'll ring Kate, I suppose.'

The mood gradually darkens between them as Amanda lets Tony know that he should have arranged something and Tony gets angry about the pressure she's putting on him. I'm uncomfortable so I go home not really caring whether Darren rings or not.

Does the building society give counselling to mortgagees who scream as soon as they see their logo? Interest rates are rising to fifteen percent. I need a boarder. The first response to my ad is from a sixteen-year-old boy who 'only smokes a bit of dope but usually just, you know, plain roll yer own smokes'.

Next a woman with a two-year-old child rings.

'I'm sorry, but I'll be studying and it just wouldn't work out.'

'But she's quiet and she does what she's told.'

'Sorry, but I haven't got enough room anyway.'

A few days later a man called Graham, who says he works at the local Gestalt Centre, rings. I haven't been to the Centre but I've heard people talk about its holistic therapies. It has a good reputation. Graham sounds suitable except that he has a dog. The dog is quiet and he does what he's told. They've done obedience training.

'There are no fences here,' I tell him.

'I could build a run for him,' Graham suggests when he comes to look at the room and the yard. I feel uneasy about him but I felt that about James too. I agree that he can move in if his references check out. I wish he wasn't so big and his dog wasn't a Doberman called Brute.

Tonight I'm going on a bushwalk with some of my neighbours and their bushwalking club. After the walk we'll all have dinner at the neighbours' place. It's beautiful in the moonlight and the company is cheerful. When the walk is over I call in at my house to get my food to share.

'Where are you off to?' Graham asks.

'Next door for dinner.'

'Oh good. I'll come too.'

I'm speechless for a while. Should I just tell him he's not invited?

'Well, it's a club.'

Wrong response. Graham turns up later with a tomato to share. He eats like this could be the last food on the planet and dominates conversations near and far. I whisper apologies to the hosts before I leave.

His pattern is to invite himself to anything I'm going to, so my pattern becomes telling him it's not open or dodging him. My days of doing school work in the lounge room are over. Anytime I want to sit there to do anything, Graham arrives. If I go to my room he follows, talking all the way. This is a mistake. How do I get him to go?

Elliott rings. He's in Sydney and suggests we have dinner together.

'We should get together again,' he says.

'Together, as in together?' I ask, surprised. I had no idea he felt this way.

'Well, neither of us has met anyone else and we get on all right. It'd be better than being lonely.'

'It didn't work before and, anyway, you're so far away now. Let's just stay friends. Um, there's also the fact that I'm about to be introduced to the man of my dreams.' I tell him about Amanda's thoughts on what's his name.

'Oh! Well, good luck with it. You deserve a nice fella. Like me.' He grins with mock bashfulness and makes me laugh. 'Here's the bill. It's your turn to pay, isn't it?'

Holidays are over. Back at school. With Maud. No-one has been appointed to replace her yet. She seems to be putting a bit of effort into her work now, though. Peter, however, wants us to start a new version of early entry for parents and kids again and he just about shouts at me when I argue against it again. I ring the union and the rep confirms that us teachers cannot be told to do what Peter is telling us to do.

'Would you like me to call a meeting?' the rep asks.

'No. I'll tell Peter what you said and see what happens.'

Peter explodes but pulls himself up just short of strangling me. I wish I could just go to an empty home and relax. Or go to Tony's office and talk about how frightened I am of being shouted at. I don't cringe any more but I freeze and struggle to pull myself into my adult being. But I haven't got Tony. I've got Graham.

'Sorry I haven't got the rent,' he says the day after it's due. 'I'll give it to you tomorrow if I sell the car. There's a bloke coming for it in the morning.'

'But you've got a job, haven't you?'

'Yeah. It's just not payday this week. Don't worry. I'll have the money. Can we share dinner? I'll cook rice.'

Neighbours provide the Graham solution without involving me.

'Looks like I'll have to move,' he says.

'Why?' How soon can you go?

'The neighbours are complaining about Brute. They reckon he howls all day when I'm not here. Have you heard him?'

'No, but maybe he does it when I'm at work. They wouldn't make it up. Brute's making a mess of the yard too.'

'Well, yeah. He needs more space.'

He's not the only one!

'I think I'll have to move.'

'I think that would be best.'

Before he goes he admits that his job is a two-day-a-week handyman one. If nothing else, I've learned to ask the right questions when I ring referees.

He's gone and that's a relief but there's the mortgage payments and uni fees. Anxious, tired spinster goes back to the newspaper to rerun her ad for a boarder.

How long until all this anxiety stops? How long until I get the right boarder? A decent aide to work with? A nice man to go out with? Stop feeling I need Tony to prop me up? Stop feeling muddled about all those issues he raised in therapy?

Out of the blue Darren rings. We have a polite conversation about nothing, then he says goodbye. Well, wasn't that fun? I could have a polite nothing chat in the vegie shop or the library. With the spuds or the books.

Next walk night it's only Amanda and me again. This is the case more often than not now. Although she's not like any of my friends, Amanda is definitely helping me get fit. All the same, I wish Tony could join us. The possibility of spending time with him is reason enough to walk.

But here we are, Amanda and me. She asks the inevitable question about Darren and is puzzled when I describe what a non-event his call was.

Back at the house, she tells Tony about it. I feel like a failure on show. I wish I could have told Tony in my own time, my own way.

'Ring and ask him to dinner,' Tony says, sipping his wine. 'Ask me too.'

I laugh but Amanda retorts, 'Oh, don't be a stupid fool. Why don't you get off your bum and ring him yourself?'

'I work it off all day, in case you haven't noticed,' Tony replies sarcastically.

I feel sorry for him. He does work hard and Amanda hasn't got a job yet. I'm uncomfortable. 'I should go,' I say. 'Good-night.' I let myself out. I'm fumbling in my car for the ignition keyhole when Tony knocks on the window. I roll it down.

'Give us a kiss,' he says. I can smell the wine on his breath.

'No!'

'Oh, come on. Just one proper one.'

'No.' I find the keyhole.

'You know what I want to do?'

'No. I'm going home.' Quickly.

'I want to come around to your place and be rude with you.'

'Goodbye.' I drive away.

What on earth is going on? He's always been a person who tells me to value myself and not accept less than the best. If

361

I didn't know better I'd call him a sleaze. I'm shaken and confused. Why did he do it? He must be drunk. I daydream about him wanting me but not when he still lives with his wife, even if their marriage is obviously failing, and not because he's drunk. I hope he doesn't make the same suggestion when he's sober. It'd be hard to keep resisting. But he wouldn't, would he? When he's sober, he's my therapist.

I take my therapist's advice and invite Darren to lunch. He seems delighted. Why is he so keen now when before it was as if he was talking with a dish mop? I ring to invite the Bentons too. If Darren is as bad at conversation as he seems, I'll need all the help I can get. I just hope the Bentons don't argue during lunch. Tony answers the phone and I get anxious. I tell him why I've called.

'Well done,' he says warmly. 'You'll really like Darren. He's a gentle, intelligent person. The kind of man you deserve.'

There! It was just the wine talking. He's not going to get out of control.

I start getting anxious about the lunch. Amanda talks a lot about Darren when we go walking next, which doesn't help. She also explains that, although she and Tony have split up, they'll still join me and Darren for lunch. Tony has moved into their granny flat but he still likes to appear a happily married man in public. Why? This is crazy! There'll be two people pretending to their old friend that they're happily married while they're watching how I behave with a strange man who I might want to impress but who gives confusing messages. It's worse that I love one of the couple and that he knows all my secrets but doesn't know that I know that he and his wife aren't together any more. Woody Allen himself could have written this scene. What am I doing in it?

Amanda and Tony arrive with Darren and they put on a pretence of getting on well. Darren is quiet and seems more interested in talking with Tony than with me. Amanda is keen to talk with me about a job she's applied for. Everyone has an agenda different to mine. I just want to get to know a nice, available man and I want our mutual friends to help that happen. I want to get over my feelings for Tony.

After lunch we go for a bushwalk. This must be when I'm supposed to manoeuvre things so Darren and I can talk. I try to but Amanda walks with me and I can't get free. Darren hangs back, still talking with Tony, who does nothing to help. This is stupid! Darren obviously doesn't like me and the feeling is mutual. I wish they'd all push off. I'm getting more angry and can't keep pretending this is going well.

At last they go. I sit on my lounge and fume. Why did I put myself through that? Why did Darren come here to my place at all? If he wanted time with Tony why not go there? And why not even try to get to know me? Why was Tony so unhelpful? Amanda too? Why am I so hopeless at flirting? They'll all think I'm an idiot! When will I ever be normal? Over Tony?

Chest tightens. Heart racing. Breathe. Remember to breathe! Too anxious to sit. Pace about. Too much energy. No air. What's happening? Heart attack? Going to die. Need help. Call Tony. Get help. No. Thinks I'm an idiot. Make it worse. Breathe. Try to calm down. Hands shaking. Breathe. Feel cold. More pacing. Remember, breathe. Pick up the phone.

'Amanda, it's Kate.'

'That was nice today. Did you enjoy it?'

'No. I hated it. Is Tony there?'

'Are you all right?'

'No. Is Tony there?'

'Hang on. I'll get him.'

Waiting for ages. Trying to calm down.

Hurry up, Tony!

'Hello. Amanda says you're upset.' At last.

'I'm a mess,' I cry. 'Today was horrible. I hated it. I was so bad. Hopeless.'

'It was all right. What was the problem?'

'It was terrible! I didn't know what to do and Darren didn't like me and I still have these feelings for you and I can't handle it! Don't know what to do. I need an appointment.'

'Would you like me to come over?'

'Come over?' House calls? That's right, he treats some woman up the hill from my place. 'Yes! Could you?'

'I'll be there soon. Just have to finish up here. Will you be all right?'

Try to get calm. He'll be here soon, know what to do. Hypnosis or something. Have to keep pacing and remembering to breathe. Heart slowing. Calming down. Deep breaths. Like the panic I felt in that age regression thing. Sit down, eyes closed. No, don't get up. Sit and breathe deeply. In. Out. In. Out. Getting calmer. Heart slower. Tears pouring out with confusion and frustration at my inability to cope. Hurry up, Tony.

A knock at the door. At last. He puts his arm around my shoulder. I feel like I'll explode.

'Feeling anxious? Let's sit down.'

His support is such a relief. We'll talk and he'll tell me what to do and find out why I panicked.

'Tell me all about it.'

'I'm so confused. Darren was a non event. I felt so stupid. You didn't help and my feelings for you are supposed to go away and they haven't. I'll never get sorted out. I'm a mess. What's happening to me?'

'I know what we could do,' he says, moving closer.

Ignore that. It might not mean what I think it does. I can't think straight, trying to fathom it all in my confusion. 'The other night when you said you wanted to come over, well, that made everything confusing. The feelings are supposed to be resolving. Why did you do it? It made it hard to sort . . .'

'Oh, sorry about that. I was very drunk. I was sorry afterwards.'

'I wish you'd told me. I didn't know what was going on. I've got these blasted feelings and you haven't.'

'Look, I was drunk but I meant what I said.'

'What?'

'I meant what I said. I'm very attracted to you.'

No! It's real out here too. Could I be this lucky? Tony loves me out here in the real world! He's not going to tell me to get over my feelings. Not going to say he feels respect and empathy but not love? Hope and hormones rage. How can I resist when the nicest man I ever met is whispering in my ear, 'I know what we could do?'

He kisses me. I don't turn my cheek to him this time. I was so certain this would never happen. Tony Benton, who tells me I'm wonderful, intelligent, attractive, who listens respectfully as I bungle through the collision of my past and present lives, loves me despite it all! He's here, kissing me, pushing me gently backwards, whispering, 'If we keep doing this I can't be your psychologist any more.'

The sense of loss is instant. 'But what about all the work I still have to do?'

'Oh, we can do all that as friends,' he says, kissing me as if to confirm that we'll find the balance between therapy and real love. I can't think clearly about the dynamics of psychotherapy and transference. This isn't the time or context. I trust Tony. I'm not betraying Amanda. She doesn't love him. They've split up.

'Let's go to the bedroom,' Tony says.

No violins in the bedroom. Not even a slight movement of the earth. It's over so quickly. The earthmoving and the violins must come later, after we've had time to adjust.

'That was nice,' Tony says, getting up and dressing.

'Where are you going?'

'Got some work to do. You know, the contract. But we'll see each other again soon.' He kisses me lightly and goes.

I counter the hurt with the knowledge that at last I'm loved by a man who truly knows and understands me, who I don't need to hide from or be anyone but me with.

In the morning I feel ambivalent. Have I done the right thing? Should I have waited until Tony and Amanda are divorced? Will he be able to be objective enough to continue therapy 'as friends', as he said? When I try to imagine therapy between work and a date, it doesn't seem possible. And what if we were having a relationship problem? They do happen even when people know and respect each other like we do, don't they? Well, Tony would know what to do. He's a psychologist. Best to be positive and concentrate on being loved, warts and all.

After work I dash home expecting him to ring. He doesn't but comes over for a while. 'Is all our time together going to be like this? Short and sweet?' I ask.

'Has to be for now, but don't worry. I'm planning a day off soon. We can spend it together. Do something nice.'

Meanwhile, my ad has been answered by a midwifery student, who rings back to say she has decided to move in. Her name is Ellen. She's energetic, cheerful and looking forward to the bush setting and the quiet ambience of my house. She'll be studying here until she returns to the Northern Territory when the course is over.

Days pass and I hear nothing from Tony. Well, this is the nineteen eighties and it's all right for women to ring men. I pick up the phone nervously, hoping I won't sound too desperate or pushy.

'Oh, hello. I've just been thinking about you,' he says. 'How have you been?'

This 'how have you been?' lacks a certain quality that the same question had when I'd arrive for therapy. This one is quick. Tony is at work and I'm not his client.

'I'm fine. How are you?'

'Oh, better than okay when I think of the other night. I'm better than *okay*. We must do it again.'

What? Was it just something nice to do after a busy day at work? No! It was, is, love. That's why he's feeling so high. How stupid and insecure I am. Lost my sense of humour. 'When will I see you again?'

'Well, we've got to finish the draft for another contract tonight so it'd be late if I did come.'

'That's all right.'

'Well, we'll see. You go to bed if it gets too late.'

He doesn't come and I feel rejected. Second best. But he has to keep working hard until the business is established. Then I won't be sitting around hoping and daydreaming.

During the weeks that follow I fluctuate between wondering if, to Tony, it's all just about sex, and telling myself not to be stupid, that he's the same person he was in therapy but he's busier now.

Ellen and I get on so well I wonder why I didn't just wait for a woman to answer my ad in the first place. I don't tell her much about my work but it's nice coming home to someone cheerful. I suspend thoughts about my grief for my mother, my feelings about my father's abuse and the issues in my Burnside file. I can't afford to get into any of that again until Tony has time to be supportive. I'll be patient. Keep pushing my questions away.

Sometimes Tony's visits coincide with my getting down about him. He comes often enough to keep me hoping but infrequently enough to make me know I'm not his most important concern. Don't people who've just fallen in love want to be with each other at every drop of every hat? I need Tony to define me in this new relationship.

Amanda rings and I feel guilty, although I know she isn't living with Tony any more.

'I've got a job,' she says. 'The pay's better than I thought and I'm hoping Tony will come back and we'll make a go of it now that there'll be less financial pressure.'

'What? But I thought you wanted him to go.'

'Oh I did but things change. People change.'

That quickly? No, I don't think so.

She talks for a while and I don't know what to say. Should I tell her about Tony and me, or have I not seen him because he's back with her or negotiating a return? I'm so confused and guilty and anxious and then we're saying goodbye. I have to talk to Tony.

'Hello. Good to hear from you,' he says cheerfully when I swallow my pride and ring.

'I thought you'd be busy,' I tell him.

'Ring me anytime. What are you doing now?'

'Nothing much.'

'Good. I'll be there in twenty minutes.'

So he isn't back with Amanda. What a relief! He arrives as Ellen is getting ready for night shift. I introduce them and tell Tony that Ellen is a midwifery student.

'Wow. That's a great job. Have a good night, then,' he says. 'Bring out lots of lovely little people.'

'What a fantastic bloke!' Ellen whispers with a grin before she leaves. I feel proud that he's my bloke.

I expect my bloke to ask how work is going and how I'm coping.

'Where's the wine?' he asks instead.

'I don't have any. Would coffee do?'

Conversation doesn't come easily. This Tony isn't the concerned psychologist. He's just the tired overworked man who soon says, 'Let's lie down.'

Before long he's snoring as if he wants to wake the neighbours, if not the dead. Thank goodness he doesn't live here. I'd never get any sleep.

He's awake again and leaving.

'I'd like to spend more time with you,' I tell him.

'We will. We will. But for now I have to get the work done and the office set up.'

'I miss you when I don't hear from you.'

'That's nice,' he says. He rushes off and I feel lost.

At school the kids are settling in and Maud has got over her initial enthusiasm. She's slacking off to her more usual level of involvement. Tension is rising again.

This year I'm going to do something about all the basic equipment that's missing from the centre. Alma usurped control of the budget years ago and I'm going to take it from her.

'We need a budget,' I suggest at our staff meeting with Peter. 'We're missing some basic equipment.'

'What equipment?' Peter asks, disbelieving.

I show him the list of missing or damaged equipment.

'Hmph. Where is it all? If we should have it, we should have it!'

Alma is seething. 'We've been here so many years, Peter. Things have broken or worn out.'

'They should be replaced from your fee collection!'

Red, angry Alma rages, but I now have a new tension release when she undermines and challenges me. I float her, using the idea of a salesman who's surprised to learn she isn't the principal of the school. 'Blimp', he'd scoffed. Alma with her pleated skirt and matching jumper, shoes and earrings, drifting in the sky like a blimp, anchored to Earth by an umbilical cord of congealed glitter glue.

Going home is great now, whether Ellen is there or not.

'I feel guilty taking your money when you're such good company,' I tell her one day.

'Well, if you weren't taking it someone else would be,' Ellen laughs. 'How are you and Tony going? He's a beaut guy.'

'I wish I could see more of him but he's always at work or working at home.'

'Oh, bad luck. Change him.'

'Into what?'

'Anything that isn't a workaholic,' she laughs again. 'Life's too short.'

Uni starts soon. How much time will we have together then?

A few nights later I'm woken from a deep sleep by footsteps on the verandah, then tapping on the window. It's Tony and he's drunk. I feel insulted but it's just that he and Vlad have celebrated.

'Report's finished,' he announces, nudging me towards the bedroom. 'Asleep, were you? Good. Go back to bed.'

'Shh. You'll wake Ellen!'

'I don't care.'

'I do. Shh.'

Soon he's snoring and I'm lying beside him thinking this is not what I want. But it'll get better now that the report is finished. He wakes himself and gets up to go.

'Will you stay one night?'

'I did stay.'

'No. For a whole night. And have breakfast together.'

'Why?'

'More time together. It'd be nice. I love you.' I want you to prove I matter enough to spend time with.

'Oh, we're not going to play married couple!'

I'm too hurt to speak.

'You're too special for all that,' he croons. 'Marriage isn't all it's cracked up to be. All that sleeping over just spoils good relationships.'

He doesn't say he loves me. I hear that so loudly. But he does value our relationship. Will that do me? Being special to him? It'll have to do for now. Tony is just hurt because his marriage is over. Books say that men don't talk about feelings; they just leave us women to interpret their actions. Just because he doesn't say the words it doesn't mean he doesn't feel the feeling. I'll be his special person and support him through the period of bitterness, then when he's over it, things will be different. None of the others told me I was special.

Saturday sleep in. I wake late and do the usual weekend things. The day passes quickly and as the sun goes down I don't have to fight the Saturday night blues. Tony will probably come over, though we didn't plan anything. I sit on my verandah and watch the sky and the cars go by. Yes, here's Tony's car. I know his numberplate so well now. Tonight I'll be like everyone else, instead of a lonely spinster at home by herself.

He's passing by! Going up the hill. Must be going to another emergency at that woman's house – he's told me that her alcoholic husband makes life a misery for her and her child. He's so good the way he helps there, even on Saturday night. It's getting cool out here so I'll wait for him inside.

Evening turns to night and my heart sinks. He must have been too tired to call in. I know I won't always be second in line for his time. He's told me that. But I wish so much that he was here now. I miss therapy too, with the constant reassurance that I'm a worthwhile person. I'd like to talk to my therapist about how insecure I am in this relationship but I don't seem to have a therapist any more.

The next day Tony calls in looking haggard and stressed.

'What's happened?'

'One of my clients has made some accusations. She's making trouble for me. Big trouble. She's got it all wrong.'

'What accusations?'

'Nothing you need to worry about. She's just misinterpreted some treatment I gave her. When you're a therapist you have to play roles sometimes, to help people understand their reactions.'

'You did some role playing?'

'Something like that. She's got it all wrong and she's making trouble. Nice to see you, anyway. How about some coffee?'

Stupid woman! She ought to know what an ethical person he is. He wouldn't do anything that wasn't in his patient's best interests! At least I can give Tony support, like he's given me. He says he doesn't want to spell out the details. He just wants to forget about it for a while and relax.

Tony's contact remains erratic. In my journal I write about spending more time feeling anxious about it than enjoying his company. It isn't what I'd hoped for. My ego-strengthening work is frozen in time. Tony's time. The uni term begins and I want his reassurance that I'm capable of a Masters. Am I about to make a fool of myself? Will I have to go to Peter and tell him I've failed but thanks for supporting my funding application, anyway?

In his time, Tony rings. 'How about coming out for a drink?'
We meet at the local pub. 'Don't sit next to me!' he hisses.
'Why not?'
'Someone might see us. Sit opposite so they know we're just acquaintances.'

I want to go home, alone, and howl. How much longer does this stupid pretence about being a respectable family man have to go on?

'When I move it'll be different but for now I need to keep the reputation.'

My course keeps me occupied and the standard is not much higher than undergraduate work. The work is challenging but not too much so. I don't have much free time but more of it is spent wishing for Tony's company than being in it. I'd imagined us discussing child psychology, educational theory and practice, Tony proofreading my papers, critiquing, suggesting, arguing and encouraging.

Time to admit, sadly, that he doesn't value the relationship the way I do. If he did I'd get more than scraps of his time. I'm too tied to him to forget it and too lacking in understanding to be sure that it's not just me being too demanding and needy. I want the Tony I knew in therapy. Floating the blimp works temporarily for the school stuff but it's not a real solution. How can I get help from Tony who can't be my therapist any more? Sometimes I cry, then find myself wanting my mummy. I could easily spiral down into depression again. Tony. I need the therapist, the person he seemed to be.

Every entry in my journal seems to be about how unsatisfied, anxious, confused, angry, undervalued I feel. I stop writing regularly. Tony's apparent lack of care starts to negate the gains I made in therapy. Ego strength wilting. Self-esteem plummeting. Work situation still challenging. Depressed.

Joan, my neighbour, invites me for afternoon tea and we talk about gardens and careers, then specifically my work.

'It's still as awful trying to get on with the others. Whatever

I do gets misinterpreted.'

'Well, dear, you just have to put in all in the top drawer,' Joan says, topping up her husband's tea. 'Just keep doing your best. That's what my mother used to say and I think she was right. Put it all in the top drawer and keep doing what you know is right.'

'The top drawer's getting pretty full, Joan. And it doesn't have a lock. Can I move down to the second top drawer now?' The problems gnaw away at me every minute of every day that I'm at work and putting it away feels impossible.

Resign. Is that possible? I'd have to go for a job interview and sell myself. That terrifies me as I remember the only other one I've had. No confidence. No sale. No job. No house. How can I move on?

'As I see it, these are your options,' the financial adviser says after we've looked at my position. 'Sell your house and rent, then you could afford to earn less and take a career change. Or keep working and earning but change to a career course that would open up your work options. Do casual teaching but, as we've seen, you'd need to work five days a week, anyway, with interest rates as they are. Or get married and share your expenses.'

'Know any millionaires?'

I don't want to lose my house, so I'm trapped at work. There aren't any real options. Ellen will only be here for another month or so, then I'll have to get another boarder.

What a fabulous surprise at work on Monday. Maud is resigning! The load seems lighter.

'Peter reckons someone's about to be appointed, so I'm gettin' out before they chuck me out,' she says. 'Got a job in a dress shop. Good bludge, I reckon.'

'Oh, I've applied for a transfer myself,' says Alma, not one to miss an opportunity for attention. Could all my Christmases be coming at once?

Weeks have passed since I saw Tony. Will I ring and tell him about Maud? No. I won't pressure him. It might drive him away. I'll just wait through all the disappointments and be glad when he's here. Things will change.

Tonight he arrives after Ellen has gone to work. He's been flat out and hasn't had time to call in. He asks how uni is but interrupts my reply with, 'Keep working on it. You'll be okay.' Then he picks up my guitar, strums and hums softly to himself.

'Let's go to bed,' he says. Then he stops suddenly and whispers, 'Shh. Someone's coming!'

'I didn't hear anything. I'm not expecting anyone, but I suppose they'll knock . . .'

'Shh. There's someone there.'

He walks quickly back down the hall and picks up the guitar. There's a loud knock at the door.

'Kate,' he calls. 'Someone at your door.'

Why is he yelling when I'm just beside him?

'Hello Kate,' Amanda says wearily as I open the door. 'Is Tony here?'

'Yes, he's here.' Why are you?

They're separated, hate each other, but she's here asking for him as if she has a right to know where he is. What should I do? 'Uh, do you want to come in?' I ask, hoping she'll decline.

Tony stands up slowly. He looks so old and careworn! Not angry or puzzled or anything predictable. Just beaten and pathetic! Amanda looks furious.

'So this is where you come with your lies now, is it?'

Lies? What lies and why is it her business where Tony is? She's not his wife any more. I leave it to Tony to answer her. To Tony, who's slowly making for the door as Amanda continues shouting something about others throwing him out and him heaping shit on me now.

What others? What shit? What's happening?

Unbelievably, Tony walks out the door without a word! I want to shout at him to come back and explain what's happening, deal with Amanda, not just leave me with it all.

Amanda stops, huffs a sigh, then turns to me.

'Has he been here long?'

'Not tonight. But . . . What's going on?'

'Has he been here before?'

'Yes. What's going on?'

'Oh, sorry,' she says, calming down. 'I wondered who he'd go to next. Hoped it wouldn't be you. I followed him. I guessed he'd be here.'

'Followed him? Why?'

She sits by the heater, closes her eyes and begins telling me they had split up but had got together again. They've just had a huge argument and he's leaving again.

No! I don't believe it! I must have misunderstood her. Tony wouldn't do that to me. I'm cold and shaking.

As Amanda talks on and on, I want to vomit. Or jump off a cliff and be nowhere. I try to listen but I try to understand, too, why she's here saying such vile things about Tony. Why would she live with a monster like that and take him back time and again? I can't think it through with Amanda talking on and on. I wish she'd go so I could do a reality check.

'I know he's attracted to you, so you be careful . . .'

Is that it? Is she making it all up because he's attracted to me, not her? Because she wants to turn me off him? Now she's talking about the woman up the hill but Tony told me about that. It was a misunderstanding that he expected to blow over.

At last there's a break but I don't know what to say or do in it.

'Anyway, I'd better go. Sorry about all this.'

I flop back into the chair, frozen, stunned. Have to think. Be logical. Where on earth to begin!

Tony is living with Amanda? Of course he's not! He wouldn't lie to me. He wouldn't have been sneaking away from her to come here! Is that why he never stays? No! He wouldn't! I trust him. Trusted . . . no trust Tony. Or have I been used by some-one I only thought I could trust completely?

No! Stop. That's repulsive. It's not Tony.

He'll come over and explain everything. I'll just have to suspend judgement until I see him and hear his explanation. I'm exhausted and the truth is hard to find. I go to bed and cry. Too many tears for journal writing tonight.

Tony doesn't ring or call in for days. Wouldn't he want to see if I'm all right and to clarify things?

It's stupid to keep wondering. I need closure if it's over. The thought of no Tony makes me sad but I need to know. I ring him.

'Oh hello, love. Been meaning to ring you.'

'I assumed you would when you had time,' I say, trying to hide my desperation to know what's happening, trying not to get hooked by his warmth.

'I have been flat out. I've missed you.'

'Could we meet? Have coffee and a chat?'

'That'd be good.'

He comes to my house and tells me he's wrung out and sad. He's deeply lonely and knows what I've been talking about now. That hooks me. It's hard to distance myself when he's so willingly showing his vulnerability. He and Amanda are definitely divorcing.

'Did you go back to her?'

'Oh, I went back into the house but I wouldn't call it living together. A marriage. We've done it all before. It's all over now, though. For good. All over.'

He sounds sad and flat. And he just lived in the house but not in the marriage.

'I just don't know what to do. Can't afford a flat at the moment.'

'It must be difficult.'

'Difficult, to say the least. What do you think I should do?'

I'm flattered that he wants my opinion. I'm tempted to invite him to move into my study but I'm not ready to have him here when I don't know the whole truth, or whether we could live happily ever after. I've thought about it but we've never discussed it. It's too soon for me. 'I think you should get any kind of flat you can, even a dump for a while, and move out straight away. It must be so unhealthy staying around a person who . . . isn't very fond of you.'

He talks and makes himself more vulnerable by telling how fragile he feels. I feel sad for him. I want to help him get happy and I'm glad I can be supportive.

In the weeks that follow I assume he's moving and sorting his new life out. When he's settled he'll ring. I wait and wait.

TURN AROUND

'How about Saturday?' Tony says enthusiastically when I ring and suggest lunch. 'It'd have to be here, though. I've got a client coming. Let's see,' he mumbles as he reads his diary. 'How about eleven?'

'All right. If that's all you can fit in.'

'I've missed you, love,' he says pensively. 'I'll look forward to Saturday.'

'Me too.'

Do I really want to stay waiting, hoping he'll come and being disappointed more often than not? No. But he missed me, called me 'love' and he's probably got his life together at last. He sounded more like his old self. I still have feelings . . .

'Phone for you, Kate,' Ellen yells on Friday night.

'Hi. It's Amanda.' I haven't seen or heard from her since she came to my house.

'Hello. You sound upset.'

'It's Tony. He's left me. I thought we could work it out but

378

he's moved in with another woman.' Amanda is crying as she's talking. I don't understand.

'Oh!' But he hasn't moved in to my house.

'Someone he met at a seminar.'

I need to dash away and howl.

'I have to go,' she says and hangs up, apparently to do what I need to do.

What woman? Did he just invent moving in with another woman to stop Amanda trying to get him to come back? Tony wouldn't lie to me.

Oh, wake up, Kate! Face what you know is the truth. The other woman is not you. What now? Apart from cry and shiver. Freeze until tomorrow. Don't hurt yet.

Tony welcomes me warmly at his office. There! He's not a liar or a cheat. He makes coffee as we chat about how uni is going and how the business is picking up. I can't keep it up. I have to know the truth.

'Amanda rang me last night,' I tell him.

He blanches. 'Oh yes? What did she have to say?' he asks. Angrily?

'That you've moved in with another woman.'

'Amanda's wanted me to go for ages,' he says bitterly. Then he turns into a person I haven't seen before. Rage in his eyes. 'Yes, I've left her, and yes, I've met another woman, moved in with her. All right?'

Don't leave me. Please don't leave me.

His 'all right' has never been a knife in the heart before. I thought if this had to be done he'd at least do it civilly.

'I thought I'd be . . . that you and I . . .' I don't know how to say it. I feel foolish, small, hurt, confused. Why is he turning on me?

'I met her months ago,' he sneers, raising his head as if in triumph.

While I reel I hear him bullying me about how he is my therapist and I should tell him what I'm thinking now. What

I'm feeling. Why? Why is he insisting he's my therapist all of a sudden?

'You said you couldn't be my therapist any more.'

'And now I am your therapist again. You should be talking to me about your feelings.'

'It's different now.'

'Why is it different?' he snaps.

'You're not my therapist. You're my friend. Or were.'

'I'm your therapist.' He's trying to sound gentle again but it doesn't work. 'Tell me what you're thinking.'

'I can't. It just doesn't feel right talking to you about you. I'll have to find someone else to work with.'

'I am your therapist.' He raises his voice, emphasises 'I'. 'I'm the person you should be talking to. No-one else.'

Am I going mad? I'm too confused to think about leaving.

'Cut the bullshit. Talk to me. All right?' This time 'all right' sounds like a drop of sickly sweet syrup. 'Oh look, Amanda's giving me a hard time. I'm just strung out. Sorry.'

I stay quiet. Frozen. Can't think.

Tony breaks the silence. 'I haven't done this before and it won't happen again. I talked to a senior colleague about you last week,' he says. He seems to have moved to a different conversation, measuring his words in this one. Done what exactly before? I feel outrage that he discussed me with a stranger. But what does it have to do with anything? 'He says I haven't been wise but I shouldn't worry about it.'

Worry about what? What is he talking about?

'Well, I just thought that you and I might be together when . . .' I blunder along, trying to keep on track.

'You!' He slams the word into my face, his attempt to stay calm and civil failing violently. 'Look, when I go out with a woman I want someone who looks like a woman, not like someone's mother. Yes, I've got another woman,' he snarls, poking his angry finger in my face. 'She knows how to be a woman.'

Where is the venom coming from? What have I done?

'You wouldn't know how to be a woman. The way you present yourself makes people want to stay right away from you.'

'That first night you came over –'

'Oh, it started long before that!' he interrupts with an ugly smirk. 'Long before that.'

What does that mean? That he set me up? I remember telling him how I didn't want anything to do with falling in love with my therapist. I even told him I wasn't attracted to him. There isn't time to keep thinking. He's raving, hurling abuse, getting up menacingly. I flinch.

Stop it! Stop! Don't leave me.

He doesn't stop. There's more. Much more he wants to shout at me. I don't hear a lot of it. Can't think. Want to run away in circles and scream.

Don't leave me! Please don't leave me!

He's raving, on and on. Mad, angry taunting.

Stand up slowly, a calm, detached part of me says. Pick up your bag slowly and walk slowly out of the room. You don't have to stay and listen to this.

It's as if a different me is taking control and getting the frightened me moving.

Tony follows. I used to like his huge bulk. Not now. Will he thump me? Shove me down the stairs? I feel small and frightened, like when they beat me as a child.

Keep walking. Don't turn around. You're doing well. Taking control like a wise, strong woman. Keep going. Don't listen.

As I reach the bottom of the stairs I turn back to see if the thing at the top, still spewing abuse, is real. It is. It glares at me, ugly, like a Dorian Gray portrait.

'Look at you, walking out like a stupid little girl who can't bear to hear the truth.' He delivers the final blow: 'Well, I'm laughing at you!'

Tears at last.

Turn away. Keep going. Don't stop. Just get out.

'Yes I am. I'm laughing at you!'

381

Get to the car. Fumbling for the key. Get in quickly. Lock the door and drive. Doesn't matter where. Just get away.

Drive until I have to pull over. Can't see. Shaking and cold. Howling. The humiliation fills the whole world. I'm such a fool. A drab, boring, stupid fool. And Tony has rejected me.

Strong Kate challenges: what are you thinking? Do you want the ogre you've just seen? You've had a lucky escape.

Can't concentrate. Feel small and hopeless. Have to get home. Shut down. Ellen will be there. Don't want her to see me humiliated. Don't want anybody to see. Ever. Pull over and try to compose myself. Drive on.

'You're back early,' Ellen says cheerfully. 'Oh, Kate! What's happened?'

'Nothing,' I blurt out.

'Nothing doesn't do that! What's wrong?'

'Tony said horrible things and . . . it's all over.'

'Tony? That bloke I met? Oh, he didn't mean it.'

'I think he did. It was terrible.'

'What did he say?'

'That I'm . . . that . . . he's laughing at me. I look like someone's mother.'

'Oh, don't cry! What's wrong with looking like someone's mother? Mine's gorgeous!'

'He didn't mean the gorgeous sort!'

'Oh, he didn't mean it. You look great.'

'He was raving like a maniac and I was so scared. Oh, sorry. Think I'll have a shower.'

Alone in the bathroom I cry some more as Tony's words echo around the tiles. 'I'm laughing at you.' 'You make people want to stay away from you.' 'It started long before that.' 'I'm laughing at you.' He really knew how to hurt, how to push me away. Thank goodness Ellen's going out. She still thinks Tony is wonderful.

The days pass in a fog of despair and sometimes in hope that Tony will come back, apologise and explain that he has a weird version of Tourette's syndrome or something. I go through the motions at work and take a different route home and shopping so I don't have to go past his new office and dissolve in tears.

Sometimes I'm very sure I don't ever want to see him again but other times, most times, I remember good Tony and I want him back. I want the Tony I knew when I was his patient and he valued and respected me. Or made me think he did.

In a period of wanting him to come back I write to him. Maybe if I show him that I'm mature and can take criticism and move on, he'll want me back. I write a pathetic letter that is such an embarrassment to me now.

As I fold the letter I remember what he said about talking to a senior colleague who judged that he'd done nothing wrong. What was that about? He must have been worried that I'd make trouble for him, like that other woman who didn't understand what Tony had intended. But I'm different to her. My wonderful, caring, respectful psychologist had fallen in love with me and I with him. He offered me a choice of therapy or a relationship with therapy 'as friends'. I made my choice. I knew what I was doing but I was stupid enough to think I was good for Tony.

I add a PS, in which I tell Tony that I have no intention of making trouble. Why would I when he'd done nothing wrong?

After I post it I regret having sent the letter. It is pathetic.

Did he set me up to be used and then dumped when he'd had enough of me? No, he wouldn't have. He was so nice! Did he just use me for sex? No. The caring, the strong positive feelings, the love, was not just a Tuesday thing. It was real. He said so himself.

How will he respond to my letter? Will he laugh at me again? Will he think I'm more foolish than he already does? Am I pathetic wanting him to remember the me he said he was attracted to? Was he lying about that? Or was it real but I'm just too boring to have maintained his interest?

Tony doesn't reply. It hurts, but on the days when I remember waiting for him to arrive and being disappointed, I can see that my life now is more even now. Evenly depressing. I bury my Burnside file among some old papers and don't look at the photo of my mum much. It reminds me of when Tony valued me. I feel like a mangled mess. A quiet, flat mess. The curtain across my memories had better stay firmly closed. I've locked the window and eliminated any breeze. I hope.

Thank goodness school is more pleasant these days. I'm about to get information that will make my experience with Tony somewhat more hideous.

Felicity will be away for a few days. Nan, an older casual teacher I first met years ago, comes to take her class. Nan is wise and experienced. She's good at giving advice when it's asked for or when it's needed. We work back late and Nan starts talking.

'How is it for you here, Kate?' she asks.

'Ah, it's not like the other places we've met.' I give her a brief, slightly diplomatic account of how it is. 'I've tried to fit in.'

'Oh, don't blame yourself! There have been problems here for years. Some are still here, I see. But believe me, it's far better now than it has been. You've done well.'

As Nan describes the history of problems at the preschool, and the difficulties experienced by other teachers here, my eyes burn but I try not to cry. I don't want her to think I'm a sook.

'It's such a relief to hear all this. I thought it was all my fault because I'm too inflexible or something.'

'You do what a good teacher should do, Kate. I can see you've learnt so much since you started out all those years ago. You're a natural.'

When she goes, I let the flood of tears flow. If only I'd heard this a year ago. I might have understood what I'd walked into. I might have done things differently. Might not have got so insecure. Above all else I might not have gone to see Tony Benton.

I go home exhausted again. I miss Tony, the Tony I had thought he was.

Elliott stays over on his way home from his mother's house. She's gravely ill and he's finding it hard to cope with seeing her in pain. It's made him more sensitive.

'You seem sad or something,' he says.

'I don't want to burden you with my stuff.'

'I don't mind. I can't think about mum all the time. In fact, it might be good to take my mind off her.'

'Well, you know that psychologist I was seeing? Well, it turned into a relationship sort of thing.'

'Oh!'

'Yeah. I thought I loved him and he loved me. But it ended a couple of weeks ago. He said some horrible things and I'm not coping too well.'

'Bloody psychologists! They think they can trample all over you. All they're really after is your money. They keep you feeling inadequate so you'll keep coughing up. I don't know why you bothered going to see one in the first place.'

'I needed help. I thought he was helping me understand things I didn't understand. Then he said such horrible things.'

I'm crying. Elliott holds me and waits.

'Sorry, Elliott. I shouldn't be howling all over you.'

'It's all right. You said yourself it's what friends are for. Do you want to tell me what he said?'

'No. It was too horrible. It was humiliating. I felt ridiculous.'

'Humiliating! Ridiculous? That's not you. What have you got to feel ridiculous about?'

'Oh, stuff like he said I make people want to stay away from me.'

'Hmph. He hasn't seen me waiting to grab a dance with you, has he. Just don't take any notice. He's the ridiculous one. You're definitely not.'

'Thanks. He was raving like a madman and I was so confused and scared he'd do me harm – you know – clobber me or something. I walked out.'

'Good for you.'

'He said it was childish. That he was laughing at me.' I cry again and Elliott waits. 'He said he'd been laughing at me for ages.'

'Bastard! You don't believe him, do you?'

'Don't know. You can't just believe the good things someone says about you without considering the bad things.'

'You can if they're stupid.'

'But what if they are true?'

'They're not. People don't want to stay away from you. What about your house warming, all those people? He was there, wasn't he? He saw them all. And your friends at the farm? He's wrong. Surely you can see that.'

'It just hurt so much. And scared me. No-one's ever spoken to me like that before. Not the adult me.'

'What do you mean you had a relationship anyway? Did you sleep with him?'

'Yeah, for a while.'

'But he was your psychologist.'

'I know, but he said he'd still help me as a friend when that started.'

'Some help!'

We go for a long walk and don't talk much. We buy takeaway on the way home for dinner. 'I hate this time of day, when the sun's going down. Makes everything seem worse,' Elliott says.

'Really? I thought I was the only one that happened to. I know exactly what you mean.'

The thought of Elliott being so far away saddens me more. He's a good friend, but after he's gone I regret having told him about Tony and my humiliation. Have I compounded it by telling someone what a fool I was? Yes. I cry again.

At school my new aide, Clara, is cheerful and loves kids but has no long- or short-term memory regarding her daily routines. Well, she's probably nervous, being new. I'll be patient. She tries hard and her positive determination gives me hope. She listens intently.

'Kids learn best if they choose their activities rather than us telling them what to do all day. Our job is to help them learn while they're playing. So if they want to build, we can teach them about balancing, counting and finding shapes to fit their plan. That's maths. Or we get them to find balancing blocks. That's science.'

'Yes. Yes, Kate. I understand.'

'And if they choose to play in home corner we can role play and get them thinking about other people's points of view.'

'Yes, Kate. Yes.'

Then off she goes and forgets. Still, she's so positive, I can't stay cross for long.

Lunchtimes are very different now as Clara, oblivious to past friction, regularly declares that she loves working here and is having a fabulous time. She is impressed by how much the kids love me. Alma often chokes or is speechless, and I find that she doesn't have to be floated much these days.

Months pass and I think I feel less attached to Tony and more objective about him. If I were to bump into him, what would it be like? When I answer that I'd crumble, I know I'm not doing as well as I thought. One day at a time. Time heals. Learn and move on. Between all these cliches that I chant to myself, I tell myself that I'm a pathetic, stupid woman and it's no wonder Tony didn't want to be around me. I still cry and Ellen doesn't mind.

'You'll be right. There's plenty more fish in the sea. I don't know where but they must be there.' We've often joked about where single men hide.

'They can stay there for all I care. I've had the complete cure,' I tell her.

The future looks very gloomy. I'm always tired at work and I'm trapped with a mortgage and the endless procession of boarders I'll have to have. Will interest rates ever stop rising? Seventeen percent! How can I cope? If all the boarders are like Ellen it won't be a problem, but what about the Jameses and Grahams! Uni and work keep me busy but Saturday nights are harder to bear than ever. I remind myself that I rarely saw Tony on Saturday nights anyway but it doesn't help when I realise that for the next thirty years or so every Saturday night will be like this.

Humiliation stops me talking with friends about Tony. I keep the shame locked away and babble on about uni and school.

As the year comes to an end it's getting easier to pass Tony's office without panicking. When I do well at uni and am offered a position in the Honours program, I'm only slightly sad that I can't tell him.

Another holiday at the farm where long quiet walks, affirming company and golden sunsets give me the space I need to think without reminders or distractions. I'm still too humiliated to talk about Tony with Leonie and Col but I'm clearing away some cobwebs and looking at him more objectively.

He was a professional I went to for help. Why have I got more baggage to drag through my life now? If I hadn't decided to see a psychologist, I'd never have met him, let alone become involved with him.

I should have worked the school problem out myself. But I tried and failed, went to Peter and failed. Shouldn't a person be able to go to a psychologist and trust him? I had rung two professional organisations to make sure Tony belonged to them. Do they just let anyone who pays become a member?

Tony's training enabled him to build my trust, manipulate my feelings, then take advantage of me when I was most trusting. Was my so-called therapy just an ego trip for him? A Tuesday barometer of how ready he'd got me for exploitation, then humiliation? A Tuesday collection of my vulnerabilities that he could use to stick the knife in and twist it when he'd had enough? Here on his garbage heap it's a very poor view I have of myself.

Crying again. Gullible fool. Gullibility, the silent partner of trust. Am I the only person who had to learn that the hard way? Or are there others? Let's face it, I'm hardly an irresistible femme fatale, so if he used me, wouldn't he use other patients as well?

Or have I got Tony all wrong? Is he who he seemed to be in

therapy? He was kind. Wasn't he? He was caring. Wasn't he? He insisted that our feelings were real, nothing to be ashamed of or to hide, or hide from. Was that horrific ogre I saw at the end just a good man having a one-off temper tantrum when he was under incredible stress? Or was Tony in therapy just an act that I bought and paid for?

I'll never trust a shrink again! But you should be able to trust them.

The argument keeps going around in my head for months and I come to believe that I've been abused. Again. Not as a vulnerable, trusting child this time, but as a vulnerable, trusting adult patient. Abused by a trained professional, a manipulator who even boasted about his skill. Was he laughing all along? I'll show her what a joke she is telling me I'm not attractive. That I don't do therapy the way she says I should.

Stop thinking about it and prepare for school and find a new boarder now that Ellen's gone. I try to spruce myself up. Stylish new haircut and some new clothes. Sometimes I start believing ogre Tony again and it hits me that I'm fooling myself, that I can't look nice because I'm just plain ugly. I argue with myself. I become obsessed with my appearance. I stay home because I don't want to be seen. Then I fight Tony off, look in the mirror and go out. Although I'm more objective about him now there are issues that won't resolve. *Katherine is a rather plump girl . . .* Tony thinks I'm dull and boring and he really knew me. I wish I could stop the eternal debate.

Thora, a neighbour I've become friends with, walks with me in the evening now. We're going to get fit. As we walk we chat about our lives, her kids, my work and I wonder if I could talk to her about Tony. She seems to be more concerned about my isolation from my family than I am, but she tells me how lucky I am, too, to have no ties and be completely free. Oh, if only she knew. No, I can't tell her about Tony. Not yet. I'm not sure that she won't just tell me I'm a fool. Better to keep walking and chatting about other things. I'd love to be able to talk with someone, though.

I try driving past Tony's office on my way home. Fine. No, wait! He's up there doing what he does! Is he setting up another patient for abuse? Who'll warn them? Who'll stop him?

Well, I can't do anything. Too busy at school and finding a boarder. I want to make sure I'm doing a good job at work, being the kind of teacher I used to be. Happy, interesting, creative, understood and respected. I want to hear kids say, 'You love me, don't ya?' And when I joke and say, 'Nuh,' I want to hear them argue that I do, because they know I do.

Thoughts of school lead me to wonder about issues of professional accountability. Teachers are accountable to principals, who are accountable to superintendents and so on. Who are psychologists accountable to? If one psychologist can abuse his patients, how many others are doing the same? Isn't there an assessment process that screens out predators? Who administers it? Psychologists would surely be able to identify them. I still struggle with thinking of Tony as only an abuser. Who is the real Tony Benton? The one I thought I loved or the one who humiliated me? They're poles apart. And I wonder what happened with the woman who misunderstood him and made trouble for him.

Now I'm remembering that at uni, in an undergraduate course, we discussed a definition for rape. We decided that it is the forcing of sexual contact by a more powerful person on a less powerful one for the gratification of the more powerful person. Physical aggression doesn't have to be part of it, nor does an age differential. Power is the defining issue. Was I raped? Spiralling downwards. Who will understand? I so want to talk to someone and clear my thinking.

Meanwhile, I've found a new boarder, Reggie. She seemed loud and cheerful at the interview but said she needs a quiet place to live. Just so she can noisy it up? Coming home exhausted is a nightmare of noise now.

'Oh you're home. Come and watch "Monkey" with me! It's amazing!'

Just what I need. A crazy Japanese show for kids.

'Thanks, but I've got to work. Can I turn your radio off?'

'What?'

'Can I turn your radio off?'

'Radio? Oh, don't you like it?'

'Not when the television's on too. Can I turn it off?'

'Okay. Turn it off,' she says as if I've just popped in from the outer limits of the solar system.

I can't wait for Thora to get home so we can have a quiet walk around the quiet streets and have a quiet chat.

'Reggie's a bit deaf but she doesn't seem to know.'

'Oh, I couldn't stand that. What will you do? Ask her to go?'

'It's hard to know whether I'm being unfair. I mean, she lives there too. And I need her board. Anyway, I've agreed to let a friend of hers stay next week so I can't do it yet. Tricky when I've got an assignment to do.'

'Come down to my place if you need to.'

After a few days I'm fantasising about moving to Thora's place permanently.

The mess and noise at home make it resemble a zoo. I'll just have to ask Reggie to go. Asking her to turn the volume down is like asking a bull elephant to sneeze quietly. I'm nervous about how to state my case amicably.

We sit down with our drinks. I'll say 'Reggie this is difficult but I have to say it. You and I have different needs with how we live here.' Sounds all right, I think.

As I take a sip of coffee to fortify myself, Reggie says, 'Do you think it's working out? You seem to ask me to be quiet all the time.'

Phew! 'Yeah. No, it's not really working. I like more quiet and you like more noise. I like more tidiness and I think you're not as fussed about it.' That sounds okay.

'That's true. Can we do anything about it?'

Yes, yes, yes. But take it slowly and diplomatically.

'The thing is, I need the quiet, especially when I get home from work. If you could limit it to one thing on and softer. But you like it all turned on and loud, don't you?'

'What? The radio and television? Oh, I love all that energy and action.' She grins and shimmies her shoulders. She wipes the spilt tea up with her sleeve.

I force a smile and say, 'I noticed. But I need quiet because I'm out of energy and I've got school and uni work to do. I don't think we could work a compromise. We're just too different.'

'I don't want to have to watch all the volume levels and creep about,' she says good naturedly. 'Okay, well, I've got some friends who want their house minded. How about I move out to there?'

I love your friends. Love them. Love them. Love them.

'I don't want to be mean but that'd be best. Sorry.'

'Oh, don't worry. But they want me there on the weekend.'

Can she hear me shouting hurray on the inside? I'm grateful to Reggie that we got through it calmly.

Now I'm living alone quietly again, financially challenged but I'll deal with that somehow. It's easier without therapy bills. Alone is what I need. Coming home is bliss. I can keep up with my school work, uni work and sleep.

Where's my life going, though? Nowhere. I'm a mess, really. All those issues Tony raised in therapy that never got dealt with. When am I going to sort them out? All the issues he raised later! How can I repair the damage?

How can I stop it happening to other people?

A few weeks later I'm washing up. Someone knocks on the door. Surely Thora doesn't want to walk now! It's nine thirty.

'Hello, Kate,' Amanda says as I open the door. 'Is it too late to call in after all this time?'

Amanda! Why is she here after all these months?

'Uh, no. Hello. Come in.'

I make us coffee. While we do small talk I wonder if I'll tell her what happened with Tony. I'd like to say I'm sorry I got involved but I'm afraid of how she'll react. I'll see if they're together again.

'Have you seen Tony lately?' I ask.

'Tony. No! I told you, didn't I? He left me for someone else.

All our contact is through lawyers these days.'

'You're getting a divorce?' Is there any point telling her, then?

'I know what happened between you and Tony,' she says gently.

I stop breathing. Marvelling that she isn't furious, I want to cry with relief. 'You know?'

'Yes. I don't blame you or hold it against you, Kate. You were vulnerable. You were his patient.'

I can't think of anything to say but I want to howl. I'm so tense I hardly hear what she's saying. She seems glad to be free of Tony.

'I wish I'd never met him,' I say. 'I rang that Psychologists Society thing before I went to him. And the hypnosis lot. They didn't let on that there was a problem.'

'They probably didn't know. Are you going to tell them?'

'I don't know. I've thought about it. But . . . Oh, I don't know. Sometimes I just want to put it all behind me and forget it ever happened. But then I think he might be doing it to someone else. But everyone isn't as gullible as I was.'

'You're not gullible. I'm sorry it happened to you.'

'I'm sorry too. How are you coping these days?' I ask, not wanting to be the focus of the conversation.

Amanda tells me that some days are good and others are hard. Her job is great and Vlad has been counselling her. His business with Tony is finished. Vlad is a nice man, she says, and if I want to talk to him, she's sure he wouldn't mind. He's a really principled, ethical person.

'I've heard that before!'

'Yes, you would have, I'm sure,' she says bitterly. 'But Vlad really is.'

Soon Amanda leaves, wishing me well, and I wish her well too. We're both getting free.

The next time Thora and I go walking I decide to tell her about Tony. She's good at looking at both points of view and it might help me decide whether to take any action against Tony. Thora's response is astounding.

'I have a friend who that happened to.'

'Really! Who was it, the psychologist, I mean? No, hang on. Don't tell me. It might be defamation. Um. Is his first initial T?'

(No, dear reader, we didn't use initials, but the lawyers made me do it.)

'No. I think it was A. I don't remember. But she was absolutely devastated. She had a breakdown.'

'Is that why she went to a shrink?'

'No, the breakdown was after. Because the shrink did what yours did.'

'Oh, I don't believe it! No, I do, but I thought I was the only person from here to Iceland who it'd happened to. Yet someone in my own street knows someone.'

'Well, I don't see that friend much any more. She can't go out or anything.'

'Is she going to report him?'

'No, Kate! She's had a severe breakdown. She can hardly put one foot in front of the other.'

Is that going to happen to me? Can it happen without you knowing it has? I don't think it's happened to me. A breakdown.

'The poor woman. I'm thinking about reporting.'

I'm outraged that abuse is more prevalent than I'd imagined. I'm more sure that I want to report Tony now. He could have ruined me, like A did to Thora's friend. Something has to be done to stop these psycho-bloody-chologists treating us like trash.

I ring Vlad nervously. Better the devil you know, vaguely. Amanda's admiration for Vlad did seem sincere.

'I thought you might ring me one day,' he says. 'Amanda said you'd talked.'

I try to slough off resentment and get to the point. 'Well, I'm not happy about being discussed but I need to talk to you. But not when Tony's there. Does he ever go there now?'

'Sometimes. You could come to the house.'

'Your house!' You must be joking!

'My wife and kids would be there.'

And Tony wouldn't. 'All right. On my way to uni.'

At his house Vlad introduces me to his family, who then leave the room discreetly.

I outline what happened with Tony, and tell him I'm thinking of reporting him but I don't know how. 'That's why I've come to you. Do you know?' Vlad looks concerned. He believes me. He wants to help.

'I could get the information for you, if you like. It'd be the society, I would think, but I'll check with my contacts. And if you go ahead, I'd like you to think of me as a supporter. If a statement from me is required, I'll give one. And if I can help to counsel you . . .'

'Uh, no. Thanks. I can't afford counselling. And I don't know that I'd trust you either. Sorry, but I don't know if I'd trust anyone.'

'I can understand that, but the offer stands, should you change your mind. Just think it through and let me know.'

A few days later he rings.

'I don't want to pressure you but I've got some information about how to make a report, if you choose to.'

'Thank you. I'll get a pen. Okay, Psychologists Registration Board. Rawson Place . . .'

He tells me I need to outline what happened in a statutory declaration and send it with a covering letter to the Registrar. He thinks the process is that the complaint will be tabled at the next meeting of the Board and it will decide what should happen next.

They won't believe me. Why would they? They'll say I'm making it up. It'll be an old boys' club protecting its own, like people reckon the police do.

I wait a few weeks, to assure myself that it's the right thing to do. It's an easy decision if I think of the last time I saw Tony. What will he do to me if I report him? Will I be safe? But I can't let him just treat patients the way he did me and get away with it.

When I feel as ready as I'll ever be I sit down to begin the statutory declaration. I word and reword it until it's concise but tells the essentials. I push the question of who I thought he was away.

At last the stat dec is finished. When I did them in the insurance company years ago I used to include 'I declare that I am of sound mind'. I leave that out.

Oh no! It has to be signed in the presence of a Justice of the Peace! What if he insists on reading it before he signs it? The embarrassment will kill me! Should I write my will before I go? I find the listing for JPs in the phone book. Should I get one away from this community, in case he does read what I've written? Haven't got time. I have to present a paper at uni next week.

I go to a local person. His eyes move slowly down the page as we walk inside.

'I'd like you not to read it, please,' I tell him. 'It's embarrassing.'

'Oh, all right. I'm only required to witness your signature,' he says blandly.

Now it's ready to post. I take it to the post office twice and I bring it home twice. Am I a coward? Probably. I'm a coward who can't bear the thought of Tony confronting me or worse. I feel wretched about my cowardice but I'll feel wretched if I send the report in and wait for the retaliation. Feelings. I'm making the decision based on feelings. What if I try cognition instead? No, it doesn't get me back to the post office. I'm too stressed already, without that adding to it. I'm barely holding my shattered self together.

Driving home from school one day I hear a radio interview with a person described as a well-respected psychologist, and he practises in our area. Will I go to see him to help me rebuild my life, sort out the damage? Him! That's the problem. But if I don't see this person, it'll be a lucky dip in the phone book. I'd never let what Tony did happen to me again. And I don't want to go around thinking all male psychologists are predators so if I could work with this person . . . But I'm sure I couldn't trust him. But he could work with that.

Before I can talk myself out of it I make an appointment. As soon as I'm in his room, cold and shaking, I know I've made a mistake. Telling him about Tony is a relief but it's also making me more nervous. Am I just saying 'Here I am, a vulnerable fool ready to be exploited again'?

'Look, you really don't need to see a man, do you?'

'No. Sorry. I thought it would be good if I could work it through, but I can't.'

'How about I give you the name of a woman counsellor?'

'Yes please.'

'Have you reported this person you told me about?'

'Not yet. I've got the stat dec ready but I'm not ready to send it.'

'You need to send it, to report him. I'd have to if you weren't going to.'

I leave with the woman psychologist's number on a card: her name is Neroli. I put away the card and decide I'm not ready to see anyone yet. That man said he would have had to make a report, so the profession must have some standards of practice. That's encouraging. Will I send the stat dec now?

Surely Tony wouldn't drive from where he is now, in a rage, to confront me. Before I have time to change my mind, I dash to the letter box and throw the letter in. I tell myself this is a good thing to do because he won't be able to abuse anyone else. I tell myself that he probably won't come after me and he won't even know what I've done for a month or two.

No acknowledgment comes after I send the stat dec, so I ring the Board. I'm told my letter hasn't arrived yet but that nothing can be done for some time, anyway, because the Psychologists Bill is currently being debated in parliament; the Board will have to wait for enactment before it proceeds. Good. That gives me time to brace myself for whatever happens next.

When a letter arrives two weeks later, it acknowledges receipt of my complaint and tells me I'll be contacted again when the Psychologists Board has considered my allegations. Will they believe me? What have I let myself in for? Will I ever stop feeling anxious? At least if they don't believe me, it'll be over. But what about all those other women?

I have to try to put it out of my mind for a while, pretend I haven't lit a fuse.

My face is about to explode. I've got a cyst between my eyes, and it gets attention at work. Parents make sympathetic comments that make me feel cared for and kids think the patch I wear is a pirate patch gone a bit awry. It feels so good to laugh again. I'd forgotten what it's like.

Alma is accepting a transfer. I try not to appear too enthusiastic but I'd leap for joy if my face wasn't so sore. Am I sad that I've booked the operation to have the cyst removed on the day of Alma's farewell party?

Her replacement, Jessie, is a quiet woman who smiles easily and has a mischievous sense of humour. Mischievous because it jumps in and surprises, not because it stabs backs. School is a happy place at last. We laugh a lot and I forget the other thing at least at work.

Home is a contrast. I become tense and suspicious that Tony will appear from nowhere and there'll be a scene. As my fortieth birthday looms I grieve for the babies I won't have. There's some relief in that too, though. I don't have to find a mate. A mate has as much appeal as sticking my head in an active bee hive. Home church gives me a lovely birthday dinner that shows me how much I need my closest friends. I miss the openness I usually have with them but I still can't tell them about Tony.

EVIDENCE

Just as I used to shudder when the building society logo popped up in my letter box, I shudder when the Board's envelope appears. The shudder turns to a constant tremble when I read that it has referred my complaint for investigation by the Complaints Unit of the Department of Health. The Board must believe me!

What now? It means it isn't going to go away. Health Department? At least if it's a government department it probably won't be old boys protecting their own. A whole unit devoted to complaints. What's the world coming to? What's my world coming to? Well, I'll try to forget it for a while, until they contact me. The 'while' is very short.

'Hello, Mrs Shayler?' an unfamiliar voice asks. Only telephone sales people call me that at home. My nerves are twanging and I'm ready to tell him to get lost, to stop disturbing my peace.

'Brendan Green from the Health Department Complaints Unit calling.'

'Oh!' Oh no! 'Have you got my letter already?'

'Yes. Your complaint is here on my desk. I'll be dealing with the matter, so I'll need to go over your statutory declaration with you. We need to get the details clear.'

'Now?'

'Well, it would be better if you could come in, but if you'd rather do it on the phone, we could.'

'No! I'd rather come in.' Better than spelling it out here beside the kitchen window where neighbours or friends pop up at will. We make an appointment.

The day is a nervous one at school and I lose my patience and snap at Clara for the first time when she forgets to get the kids' drinks ready. I don't feel good about it.

Brendan Green is so young! I expected to feel awkward but I'm just about old enough to be this man's mother! What would he know about being an older, single woman? Or vulnerability? Or humiliation?

He talks respectfully and says he knows this will be difficult but it's important that he gets as much information today as he can. We need to be thorough and then an investigation may be carried out. The tacit message that I will not be believed automatically makes me want to stamp my foot and shout that what I've said is true, that he has to believe me, that I'm not making it up. I want to have a tantrum! But then I have to admit that it's fair. To Tony.

'How long will the whole thing take?' I ask.

'We try to get matters dealt with as quickly as we can. For the client's sake, and in fairness to the practitioner and the public.'

'A couple of months? Six months?'

'It depends on how long it takes to gather the evidence. Depends on how quickly people reply to letters and phone calls, that kind of thing. When we've got all the evidence we need it's given to the Board to decide whether to take the matter further. There could be a hearing before a Professional Standards Committee or they could decide on a lesser action, depending on how seriously they view Benton's behaviour. It's not a quick process but we'll do what we can to expedite the matter within a reasonable amount of time.'

'So how long?'

'It could be as long as twelve to eighteen months. I can't be specific.'

'But is Tony Benton allowed to keep practising for all that time?'

'We can't stop him until the case against him is proven.'

'But what if he's abusing someone else right now?' I ask. Squeak is more like it. 'Can't you stop him? Oh, innocent 'til proven guilty, isn't it?' Okay let's get on with it, then, before I go mental.

Brendan explains that statements from both parties will be taken and the Unit's investigators will gather other evidence as well. Peer reviews will be sought.

'What are peer reviews?'

'We send yours and Benton's statements to respected peers of Benton's for comment. They express their opinions based on their understanding of the Code of Conduct and on their professional judgement.'

'Is there a code for conduct? I mean, a document or something.'

'Oh yes.' He explains that the code can be open to interpretation. The Unit gets opinions from respected people in the field because they reflect the profession's view of what behaviour is and is not acceptable under the Code.

Now the hardest part begins and I start blushing more brightly than I've ever done. I'm questioned about the sequence of events and the details of my dealings with Tony. Brendan needs more detail than I've given in the stat dec. Times and dates are very important but I don't remember those. I'll get them from my journal. I never imagined it would be used for anything like this. There are some questions I can answer easily and others that make me wish I'd dissolve into the carpet. Brendan remains calm and clinical, assuring me that nothing I tell him will shock him. This is what the Unit does: investigates complaints against health workers day in and day out!

The Psychologists Registration Board has recently been reformed in response to the Psychologists Bill being enacted. Although the experience of investigating a psychologist is new for the Unit, my story, the essence of it, isn't. It's similar to others involving doctors, psychiatrists, nurses and even dentists. People in positions of trust sometimes abuse their power. The Unit exists to protect the public from them.

'Good. You can stop him.'

'Kate, you must understand that we are not here for revenge or to carry out vendettas. While I do understand you might want revenge, we are here to protect the public and ensure that proper standards are maintained in the health professions.'

'I don't want him to be out there doing to other people what he did to me,' I say quietly, forcing the words to come slowly.

'That's what we want too. Now, do you know of any other people who might be able to substantiate your claim?'

'I'd have to check with them but I think Benton's ex-wife and ex-business partner will cooperate. I haven't ask them.'

'All right. If you could check with them and get back to me, we can look at that.'

At last the questions stop, except that Brendan asks, 'Any questions before you go?'

'How long have I got before Tony Benton finds out about this? I'm scared he'll want to confront me.' I feel like a sook.

'He's not allowed to contact you at all during the investigation.'

'But that mightn't stop him. He's got an awful temper. How long have I got?'

'Mm. First, we need to get your version down fully and accurately. Then we give Mr Benton a chance to respond to it.'

'You send him my stat dec! Can't he just write his own, without reading mine?'

'He has to be given the chance to answer your allegations.'

'Do you think he did wrong? I mean, if what I say is true?'

'If what you say is true, he's behaved outside of the Code of

Conduct, as I see it. But it's not for me to say. The Board will determine that. Have you seen the Code of Conduct?'

'No. I didn't know there was one until you mentioned it.'

'It's the code that psychologists agree to practise under,' he says, rummaging through papers on his desk. 'I can't put my hands on one right now but I'll send it to you, if you like. Oh here. I'll need to keep this but just glance through it. Let's see. Where is it? Yes, paragraph five.' He passes it to me.

Psychologists Registration Board, I read. *Code of Conduct*. I scan until I reach paragraph five. *Psychologists must not exploit their relationship with a client in any way. In particular there must not be a sexual relationship with a client during the professional relationship.*

'This is so clear! Everyone should be given this when they go to see a psychologist,' I exclaim. It's so clear it makes me angry.

'It is clear,' Brendan agrees. 'As you can see, those dates you need to look up when you get home are critical. We have to be very clear about when the professional relationship ended.'

'Yes, I can see that,' I say angrily. 'It ended when he was on top of me, to put it bluntly.'

I read the rest of paragraph five. *When the professional relationship has ended, the advice of senior colleagues should be sought before beginning any other sort of relationship.*

'Look at this part about having a discussion with a colleague! We didn't have a discussion! It all happened on the same night.' I could shed angry tears but my cognitive functions are on overdrive. 'Oh now I know why he said he'd talked with a colleague. He said it when he was telling me off at the end. He said he did it in the previous week, when the relationship ended, not started. And I certainly wasn't there for it.'

'Good, well, write that down and it'll go in the stat dec too.'

It's as if this Code was written for me, to confirm that what Tony did was abusive. He has to be stopped. 'What happens next?' I ask, feeling more determined, energised by my anger.

'I'll make up a new stat dec based on what you've told me and get it out to you as soon as I can. I'll be discussing the case with Merrilyn Walton, the Unit Director, as we go along. I'll include the Code of Conduct with the stat dec. I believe there's a more recent version than this one. Have you been given the brochure about how the Unit works? No? All right, here it is. I suggest you read it through. And if you have any questions or concerns, please feel free to ring me. If I'm not here just leave a message and I'll get back to you. Have we got your number on file?'

'You can't ring me at school, not while I'm teaching. I'd have to ring you back after classes.'

I leave utterly exhausted. On the train I start to read about the Unit but I fall asleep.

'Hey, are you getting off?' Thora is waking me up. She waits on the platform as I stagger off the train, clutching my bag and papers.

'Been to uni?' she asks.

'Something like that.' Will I tell her? No. This isn't the place. I'll wait 'til our next walk.

At home I start reading again. The brochure covers the purpose of the Unit and the procedures. If a *broader investigation* is deemed to be needed – yes, that's me – *sign an authority . . . following initial information . . . additional questions . . . further information* – that'll be next. Opinions of *experts sought . . . fair and objective assessment* – that's the peer review thing Brendan mentioned . . . *copy of the complainant's letter is usually sent to the service provider for comment.* Service provider! Ha! Not looking forward to that part but at least it'll be getting close to the end then, won't it? Yes . . . *may take weeks to months . . . waiting time is difficult . . . will keep you in touch.*

It will be difficult, is difficult, but at least it's only months.

What's next? . . . *where the Department believes no further action is necessary* . . . Hells bells! Surely they won't decide that, will they?

I can't help thinking about kind and caring Tony in therapy. I did make some gains. He sent me to my mother's grave, let me grieve, well, sort of. He let me talk and made me start believing in myself again. Am I destroying his career just because he blew up once?

But there's the Code of Conduct. No sexual contact. Discussion with colleague. Remember his parting words, the defensive statements he made about never having done this before and so on. These assure me that he deserves what he's going to get. He helped me. Yes. But he took advantage of me too.

I finish reading the brochure . . . *believes further action is needed . . . referral will be made to an appropriate disciplinary body . . . the Unit does not pursue matters in relation to financial compensation.* Hadn't thought of that. I just want him to be held accountable and stopped, to have this dealt with and out of my life in the shortest possible time.

I ring Amanda to ask if she'll give a statement and if I can give her details to Brendan.

'Give me his number and I'll ring him myself.' She seems to think that what I'm doing is right and is surprised that it will take so long.

Will I make it through the stress, or crumble and lose my patience with Clara again? What if I start snapping at the kids? That would be devastating. Uni work is always waiting behind whatever I do too. It's all too much.

Where did I put that phone number for what's her name, the psychologist? Might as well go and see what she's like. She might be helpful, but if her methods are anything like Tony's, I'll leave. I'm more nervous about it than I thought I'd be. I feel like I'm asking someone else to pour molten lava down my back.

The waiting room is sunny, there's beautiful choral music playing softly, and a delicate aroma of incense or oil in the air. I hope Neroli isn't a new-age airhead!

'Kate? Come on in.' She is tall and slender. She smiles slightly and speaks quietly.

We sit down and Neroli asks what she can do for me. Her gentleness and apparent concern make me feel weepy already.

'Before we go any further, do you know Tony Benton?' I ask, suddenly frightened that she'll be a friend of his and she'll laugh at me and send me packing.

She looks surprised. 'No. Should I?'

I tell her who he is. She doesn't interrupt but lets me know she's listening.

'That's shocking,' she says, slowly shaking her head. 'So you've reported this? Good, because if you hadn't, I would. Let me know if there's anything I can do to help. Anything at all.'

Assuming that's a platitude, I move on. 'I have more to deal with now than I had when I first went to see him.'

'Tell me about what you want to achieve here.'

What I want to achieve! Not what she thinks I should do. This is different. Well, it'll be hard to articulate what I want.

'Well, Tony made me think that a person with my background is a mess. So probably most of me needs fixing.' Neroli doesn't smile. 'I want to sort out the feelings that I had and the ones I have now for him. I want to find ways to get me through the investigation sane. And I want to work out how my childhood traumas affect me now. Well, I don't really but Tony said I should, before he turned bad. And, um, I want to learn how to do relationships with men differently. I keep getting them wrong. And my work situation is better than it was but it's still got a few problems, so I'd like to work those out too. The main thing is dealing with the complaint. Oh, and I got my file from my childhood and I might want to work through that too. Tony thought it wouldn't affect me but it did. It made me depressed. More depressed.'

At last I stop. But I know I haven't mentioned the most difficult part of my baggage. 'I want to get some self-respect back.' And stop this teary thing happening all the time.

Neroli has been listening and nodding. She made some notes but not intrusively.

'It's nice to be asked what I want to achieve. I thought you'd tell me what you think I should do.'

'Clients usually know what they need. My role is to help them find their own solutions. It's no use me telling you what to do when you know yourself so much better than I do. You know what's appropriate for you. I don't believe I have all the answers and clients are just here to listen and obey me.'

Clients. Not patients. It sounds more respectful to recognise that I have something to bring to the process.

'What if clients are too messed up to find answers?'

'How do you mean too messed up?'

'Well, Tony Benton seemed to think that I was, oh, you know, damaged goods. Not the full deck any more. Because of my childhood. He thought he could fix me, I think.'

'Mm. It sounds like a kind of Freudian approach where the client is pathologised, so the psychologist's role is to diagnose, then treat the patient to restore the damage. I don't work that way.'

'I suppose if all childhood trauma led to damage, there'd be hardly any sane people walking about. Only people who could afford the treatment would be sane. But that's not how it is.'

Neroli asks me to tell her my history, and when I finish she doesn't predict gloom and doom and years of agonising scrutiny. She believes that how we think about ourselves is the important thing that guides our behaviour as adults, not what kind of childhood we had, though that can influence how we think, of course. She invites me to notice my thought patterns and how they relate to my behaviour. She calls it 'self talk'. If I find behaviours I want to change, we'll work on those by challenging the assumptions behind them. We'll work with my self talk.

She asks me to elaborate on what I need help with, regarding the thing with Tony. I tell her about the shame I feel, the humiliation, and the fear that the picture Tony painted of me in his final assault might be true. I talk about how much the betrayal hurts and how angry I feel about it all.

'Let's look at some of those things. The shame you feel. Why do you feel shame?'

'Because I think I compromised my values and I did such an incredibly stupid thing getting involved with him. Socially, I mean.'

'Why did you do those things?'

'Because I thought he loved me and I loved him.'

'And why did you think those things? What evidence did you have?'

'He told me the transference thing was real and then I thought it was real outside therapy because he wanted me. Or I thought he did. No, he did. Oh, I got so confused.'

'You know that we are not supposed to blur the boundaries between professional and social contact with clients, do you?'

'No. Well, sort of. It's in the Code of Conduct, isn't it?'

'We don't have social contact at all. That helps clients understand the limits of the relationship, so that that confusion can't happen. I won't, for example, come to your house or have coffee with you at the shops. If we bump into each other, I'll just say a friendly hello and leave. Tony Benton, I suspect, allowed the boundaries to become blurred and confusing. He led you to think those feelings belonged outside the professional relationship, when, in fact, they had no place there.'

As she talks I remember and let the tears fall. I'm so stupid.

Self talk comes automatically. As yet unchallenged.

'Kate, you were manipulated. Can you see that?'

'I think so.'

'Were you stupid to trust him, a professional person?'

'No.'

'No. So who should be feeling shame?'

I know the answer but it's too soon to let go of the shame.

This is work. We talk through more issues but time is up so quickly. Before I go, Neroli says I'll be able to turn my anger into courage. I hope she's right. There's so much of it.

I leave feeling lighter, not as if I've been through the wringer like I did when I left Tony's room after my first session. Is Neroli going to be helpful? I like that she doesn't play God and that she asked what I hope to achieve. She made me work, too, and find things inside myself. It's good to have an objective female to help sort myself out. I think I'll come back, at least until this round of health-fund rebates runs out.

Another letter box shudder at the end of September. Brendan has sent a revised stat dec with a letter asking me to read it carefully and make whatever changes I feel are necessary. Heavens! I've given him so much detail, it'd have to be accurate. This won't take long, then I can get back to trying to pretend it's not happening.

The other thing in the envelope is alarming. It's a consent form for me to sign so that the Unit can access Tony's records of my therapy. When I sign that, they'll contact him and my very tenuous grip on feeling safe will be broken. I know! I just won't sign it until I'm ready.

I can't deal with this now. I have a uni paper to finish. But concentrating on research into social isolation in early childhood proves impossible when the stat dec is glaring at me from the shelf where I tossed it.

Heart races as I begin reading.

No, that's not right. I want it understood that Tony and I did not decide together to explore my history. He pressured me into it and he decided I needed long-term therapy.

Driven by the need to have every little detail accurate and understood, I make corrections until my back is aching. I look at the clock. It's after midnight and I still haven't finished.

Go to bed. Leave it for the weekend.

Friday afternoon. Home exhausted. Check the mail, then I'll collapse for the night. Junk mail, electricity bill, blue envelope. I don't recognise the writing. I turn the letter over. Small spiky letters say, *T. Benton. Suite 21. . .* Every fibre of my being panics.

I tear the envelope open, and have trouble reading the spiky little words.

Dear Kate,
It was with dismay that I learned of the action which you have taken against me. It was surprising in the light of the two personal, supportive letters I have before me, which you sent to me at the end of last year.

This action pales when compared with another letter sent to me today, one very damaging to my professional reputation. It was addressed to a well-known professional colleague of mine and refers specifically to your complaint against me.

I have passed a copy of this defamatory letter on to my solicitor.
T. Benton.

What letter? What colleague? What are you talking about? I try to read it again. I look around to see if he's watching, then run inside and lock the door. Squeeze the tears away and read again. My hands are trembling. He's going to sue me for defamation! I'll lose everything. How did he find out about my complaint? Brendan said it'd take longer than this. Have to ring him. Five thirty. Too late! I find the number. Try it anyway. Hardly breathing.

'I'm sorry. Mr Green has gone home,' a woman says with a finality that suggests I should know the time.

'Well, I have to talk to someone! I've made a complaint and I've got a letter and I need to . . .'

She tells me that I should wait until Monday.

'I can't wait 'til Monday!'

She tells me that genuine complaints to the Unit are covered by qualified privilege, which means complainants can't be sued for making them. But I really should wait until Monday and talk with Mr Green. Meanwhile, try to be calm and put it aside.

Can't be sued. Qualified privilege. Monday.

I read the letter again. Details are starting to get through now. Tony's dismay isn't in the light of the precious friendship we had.

No, it's in the light of two letters he can threaten me with.

Anytime I start feeling soft about you, Tony, I'll remember this threat.

Did I write to him at the end of last year? Twice? Surely I'd remember. I was depressed but surely I'd remember writing. They wouldn't have been supportive, though, not like the Christmas card I gave him or that letter I'm too embarrassed to think about now. I'd imagined him screwing that up and chucking it away. Like he did me. Did he keep it because he knew what he did was wrong and he'd use my letter if I took action? That makes me angry, makes me glad I've done what I've done.

I know beyond a shadow of a doubt that I didn't write to his colleague. What colleagues have I ever met? Who did write then? Amanda? Vlad? They're the only other people who know about the complaint.

Will I let Tony's letter intimidate me and withdraw my complaint? Peace! I could move on.

No, I couldn't. He would have won and I'd feel cowardly. And worried about the other women. And Tony wouldn't have the Unit telling him to keep away from me.

I'm trapped. No going back. I check all my door locks and windows and go to bed. Have to get some sleep so that I'm ready for the working bee at school tomorrow. I arranged it, so I have to be there.

Jessie comes to help too. Young, feral-looking fathers come to lay sleepers and turf and clear the gardens. They grumble good-naturedly about the lack of beer. I'm grateful for their help and their humour, though some of it I don't understand and I notice Jessie's eyebrows are pretty busy going up and down between blushes. At the end of the day they say they enjoyed coming, apart from the big dry, and ask when we want them to come again.

I stay and tidy up for as long as I can. I go home as late as I can, exhausted. The closer I get to home the more anxious I get. Will Tony be waiting? I listen outside my door, then creep inside and check each room. I keep the curtains closed and my ears trained. When cars pull up in my street, I peep through the curtains.

Must get my paper ready to present at uni. I'm working on prevention of child sexual assault. I unplug the phone and spend hours reading, writing and thinking.

The statistics for girls abused in childhood are depressing and infuriating. One in three, some people say. Is this what being a woman is? Being abused as a child and living with the consequences for the rest of your life? What gives men the right . . . oh, better get back to the prevention programs. Then I'll try to finish that stat dec.

When I do there's still so much rewording, remembering, referring to journal entries and the calendar to do between pacing around trying to calm myself.

Ring Gen for support, that's what I need to do. Neroli thinks I might need to be more trusting of friends' offers to be there for me.

'Hi, Gen. Me again. Are you busy? Is this a bad time?'

'No. Just got the kids to bed. What are you up to?'

Good decision. Thanks Neroli. 'Well I hope you mean you've got time because I need to tell you something awful.'

'Yeah. I've got time. What's happened?'

'Remember Tony Benton the psychologist. Well I got . . . sort of involved with him . . .'

'A relationship do you mean?'

'Well, if you could call it that. Yeah, a sexual something or other.'

'Is that wise? I mean he's married and he's your psychologist.'

'No. Yes. Oh well, he's getting divorced but it all went wrong and horrible and I don't see him at all now.'

'Oh good.'

'Yeah. Sort of. I'm a mess though and I can't keep it to myself any more. He said some dreadful things to get rid of me.' I'm getting weepy and can't hide it.

'That bastard!' Gen seethes.

'I'm reporting him to the Complaints Unit so that is sort of prolonging the agony.'

'Good for you Kate. Can I tell Paddy? He's just here.'

She tells him what I've said.

'He says to let him know if you need anything.'

'I'm just scared Tony'll come and confront me.'

Gen reckons Tony wouldn't drive all the way here to confront me. He'd assume his letter would stop me. Paddy thinks so too. Their loyalty and reassurance are calming, at least until I hang up. All right, I'll test it and go for a walk tomorrow.

Will I invite Thora? No. If Tony does turn up I wouldn't want her to be involved. I go by myself.

What on earth am I thinking wandering about here by myself? I turn around quickly and rush back to my cage.

Monday at last. 'Hello, Brendan? I got a letter from Tony Benton. He knows about the complaint. Oh, it's Kate Shayler. Sorry. I'm nervous. He's going to sue me. I thought you said it would take longer . . .'

'Hello, Kate. Just calm down. I haven't contacted him yet. What does the letter say?'

I read it.

'Did you write to his colleague?'

'No. I thought you must have.'

'You definitely didn't write to any of Benton's colleagues?'

'No. I don't even know who his colleagues are, apart from Vlad. I don't remember writing letters to him either. I wrote one letter to Tony but that was before he says.'

'All right. Now, you've made a complaint to this Unit in good faith, so you're covered by what we call qualified privilege. That means, in effect, that he can't sue you. It's not defamatory to lodge a bona fide complaint with us.'

'What will I do?'

'Send a copy of the letter to me and I'll write to him and advise him against contacting you.'

'Will I write as well?'

'To Benton? No. Definitely not. We advise no contact between the parties involved during an investigation. Just leave it with me.'

I appreciate the clear, simple answer. I go back to work.

At home I finish the stat dec and send it and the consent form to the Unit.

Will I tell Peter what's going on in case Tony rings or turns up at school to make trouble? No. He hasn't been much help so far and I doubt he'd understand this. Things have settled down nicely, too, and I don't want him to think I'm a series of disasters waiting to happen.

School is like an oasis. I'm so busy getting real teaching done I don't get time to think about anything else here.

'Come and see me bridge,' Jason says. 'Cars can go over and boats go under.'

His little round face is beaming with pride and I can't help cupping it in my hand as I say, 'Good planning. Good for you.'

'You love me, don't ya?' He grins.

'Nuh.'

'Yeah, you do.' He pushes my hand more firmly against his cheek. 'You do so,' he declares, then tosses my hand away and revs up his truck.

It's nice to see Elliott again because he's a friend and because he's a male. If Tony turns up, Elliott, although he's a very gentle, quiet man, just might scare him off. We go to a movie and on the way home I tell him about my complaint to the Unit so that he'll understand what I need him to do.

'But surely it takes two to tango. Why should this bloke, even though I think he's a cretin, why should he get into hot water over it?'

I'd assumed Elliott would understand. I try to explain.

'When you go to a doctor, you trust that they'll do the medical things you need to get well, don't you? You don't expect them to manipulate you into a sexual relationship.'

'That I should be so lucky!' Elliott laughs, making me cranky, disgusted.

'Can't you see that it's not a normal healthy relationship we're talking about, where you meet socially and get to know each other and then decide to go further? It's one person who has power taking advantage of a vulnerable other person. Who they can manipulate. Using their professional position to meet their needs, not the patient's. Can't you see the betrayal of trust?'

'Yeah, sure. But you're a strong, mature adult who chose to get involved,' he replies with some reservation.

'Yes I am an adult, but I was vulnerable, needy. Not strong. That's why I went to him. He made me more needy and dependent. I was manipulated. He could do it because of his training, his professional position.'

'I can see that but I still say you made choices too. I'm really sorry you were treated so badly, but from his point of view it seems he's taking all the blame.'

'Yeah. I know what you mean about me making choices, but I was vulnerable to manipulation because I trusted him. He was a professional. It wasn't like choosing which shoes to buy or what movie to see. He had all the power. Anyway, the bottom line is that it's against their code of conduct.' And your not understanding is such a disappointment.

We finish the trip in silence. This is a good warning for me not to tell anyone else about it. If Elliott can't see, will anyone else? He thinks I'm strong. Well, he didn't see inside my head, behind the coping exterior. No. I won't tell anyone else. I'll keep my coping exterior and just talk with Gen, Paddy and Thora. And Col and Leonie when I go to the farm.

Each afternoon I'm a little more relaxed about going home, although the letter box feels like a time bomb. The final version of the stat dec comes near the end of November with a covering letter assuring me that Tony has been advised not to contact me and that my complaint has qualified privilege.

My next appointment with Neroli is at a useful time. I need to talk to her about all the fear and frustration that drains me. She suggests I need to access my personal power. Me? Power? Where?

'Can you think of times when you feel powerful?'

'Um.'

'When you've felt in control, made good decisions?'

I have to dredge the barrel to find times like that. Neroli sees my leaving the insurance company and going to tech as a time when I must have felt strong and in control. I don't. I see it as a time when I drifted around with a safety net always below me.

As we talk about personal power, taking risks, speaking my mind, Neroli often asks, 'What evidence do you have for that?'

'Sometimes I do things because I don't want people to think I'm awful. Like if I'm asked to babysit. I hate babysitting but they'll think I'm horrible if I say no.'

'What evidence do you have for that?'

'Um. None.'

And: 'I don't like people knowing I'm single, because they'll feel sorry for the poor spinster and wonder what's wrong with me.'

'What evidence do you have for that?'

'Um. Er. None.'

'So how could you change your thinking on that?'

'I'm single. So what? But I'm single and I'm lonely, that's what.'

'What can you do about that?'

'Nothing.'

'Nothing?'

'Nothing! No-one asks me out. I can't catch a fella. I don't even want to any more.'

'Is a fella the only solution to loneliness? Do you have to wait to be asked out? You have women friends.'

'Oh, good grief! It's so obvious when you say it. Invite my women friends out. Gosh, I'm stupid. What's the matter with me?'

'What is?'

'Nothing?'

'Nothing. Just think about it differently, the way you just

did. Invite your women friends over.'

Neroli doesn't tell me what to do. It's harder work than that. I have to find my own solutions. Sometimes I'm lazy. 'Can you just tell me the answer?'

'You've got the answer. I think what's happened is that you've been out of touch with your personal power for some time. You were given a very strong message about not being okay. Your recent experience has got you away from your sense of self worth, but you are okay. More than okay. What we need to get you to do is to notice when you are strong or wise or resourceful. To get you to realise that you are okay and that you do have strengths. Many strengths.'

'It doesn't sound like me, the strong, whole person,' I tell her.

'You are whole and strong. Let's look at the most obvious evidence.'

'Um.'

'Kate! It took enormous courage and strength to make the report about Tony Benton. I'm honoured to have a client with the courage to do that.'

I look shocked. My evidence is that Neroli goes on to explain herself, then she says that her colleagues here would feel the same way. They'd applaud my action because they don't want people like Tony out there denigrating their profession. 'If my colleagues were in this room now they'd be cheering for you. Congratulating and supporting you. Remember that when you have doubts.'

'Wish I could bottle that and take it home. I feel weak most of the time. And I feel guilty about destroying Tony's career.'

'You're destroying it?'

'Yes. Well, might be.'

'You're destroying Tony's career?'

Is Neroli deaf? I've said it twi– . . . 'Oh, I see. I'm not, am I? He destroyed it himself!'

'He did. He chose to behave so disgustingly. He chose to end his career.'

I'm crying with relief. Neroli gently rubs my back and hands me a tissue.

I go home with so much homework. I have to keep asking myself what evidence I have and how I can change my thoughts and behaviour. Well, to start with I can make Tony responsible for his behaviour and only take responsibility for mine. And at work I can stop thinking it's my fault for not explaining things well enough to Clara, who's still very forgetful. Sometimes the recognition that I've done well at work empowers me. Sometimes there are challenges to chuckle about.

'Oh, go away bees. Don't start swarming again!' I say as we're outside playing at preschool.

'Bees are dumb shit, aren't they, Miss Shayler?' Michael says as we watch them.

'Why do you think bees are dumb?' I ask incredulously.

'They don't know nuffin', do they?'

We've just finished a unit of work on bees after they swarmed in our downpipe. We've seen honeycomb, tasted honey and cooked with it. We've watched films about bees and we've watched bees. We've played bees dancing to tell the others where the flowers are and scared off intruders to our pretend hive. We concluded that we can't make honey. Only clever, unique bees can.

'They can sting ya too, eh!' Michael adds.

Someone further down the track can help Michael understand bees. I've tried and now I'll let it go.

Uni is over for the year and I've done well. I have a free Saturday night and no-one has asked me out. Remembering my session with Neroli, I invite Thora over for dinner and a video. To my surprise she's free and keen to come. She rings back later to ask if she can bring one of her friends who's recently divorced. The numbers swell to five when I ring Robyn, a friend from Sydney who has moved here too and will bring a friend of hers. We decide on a Chinese takeaway. That's how a series of light, happy Saturday nights at home begins. Easy. I hardly notice daylight fading outside. Why didn't I think of this before? Where have I been?

Christmas cards begin to arrive and my letter box becomes a sometimes shudder-free friend. I reply to the cards but tell no-one about what's happening.

I go to the farm again for Christmas. This is family for me. Always here. Always welcoming. Always supportive. Will I tell them about the complaint? What if they do what Elliott did? But when I remember their reactions years ago, when I told them about my father's abuse, I know they'll understand. It's time to talk openly. I need to.

When I finish talking, Leonie and Col stay quiet for what feels like long enough for a glacier to carve out a valley. The Tony story seems worse than anything else I've told them. I wait.

Words of regret that I've been so badly dealt with come slowly and sincerely. It's as if I'm listening slowly and hearing exactly what I need to hear. I won't be rejected or humiliated. I'll be supported and nurtured, having learnt a very hard lesson.

'Were others abused?' Leonie asks.

'I think there must be. If he did it to me, he'd have surely done it to other people too.'

'Is anyone else reporting?'

'No. Not that I know of. It's just me.'

'Well, you are so brave. If you get frightened, just get in your car and come down. Anytime. We're here for you.'

'Could you move your here a bit closer?'

We laugh and I feel incredible relief that I'm not hiding from them any more. Trust fits here.

I go home and have a late Christmas with Gen and Paddy. While we wash up I tell Gen my latest news about the Unit. 'How did I get sucked in?' I groan.

'Oh he was so charming! Remember at your house warming! I knew he was up to something,' she says.

'Yeah. I should have listened to you, not him. I just got caught up in the flattery, I suppose. And manipulation.'

'Well, you expect to trust professionals, don't you? You be careful now. If you need to come and stay with us, you know you can. He doesn't know where we are, does he?'

'No. Oh no! He's got your address and number. I gave it to him as next of kin. Remember?'

'Oh, that's right. Well, what can he do! He wouldn't know you were here.'

Friends! Where would I be without them? Where would I be if I'd believed them when they said I was okay, before I met Tony?

It's been two months since I sent the stat dec back and Tony was to respond by the end of January. I'm impatient to hear what he wrote. I write to the Unit, pointing out that the case has dragged on for nine months. I don't remind them that a whole human being is made in that length of time and that surely they could have made just one letter in the same period.

Proud that I'm brave enough to confront the thing, it disappoints me that I'm still afraid too. I try to believe what people tell me, that I'm stronger than I realise. If it is true, then my strength is mine. It doesn't come from dependence on a psychologist playing God. Only God is God now. Neroli insists that I use my strength, my resources, not her, to analyse, decide and move on. Her constant asking of The Question of evidence begins to feel like a parent pushing a clinging child gently, reassuringly to independence.

She talks about my inner child. 'When you feel sad, ask the child what she needs.'

Inner child! No. No immaculate conception here!

But as I listen something starts to gel.

'The child you were is still there and if her needs were not met, the needs are still there too.'

Yes, I recognise her! She was there at the cemetery, forcing me to stay and find my mother.

420

I'll learn to acknowledge that persistent little girl who wants to be cared for, to be given attention, to know she matters and to be loved.

I write notes as we talk. 'Don't accept what the matrons said. Challenge it.' 'It's all right to make mistakes. Learn from them.' 'I am good. I am whole.' So much of what I write is what I teach the kids at school. How could I have not understood this before? Where have I been?

Neroli talks about the inner parent too. I'm out of my depth with parenting. No, I'm a good teacher. I know about care and nurture.

The pig parent who is negative, always criticising and presenting 'shoulds': You should do a degree. You should be thin. You should be nice to everyone. The nurturing parent who is constructive and kind and looks at 'need to' rather than 'should': You need to be healthy. You need to contact your friends when you need support.

I read over my notes at home and an inner dialogue begins as my mind makes connections. I want my mummy. It's okay to want her but what will I do with the wanting? What would Mummy do? Nurture. I am a strong adult too. I will be the inner child's mother. How? I don't know how to be a mother. Yes you do. Give yourself, your inner child, the same care and compassion you give to kids at school. When my inner child tells me she is worthless and no-one loves her, challenge her and tell her lots of people do. Most of all tell her you do yourself. Well, you're learning it anyway. She'll have to learn patience. *Needs* to learn patience.

It all makes sense like nothing else has. The contrast with Tony's treatment, especially after my visit to the grave, is astounding. Cry about it, then squash it down? Or cry about it, understand the child who was left alone, then nurture her and teach her that she is okay and that I can look after her now? Don't be afraid to look when the curtain blows. The child might be telling you what she needs, and you can manage it. Don't be afraid of her.

It's hard to shut the pig parent up and let the nurturing one get a word in sometimes. You're too stupid and childless and single to be any use to a child, the pig says. But I'm going to keep trying and keep challenging it. I am a strong, intelligent adult, and I have evidence of that.

RICH SOIL

'Hello, Kate. Had a good day?' Wendy, a neighbour, asks, smiling expectantly.

'Lovely, thanks. Been walking to The Rock.'

'Well, you should have stayed home!' She mocks a scolding.

'Why? What happened?'

'You had visitors.'

'Oh. Who?' Don't let it be Tony!

'Two women who said they're your relatives.'

'Oh. But I don't have any relatives. Not who'd visit. It wasn't my sister, was it? You know, you met her once. She wouldn't just turn up, though.'

'No. No, it wasn't her. It was a really little, old lady and a middle-aged woman with mousy hair. I didn't get their names. I thought you'd know who they were.'

'It doesn't sound like anyone I know.' Sometimes Genevieve says she's my sister but the description doesn't fit her.

'Oh well. They said they'd try again another day.'

'I'll just have to wait for their next appearance, won't I?' I'm curious about the visitors but I don't have time to contemplate further.

My knees turn to jelly when the Unit's logo is among the envelopes in the letter box a month after my letter to them.

Breathe. Can cope. Am strong.

The letter asks me to comment on the enclosed copy of Benton's response to my statutory declaration, and to *contact the unit as soon as possible in order to finalise the matter*.

Finalise! That energises me despite the churning in my stomach. My determination borders on mania as I sit down to read and respond. The letter is bulky but it includes case notes from my therapy sessions. Tony's actual response is very brief. Well, it would be, wouldn't it? He'd just have to agree that what I said is true. This won't take long. Finalise! Finalise!

What? He denies that he has done anything wrong. Good grief! Hasn't he read his Code of Conduct? At least he doesn't deny that it happened.

I read on. No. This is not the story I lived in! What's he doing? We realised we were attracted to each other, decided we'd have to stop therapy and seek advice from a supervisor. We waited for a reasonable period of time before we started the sincere, committed relationship which led to our often discussing cohabitation and which ended when Amanda intervened. Now Amanda and I are working together to destroy him, his property and his reputation.

Tears pouring out. Angry, hurting tears. How could he tell such outright lies on a stat dec? Anywhere? Fancy getting so upset by the first lie when there were so many more to come. Each one is a slap in the face. Another betrayal.

Got to ring someone. Ask if I'm going mad? Have I lived in two different stories and only remember one?

No, use your own resources and calm down. Be an adult and think about this rationally. Be angry and be adult.

Why has Tony told this story and not the real one? Supervision. Reasonable time period. Oh, I see. He's created a story to

fit the Code of Conduct! A series of lies to show that he's ethical.
I loathe him.

But will the Unit believe me in the light, no, in the darkness of
this fiction? I have told the truth. Honestly. I have. You've got to
believe me.

Don't leave me.

I cry, stare at nothing, feeling as if I've been dropped onto a
strange planet. The truth wins through on my home planet but
I've never tested it against this level of deceit. This isn't the world
I live in.

Talk to someone. Who haven't I burdened for a while? Too late
to ring anyway. Lucky friends!

Journal! Faithful friend who can't get sick of it all. Poor you.
I write for a long time and fall asleep.

When I delve into Tony's fiction again, I find copies of the
two letters I sent him. Oh yes, now I remember. The second one
too. I told him about a garden flat I'd heard about. I'm so embarrassed to have written either of them now. Embarrassed that
I was so needy and dependent. Grateful that Neroli isn't creating
dependence.

Could I have forgotten events Tony claims happened?

Well, I remember that first night as clearly as if it had happened five minutes ago. The first kiss and then his exact breathy
words close to my face: 'If we keep doing this I can't be your
psychologist any more.' Exact words.

Exact reply: 'But what about all the work I still have to do?'

Exact response: 'We can do all that as friends.'

Second kiss.

Is that a discussion? Did we lie on my lounge for the seven
weeks he claims we waited, repeating those three sentences over
and over? And did we discuss it with a third party as we lay there?
When did we ever discuss living together? Remember the
boarders, Tony? The second letter about the flat, Tony? And let's
be blunt about the ending. It ended because you found someone
else. Who didn't look like someone's mother.

Refuelled with anger and the word 'finalise', I march to my desk and begin typing, anxious to spell out the truth in detail and be believed. I deal with each lie systematically, feverishly scribbling notes. I don't need my journal yet. These events are in my head. My intelligent, clear thinking, strong, angry head.

Typing the truth. Again. Clearly. Thoroughly. Finished. Posted.

Finalise! It keeps me energised for a while. After Amanda and Vlad give their statements a peer review will be done, then the Psychologists Board will stop Tony. It's going to be over soon. One way or another. I'll be pretty devastated if I'm not believed. And Tony keeps doing what he does. But I can't think about failure now.

Brendan rings me to explain two critical points that I need to make clearer. How could he possibly want more? The first point is about the ending of the professional relationship before beginning the personal one.

'We need to know exact dates.'

'I've got dates written in my journal.'

Some of my dates don't match Tony's by a day or so. Well, I wasn't writing evidence, was I. Sometimes I wrote up a week in one night and had to work backwards for dates. What difference does a day or two make in the scheme of things?

'The other point we need to clarify is that Benton says this complaint is one of collusion.'

'What's collusion?'

'He claims you've lodged the complaint, to be vexatious, with certain other parties. He's suggesting you're doing this just to cause him grief, really. You want revenge.'

'We've been through all this, haven't we? I want him stopped. I made the complaint because I chose to. Amanda and Vlad have nothing to do with it. It's totally my own action. I don't even see them. Haven't since that June.'

'You're sure there's no collusion.'

'There's absolutely no collusion.'

426

'And you haven't had any contact with either Vladimir Ukanov or Mrs Benton since last June?'

'The June before last. None! Except when you asked for their addresses and phone numbers. That's all.'

'All right. Put it in a letter and we'll contact the other parties for their versions.'

Versions! I wish he'd express it differently and show some understanding of what I'm going through. Well, let's get through versions and onto my favourite part. Finalise.

Back to my journal and calendar to check dates. For hours I relive events and I only leave my desk to turn the light on.

Finally, I set out my reasons for making the complaint. I don't need Amanda's reasons. Or Vlad's. I have plenty of my own.

Thank goodness I have Neroli. I tell her about the lies and the picky questions about dates.

'Kate, I believe you,' she says.

I talk again and she repeats, 'Kate, I believe you. You don't need to present every bit of evidence to me. I believe you.'

'Oh, sorry. Don't know why I go on like that.'

'It is one of your patterns. What does the child need here?'

'To be believed.'

'I believe you.'

'Thank you.'

Our work together is often challenging as Neroli encourages me to open the curtain and look behind it. I'm still afraid.

'Remember it's old pain, Kate,' she says gently but firmly. 'It can't hurt you any more.'

I relive some of the matrons' cruelty but I reprocess it using the nurturing skills I have and my adult judgement. Now I undestand that I have interpreted criticism with my childhood perceptions. I feel the pain and fear of the child who was told she was filth by omnipotent adults. I need to challenge that and reconnect with my wholeness. I need to accept that powerful people make mistakes.

'You won't ever see yourself as a powerful person unless you understand that they can and do get things wrong sometimes. You can and do make mistakes and it is all right.'

That stands out like a beacon until the next light comes on.

'Being alone is not punishment for being bad.'

It's such a relief to make that connection, to understand that aloneness is not punishment, not proof of worthlessness. It's just a lack of company at that point in time. I can pick up the phone and have company if I choose to. Good, caring, nurturing company.

Next light. 'Will your friends leave you if you're a few pounds overweight? Will they think you are worthless? Do you have evidence of that? Apart from in your childhood.'

'What evidence do you have that people are driven away from you? What evidence do you have that people like you? All right then, why not assume that others like you when you meet them? What do you need to do about the assumption that you have to work to make them like you?'

Remembering tech and uni and church, I see that people liked me even when I didn't try to be impressive. I lost the sense of being likeable with Maud and Alma but now I can see that was about their agendas. Right, I'm reclaiming being likeable but with more confidence.

None of Neroli's questions are rhetorical. She demands that I do the reprocessing and answer accordingly. It's refreshing, exhausting and also empowering.

Come on, Tony. Just take me on!

While I wait for the Unit to contact me again, I concentrate on enjoying my life. I rejoin the bushwalking group and test the assumption that I don't have to make people like me. I relax and chat as we walk and soon we're laughing and I'm asking when the next walk is. They don't mind that I'm slow because my torn ankle ligament hurts. That injury is a reminder of past bushwalking fun. My long service leave is due soon and so I'll have the recommended operation.

Long Service Leave! What a fabulous idea. And I won't mind

coming back to work after it's over. Elliott and I are soon camping under the stars in the Red Centre, awestruck by the huge sky and the ethereal Uluru at dusk and dawn. We go on to the Kimberley, camping all the way, swimming in waterholes and photographing to our hearts' content. How could the land be this red, the sky so full of stars, the self so calm?

Elliott had been hoping we'd be a couple again but I had no idea. Or interest. I'm cured, I tell him. We remain friends and I come to appreciate his eye for textures, shapes, contrasts and composition in photography. He enjoys showing me the outback through his eyes and I feel incredibly lucky that he is my friend.

We love mighty waterfalls and nature's way of being quiet, which is often to fill the air with glorious or raucous bird calls. The sense that the land is ancient hangs in the air as we gaze at rock art that we happen upon. We feel connected to ancient people who decorated caves and rock shelves. Sometimes we feel a forboding presence that makes us quiet and reluctant to stay in some places.

I'd love to stay out here travelling but there's the mortgage and the Unit. And the operation.

I fit in a session with Neroli before I go to hospital. I'm glad there was time because when Elliott said goodbye I got that awful don't-leave-me feeling again. I want to work it out.

We talk about my mother's death but it doesn't seem to relate to that. I didn't see her leaving, so I couldn't shout at her to stop going.

'Tell me about your father leaving you at the home.'

'I hardly remember anything. Just that I was put in the dining room until I stopped crying.'

'When was that?'

'After he left us.'

'After he abandoned you.'

'He didn't abandon . . .' Tectonic plates shift my comprehension.

'It's about what you felt as a child, not what your father did or intended.'

The curtain is drifting.

'He abandoned me!' my small voice says. 'He walked away and he wouldn't come back. I was lost and so alone. I felt like a nothing.' I'm crying. Walking around in a dark place on the other side of the window.

Don't leave me, Daddy. Please, please don't leave me.

And the more I cried, the further away he went.

Neroli waits while I sob. 'It's old pain, Kate,' she says quietly. 'It can't hurt you any more. You don't need to be afraid.'

Wipe my eyes. Blow my nose. Sigh deeply.

I don't need to be afraid of goodbyes. I am learning to care for myself. How can I describe the relief? With tears, of course.

'What does the child need when you feel abandoned?'

'To belong. To be cared for. To be loved and protected.'

'How can that happen?'

'I will care for myself. And I'll be okay when people go home.'

At home I put stickers around the house to remind myself to nurture the child within and remind her that she matters and will be cared for. One on the mirror. One on the wardrobe. One on the kitchen window. They remind me to notice my self talk and protect the child from the pig parent. They remind me to connect with my whole adult self.

I have my ankle reconstruction and Wendy brings me home. 'Pick you up for shopping on Thursday,' she says as she leaves.

As she parks at the supermarket I tell her not to worry about staying with me. I'll be all right.

'No, I'll stay,' she says cheerfully.

I can push the trolley along with my body while I hobble along with crutches. Biscuits from a low shelf. Easy. Baking powd– whoops! Dropped the crutch. Clever Kate is now learning that shopping is impossible when you need both hands to hold your crutches. 'Um, thanks, Wendy. You knew about this, didn't you?'

'I've got sons, remember!' she grins.

At home I have a series of stopping places for my making-coffee-and-getting-it-to-the-lounge ritual. Kitchen bench, step, dinner table, step, ironing board, step, other end of ironing board, step, coffee table. Sit. It's the same with the meals Robyn drops in. My inner child and my adult are so grateful for friends.

I sit with my plastered leg up as the doctor advised and wonder if I should ring the Unit and find out what's going on with the investigation.

'It's Kate Shayler calling. I'd like to speak to Brendan, please.'

'Who?'

'Brendan. He's handling my complaint. Brendan Green.'

'Oh, Brendan. He doesn't work here any more.'

Don't leave me. Don't go and leave me with this.

It's all right. You can manage.

No offer is made to put me through to anyone else. Have they decided not to take my complaint further, and not bothered to tell me? Someone has to take it! And finish it. And stop Tony.

'Who's handling it now?'

'Let me see. What name is it again? Shayler. Yes.' She rustles some papers then tells me that no-one is handling my complaint. She offers nothing more.

'Do you mean it's just sitting there?' I ask hysterically.

'Someone will be assigned and when they are they will contact you,' she says as if it's none of my business.

'Can I speak to anyone at all about it? Today?'

'Well, Brendan would have known about it but no-one else would. Not yet. They will contact you later.'

'When?'

'I can't say.'

Pull yourself together, Kate Shayler. It will go on but with a different lawyer, that's all.

Meanwhile, I'll sit here with my leg up getting bored. I ring after a week and try again.

'Mr Johnson is our senior legal officer. He's out for the rest of the day.'

'Would you ask him to call me, please?'

'All right but he'll be out for the next two days.'

She takes my details and we hang up.

My ankle is throbbing and my leg is swollen inside the plaster. The doctor advises me to go to the surgeon urgently because there might be a serious problem. Thora drives me to the surgeon's rooms and he sees me straight away.

'Come in, Katherine,' he says. 'You're having a problem with the cast? Get up on the bench, please.'

'Um. How?'

'Oh! Sorry. I'll lift you,' he smiles kindly. He's very small. I don't know how I got here by myself but I'm sitting on the bench.

Even the most delicate touch of his small, cool hand is agony. Soon he's sawing the cast. He looks strained as the saw buzzes through. I nearly faint when my leg is released.

'Oh dear, oh dear. I think we have a thrombosis. We'll get you scanned straight away and get you to the hospital. Go into the Centre next door and they'll see you as soon as they can.'

I hobble next door with Thora, holding back tears and panic. I'm taken in ahead of the people already waiting. I'm getting frightened. Everyone is being kind and acting urgently. The scan shows a deep vein thrombosis.

'You don't have time to go home for your toothbrush or nighties. This is life threatening,' the doctor says. 'You must go straight to hospital.'

Thora drives me there. Alone in the hospital bed I sob. I can't die now! I wanted to not long ago but not now! Not when life is getting better and I'm strong and I know who I am. Not now, God. Not now.

The clot is dissolved with medication and I'm eventually sent home with instructions to have regular blood tests.

I'm not going to die. I thank God for Thora who was so loyal and helpful when I needed her. And Wendy and Robyn. Well, now I just have to stay well. I'm not going to worry about the Unit. It can wait until I'm absolutely fighting fit again. Unless someone gets assigned to it and contacts me.

A new social group is starting in the neighbourhood tonight. I decide to give it a try. A broader social network might be nice. Saturday nights when Thora and the others are busy with their families are still a bit lonely. This group couldn't be any worse than the other one I went to, where the men lined the walls and leered.

I can't fit a shoe on yet but a sock will do. We're meeting in a restaurant, so no-one will notice.

Alas we stand around with drinks first. My foot starts throbbing. I feel very protective of my toes and back off if enthusiastic people come too close. I show my sock so they'll understand. It's a good conversation piece and we laugh at my foot fashion sense. People are animated and we chat about what we want from the group and laugh at our experiences with other ones. Most of us just want a nice group of people to go out with.

At last we sit down and announcements begin. Malcolm tells us he and his friend Frank want the group to be social not a matchmaking concern, though of course if that happens, no-one will complain. They hope we'll get together on Saturday nights and go to movies, dances, dinners, whatever we like. Malcolm is modest but articulate and very funny.

'So, in the best of traditions, let's form a committee!' he says, twitching his eyes comically then squinting at possible volunteers.

We sit at a large table and we swap places between courses so that everyone meets everyone. I have a wonderful night and it's not until I get home that I realise I was relaxed and didn't have to earn anyone's approval.

A happy round of regular socialising begins and, if it weren't for the complaint in the Unit always looming, I'd be content.

It's probably time I rang the Unit.

'Mr Johnson is handling your matter.'

'Can I speak to him, please?'

'I'm sorry. He's out but I'm sure he'll ring you when he's been over the file.'

'When is that likely to be?'

'I can't say.'

Weeks later, Mr Johnson rings. He's sorry for the delay. He sounds sincere and is clearly committed to stopping misconduct. I'm surprised that he has more questions, though. He wants me to clarify my story in respect of the seven-week plan that Tony alleges he and I made prior to the social relationship, and Tony's claim that we had planned to live together.

Back to reliving and rewriting but with more detachment. There could not possibly be more questions, unless Mr Johnson needs to know my shoe size.

Back to forgetting about it. During the next inevitably long wait I get on with enjoying myself.

Later I have an incredible dream that seems to mean something. I tell Neroli about it.

I'm walking down a path where some road construction is happening. I look into a hole where an earth mover is digging rich dark soil. In the hole is my naked body, lots of them. They are being churned slowly about in the soil but the machine isn't damaging them. I feel puzzled, a bit anxious, so I go to a coffee shop where my friends are meeting me. The owner says I can stay for as long as I need to. My friends gradually go and I'm left there as the owner shuts the shop. 'Sorry, but you'll have to go now,' he says. 'We have to close.' I leave but I don't want to go back to the hole where my bodies are. The driver of the machine looks at me blankly but I take it as a warning not to come near. I go back to the cafe, and the door is open. I go inside and sleep, knowing I'll go back to that soil some day.

'The earth is black and rich? And the bodies are naked but they're not being damaged?'

'Yes. They're all me but how can that be? And they're sleeping or something. Not dead, though.'

Neroli thinks it means I need to stop delving for a while and spend time doing things I like, taking with me the discoveries I've made, to build on. This interpretation feels perfect. It makes sense. Neroli and I say goodbye and we know I'll come back later to do more work if I need to.

School begins, the kids settle in and I'm happy enough to be here for another year. But soon I'm visited by a teacher who wants my job because it's closer to her new home. I want her job when she tells me it's closer to mine. Would we be lucky enough to get a swap?

While I wait to hear if my work transfer will be approved, a Mr Fielder rings from the Unit.

'There's been a delay in the processing of your complaint,' he announces.

'There've been a few!'

He ignores that and goes on. 'Benton is arguing that because the events you've complained about took place prior to his registration under the Psychologists Act, his behaviour can't be judged under that Act.'

'I don't believe it! Can he? I don't believe . . . I put the complaint in nearly two years ago and now this. It could all come to nothing?'

'It's only just been raised. We think the matter can be heard but we're getting advice from the Solicitor General.'

'How long will that take? What if the Solicitor General agrees with Tony Benton?'

'We're waiting on advice. If he finds in Benton's favour, then we can't proceed. We'll have to wait and see.'

'What does that mean, can't proceed? Can't do anything? He'll get away with it? Keep doing it?'

'If it comes to that. But you could try legal action.'

'I'm trying legal action, aren't I?'

'Through the criminal code rather than the Professional Standards Committee. I can't advise you on that, though. You'd need to see a solicitor.'

A solicitor. That would mean police, court! Me? That's not

who I am. I don't belong with the police and crimes, do I? And I can't start all over again. I can barely manage this.

'Try not to worry,' Mr Fielder says. 'We haven't given up. Our argument is that professional standards were the same prior to the Act. The Act just got them formalised.'

I'm certainly learning a lot and on one level it's fascinating but what I really want is for this complaint to be over with and for Tony to be stopped. If the law can't protect people from health workers who are predators, then the law really is an ass. I'm going to – I need to – pretend the complaint doesn't exist again. When friends ask how it's going I tell them I don't know. The Solicitor General has taken it for a nice holiday of indeterminate length.

Meanwhile, there's a little group of us in the social club who love board games, especially Pictionary. We meet weekly for dinner and a game or six. We laugh ourselves silly for hours on end.

My first word tonight is 'philosophy'.

'How do I draw that?'

The opposition laughs wildly as I draw a head with the brain showing through.

'Lobotomy!'

I draw a thought bubble.

'Hat. Lobotomy hat!'

Not working. Try a different tack. I draw a glass half full.

'Times up!'

Maybe the glass was half empty. I never want these nights of laughter to end.

At school Peter calls me into his office to tell me that I'm being transferred to the position I want. He wishes me well and says that, despite our differences, he can see that there have been improvements since I came to the preschool. Now he tells me! Three years late.

My new principal, Vivian, is passionately committed to improving the long-term prospects for the kids in this very depressed area. She's new here too and is going to make her mark. The preschool is a huge concern because it's been neglected and is in a state of chaos. Sounds familiar!

'I wouldn't send a child of mine there!' she tells me. 'I want it cleared out, cleaned and organised. I want any book that shows gender stereotyping thrown out and any equipment that doesn't work . . .'

I see what she means but she can't imagine that I'm even more keen than she is to get some order here. For months I use my old routine of working until dark, cleaning, sorting and filling garbage bags after the kids go home. They miss their old teacher but we soon become friends. It's great to be able to do what needs doing, with Kirsty my assistant. Kirsty, a breath of fresh air! She's intelligent, creative and has a wonderful sense of humour. We all laugh our way through days and I feel like my old self. Days of laughing and working hard with someone who knows what she's doing! How did I get this lucky? Kirsty's musical talent is not the least of her assets and I love her willingness and enthusiasm for using that talent when I have none, musically speaking.

A few of the parents make comparisons with the previous teacher and some criticisms are voiced to Vivian.

'Look, you're doing a great job and I told them that but try and see it from a parent's point of view . . .'

That is who my new boss is. Fair and forthright. When she's too busy, she can be more forthright than fair but it isn't personal. She has the kids' best interests at heart. I admire that.

Thora and I go for a walk.

'How's your friend who was abused by A? The one who had the breakdown.'

'She's still not well. I ring her sometimes but I don't see her. Nobody does.'

Silly to ask that question. How can I maintain my distance from the Unit now? I ring and ask what's happening.

437

'We're still waiting on the Solicitor General's advice.'

'Why is it taking so long? Why don't I get kept up to date with what's happening?'

'We can't move until we have advice.'

'Well, it's pretty poor that I've heard nothing, not even a simple update for months. Lodging a complaint is hard enough but to have it drag on for this long, well, it's unfair.'

'I can pass your comments on to the director, if you wish.'

'Would you put me through, please. I'll tell her myself.'

'She's in a meeting. And after the meeting she has an appointment on the other side of the city.'

'So, I can't talk to her at all?'

'No. But I can pass your comments on to her.'

I hang up and cry. Just when I thought I was managing, I'm disempowered. I'm just a bit of paper to be shoved around or filed away and forgotten.

Talk to the child. What does she need? To be remembered and to have her feelings considered. The Unit says it doesn't offer support, just respectful treatment and efficient handling of complaints. Who can meet the child's needs? Me. Where's the peanut butter?

How do other people manage? There must be others. How can I find them?

Soon after, a letter from the Unit advises me that they're still waiting on advice from the Solicitor General but that they will keep me informed.

All right. It's back to denying the complaint exists then.

It's my turn to tell my life story to the social justice group I'm in. We're a group of Christian friends, teachers, welfare workers, doctors and artists, who meet regularly to support each other in our various actions for social justice. Lots of people are home churchers but there are traditionalists as well. Over the years we've been telling our life stories so that we'll get to know each other better and understand where our various commitments to social justice came from.

How much of my story should I tell? I've written a bit of it down but I've never told it straight through before. How long will it take? I don't prepare. I just go along and start talking when the time comes. I tell them that my mother died, I grew up in a children's home and that my father abused me. I rush through because, although we're all aware of child abuse, I don't want them to probe and make me lose my nerve. Sometimes people interrupt and ask what the home was like, how my mother died and so on.

'I think I might be taking too long,' I say after I answer a question about starting work at the insurance office.

'No! It's so interesting. Tell us what it was like when . . .'

I feel self-conscious but these people are respectful and supportive. I enjoy telling them about Rosa, who started my support for World Vision and who first made me look at poverty.

When I finish my story, one of the men says, 'Do you know about Friends of Susannah?'

'No. Who's Susannah? Is she a local person?'

'No, she's a woman in the Bible who was raped by priests. They told her that if she reported them they'd say she seduced them.'

'Oh! Well, wouldn't all her friends be dead?' I say joking to relieve my tension.

'Funny! No, there's a group called Friends of Susannah who are advocates for survivors of abuse by priests. A friend of ours is involved. She was abused by a counsellor, not a priest, but the point is, she went through what you're going through and got him deregistered. I thought y– '

'Who is she?' I interrupt. 'Can I meet her? Talk to her? Would she talk to me?'

'I could give her your number and ask her to ring you if she's willing. I imagine it'd be good to have a supporter who's been there.'

Rita rings within a few days and we talk and talk and talk. It's so good to meet someone who knows what I'm going through and who has seen an outcome that vindicates her action. She talks in terms of boundaries, violations, grooming and predatory behaviour. It all rings true, though some of the language is new to me. Rita has a lot to say and she becomes an ally who invites me to ring whenever I want to talk.

'You don't get support from the people at the Unit, do you?' I comment.

'No. They just do their work and stay objective.'

'I wish they'd show a bit of sympathy or compassion or something.'

'No. You have to get that out here. There's someone I know who has a matter going through right now. Yeah, a psychologist. Do you want me to ask her to ring you?'

'I'll just talk with you for now, if that's all right. I had no idea there was so much of this going on. I thought I was the only one but now I'm hearing about more and more. Can you believe it!'

'Not 'til I'd been there. I didn't know anyone until my case and then some other women reported the perpetrator too. Are there any other complainants in your matter?'

'None that have gone to the Unit but there must be others.'

'Oh. I didn't have to go through it alone like you are. Tell you what, though, when he was deregistered I felt like I'd died and gone to Heaven.'

'I can't wait. If it gets that far.'

In September the Unit writes to say they are still awaiting advice from the Solicitor General. I imagine I'll have to wait until at least the end of this year before the thing will be over, so I'll try slipping back into denial and keep enjoying school and the social group.

Time to enjoy Christmas cards from people who are organised enough to get them done early in December.

I recognise Aunty Marj's beautiful handwriting instantly.

Freda and Karen said they went to see you a while ago but you weren't home. They were so disappointed. Will you give them a call? I know they'd love to see you.

Freda and Karen? They must be the women Wendy told me about. I ring Aunty Marj and she talks as if I know them. I'm too embarrassed to say I haven't a clue who they are. I put their number beside the phone but I'd feel too stupid ringing strangers and asking them who they are. I'll do it in the holidays.

Among Christmas cards there's a letter from the Unit advising that advice has been received. At last! No, wait. Further advice has been sought. It should come in the near future. Denial again.

Time for a holiday at the farm, where I tell Leonie and Col that nothing has really happened all year as far as the case is concerned but school is great and so is the social group and the work I've been doing with Neroli.

'And, how's your writing coming along?'

'Haven't had much time with uni and school and all but I've done a bit. I just don't know who'd want to read it.'

'We would! But other people would too. You must do it when you finish uni. When will that be?'

'A year to go!'

When I get home I ring Freda and Karen. What have I got to lose? They must be relatives, but I haven't had them for most of my life, so if it doesn't work out, it won't matter. On the other hand, it would be interesting if they could tell me about my mother and when we were small. They could be the family of Charlie, my mother's brother, but he hasn't been mentioned. If it is him, he'll be able to tell me about their childhood and their parents and whatever else there is to tell.

'Hello. My name is Kate Shayler and I g– '

'Oh, Kate. Is it really you?' an old woman asks excitedly. 'This is Freda. Your Aunty Freda. Karen, Karen come here,' she shouts. 'It's Kate Shayler. She rang us! Sorry, dear. I'm just calling Karen. Oh, it's so good that you've called. Oh, we've been waiting for this. Karen! Come on. It's so good that you've called.' She talks and talks and enthuses and I hardly have to say a word. Aunty Dot has been telling them about me every Christmas, after she and I exchange cards and news. Aunty Freda's so proud of me for going to university and becoming a teacher. Proud of me? But she hasn't been in my life, so why be proud of me? It feels nice to have someone say it, anyway. 'I'll put Karen on now and you can talk to her.' She's gone. I've done the mental calculation and worked out that this must be my uncle's wife and Karen is their daughter, my cousin.

'Hello. This is Karen Lyford speaking. Is it you, Kate?' a younger, hesitant voice asks with a formality that was totally absent in Aunty Freda. She said Lyford, so they must be Uncle Charlie's family.

'Yes. This is Kate.'

'Oh. We hoped you'd get in touch. We called in to see you some time ago but you were out. We met your neighbour.'

This is so stilted. No spontaneous energy. It's hard to drag words out. My cousin answers in monosyllables and reminds me of myself as a teenager.

'My neighbour is lovely, isn't she?'

'Yes.'

'Did you see my house?'

'Yes.'

'Nice, isn't it?'

'Yes.'

'Tell her to come for lunch!' Aunty Freda shouts in the background.

'Yes. All right, Mum. Did you hear that, Kate? Mum would like me to invite you for lunch, um, if it wouldn't be too much trouble.'

'Yep, I heard her. My neighbours probably did as well, so they'll come too!'

'Really?' Karen sounds alarmed.

'Oh no. I was joking. I just meant Freda's got a voice like a foghorn!'

Karen roars laughing and the ice is broken. She tells her mother what I said and I hear Freda laughing too.

'Would you like to come? Without your neighbours?' Karen asks. 'I know it's a long way but we'd like to meet you.'

'I'd love to come,' I reply. 'When's a good time?'

We plan for the following Sunday. There was no mention of Uncle Charlie but it must be his family. Who else could it be? I'll probably meet him at lunch.

My cousin and aunt live at Castle Hill. Aunty Freda asked me to come at midday, so I leave in plenty of time to get lost and find my way again. That's what I thought but my street map doesn't show some new roads and I get hopelessly lost and arrive half an hour late, having stopped to ring and tell them I was lost.

A tiny, old lady with white hair and glasses at the end of her nose, opens the door before I ring the bell. She be great in a kid's story book.

'Oh, sit down,' she says irritably.

'Who me? Can I come in first?'

'I'm talking to the dog,' she laughs. 'Kate, isn't it? Oh, you're so like Norma! Come in. Come in. Don't mind Cindy. Cindy! Sit. Oh, all right then, go through and sit down like you're told.' Freda bubbles at the dog as I come in.

'Karen! Oh, where is she? Karen!' Freda calls into the house. 'Your cousin's here.'

'She's here!'

Karen and I meet in the hall with Cindy between us wagging her tail and barking. 'How do you do, Kate? It's very nice to meet you,' she says nervously. She doesn't look like her mother or any of us three K's, not that I've seen either Ken or Kerry in ages.

'Sit down,' Aunty Freda commands happily. 'Yes, you, Kate Shayler. I couldn't help the roast drying out a bit but we'll eat it anyway, won't we?' she laughs.

'Oh, sorry I was late. I'll have to get you to show me which way I should have come later. Whose place is where?' I ask.

'Mum usually sits there and I sit here,' Karen says while her mum gets plates from the oven. Three places and no mention of an Uncle Charlie. Have I got it all wrong?

Apparently twelve o'clock lunch means the food goes on the plate at twelve o'clock on the dot. 'It's a bit dry but that's all right,' Freda says again.

'Mum was so excited about you coming.'

'What's that, dear?' Aunty Freda asks.

'Oh, Mum, turn your hearing aid on!' Karen yells and taps her ears. Then she whispers, 'She can hardly hear a thing. She's nearly eighty.'

'Gosh, you've got lots of energy for an eighty-year-old,' I shout.

'She still mows the lawn. Has done since Dad passed away,' says Karen.

'Passed away?'

'Yes, didn't you know? What was it, eight or so years ago?' Then she adds in a loud voice, 'I'm just telling Kate that old Charlie died, when was it?'

Freda tells me the exact date and then, 'It's such a pity you didn't meet him. Well, you did, of course, when you were a baby!'

'We've met before?'

'Yes, don't you remember? No, I don't suppose you would. You were very small. Your mum brought you over sometimes.'

'Oh so you and my mum were friends then.'

'No. Oh sisters-in-law, you know,' she says as if she's getting a bit muddled. She changes the subject. 'But you do remember us visiting you at the home, don't you?'

'No.'

'Oh yes, we came up to see you once or twice. Charlie didn't want us to. Said it would upset you.'

'Charlie?'

'Yes. Your dad.' Freda puts our meals down and sits down too. 'Well, there it is. Your favourite. Roast lamb.'

'Mm. Thank you. So Dad told you not to visit us, did he?'

'Oh, not in as many words, but after your mum died, well, we'd had some troubles. I wanted to take you, you know.'

I've lived in this scene before. Aunty Dot had said the same thing years ago when I visited her as a frightened teenager. Now I listen calmly, interested, as Freda tells me that she had been pregnant when my mother was pregnant with Ken but that her baby had died. Then she became pregnant again with Karen but had nearly died in childbirth and was ill for a long time after. Karen was born two months before me.

'So you see, I couldn't take on three little kids as well as Karen. You can understand that, can't you?' she asks, almost pleads.

'Course I can,' I reply, embarrassed that she's so concerned that I'll understand what she did forty-odd years ago.

'I just want you to understand that we loved all three of you but we just couldn't manage three extras, and Charlie, your father Charlie, didn't want you split up.'

'Aunty Dot told me that when I was a teenager, when I visited her, that Dad didn't want us split up.' I need to clear up who the Charlies are. 'I'm confused about the Charlies. Was your husband our uncle? I mean, was he my mother's brother, Charlie?'

They both look incredulous.

'Yes!' they reply together, as if I've just asked if the earth is a sphere.

They don't understand that the family they've been part of and taken for granted is new to me. Just as well they can't see the mental notes I'm writing. Charlie, mother's brother. Freda, Charlie's wife. Karen cousin, two months older.

'It's such a pity you never met your Uncle Charlie, as an adult.'

'I nearly did,' I tell them. 'When I lived at Meadowbank and you lived at West Ryde?'

'You lived at Meadowbank! Oh, you should have come to see us!'

'I did. But I saw an old man out the front in the garden and got cold feet. I didn't know if you'd want me to just drop in. I thought I might be too much of a shock. Aunty Dot always said I look like my mum. He might have thought I was a ghost or something.'

'Oh, you should have come in! That would have been Charlie you saw. He would have loved to have met you.'

'I thought it was him. He was a bit bent, not very tall, snowy white hair.'

'That's him. Oh, you should have come in.'

How can I explain that I didn't know if they would want me in their lives? They hadn't contacted me, and Aunty Dot always knew where I was. How can I tell them that a person suddenly dying of a heart attack is as much a part of my instinctive world view as sliced bread or knots in shoelaces?

We eat our first course among slightly uncomfortable silences and as soon as the last mouthful is swallowed, Freda whisks our plates away and brings dessert.

'It's only apple pie,' she announces.

'Oh, is that all!' I say, risking a joke.

'Ha! That's just what the old man used to say, isn't it, Mum?' Karen laughs. 'You've got exactly the same sense of humour as Dad had. Hasn't she, Mum? I say, Kate has the same sense of humour as Dad!'

'Might be because we're related,' I say.

'Yes, he would have said that too!'

I want these two to keep on talking, to tell me every minute thing they know about our family, especially the part my mother and us kids were in.

'There's not a lot to tell, really,' Freda says. 'We were just ordinary people.'

Tell me the ordinary, the banal, the trivial, the irrelevant. Everything. The more they don't understand how much I want to know, the more I want to know. I've developed an enormous thirst for it. I want to open their memory curtains and wander around inside their heads, uninhibited by their judgement of what's important or interesting. Freda and Karen would rather talk about the present and about me.

A rough outline will have to do. Their questions keep coming and I keep fobbing them off to get back to the real questions.

Freda dots the conversation with expressions of hope that my life has been happy. She's very keen to have me understand that she tried to do what she could when my mother died. All right. I understand that but tell me every single thing you remember about my mother.

They don't think it's odd that I haven't married, and I find that refreshing. Karen hasn't married either. Here's a chance to get away from my story and back to the family one.

'How did you meet Uncle Charlie?' I ask Freda.

Her eyes light with a mischievous sparkle. She's going to enjoy telling this.

'Well, I wasn't so young by then! But nor was Charlie,' she laughs. 'I'd been looking after my mum and when she died I got a job in a nursing home. I was good with old people, you see. Anyway, I had to get the train to work and every morning I'd see this serious-looking man, very nicely dressed he was, waiting for the train. Very handsome, I thought, and he didn't wear a ring. I used to say good morning to him and he always said good morning back. Nothing else. He seemed shy. So I thought, oh well, in for a penny, in for a pound. One morning I asked him what time it was and he didn't seem to mind telling me.'

'Hard work flirting with him!' I say.

'Hard work, all right. His watch was beautiful, so I decided he wasn't poor. Anyway, a cousin or someone, I forget who, was having an engagement party, so I decided to ask him to accompany me. You could have knocked me down with a feather when he said he would! And that's how it all started.'

'Maybe we should get the train to work instead of driving,' I say, and Karen and I laugh.

Freda says that Charlie had just lost his mother too and was a bit lost.

'His mother. That would be our grandmother Mary. I saw her name on my mother's death certificate. My middle name is Mary. It must be after her.'

'Oh, mine is too,' says Karen.

'You didn't meet her, though, did you?' I ask Karen. I realise it's a stupid question as soon as I've asked it. I just didn't do the mental maths quickly enough.

'No. Dad used to talk about her, though. She was born out at Tarana on a farm where they grew potatoes and raised cattle. Then when she married Fred they built the house at West Ryde. Yes, that one that you saw. Dad and your mum were born there.'

'Let's sit in the lounge and Karen can play for us,' Freda suggests.

It'll be nice to have a chance to sit and let it all gel. The lounge room is taken up mostly by a baby grand piano. Freda and I sit on chairs and Karen sits at the piano.

'What would you like to hear?' she asks shyly.

'Oh, um. I don't know much about music. What do you play?'

'Classical mostly.'

'She's done her certificates. We had her taught when she was little. Piano and ballet for a while. Play something soothing, Karen.'

Karen plays and I listen. It seems stiff, not soothing.

'Sorry, I'm so out of practice. I don't do it as much as I should. I'm knackered when I get home from work. I'd rather paint.'

I try not to feel jealous that my cousin has learnt music and painting and ballet and bonsai and goodness knows what other lovely things. She doesn't boast, though, and still seems nervous and shy.

'Well, thanks for a lovely afternoon. I've really enjoyed meeting you both but I'd better be going. Who knows how long I'll take to get home. Could be years!'

'Oh, I don't want you to go,' Aunty Freda says, squeezing my hand. 'You make sure you come back and see us, won't you? We've got a lot of time to make up for.'

'Yes, you must come again,' Karen agrees.

'I'd love to. If I ever find my way home again. Which way would you go?'

'Oh, we don't go out much.'

Wish I hadn't parked in the driveway. Would backing over

their letter box detract from other family reunions? 'I'm not much good at reversing,' I say.

'It's in our genes,' Karen replies.

Driving home is like driving out of one life into another. It's been so good to have forgotten my complaint so completely for a while. Wish I'd got some specific questions ready, though. Ones that would have got them talking about what I wanted to hear. Still, I don't think Aunty Freda needs much encouragement. When the subject isn't my mother.

Looking at the photo of my mother doesn't connect me to Tony like it used to.

'Hello, Mum. Do you have secrets that Aunty Freda might tell me?'

I don't have time to visit my aunt and cousin again before school goes back.

It's been years since I've been this pleased to get back to work. I'll completely ignore the Unit until they contact me. I'll have a great time at work and when uni starts I'll go with more energy and enthusiasm than I've had before.

Aunty Freda rings to ask me to come for lunch again during term. I arrive at Castle Hill a little late from having got lost again, and I have some questions ready. Most are about my mother.

'What was my mother's personality like?'

There's some hesitation and then Freda replies, 'Well, she was very strong willed, knew her own mind. We didn't see a lot of each other because she lived over with your father.'

'How did you two get on?' I ask my aunty.

'Oh we had our moments. But we had you kids so we made an effort.' That is all she wants to say apart from, 'She had her sense of humour, like Charlie and you, but, oh, I don't know, just different personalities, I suppose.'

'It's all gone and forgotten,' Karen says.

I wait, hoping for more, 'She loved you kids so much. She knitted all your clothes and sewed too. We couldn't believe it when she died. Just couldn't believe it.'

Aunty Freda doesn't weep as Aunty Dot had all those years ago but I like the way her words affirm the emotions I've uncovered recently.

Karen brings some photos in that she has taken out of an album in another room. I hope she'll have some of my mother but she hasn't. She shows me her father and I'm surprised that there is absolutely nothing about him that resembles anyone I know.

The next photo jolts me back to my father's house when Ken and I had cleared out some old photos. We threw them in the garbage because we didn't know who the people were. I particularly hated one of a severe old lady who looked like she would have gone well as a matron at Burnside. Here she is again in Karen's album.

'Who's that?'

'Aunty Mary,' Karen replies. 'Dad's mum. Our grandmother.'

'You call her Aunty Mary?'

'Yes. Dad did too but I don't know why,' Karen replies.

'She looks witchy,' I say. 'Did you know her?' I ask Aunty Freda.

'No. She died, when was it? Your memory goes when you're nearly eighty. It was before I met Charlie, anyway. He said she was a lovely lady. Funny too! Show Kate the photo. Not that awful thing. The other one.'

The other one is of a buxom matron beaming a huge smile. She's wearing a large hat and a coat with a gold horseshoe brooch on it.

'I've got that brooch at home!' I exclaim. 'I took it when my father died because I liked it! I thought it might have been my mother's.'

'Well, I'm glad you got something of your grandmother's, dear.'

We look through photos of Karen as a baby at the house at West Ryde. There is a close-up of her sitting on a man's lap. The man's face is concealed by his hat. I know that hat! The world turns upside down. That huge leathery hand that supports my little cousin as she sits on his knee! I want to scream. Did he hurt Karen too? Make her cry? Make her frightened of men? Is that why she's like me? Single. I keep the screaming and the questions inside as the stream of photos are thrust quickly in and out of view. Karen is self-conscious and doesn't like all the attention focused on her.

'Show Kate your paintings,' Freda suggests.

'She doesn't want to see them, Mum!'

'Yes you do, don't you, Kate?'

We go to the sunroom and Karen shows me one she did of her parents and one of Cindy, who obviously thinks she's a person too. I have a cousin who paints very nicely. I hope that's in our genes.

Freda is so proud of Karen. I feel jealous of their relationship. Now Freda is sitting beside me. Every now and then she smiles and pats my hand while Karen plays Bach.

At last we say goodbye and it's a while before I find time to visit again. School and uni keep me busy.

The preschool parents are running fundraising street stalls and helping with our programs – I'm not doing anything differently but Kirsty and I have won them over. With Kirsty's musical talent and the happy ambience we have now, we decide to start a weekly singalong with parents so that they'll learn the songs we teach their kids. The parents are slow to come, then too self-conscious to sing. My voice helps them realise they don't need to be good singers to enjoy it, and after a month or so we spend the beginning of Friday classes singing our hearts out.

And at uni, I feel so different this year. I'm freer and more able to think and argue clearly. I'm going to work on a research project within my school where we're trying to adjust the gender bias so that girls get better educational outcomes. My project will be a study of gender construction within the school families, and it will mean surveying and interviewing parents as well as closely observing the behaviour of kids while they play in the preschool.

Most parents cooperate and enjoy doing the survey, though some say they're glad it's anonymous. I bundle up the paperwork and file it for analysis later.

By June I'm wondering about the Unit again, so I ring to ask what's happening. Mr Johnson is out. What a surprise! He will call me back when he can. He hasn't called when second semester at uni starts and I decide to put it aside again. This semester is a big one, in which I have to collate my research, write it up and submit my report. There's masses of reading to be done and I'm relieved that I don't have to deal with anything extra. After school I come home to work on my research. I'm racing towards the finish line as the semester draws to an end.

Today I'm thrown off balance by a letter from the Unit. Great timing.

The letter starts with an apology for the lack of contact and a comment that Mr Johnson has been trying to phone me for some time. Then the news I want to hear. The Solicitor General has advised that the complaint can indeed proceed under the Psychologists Act. Counsel, Ms Parker, has been briefed, will advise on the evidence and prepare a draft of the formal complaint for the Psychologists Board. Mr Johnson will contact me soon to arrange a meeting with Ms Parker.

It's three and a half years since I lodged my complaint and Tony has been practising for all that time. Well, it will be over soon. Finalised.

What if Tony wins? Suddenly I'm re-connected to all the doubts I've put aside. I feel smaller than I've felt for a year. Battered by doubts.

Why now? A year of nothing, then when the pressure is on at uni, this! I can't cope. I'm cracking up.

Talk to the child. Challenge the pig parent. What evidence do I have for not being able to cope?

I can cope. I will. I have coped this far in my life and I am strong. I need to put the complaint aside until Mr Johnson rings.

Back to my research. Eventually I finish my project and post two copies in for assessment by two academics. Finished!

School ends with a Christmas party and I feel my eyes burning as we say goodbye to the kids and parents. That hasn't happened for years!

Christmas card time again. Aunty Marj's card is early as usual but this year tells me that Karen has been having a terrible time with breast cancer but that she seems to be all right at the moment. Breast cancer! Why didn't she tell me? Well, why would she? We hardly know each other and you'd want close people around with that, I suppose. I ring to see how she is and Aunty Freda says it's been shocking but they think Karen is on the mend.

'Will you come and see us? Yes, after Christmas? Good.'

Her voice wavered during the conversation, especially when she told me that the doctors said the cancer was at an advanced stage by the time Karen got it checked. She's been through a radical mastectomy and chemotherapy. Do I want to get closer to this? I feel drawn in by my fondness for my aunty. I'm glad Karen is doing well and I decide that if I can help and support them both, I will.

My Christmas present from the Unit is a letter telling me that they have received advice and a draft complaint from Ms Parker. The formal complaint is being engrossed. Engrossed? Fattened up for Christmas dinner at the Psychologists Board?

I ring Mr Johnson but he's gone on holidays. Good. So will I.

Before I leave for the farm I write more of my life story because I'm sure Leonie and Col will ask about it. I've got my life down on fourteen pages. That's the best I can do for now. All my writing this year has been for uni.

At the farm, when my friends ask about the writing, I hand over the folder containing my short life story. 'Oh you've done it,' Col says, weighing the envelope in his hand.

'Been busy,' I say. 'But the basics are there.'

A few days later Col and Leonie have both read my story and Col returns it to me.

'It's interesting,' he says. 'But, Katherine Mary, I think there's a lot more to it than this.'

'I suppose there is but I just haven't had time or energy.'

'Well, this little outline shows there's a story there if you want to tell it.'

Soon I'm home again, and then I'm off to my relations' house. I'm more content to let the conversation flow and not probe for family history. Karen wants to talk about her illness. She says she had thought the odd shape of her breast was caused by the seatbelt pressing on it as she drove to and from work each day, and Freda had thought that sounded right. That's why she left it so long to be checked. 'I don't watch television or read magazines. I just don't mix with people who talk about breasts! Well, I didn't used to. I didn't know about breast cancer.'

For once I'm grateful that I haven't been as sheltered from life as my cousin has. This thought will be repeated constantly as we get to know each other. Karen says she's feeling all right now and that she's glad chemotherapy is over. She's lost some movement in her arm and shoulder since the operation but she's improving all the time, and she'll only have to wear 'the rug' on her head for a little while longer.

'The big C is not going to kill me. Us Lyfords die of heart attacks, not cancer, don't we?' she says, mimicking her mother's determination.

'You'd better mean that, Karen. I don't know if I could go through that again,' Freda says.

We chat about work, and Karen is keen to know about how I got to be a preschool teacher.

'I'd like to work with little kids,' she says. 'I was so sick of where I was before all this and, anyway, it's winding down, so I'll be out of a job eventually.' She's been working in a chemical plant for most of her working life and is very worried about changing jobs. She's surprised to hear that I know the feeling, and giggles uncontrollably as I describe the only job interview I've ever done.

'You'd be great with your music with little kids,' I tell her.

'I'm not open and confident like you are, though. I'm reserved. I don't now how you could do that social group thing you belong to either.'

'Kids are easy to get on with. If you treat them well, they want to please you.'

Will I tell her about therapy with Neroli, and how I've learnt to assume people like me, rather than assume they don't, and avoid getting on the treadmill of earning approval? No. I don't know how they'd cope with a relative who needed psychotherapy. And Freda is still anxious to know that my life has been good since my mother died. I can't disillusion her. I like her feisty spirit and her humour and determination to keep going as long as she can. Today she's not as energetic as she has been.

'Got such a belly ache,' she says. 'Ah well, I suppose you can expect these things when you're eighty and still mowing the lawn,' she laughs.

At home that night the phone rings.

'Hello. Is that you, Kate? It's Freda. Your aunty.'

'Hello, Freda my aunty. Long time no see!'

'I just wanted to tell you that I love you and I'm going to be your mother now.'

'Oh, thank you. Um. I don't know if I know what to do with one! It's nice having an aunt, though.' Oh dear. Was that ungracious? Hard to know what to say when someone springs that on you!

'I couldn't be much for you when you were small but I want to make up for it now,' Freda continues. 'So you be sure to stay in touch and remember we're here if you need anything.'

'Thank you.' I can't imagine what she has in mind but I'm moved by her wanting to be there for me, wanting to be my mother.

STOP. START.
STOP. START.

'How's your complaint going? It must be nearly over,' Gen asks as we recover from our Christmas dinner.

'Still dragging on. I actually got a letter last week and that's pretty good. Only got two in the whole of last year with that Solicitor General delay.'

'They're still working on it, then.'

'Yep. You'll hear me shouting from the rooftops when it's over. It will be soon, I think.'

'Is Kirsty still as good at school?'

'She's much better than good! I can hardly believe it after those years with Maud. I nearly didn't want the holidays to come this year.'

'You're mad.'

'Probably.'

Sleeping in is the best thing about holidays for someone who might be mad sometimes. But today the phone rings early.

'Hello, Kate. It's Aunty Dot. I'm well, thanks, but there's bad

456

news, I'm afraid.' She hesitates. 'Freda passed away during the night.'

Passed away? Died? But she mows the lawns. She said she would keep go– . . . silly as it seems now, it hadn't occurred to me that Aunty Freda might die soon.

'How's Karen?' I ask.

'She's pretty distressed, as you can imagine. They were very close, as you know.'

'Is there anything I can do?'

'Just keep in touch with Karen, will you? You've become a good friend to her and she'll need you.'

'All right. Does she want me to come over? I could stay if she needs company. I'm on holidays.' I don't know what made me say that. Perhaps I see Karen as a frightened child. She'd want people who are closer to her than I am, though, wouldn't she?

Aunty Dot asks Karen. 'Yes, she'd like you to come, if you wouldn't mind. Are you sure? That's good. She hasn't been alone before. She's always had Freda.'

Karen looks much older, sicker. She tells me she hasn't slept since the night before. Freda had had unbearable stomach pain on the previous afternoon and Karen had eventually called an ambulance against her mother's wishes. Tests revealed a perforated bowel and surgery was recommended.

'I told her to hold on because I need her, but she just whispered, "I don't think I can," then she died in the operating room.'

She tells me without shedding a tear. I wipe my eyes and feel embarrassed.

'I'm no good at crying,' Karen says. 'I suppose it'll all hit me sooner or later and I'll blubber like a baby, but now I'm just numb.'

'Just take it as it comes, I guess,' I say.

'You've been through all this, haven't you?'

'Yeah, but not for a long time.'

We take Cindy for a walk and when we get home the dog whines when she can't find Freda. She sits by her bed and waits.

Karen and I chat sometimes and sometimes we sit quietly with our own thoughts.

'Oh well, I'd better make us some tea,' Karen announces. 'Are you game?'

'What do you mean?'

'Mum wouldn't let me set foot in her kitchen and I haven't got a clue what to do,' she replies.

We sort out a meal and eat it among halfhearted jokes about food poisoning. Karen is almost asleep before we finish but she's afraid to be alone, afraid to go to bed, afraid of the dark.

'You can leave the light on. You need to sleep and stay well. You'll be all right. What could happen while you're sleeping? If you wake up sad, cry. You'd be a pretty strange bird if you didn't feel that way, wouldn't you? Wake me up if you want to.'

I don't understand why she's so afraid.

'Do you believe in ghosts?' she asks.

'No. Why?'

'I do,' she says shakily.

'Oh! Well what do they do? What are they?' It seems very odd to me to believe in ghosts and, more to the point, to be afraid of them when your mother, who loved you, has just died.

'I don't know but it's scary,' Karen says.

'Uh, I don't know anything about them. Never had anything to do with them.'

'What would you do if they were here?'

'I don't believe in them.' But she wants an answer and I'm concerned that she is afraid. 'I suppose I'd pray.'

'You believe in God?'

'Yeah. Do you?'

'No. Well, if I see ghosts I'll let you know and you can pray. Goodnight.'

In the morning Karen says she got some sleep but Cindy's whimpering for Freda disturbed her.

I stay a few days until Karen thinks she wants to be on her own. I've taught her to escape loneliness by reading, listening to

ABC radio or watching television. She didn't know there were such fabulous wildlife documentaries and I leave her watching one about howler monkeys.

She rings a few days later to tell me about the funeral arrangements, and says she's scared of going to the funeral home to see her mother in the coffin.

'Do you have to go?'

'No, but I want to, sort of. To make sure it's the right, you know, that it's Mum in there. Would you come with me? I shouldn't ask but I'm so scared.'

I meet her at the funeral home and we're ushered in by an obsequious man who makes me want to giggle. He's such a cliché. Karen is too tense to notice.

'Your mother is resting in this room,' our guide says with a slow sweep of his arm. 'It's quite all right to touch her or say your goodbye in whatever way you see fit. Perhaps you'd like a few moments before you go in?'

'No. We're all right,' Karen says quickly. 'Just give us a few seconds, then come in. I want you to put the lid on while I watch.'

Why is she so insistent on watching? It must be about ghosts but if Aunty Freda's in danger of becoming one, I can't imagine she'd be anything but a comical or benign one.

The coffin and flowers are the only things in the room. I stay back to let Karen do what she wants. 'Come with me,' she says.

She looks in nervously and steps away, shocked. 'Oh, she was so old! I didn't realise she was so old.' Then she makes for the door to call the attendant.

I don't want him to come yet. I want to hold Aunty Freda's hand and say a quiet goodbye and thank you. I want to tell her one last time that I understand why she wasn't there for us kids when our mother died. I'll have to do it quickly.

When I stand beside the coffin I'm absolutely astounded by the difference the lack of life makes! Freda isn't here. This is just a body. A shell. But it's all there is for me to say what I need to say to. The attendant comes too soon with a tool to screw the coffin lid down. We watch, then Karen leaves quickly. I stay back and whisper my words to the lid.

Freda's funeral is quiet and her life and spirit are celebrated. People from Karen's work are here and they are kind and concerned for Karen. Aunty Marj's family are here too, though I don't recognise any of them. It's been thirty years since I've seen them. Afternoon tea is served by the family at Karen's place, which seems eerily quiet when everyone leaves.

I need to go home because Mr Johnson will probably be trying to contact me. But should I desert my cousin?

'I didn't know it was going to feel this lonely without the old girl,' she says but she still doesn't cry.

'Pretty gloomy,' I say. 'It'll get less mournful over time. You just do your grieving and get through it. Do you want me to stay?'

'Um. Will you be offended if I ask you to go home? I think I want to bawl now and I can't do it in company.' She tries to smile but it doesn't work. I leave quickly so she can get on with what she needs to do and so I can do it too. I'm good at crying.

Notification comes from uni that my research project has been assessed. One examiner thinks my statistical analysis is a little weak but my theoretical base is solid. The other thinks my statistical analysis is strong and my work could be improved if my theoretical base was a little stronger. Oh no, I'm going to fail. No, wait! Both examiners have given me a pass and I'm to graduate in June! No need to fathom the examiners' contradictions.

I can't wait for the ceremony. It'll be in the fabulous Great Hall at Sydney University. There'll be a procession, trumpets and robes and I'll be in the middle of it all.

As I'm imagining telling Tony, the person I thought he was, Mr Johnson rings. We make an appointment to meet Ms Parker after school on Wednesday. Now I imagine telling Tony that uni was not a social whirlwind or even a breeze and that attaining my Masters has made just a small difference to my self-concept and none to my standing at work.

Ms Parker is cool and efficient. I can't imagine her ever being vulnerable or making bad decisions. Her immaculate presence is enough to make me weepy. Can't there be a bit of caring? No, I'd just cry if she was kind and we'd never get through the work. Better to be detached. Efficient. Except that I have to keep struggling with the thought that she must think I'm the most stupid woman she'll ever meet.

She questions me so thoroughly I'm sure she's about to ask for my shoe size too. There are still things I need to check in my journal.

'All right, look it up when you get home and let Mr Johnson know. Now, about this matter of . . . tell me how . . .'

She and Phillip, I've decided to call him that because he calls me Kate, discuss some issues without me. Sometimes I catch sight of a raised eyebrow that makes me think Ms Parker is on my side, but there's never direct words to that effect. Sometimes Phillip's voice suggests caring. I know now that he believes me and is committed to stopping Tony abusing anyone else. Here he is clinical too and I'm forced to stand on my own two wobbly, adult feet. At last it's over and I'm going home, wrung out but looking forward to finalisation.

I send answers to the questions to Phillip and his reply is prompt. It ends with: *When the matter is listed for hearing you will be formally requested to attend.*

I can bear the waiting now, nervously. I've waited this long, haven't I? I'll use the time to get strong and ready to face Tony. I'm dreading the hearing. Something akin to terror strikes when I think of coming face to face with him. All the old vulnerability courses through me and turns me into a blubbering wreck. I make an appointment with Neroli.

'Kate, who is the powerful one in this scenario?' Neroli asks.

'Tony,' I reply mischievously.

'Who is forcing Tony Benton to a public account of his actions?'

'I am. I know, but I feel so frightened of seeing him, standing close to him.'

'He's a coward. He won't do anything in a public place. Put yourself in his position. You've behaved appallingly and you know you have. Your victim is calling you to account in front of your peers. Do you really think he has any power?'

'No, he doesn't, does he?' I'm grinning at the thought of my power. It sustains my optimism and I resolve to keep this argument about power at the forefront of my thinking while I wait.

'I've done the report for the Unit,' Neroli says. 'I'd like you to read it before I send it.'

Her report reconnects me first to my vulnerability and then to my strength as I realise how far I've come.

'It's great,' I tell her. 'Let 'em have it.'

I'd better tell Kirsty about my complaint and the hearing, briefly, so she'll know I'm not just taking sickies when I have time off.

'Good heavens! I don't know what to say,' she says. 'I can't imagine any such thing. You're such a strong person, I just can't see you being taken in by a jerk like that.' Then she adds with a mischievous grin, 'I mean it in the nicest possible way.'

'I was different then. I'll tell you all about it one day. Not now, though.'

'Soitenly,' she replies and my mind flashes back to Jane's humour. 'Meanwhile, back at the ranch, do you reckon I could hive off from the staff meeting?' Sometimes we both 'hive off' and no-one seems to notice. It's tempting.

'Better not. Vivian said to make sure we're there today,' I say reluctantly.

Vivian invites the whole school staff to discuss applying for a Quality Assurance review. She convinces us that it would be worth doing because the community would be assured that we are accountable for what we do in the school. We discuss the parameters and the application goes off within a week or two.

Quality assurance. It should be mandatory for all psychologists. What if the hearing collides with our school review? We don't have to do anything special for it because the panel assesses our regular practice but I'd have to be there for it. I let the Unit know that I won't be available for that period of time.

First comes graduation day. A couple of friends from the social group who do shift work come with me and I'm glad. They'll be my substitute family. Gen and Paddy have to work and the farm is too far away for Col and Leonie to come.

There are hundreds of people here and, as I dash off to hire my robes, my friends leave to find a place in the Great Hall. The Great Hall!

I feel proud in my robes. We're handed a booklet that tells us what to do when our name is called. Bow to the senate, nod to others, shake hands with the chancellor and move your tassel to the other side of your mortarboard, bow again to someone, then soft shoe shuffle to exit stage right! I'll never remember all this! At least I'll be able to watch people ahead of me if they do this alphabetically. Aaron Aardvark will be in trouble.

I don't know anyone else here but the woman beside me wants to chat. 'What degree have you done?' she asks.

'Masters in Early Childhood. How about you?'

'Doctorate in . . .' and she lapses into a foreign language, I think.

The trumpets sound. We turn slightly to watch the procession. Procession! They're dawdling down the aisle, in all their finery, like a mob of Brown's cows! No lines, no procession, just a wandering mob, chatting awkwardly. Whatever happened to pomp and ceremony? I abandon all intent to do the bowing and nodding properly. When my name is called I walk up, without tripping over nothing, and shake hands with the chancellor, who asks, 'Are you going to go on with Honours, Katherine?'

'Oh no! I've had enough.'

How very academic of me! I flick my tassel over as I exit stage right with my degree tucked under my arm.

I find my friends, who tell me they didn't see a thing because there were too many people crammed in, but they heard my name

463

called. I'm glad to have had them here, anyway. I have a photo taken and the photographer insists on twisting my head so the sun won't reflect in my glasses. I look as if I'm wondering where I am and what I'm doing here. Karen is so proud she hangs the photo on her lounge room wall.

Soon after, Phillip tells me that a meeting of the Professional Standards Committee of the Board will meet and fix a date for the hearing this month. Good. It's been four years since I raised the alarm and Tony has been doing his thing the whole time. In August I'm given actual dates in November.

November! Why was I worried about missing the Quality Assurance review at school? I'm so glad I didn't, though.

We're to be assessed on record keeping and community participation. I've developed my skills in assessment of kids and record keeping over the years and I'm happy with my system, though I think a loose-leaf binder is more efficient than the computer I use, just to show I can.

I've asked our regular singalong parents to make an effort to get here this week if they possibly can. The Quality Assurance team arrives just as our circle of parents and kids settles. People move to make room for the visitors and we start singing. We sound like a seriously untrained yet joyous massed choir! Late arrivals keep expanding the circle until we run out of chairs and have to use tables. Singing circles have been large but never quite like this. The assessors sing their lungs out too and leave laughing and saying they haven't had that much fun for years. I want to hug those parents for their support. They're fantastic and they had a ball too. I love my chosen career!

Karen is on sick leave from hers and she comes to preschool sometimes to play with the kids. She's talking about doing a Child Care Certificate if she lives long enough to be made redundant. Markers in her blood suggest the cancer could be back. She may have to do another round of chemotherapy and even a bone marrow harvest. It's a wait-and-see game. How will she manage without Freda? I desperately hope she doesn't need chemo. I don't think I could do what Freda needed to do during the last round, cleaning up vomit and so on. And I hope it doesn't come in November. But most of all I hope it doesn't come at all.

'Would you like to come over for lunch on the weekend?' she asks. 'I've been learning to cook and I want someone to practise on.'

It's the first time I've been to the house since Freda's funeral. It's also the first time I realise that I don't know how to greet my cousin. Kissing on the cheek seems to be the way most people do it these days and bear hugs have fallen from favour. Karen is brittle with both.

'I've never liked people touching me,' she says. 'I suppose that means I'm weird?'

Or does it mean that a dark father terrified you? I don't ask but I remember the hand I saw in the photo of Karen as a child.

'No, I don't think you're weird. I didn't used to like it but I forced myself to do it so I'd be groovy. Now I like it. Just do what's comfortable. It doesn't matter what people think.'

'You've learnt so much more about people than me. Mum didn't think much of most of them. The old man didn't either, so we didn't mix, except with Aunty Marj's family at birthdays and Christmas. I wish it'd been different now. I just took up their ways. And here I am.' Her chin ripples but she doesn't let tears out.

'Are you feeling lonely?'

'No. Well, yes. Well. I don't want to be with people but I don't want to be by myself all the time either. Do you know what I mean?'

'Absolutely! Story of my life. You want your mum back.'

'Yes. Yes I do. You know when the worst time is? When the sun's going down. It feels so much worse then.'

'You won't believe this but that's the worst time for me too, when I'm low. It's like darkness outside makes you dark inside.'

'That's right! That's a good way of putting it. That's amazing

465

how we both feel that. Oh well, here's lunch. Charcoal chops and mush vegies. But I'm learning.'

She talks about loneliness as we eat and she's surprised that I get lonely too.

'You've got friends, though,' she says.

'Yeah, but it's not the same as family, like you and Freda were. Like being someone's number one. I'm people's number five or six, after spouses and kids, but I'm nobody's number one. Nobody's most important person. Like you were to Freda and vice versa.'

'I took all that for granted. Didn't know it meant so much having someone to come home to and natter on to. Wish I had the guts to do that social club thing you do. I've looked up the paper and there's one at the church but, oh, I don't know. I just can't seem to get myself there. Then I think, if Kate can do it, so can I.'

'Course you could! Just go and try it out. If you hate it, you don't have to go back. Just give it a go.'

'But what if they're a bunch of religious nuts!'

'Then don't go back.'

'What do you talk about with strangers?'

'If they don't ask you about yourself, ask them about them. Most people seem to like talking about themselves. Or their kids. Or work. And there's always the weather!'

'I'll think about it,' she says as she clears the plates away.

'Don't think. Just do it. What have you got to lose?'

Karen puts our dessert on the table. 'I hope you like blancmange.'

We start to eat.

'Need some secateurs?' Karen asks, giggling and bouncing the lump of blancmange on her plate. 'Maybe I should try cooking classes first, before I launch myself into a social whirlwind.'

'Uhuh. There is that! Or tennis ball manufacturing.'

We talk about the social group again and I feel very worldly compared with Karen. I feel protective of her, too, and that surprises me. I want her to be safe and happy.

'What if some creepy man decides he likes me?'

'Invite him for dinner and serve up blancmange! No. Just tell him that you're not interested.'

'But what if he won't take no?'

She's so afraid of men! Why? The hand?

Later Karen rings to say her last test shows that she doesn't need a bone marrow harvest or chemo. So, because she's going to live, she's decided to try the social group. 'I'm just telling you so if I'm found murdered somewhere, you'll know where to start looking for the killer.'

'No-one's going to do anything! Good on you for giving it a go. When is it?'

'Saturday.'

'Ring and tell me how it went. If you're still alive.'

I think of her as I go enthusiastically to my group. It's a dinner and movie night and the usual core group will be there: Evan, a divorcee who likes his freedom, Tania, a divorcee who likes Evan, Inga and Stan, who've become a couple, Vicky, divorced, Chris divorced, and me. Tania and I talk often about her ups and downs with Evan. Her ups make me start wishing I'd meet Mr Right.

There are others in the group too, among them Scott, the handsome, well-dressed widower who's been a couple of times but who doesn't know I exist.

As we walk across the park to the theatre, I slip on the damp grass.

'Got you,' Scott says.

'Thanks. Good timing.'

'Glad to get a chance to talk to you at last.'

'What do you mean? I always come.'

'Yes, I've seen you but you always seem unattainable.'

'Me? Unattainable?' Have I taken the Tony cure too far?

Scott invites me out and I accept with more enthusiasm than I thought I'd muster. We go dancing and, although he seems to have no rhythm and two left feet, we enjoy the night. The next day he wants me to go to his house for lunch.

'I want you to meet my daughter and see if my house is the kind of house you'd like to spend the rest of your life in.'

'What? We hardly know each other.'

'No. But we will. I think you and I are going to be together for a long, long time.'

'That's much too fast for me. Why don't we just get to know each other?' I've been here before with Cameron! Transference but no counter transference. At least there's something to thank Tony for. But couldn't I have just read a book about it!

Karen rings to report on her adventure.

'Oh, I don't know,' she says tentatively. 'It was all right. I suppose.'

'Were they all religious nuts or just mass murderers?'

'There was one old bloke who kept talking to me.'

'Oh, that's nice. Is it?'

'No! It was awful. He told me he likes me. He doesn't even know me! How can you like someone when you've just met them?' she asks indignantly. 'He even wanted me to have dinner with him!'

'You can like what you know so far. He didn't say he wants to marry you, did he? Just that he likes you.'

'Well, I didn't like him!'

'Did he spoil the night?'

'Not really. There was a really nice old bird there, a bit like Mum. We talked and laughed a lot. The others seemed okay but I didn't know what to talk about.'

'Will you go again?'

'Don't know. I didn't like that man but the others seemed all right.'

Karen does go again and the people become her dearest friends who help support her through the dreadful fight with the cancer that's waiting. They gradually help break down her fear of people without 'shoving religion down her neck' and they make her want to live. I feel so grateful to them. I live too far away from my cousin to be there for hands-on help.

She gives me regular updates. 'It sounds trite but I feel like a flower bud unfurling or whatever flower buds do. Blossom! That's it. I'm blossoming,' she laughs. 'And I never thought I'd be useful to anyone but Jan needs me. She's having a terrible time so she talks to me. Me! It's intriguing. She's teaching me to swim. That's intriguing too, at my age.' 'Intriguing' is Karen's understatement for fabulous, wonderful.

Scott and I keep going out. He keeps declaring his love and commitment and I keep wondering if I'll ever feel the same. He doesn't believe in a spiritual life and his biggest concerns seem to be that his belt matches his shoes and his clothes are immaculate. Well, it's nice to have a man to go out with for a change.

'See you when I get back from the farm,' I tell him on the phone.

'Oh, I forgot you were going. How long will you be away?'

'A week. I leave in the morning.'

I get up very early so I'll have time to call in on friends on the way to the farm. I also need to drop a package off to Sue, who's in the social group and is a friend of Scott's and mine separately. The package is for George, Sue's boyfriend. I drive into her street as the sun is rising. Suddenly I want to be sick. Scott's car is parked in her driveway. I sit frozen in my car.

Don't leave me. Please don't leave me.

I feel abandoned. What will I do?

No. Wait. It isn't abandonment. It's betrayal. And I will be all right.

But does this mean what I think it means? Yes, be honest. I take a piece of paper and write, *I don't ever want to see you again.* I put it under Scott's windscreen wiper, leave the package in the letter box, and go home and cry.

I'm aware of how different I am now. Instead of a small child screaming 'Don't leave me!', an adult is hurting because of the betrayal of two friends. Am I making assumptions, though? I do a reality check with Vicky.

'Oh no, Kate. I don't think you're making assumptions. How could they? What are you going to do?'

At the farm I cry and tell them what's happened. My friends are glad that I can see clearly and know what to do.

'He doesn't deserve someone as wonderful as you,' Leonie says, her arm around my shoulder.

I've grown up. I'm using my adult judgement to respond to letters Scott and Sue each leave me. They're sorry I found out the way I did that they have fallen in love. They each value my friendship. Couldn't we talk about it, because each hopes that we can still be friends? Each receives a letter telling them that I don't want to talk about it because they'll want me to say that what they did is all right because they're in love. I tell them that what they have done is not all right and that I base friendships on trust, not betrayal.

They come to the social group as a couple, so I stop going. I didn't want to marry Scott but it's too hard having the betrayal under my nose all the time.

All the activity had stopped me thinking too much about the complaint hearing in November and that had felt good. Must stay busy. It won't be long now. Not being in the social group leaves me with energy to spend more time walking and going to meetings where environmental issues are discussed. My favourite weekend pastime now is bush regeneration. Annie, the co-ordinator, and I work for hours in the bush, trying to help it recover from weed invasions and chatting as we work. I go home exhausted and welcome the descent of the sun so I can fall into bed early.

What's this in the letter box? The Unit has a new logo. It's become the Health Care Complaints Commission. The HCCC. Well, the Commission must have got sick of complaints about the lack of support for people with complaints going through, because they've appointed a Complainant Liaison Officer. Her role seems to be to inform, support and encourage people like me. Her name is Liz and she rings to introduce herself.

'I wondered if you'd like me to take you through the hearing process and it might help if you see the room where it'll be held. It could make it feel less daunting on the day.'

We meet in Liz's office and she goes through the procedure. A panel of the Professional Standards Committee will be formed to hear the evidence in a closed hearing. That means there'll only be the panel, witnesses, legal teams, the recorder and Liz, if I want her to be there. She thinks I'll give evidence on the first day. That will involve questioning by Ms Parker, cross examination by Tony's barrister, then Ms Parker can question me again to clarify anything that needs it. Tony's peers will give reports and be cross examined and then Tony will go through the same process. I'm in a daze. It's still hard to believe that I'm involved in something requiring evidence, cross examination, barristers and lawyers.

'How about we go to the hearing room now and I'll show you the layout?' Liz suggests.

By the time we reach the room my heart is racing and my mouth has dried up. As we walk in, Liz points to where the panel will sit and then where Tony and his lawyers . . .

I'm gasping for air. Can't breathe.

'Breathe in slowly and deeply,' Liz says calmly. 'Sit down here. That's right. Breathe in and out. Slowly in and out. Good. Just relax. There's no-one here but us.'

At last I'm breathing again. My heart is still racing as I remember the last time I saw Tony. I forget about talking to the inner child.

'I can't do it,' I whimper. 'He'll be here!'

'You'll be all right. Breathe slowly. Good.'

This time I don't lose control but I don't want to be in the same country as Tony, much less the same room. All the what ifs that I've put aside for years are playing in my mind again. What if he confronts me, humiliates me? I can't find the strength that everybody reckons I've got.

'If you like, I can come in with you and be a support person. We'd sit behind Phillip and Ms Parker so we can answer their questions or whatever needs doing.'

Another awful thought occurs to me. 'Where does the audience sit?'

'Audience?'

'Oh, you know, people who watch and write articles, whatever they're all called.'

'No, it's an in camera hearing. That means there won't be anyone here but the people directly involved. No press. No spectators.'

'Phew! I'd die if this was all over the papers!' It doesn't occur to me yet that perhaps it needs to be, that people need to know this is going on so they can be alerted to the possibility of predatory psychologists.

'When you're being questioned you sit at the table there.'

'I'll have to walk right past him to get to there! This is a nightmare and we haven't even got to the real thing yet.'

'Yes, you will have to go past him, won't you?' Liz says thoughtfully. 'You'll have to go past him but you don't have to look at him. You don't have to look at him at all, if you don't want to. And remember, he is the one on trial, so to speak, not you. The panel will be watching and they'll see if he tries to intimidate you.'

'I don't have to look at him. I am not the one on trial,' I repeat to convince myself. 'But what if I get in the lift or something and it's only him and me?'

'It won't happen. We make sure you're never alone with the other person. I'll be with you and if, say, we were in the lift and he approached, I'd just ask him to wait. Or his lawyer would, if he was there too. Don't even think about being alone with him. It just won't happen. Let's go through some strategies to help you stay calm.'

'All right.'

'First, remember that you aren't on trial. That's so important. All you have to do is tell the truth about what happened. Cross examination can be gruelling, but again, all you have to do is tell the truth.'

'But they mightn't believe me. He's told so many lies already. What if they believe him?'

'Don't worry. Our legal people will get to the truth. And you just keep telling it. Don't look for trick questions. Just give short, simple answers and if you don't hear a question, ask for it to be repeated. Likewise, if you don't understand a question, ask for it to be rephrased. There'll be water on the table, so if you need to, sip it slowly and let them wait.'

I scribble notes because I know I won't remember all this.

'Also remember that the panel probably know what you've been through and they'll want to keep your trauma to a minimum. Of course they'll be being fair to Benton too. He has the right to put his point of view. If you want to avoid eye contact with Benton, pick any one of them to look at instead. When you're being cross examined it'll be tricky because he'll be behind the barrister. Don't let him intimidate you. Look at his barrister, not Benton.'

I leave still in a daze and as I walk to the station new horrors occur to me. What if Tony follows me after everyone else has gone? What if he gets on my train and sits near me?

At home I ring Trish and Sam, friends in the justice group who've offered to help if they can. Sam works in the city. One of his finest qualities is his gentleness, but I'm hoping he can look threatening if the need arises.

'The hearing is on soon and I'm scared,' I tell him after we go through the minimum of pleasantries.

'I can imagine. It's pretty scary stuff. Anything we can do?'

'Thanks, Sam. That's why I'm ringing. There might be something you can do. I wondered if you could meet me after work on the hearing days and come home with me on the train.'

'Sure! I could do that.'

'No, but I should tell you why first. It's because I'm scared Tony will follow me. He's big and he's a bully, so I need you to look like a big bully.'

We both laugh, then Sam says, 'He won't do anything. People will be watching.'

'I'm scared he will. Or he'll say something to try to intimidate me or bully me. I think if I'm with someone, he won't. I'm not asking you to do fisties with him or anything. Just be seen to be with me and look truly ferocious.'

'I'll be there. Just tell me where and I'll come up after work.'

At school, since Vivian will need to know what's happening, I tell her a brief version of the story and she congratulates me for what I'm doing. 'Will you need time off to recover when it's over? Take what you need. I'll arrange a casual for the three days but let me know if you need more time.' She's very supportive and I'm grateful, but when the hearing is over I'll want to dash back to work, to get my life back to normal. Normal before Tony, not the kind of normal I've had for the last four years. No, a better, stronger, wiser normal than ever before. I might even have a celebration dinner party!

Hearing day. I wake up having got to sleep about an hour ago. I'm so nervous I have to keep chanting, 'Tell the truth. Remember to breathe. Tell the truth. Remember to breathe.' On the train I fall asleep and wake with a jolt at Central. What am I doing here? Oh.

I'm early. I wait in a coffee shop until it occurs to me that Tony might do the same. I dash to Liz's office and wait. We meet Phillip, who is kind and encouraging.

'How do you feel?' he asks.

'Nervous. And I can't believe we're here at last.'

'Should all be over soon. You've done well,' he smiles.

All over soon. All over soon.

When Ms Parker arrives she talks with Phillip first, then turns to me and says, 'Phillip has told you about the procedures? Good. Just try to stay calm and answer simply and clearly. Don't make speeches or look for tricks. Tell the truth as simply as you can. Right, let's go in, then.'

Tony isn't here yet. Thank goodness I don't have to walk past him. Breathe slowly, soon be over, I keep telling myself. Before long other people arrive. I hear sounds from where Tony's team are but I don't look. Liz tells me quietly they've sat down and are talking.

The chairman of the Board begins proceedings by describing what will happen over the next three days. Then he introduces all the people involved. There seems to be a lot of whispering and paper shuffling going on from Tony's direction. I don't look. We're here at last and moving inexorably towards finalisation in three days' time.

Within two hours I'm sitting on the train crying quietly but wanting to scream across the universe in frustration and anger.

Tony had once sat at the same table at a conference or something with someone on the panel so he challenged their position there. The panel was deemed to be incorrectly constituted. The hearing could not proceed.

How could this happen? Don't they know what the rules are? How could they do this? Even to Tony bloody Benton? If a kind stranger sat beside me right now I'd bawl all over her. I put my bag on the seat as a precaution.

At home I ring Sam, who doesn't believe it. I ring the farm, Gen and Neroli. No-one can believe it. I ring school and tell Vivian what's happened. 'So I'll be in tomorrow after all. What will happen about the person replacing me?'

'Don't worry. I'll find her something to do.'

I howl. I'm powerless to do anything at all to get this out of my life. I can't keep fighting. I ring Phillip Johnson.

'I can't stand it any more. I want to pull out.'

'What do you mean pull out?'

'I don't want to keep going with the complaint. That thing the other day, I can't go through all that again. It was supposed to be over . . .' I'm crying on the phone.

'It was shocking. We couldn't have foreseen that. I know it's hard for you but we do need your evidence.'

'Well, some of his other victims can do it. I can't any more.'

'No-one else has come forward, Kate.'

'What happens if I pull out, refuse to be part of it any more?'

'We need your evidence.'

'But I've given it. Won't the stat dec and all the other stuff do?'

'Possibly, but it can't be cross examined. Our case is stronger with you in it. We could subpoena you if we needed to.' It's not a threat but it feels like one.

'Then I'm trapped. How many more years is it going to haunt me?' I feel foolish whining like this but I can't stop. I feel so weak and small.

'Kate, I know this is hard for you and it's taken so long but don't give up now. It won't be the same long time again and if you can just hold on, we'll get him to account for himself. We don't want him out there doing this to anyone else, do we? Talk with Liz anytime you need to if that helps. Or you could ring me.'

'You and Liz can't make it go away.'

I cry some more, then grasp onto my adult self and write to the Board. You bunch of bungling, incompetent twits! First you register a monster, then you take years to bring him to account, then you stuff it up and he escapes to do the same again. You're bloody psychologists, for goodness sake! On and on I go, letting all the venom out.

I then delete the letter and write a polite one, as polite as I can manage under the circumstances. It isn't true to say I mean no disrespect. I have no respect for them. I change my letter so it's honest. *I don't mean to sound disrespectful.* I point out that for years I've cooperated and struggled with the stress of the case, always believing that everyone knew what they were doing to stop

Tony hurting anyone else. Then, at the most important and stressful time, everything comes to nothing. I ask why the bungle happened, and didn't they know the rules for the proper constitution of a panel? If not, what are they doing to better inform themselves?

But will my letter prevent anyone who reads it going on the panel? Will it prejudice them against me? I send it to Phillip Johnson and ask him to pass it on if it's safe.

Now I'll just have to get on with my life again. I make a concerted effort to stop myself every time I start thinking about the case. I hide the file on the floor behind my desk, with my Burnside file.

Back to school, where I feel so spaced out I hardly know what to do. I pull myself together as kids arrive, and get busy with end of year assessments.

I'm working with Tashan but Josh has had a week off at his Pop's farm and wants to tell me all about it.

'How about drawing me a picture of it for my fridge? I need to work with Tashan.' He goes off reluctantly and I get back to assessm—

'There. I drew some sheep,' Josh says, pushing a page in my face.

'They'll need some grass and sky and sunshine, won't they?'

Off he trudges.

'Tashan, which of these things goes wi—'

'I done it. They've got all grass there now.'

'Water! They'll need lots of water, and a fence all the way up here and down there so they can't go next door.'

Six kilometres of fencing would keep Col busy for ages!

Soon Josh is back again with a tiny piece of paper. 'I cut the paper so they can't get away.'

I'm laughing too hard to speak. Josh is grinning, asking, 'Is it my turn now?'

If only I could snip away my troubles like that! Just prior to the hearing that wasn't, Tony's solicitor had produced a thick wad of a stat dec of Tony's fiction. Now I have to respond to that. No, not trample it and rip it up and burn it. Read it and write a response. Like selecting a work of fiction and writing a book review. All right, I'll do it then put it all away and wish myself a happy 'complaint-still-not-over' Christmas.

I read Tony's story. It's so full of lies it makes him seem intellectually challenged. I almost feel sorry for him. Writing my reply is easy. It takes a long time but it's no challenge to point out lies and inconsistencies, checking my journal as I go to make sure I'm not relying on an unreliable memory. I post another bulky letter off.

Phillip Johnson is on leave but a letter comes from the HCCC saying that, as I may be aware, the complaint was set down for hearing but the dates had been vacated. Yes, I may be aware. I just may.

Christmas. Not the way I thought this one would be but I manage to enjoy myself by deliberately staying indignant, not weak.

Karen has Christmas with her new friends. She's making enormous efforts not to get too maudlin about this being her first Christmas without her mother. We have dinner together and talk about Freda through the courses. I leave her feeling calm.

When Phillip returns he writes to say the Board has set tentative dates in May for the hearing. Dare I believe it'll be over by my birthday?

Two weeks prior to those dates I ring to confirm that the hearing is going ahead. Phillip has what could be bad news.

'What this time?'

'It's a judicial point, the issue of the misconduct predating the law. Benton's arguing that the Act can't be applied retrospectively.'

'But we went through all that before with the Solicitor General, didn't we?'

This time the challenge is to the Professional Standards Committee. Weeks later it gets a ruling that it can judge Tony's conduct under the Psychologists Act. Tony has twenty days, right up to the day before the hearing, to appeal.

'Let's just assume it will go ahead for now,' Phillip suggests. 'I'll be in touch.'

Assume it's going ahead. I ring Rita for support.

'Oh, my friend, the one whose matter is going through now too, her perpetrator is appealing. I think it's being heard, oh, any day now.'

'They seem to try every trick in the book to avoid facing the Professional Standards lot, don't they?'

'Do you want to talk with my friend?'

'Thanks. I'll just wait and see what happens with my case for now.'

And keep enjoying school and the growing friendships with Kirsty and with Karen.

Keep enjoying bush regeneration, where we're joined now by other concerned people who accept my invitation to afternoon tea when we finish. I'm not testing the theory that people like me any more. I'm making assumptions that are proved true. My evidence is the laughter and chatter of bush regen days, in the bush and at home.

After the hearing in May, I'll be as happy as I can be. Mr Right? He can stay wherever he's hiding. At least until after May.

Two days before the hearing Phillip rings. 'Benton's appealing,' he says. He's asking the Supreme Court to stay the complaint before the Committee. 'I can't say the hearing is off, because we haven't got the documents yet.'

He has them at five o'clock the afternoon before the first day of the hearing. The appeal will be listed for mention at court, then a date will be fixed for it to be heard. It will take months! When I hoped it would be over by my birthday, I did mean this year's one. Didn't I?

I cancel the casual teacher's booking and scream. Again. I'm going to stay a child and have a tantrum. I think I've earned it.

Who knows when it'll be over now!

All right, I'm not going to stay home having a tantrum. I'll go to the slide night that the bushwalking group is having on the Kimberley.

A man who I've met before, a school principal, is here with the group showing the slides.

'G'day. I'm Dave,' he says with a broad smile. 'Kate Shayler? Ah yes. The P.E. teacher?'

'No. The preschool teacher.'

It's a pleasant change to meet a principal socially, even if I have made a forgettable impression on him. I'm glad I made the effort to go out. The slides were spectacular and these people are such good company.

A few months later our bushcare group is working on a blackberry invasion. We have some new members now and most of them are going to a fundraising dinner tonight for a community group that rescues native plants before bulldozers scrape them away to make way for new houses. I've thought about going but I'm too tired and it's expensive. No-one comes for afternoon tea.

Saturday night starts feeling gloomy. Take control. You don't have to stay home. Hang the expense.

I get to the dinner a bit late and the only chair left is one beside Dave, the school principal. Coincidentally, my bushcare group is at the same table so conversation comes easily.

'Housework! My dad grew up in an orphanage in Switzerland and he's absolutely obsessed with a clean house!' says Marta.

'Couldn't be as bad as the people in the boys' home I grew up in,' Dave retorts.

'Sounds like Burnside,' I say without thinking.

Dave turns to me, looks bewildered, and asks, 'When did I tell you that?'

'What? You didn't.' There's a pause while I try to work it out. 'Was it Burnside?'

'Yes!' Dave says, looking amazed.

I can't think of anything for a moment. My mouth's hanging open anyway. I am sitting beside the only person I've met, since I left thirty years ago, who grew up in Burnside!

It feels like coming home. Not like the coming home to a sense of my wholeness that I felt at the cemetery, but like meeting someone from my home town after the excitement of being in a foreign country has worn off. Someone who speaks my language and knows my culture. I want to talk and talk and I want him to too.

'I don't believe it! It's been thirty years since I left and I've never met anyone . . .'

'I haven't either. In fact, I'd forgotten there were girls there! Which home were you in?'

'Reid first, then Ivanhoe. You?'

'Ivanhoe first, then Blackwood.'

I talk excitedly and Dave stays calm, as if he's deliberately understating our discovery to balance my enthusiasm. Sometimes people interrupt and ask, 'What are you two talking about?' 'You've never met anyone else? You're joking! That's incredible.'

'That's what you're writing about isn't it, Kate?' asks Annie, whom I've told about my feeble scribbles.

'Are you writing about it?' Dave asks.

'Oh, sort of. It's almost impossible when you're working full time but I dip in every holidays and get a bit more done. Nothing serious.'

I like Dave and hope I see him again. We exchange phone numbers but I don't hear from him, so I assume, disappointedly, that he's not interested in getting together again. Funny. He'd seemed to be at the dinner. I'll ring him later.

I'm surprised when another Commission letter arrives in June. Tony's matter was mentioned in the Supreme Court and was adjourned until August. I'm asked to ring Mr Johnson.

'Hello, Kate. How are you? You got my letter?' he asks.

481

'Yes. What does it mean?'

'Well, there's some very good news.'

'The judge deregistered him and it's all over!'

'Now you know that's not the way it happens,' he chuckles. He explains that another case before the court went in favour of the Professional Standards Committee. The judge determined that the Act can be applied retrospectively. That must be Rita's friend's case.

'So Tony can't go and make the same argument?'

'He can, but he may not.' There's a precedent now, so the likelihood of a different judgement is pretty small. But he may decide to go ahead and then appeal. He could even take it to the High Court. Phillip seems to think he'd wait to see if this judgement is appealed before he decides what to do.

'So he virtually tests his options by watching what happens to the other person?'

'More or less, but the good news about the decision in that case is that it includes a lack of skill, care and judgement.'

'I'm not with you.'

'Well, remember I've told you that the Act says we have to show a lack of good character as grounds for action or deregistration? This judgement expands the causes to include a lack of skill, care and judgement. Not just character.'

The whole experience with Tony fast forwards through my mind. 'Skill, care and judgement. He certainly lacked skill. Well, of the right kind. I can see that now from working with Neroli.'

'Well, you need to be careful there. It can be just different forms of treatment. Different opinions about what the patient needs.'

'Oh, I see. Well, care. No. Didn't have that. Not later on anyway. Assuming it means care of the client not the self. And judgement. Well, whatever that means, he got a lot wrong.'

'We had a case just on character. Anyway, we'll look into every aspect of our case. You have a break from it and I'll keep in touch.'

Why is Tony making this so hard for himself? Why not just

face the music and get it over with? Even if he thinks his career as a psychologist is over, surely it would be better to have it over with sooner rather than later and start somewhere else. I'm pleased that I'm able to put blame for his career ending squarely on his shoulders. But it hasn't ended! He could just be smacked on the hand and told not to do it again, couldn't he!

Each month a letter arrives from the HCCC to keep me up to date. They also serve as a stress barometer and show me that I'm calmer than I've been for years. There's barely a twitch when I go to the letter box these days. As I add the latest letter to my ever expanding file I remember that I meant to acknowledge the improvements in the Commission. At school we don't get direct praise very often; criticism seems to be easier to deliver. I don't know if the Commissioner cares what I think but I write and tell her anyway.

I tell her the regular update letters make the complainant feel that their case is not forgotten and their involvement is respected. The new position of Complainant Liaison Officer, which Liz carries out so well, is a great step for complainants who need some support and who need advice but not necessarily from a lawyer. I thank her for understanding the challenging and difficult position we complainants are in and for acting to smooth the process.

'Hi, Kate. Rita here. How are you? That's beaut. Listen, I've got something to tell you. My friend's perpetrator's matter, you know, the appeal, well, it was lost.'

'Oh great! Mine surely won't go through the same thing, then.'

'Who knows? This other one can go to the High Court, I suppose. Anyway, just thought you'd like to know.'

Soon Phillip advises that Tony has withdrawn his appeal in the court and the Commission has written to the Psychologists Registration Board asking them to list hearing dates as soon as possible. I make a note on my file and put it away again.

There's my Burnside file. I wonder if I'll hear from Dave again. It would be nice to spend more time with him. He wasn't there when I rang before. I'll try again.

'Hello. Dave here. Oh, good to hear from you. No. I've been away diving. Didn't I tell you?'

We make a plan to meet at his house for dinner.

He's cooked a lovely meal and we talk and talk. Although he doesn't remember as much about his years at Burnside as I do, his life story is fascinating.

'Why am I writing my story? I should be writing yours!'

'No. No-one would want to hear mine. It's ordinary.'

It isn't and neither is he. He's a widower who remembers his wife with warmth and respect. He's tall, broad shouldered, often serious but he has a great sense of humour too. Dave has two adult children and three grandchildren! I keep doing mental calculations to work out how someone who looks about fifty could have ten-year-old grandchildren and be retired.

He asks about my family and I tell him, then add, 'I never see my brother. I don't know why he broke off contact but I think he has the right to decide to stay away. I can't force anything.'

'Do you know his address?'

'I only have the one he used to live at but he hasn't replied to any letters I've sent there for years.'

'Have you tried phone books?'

'There are a few entries that could be him but I don't think he wants contact. I mean, he's had my address and never written. I just don't want to force it.'

We chat on for hours about our common interests and our lives.

When I leave Dave's house I find myself hoping to see much more of him. Soon we're going out regularly and his hugs and kisses are turning my legs to jelly.

Don't rush it, Kate. This could just be a huge whammy of transference. Give it time.

Phillip gives me dates for the hearing at the end of November. Don't panic. They won't make the same mistake twice. It could all really be over by Christmas. This Christmas!

Liz has left the Complainant Liaison Officer position and Josie has replaced her. She rings to ask if I'd like her to be at the hearing with me. She sounds young and energetic. Yes, I'd like her support.

At school, we're always frenetically busy in November and it's increasingly difficult to catch Vivian for anything. I tell her quickly that the hearing is on again.

'All right. Book a casual. And good luck with it. I hope they get it right this time,' she says, as she dashes away to her office. I book the casual teacher, telling her that I might need her for one day or three. I'll have to let her know each night.

I ring my supporters, including Sam who's ready to try to look tough again. It occurs to me that Dave would be a handy companion with his broad shoulders and imposing height, but I don't want to tell him about this in case he doesn't understand. I think he would but I'm not certain. Sam is more than willing to play the part, anyway.

Reconnected with the powerless child again, I have a good cry the night before the hearing. It's interrupted by a knock at the door. It's Dave. When he releases me from his customary bear hug, he asks, 'How are you? You look a bit stressed. Can I do anything?'

I tell him my story nervously. If he doesn't understand, it'll be the end of a lovely friendship. When I finish he says, 'You were vulnerable, weren't you? You shouldn't be embarrassed. That . . . person should be ashamed. I hope you win.'

'Thanks. It'll be the pits if it all falls through again.'

'Do you want me to come and be a supporter or anything?'

'Thanks, but no. Sam's coming. Just be a supporter at home.' I want him to leave now so that I can sit and howl with relief that he understands.

Hearing, day one. Here we are assembled, but in a different room to the one in which our previous attempt to bring Tony to account was held. He's the only person who could possibly be feeling as nervous as I am but I'm not going to look at him to see.

Numbness envelops me as I wait through the introductions and opening statements. I half listen and half wonder what will go wrong this time. Will I be on the train home soon?

TELLING THE TRUTH

Suddenly I'm called to the witness chair.

When I stand up I see that I'll have to step over Tony's feet, which are sprawled out in front of him. My immediate reaction is to want to shout, 'Move your wretched feet.' But a curious calm comes over me. You have no power over me here, Tony Benton. All I have to do is tell the truth. I'm ready.

I swear the oath on the Bible before Ms Parker begins questioning me. I understand her questions and, despite feeling embarrassed by what I have to talk about, I tell the truth easily. When she's finished, Dr Steele, Tony's barrister, is invited to cross examine.

His first few questions are innocuous but soon he is asking the same question in a different form over and over again. Is he cognitively challenged? How many ways are there to say I do not know those people he's asking about? At last he gives up and moves on, using the same technique. No, Dr Steele, there was no collusion, however you phrase your question. The truth. I just keep telling the truth and he keeps trying to make me tell a story to match Tony's. This is so easy!

The questions grind on. I often say I remember what happened or that I verified what I said in my stat dec through an entry in my journal. I feel like a parrot but I don't think even the best of parrots could sit on a perch for this long reciting the same tired phrases. No, there was no formal end to therapy. No, there was no plan to wait for any amount of time before starting the sexual relationship.

When we break for morning tea I'm feeling buoyant. I've told the truth clearly and Tony has had to sit and listen. It's like Phillip and Josie said it would be. I'm not nervous. I'm not especially looking forward to continuing with Dr Steele but I'll be right. He won't get me back up there until two other witnesses are questioned. They need to get back to their businesses and it would be inappropriate to keep them waiting. I'm asked to wait outside while they give evidence.

I wander around the block, gaze into shop windows and think how normal life is out here. If anybody tries to turn you into a parrot you can just walk away or tell them you've had it. You don't just sit there behaving like a parrot. Back in the prep room Josie comes and announces it's lunchtime.

'You'll be called back after lunch,' Phillip tells me.

'Oh, more of the same, I suppose.'

'Probably. You did well. Just keep doing what you did this morning.'

'Just tell the truth,' I parrot.

'Yes, but just watch the smart remarks,' Ms Parker suggests. 'You'll get their backs up if you do that too often. Now where do we go for lunch? Oh, you have been told that the case can't be discussed outside of the hearing?'

'All right, but can I just ask who those people are that I'm supposed to know?'

'Come on, Phillip,' she says, looking as if there's no hope for me.

Josie and I are left standing like two naughty school girls.

'Whoops! Which way do we go?' I ask.

Josie checks that Tony's team isn't in the street or the cafe we go to for lunch.

After lunch I'm called back so that cross examination can continue. I'm not nervous. It'll just be more of the same.

The recurring themes of my memory for detail and my journal writing start to dominate. Then the worst thing imaginable or otherwise begins to unfold. Dr Steele, addressing the chairman, points out that my evidence obviously relies heavily on my journal.

'I'd like to call it into evidence,' he says.

Well, you can't. It's mine. So there.

Legal people make legal arguments about the laws of evidence. Do the same laws that apply in the criminal code apply here? Isn't this a criminal hearing? No. It's a professional standards matter. What would the journal be used for? Will it just be a fishing expedition?

Eventually someone tells me I'll have to hand my journal over to Dr Steele. It's like telling me I will be stripped naked in public!

'No. I won't. It's private! It's no-one's business but mine.'

Legal people make more legal arguments and finally decide that, despite my understandable objection, my journal must be handed over. Terms for its use and safe keeping are specified. I tell them again that I won't hand it over.

Well, despite your objection, we will strip you. But don't you worry, we will tell your abuser to look only at your ears.

'I won't give it to him. It's private!' I say again.

'Dr Steele?'

'Then we'll subpoena it,' Dr Steele declares. 'I'll let Mr Johnson have the paperwork this afternoon.'

Confidence blasted away. More humiliation. Degradation. Disrespect. Abused all over again.

These people are all insensitive morons. That law they used is immoral. Call themselves psychologists! This can't be happening.

Dr Steele will continue cross examination after he's read my journal. My private, personal journal that I don't even let my closest friends read and never ever will.

I leave the room devastated. Josie is outraged too. I'm glad she's there to keep the tissues coming.

'You'll have to bring the journal tomorrow,' Phillip says quietly.

'It's wrong,' I seethe. 'It's so unfair. I'm not on trial.'

'You heard the argument. We tried to stop it. The law . . .'

'The law's immoral. What happens if I refuse to bring it?' I must be able to refuse to hand over my property.

'That's up to you,' Ms Parker says. 'But I would have to caution you. The subpoena is a legal document.'

'It's not morally right.'

'Be that as it may, as Phillip said, you heard the legal argument. The consequences of not cooperating could be very serious.'

I want to scream at her and Phillip Johnson, to make them be my champions, to make them say it's immoral too. But they have the law that guides and justifies what they do. They're not here for me. They're here to protect the public and uphold the law. Sam will be here for me soon and he'll say what I'm screaming to hear.

Dr Steele's clerk hands an envelope to Phillip, who opens it, reads the subpoena, then hands it to me. A dull slap in the face.

'The subpoena,' he says. He reminds me that they can only read entries about the period of the abuse and complaint.

'They shouldn't read any.'

'I know it's upsetting. But we couldn't stop them.'

Time to retreat to the ladies room and howl.

Sam, smiling gently as usual, is waiting when I come out, red-eyed but composed.

'Hello there. How was it?'

'Hideous, Sam. This is a madhouse. Tell you when we're out of here.'

'That bad, eh?'

'Worse.'

On the train I tell him about the subpoena.

'But they can't do that, can they?' Sam says indignantly. 'It's yours. And you're not on trial.'

'Here's the subpoena.'

'Ah no. This is not right.'

We sit quietly for a while, then he asks, 'Is there anything in the journal? I mean, that you haven't told them?'

'That's the stupid thing. There isn't. They don't need it, because I've told them everything. I reckon they're just going to fish around to see what they can find.'

We sit quietly again. I'm too wrung out to cry. I want to stay on the train frozen like this forever.

At last Sam says, 'Could you try not worrying about the privacy issue and hand it over? To prove you've told the truth.'

'But there's other stuff in it besides stuff about Tony. It's none of their business.'

'Sure. But if it'll help your case.'

'But it's the principle too, Sam. Why should I be publicly stripped when he's the one who's done wrong? We don't get to read his journal, do we? Not that I'd want to.'

'Sure. It'd prove you've told them the truth, though.'

'Oh, I don't know. I feel too mangled to think straight. Those people are psychologists. How can they give someone permission to do this?'

'True. I just don't know. Can you say you haven't got it any more?'

'No. I said under oath that it's at home. Makes you wish we'd have another bush fire tonight, doesn't it?'

'No!' We laugh lamely and sit quietly once more until Sam's stop.

'Ring Trish tonight if you want to talk. See you tomorrow, same place, same time?'

'Thanks, Sam. I'm really grateful.'

'Tomorrow, then,' he smiles. 'Good luck, whatever you decide.'

Whatever I decide. I've often wished I didn't have to make a decision, wished there was someone who dispensed answers about right and wrong like jelly beans. I've never wished it this vehemently. I suppose the lawyers would say that's what they've done – made a considered decision – but they're not talking about morality. They're upholding a law.

I rip the envelope open and read the subpoena, launching the discussion I've just had with Sam into my head again. Will I burn the journal? 'Lose' it? Hide it in the bush? Refuse to cooperate? Scribble all over it in black texta so they can't read it? Give it to Thora to keep until later?

I ring the farm.

'Kate, you have got to be kidding! You won't even let me read it.' I've told Leonie that when I die I want her to burn my journal before anyone can read it.

We discuss the options and I feel respected and supported. I feel frustrated, too, that my friends don't say, 'The right thing to do is . . .' That's the price of past decisions being respected.

'You'll make the right decision. You always do.'

'Except when I chose Tony.'

I ring Genevieve.

'Oh, Kate, what are you going to do?'

'Don't know Gen. Leave the country?'

We have the same discussion I've had with the others, but Gen says, 'Forget the principle. Just hand it over and show you've got nothing to hide. You've got to get this thing out of your life. It's been too long, kiddo. What is it? Nearly six years? Five and a half. All right. Just get it over with.'

Exhausted, I go to bed. Can't sleep. I read my journal. Yes, it will prove every ounce of truth I've spoken and written. But these are my very private mental wanderings, not a legal document! They're the most private thing I own apart from my body itself. Mine and only mine. Boundary violations! Tony isn't the only one guilty of that.

As I read more of my journal I think how boring parts of it are. The thought of the hard-hitting, over-educated Dr Steele having to wade through hours of my very ordinary mental wanderings but finding nothing makes me grin. Serves him right. But the thought of the journal being read publicly, with him, the liar, sitting there listening, wipes the grin away and makes me want to vomit.

Burn it. It's the only way. I look for passages marked with asterisks to read them for the last time. A sunset when all the world was golden and I knew again that God is real. A walk with a friend when I discovered that people have incredible capacity for wholesome love. The reminders that my mother knew I was good and worthy of love. What a revelation!

I just can't burn my journal.

'Lose' it? Could I sit there, having sworn an oath on the Bible, and say I lost my journal? Overnight? No. I'm trying to stick to living out truth and honesty.

I give up on sleep and write instead, but not in the journal. I type furiously, talking to my computer, telling it how I feel, letting the anger out. Tears of frustration and disempowerment too. What they're doing, it feels like rape. I remember once again that definition: that rape is the forcing of intimate contact by a more powerful person on a less powerful one for their own grati-fication. Physical aggression doesn't have to be involved. Power is the issue. The law and the Committee have power over me.

I write to the Committee.

I am appalled that my very private journal has been subpoenaed to try to prove conspiracy when what you are here to examine is professional misconduct. There was no conspiracy but even if there had been, it would not alter the fact that professional misconduct occurred.

You are raping my mind. My journal is my most private posses-sion and you are forcing your way into it, despite my protests, for reasons that I can't justify, regardless of your legal arguments. You are doing this while the person whose behaviour is in question sits by and watches. This is not justice. It's another abuse. You are victimising the victim and probably entertaining the abuser.'

I work on it and get it into a form that I'll be able to read to them. I go to bed and sleep for an hour or two before the alarm wakes me.

Walking up Central station tunnel I hear familiar cheery music and see a friend busking. He and his wife know about the case. Will I give the journal to him and tell the Committee I don't know where it is? That wouldn't be a lie because he moves around the city all day and I wouldn't know where he was at any point in time.

No. That wouldn't prove that I've told the truth, the whole truth and nothing but. I keep walking.

Josie meets me and we wait for Mr Johnson and Ms Parker.

'Did you bring your journal?' Mr Johnson asks.

No more plotting. I hand it over, suddenly aware of what it must look like to him and to the immaculate, efficient Ms Parker. A shabby, battered old exercise book.

'I want to read a statement too.'

'What do you want to say?' Ms Parker asks.

I hand her a copy and wait while she scans it.

'Do you have to read it? Could we distribute copies? They'll have to get copies if you read it, anyway.'

Her cool efficiency unnerves me and I agree just to have it distributed, not read aloud. Josie gets copies made.

'Right, let's go in, then,' Ms Parker suggests.

Tony and his lawyers are already seated. Tony moves his feet very slowly back under his chair as we pass. I want to kick him in the shins.

My journal is handed over and then my statement is distributed. There's silence for a while.

The chairman says he understands my position, thanks me for my statement and refers to the law of evidence. He repeats the conditions of the journal's use and safe keeping. He can talk like that all day but it won't make it right.

Rather than feeling small and vulnerable as I'd expected, I feel huge with anger. I want to stand up and shout at the lot of them. I want to thump my fist into Tony's belly and stamp on his sprawled feet.

A peer reviewer is called to give evidence. She reminds me of a wise old owl. She speaks very clearly about the Code of Conduct, how she interprets it and how she believes her colleagues do. I think I've heard the arguments before, so I listen halfheartedly. Blurring the boundary between the service the client buys and the social arena is confusing for client, hard to distinguish where the limits are . . . Questionable practice to hand a document like Burnside file over without a follow-up session, profoundly confronting material . . . Should never be a sexual relationship because of power imbalance . . .

Now she's asked about me specifically. Well, I've definitely heard all that before. Let's see what she says about it.

Impacts of childhood, create vulnerability . . . Every adult she should have been able to rely on either abandoned or abused her, violated her boundaries . . . Reabuse in adult life. I'm drawn in to listen as she describes the child she believes I was, based on her reading. I shrink inside. As she describes the damage done to that child I feel the vulnerability. My chest freezes, aches for breath. I turn my face to the wall. Grief for the broken, lost child flows like it never has before, not even with Neroli. I'm too aware of my surroundings, though, and I struggle not to make a sound as I weep my heart out.

I turn back when I think I've finished.

'Are you all right,' Phillip asks.

I nod but his kindness makes the tears flow again. I face the wall.

My heart's breaking. I can't stop the sobbing. Stop her talking! Someone stop her saying it all out loud so everyone can hear. All the pain, all powerlessness of the child, repeated in the adult by Tony Benton. And now this very room is flooded with it. I hate Tony Benton. I hate you all.

Josie rubs my back, hands me tissues. Eventually I stop crying. There's nothing left inside. I'm a zombie, walking dead out from the room when the witness is dismissed.

'Rough, eh?' Josie says quietly. 'Your childhood was really something. I didn't know.'

Later, as I drift through the day, Neroli is called for questioning. She looks relaxed and answers with dignity and conviction. I gain focus and feel proud to know her and lucky that I found someone whose commitment to ethical practice is so strong. She smiles briefly at me as she leaves after being cross examined. Yes, working with Neroli is a good sensible adult thing I've done. A good decision. What evidence do I have for that? Here she is supporting ethical practice, supporting me and protecting other vulnerable people. I was not a weak fool for needing help. I was right. And I was right in lodging this complaint.

As long as I don't think about my journal.

Sam is waiting at the end of the day. We talk about handing over the journal and try to laugh about Dr Steele's homework as the train lumbers out of the city.

'I'm exhausted,' I say. 'What will I be like by the end of tomorrow?'

'It'll be over by then, won't it?'

I've been so focused on the day and my journal that I haven't really thought about it being over tomorrow. This time tomorrow it will all be over! Makes the journal issue seem a little smaller. But even that is too big.

I wake up next morning feeling the dread of knowing today is the day my journal will be used. There's only small relief that it's the final day.

Dr Steele has read my journal and so I'm called for questioning again. He makes a point of stating that he has strictly adhered to the terms of the subpoena.

Say it a million times and it'll still be a violation.

He launches his attack. In this round I repeat and repeat that

I only wrote what I wanted to write in my journal. I wasn't writing evidence.

Dr Steele reads sentences that I don't remember writing. I ask to read the entries myself and Dr Steele is kept busy walking back and forth bearing my battered book. We seem to be pitting my ability to use my words in their context against his to use them out of it. This is ridiculous. And it seems so dishonest! He's read the context. He knows he's manipulating my writing.

Keep telling the truth. Over and over and over again. Just tell the truth.

At last Dr Steele has finished. Ms Parker clarifies a few points, then I'm excused.

I storm out, not caring about dignity or grace. Josie finds me in the prep room crying yet again.

'You did so well,' she says quietly.

'Are you all right?' Phillip asks.

'Oh, what went wrong?' I snap, assuming, for no reason that I know of, that he's here to tell me I shouldn't have got angry, or thumped the table or kept saying 'because I didn't want to write it' or 'because I didn't care what the date was'.

'Nothing went wrong! You did well,' he enthuses. 'It was just what we needed. Just the truth.'

'Oh. Sorry. It was all right, then?'

'Yes, you just answered the questions and stuck to the truth. Well done.'

'Thanks.'

'Must get back in there. You can relax now. Your part is over.' He returns to the hearing and I want to shout, 'It's not over 'til I get my journal back!'

Josie and I go back into the hearing because Tony is about to be 'done' at last. It's my turn to watch him squirm. I've told the truth. What can he possibly say?

He walks to the witness table apparently calmly and sits down slowly. He's going for his regal pose. He takes the oath and looks arrogantly at our barrister, revealing what seems to be a certainty that a mere woman, Ms Parker, will not be able to trick him into telling the truth.

As Ms Parker chips away, I admire her work immensely and feel glad she's on my side. I watch Tony unwittingly fall from the position of grace he's appropriated. He seems to be unaware that it's happening! He takes the 'don't rush your answers' advice to ridiculous extremes. Ms Parker must be wondering if she should wake him up.

'It's a petit mal,' I whisper to Josie.

'Grand mal, I suspect,' she says and we giggle.

Phillip turns and mocks a frown at us. We are suitably chastened but we can't help grinning.

Tony's lies are exposed by other lies that he invents to cover still others. He blunders arrogantly along. The pauses between questions and answers get longer. Eventually there is very little coherence to his story at all. I feel powerful as Ms Parker pushes on relentlessly. All my reservations about whether she really cares depart. She's still cool and efficient but she's ruthless to the point where I almost feel sorry for Tony. He must know he's had it but he keeps up the same charade of slow deliberation that would frustrate even a meeting of sloths.

He's given chance after chance to admit that what he did was wrong but he seems to refuse them all. He thinks I should take responsibility too.

Oh, I do, Tony. But you shouldn't have let it happen. You should have kept it professional. That was your responsibility. Listen to your peers. Remember your Code of Conduct. Remember your threats and lies too. Why were they necessary?

By the time it's over I have the impression that Tony still doesn't accept that what he did was wrong or understand the issues.

The chairman thanks everyone for their participation and asks, 'Has Miss Shayler's journal been returned?'

'I'll do that now.' Dr Steele hands it over and I bury it in my bag as everyone packs up files and moves out.

Ms Parker talks quietly to Phillip. Then she turns to me and says, 'It's up to the Board now. Don't expect any particular outcome.'

I thank her, she says goodbye and strides out efficiently. I wish she'd said our case went brilliantly.

Phillip says he thinks it went very well. He thanks me for all the help I've given the HCCC over the years.

'How does it feel now?' he asks.

'Apart from the journal?'

'Apart from the journal.'

'Fabulous. It felt absolutely powerful telling the truth. The best thing was that Tony had to listen to it. You said it would be like that but I didn't understand until now just how good it is. And it was great listening to other people say what they thought too.'

'How do you think he reacted?'

'He still doesn't get it. That's what I think. And Ms Parker was amazing the way she drew out all the inconsistencies. But he still wouldn't relent! I wouldn't want to cross her, tell her lies!'

'Well, Kate, you can go home and relax now. We'll be in touch when the decision comes through.'

'Thank you for all your work. Couldn't have got to this point without you.'

'It's been a pleasure. Let's hope we get a good judgement now. I'll be in touch. Can I say something before you go? Something personal?'

'Um. All right.'

'I just want to tell you that I think what you've done with your life is pretty incredible given your beginnings. Well done.'

Now I want to cry again. It's hard to know what to say. Phillip Johnson has worked on the case for years and been an important part of my journey from humiliation to the quiet sense of triumph I feel now. He has a heart of gold. I should have known. He's been objective and apparently detached. He's listened to me cry, grumble, argue, complain and sometimes laugh. He can still see me as he does. I'm deeply moved.

Josie returns and says goodbye. 'Go home and put your feet up. I'll ring and see how you are.'

'Thanks for your support, Josie.'

'Pleasure. Bye now.'

'Looks as if things went well today,' Sam says.

'Did they ever! It's over, Sam! Can you believe it? It's over.'

'That's great. So what happens next?'

'How about we get a huge bar of chocolate to celebrate first? Then the Committee has to go over the evidence and make a decision about what the truth is and then what penalty to apply. I think it takes a couple of months.'

'Well, you made it. Congratulations.'

That evening, Dave calls in with a bottle of champagne. 'I thought we'd celebrate that it's over even if it went badly. How did it go?'

'Not badly! Very, very goodly, I think.'

A few days later he says he has some news that might cheer me up or at least take my mind off the hearing, especially the journal part.

'I told you I'd try to help find your brother if I could. Well, I've looked through every phone book at the post office and here's a list of all the K. Shaylers in them. You could write to them and see if that tells us anything.'

'Oh, thanks. I can't cope with that just yet, though. I'll do something in the holidays. But thanks.' The thought of doing anything beyond sipping champagne and surviving the rest of term is just too daunting.

'There's no listing for Grafton where you had that address for Ken but I've got an idea,' he says enthusiastically. 'Let's go there anyway and see if anyone knows him. In the holidays. We could explore some National Parks while we're up that way.'

'That sounds nice. Thanks. I'm going to the farm for Christmas but maybe after that.'

Weeks later, when I've had time to stew over the subpoena and calm down a bit, I decide to write to the Board detailing how damaging and unfair it was. I haven't been able to write in my journal since the hearing. Just picking it up makes me anxious and angry. Now I open it to remind myself of the inspiring points before I launch into how Dr Steele used quotes from it unfairly. I don't care that each of his claims was refuted. I'm here about the principle now.

I don't remember this mark. What's it for?

Oh no! I wouldn't draw attention to that. Other pages are marked as well. Traumas with Tony Benton all marked for attention! My asterisks have been upstaged by Dr Steele's marks! When will all the violations stop!

My letter is angry and thorough. So are my tears.

Josie replies, telling me that, although I was obviously distressed, I remained a credible witness. She reminds me that Tony had the right to any document that might let him substantiate his line of defence. I want to scream, 'My journal, my mind, is not a document!' And he did the abusive stuff regardless of what I wrote about it! Why can't anybody see that?

Some of the Committee are psychologists, Josie goes on to say in her letter, but their primary function at the hearing was to acquaint themselves with all the evidence, within legal parameters, regardless of their personal views. Well, I think he who pulls the trigger is just as responsible as he who gave the order.

Josie also asks whether I'd have kept going with the complaint if we'd known earlier that my journal would be used that way. Yes, I think I would have, and I'd have had time to prepare myself and understand the legal position. Or lose the journal properly.

I write all this down for Josie, thank her for her support again and post the letter.

Time to have dinner with my women friends. We go out tonight instead of watching a video with Chinese takeaway at home. None of us wants to join a singles group and we often say how much we treasure living alone for the freedom it gives but sometimes it would be nice to have a special someone. Sometimes. Odd that I've been single for the longest time and now I'm becoming the odd one out.

'How's Dave?' Robyn asks.

'Gorgeous!' Thora replies.

'Oh! Does he have any brothers?'

'He'd need four to be fair, wouldn't he!'

Among other things, we talk about the hearing and my friends are appalled when I tell them about the journal. Thora usually explores the other point of view in our discussions but even she can't justify the invasion of my most private possession.

I go to the farm still seething about it. Why is it that friends can see my point so clearly but the law can ignore it? Leonie and Col tell me about a news story they have been following that connects with mine. Di Lucas from Canberra's Rape Crisis Centre has refused to hand over counselling notes in the trial of an alleged rapist. She argues that the notes are a kind of record of the victims' exploration of ideas about a host of subjects, including what they might have done differently to avoid being raped. The notes are not evidence and the words are not necessarily factual.

Di Lucas is being held in a cell until she agrees to comply with the court orders to hand the notes over. I want to cheer from the hilltop for her. I wish I'd had her courage and refused to hand my journal over. She and her supporters understand that a person's thoughts and comments are very often explorations of ideas, not declarations of belief or intent. They understand. Victims, trying to be survivors, understand. Even rapists understand that, I'm sure. But the law does not. I write to Di Lucas applauding her action. She eventually hands the notes over in a locked briefcase, leaving the lawyers to work out how to gain access to them. Di is released from her cell to fight on. I might fight on sometime, but for now I need a break.

Dave and I go to Grafton when I come home from another lovely Christmas at the farm. He knocks on the door of the house where Ken once lived, while I wait in the car. No-one answers, so he goes around to the flat at the back, and returns a few minutes later, laughing.

'Have you found something?' I ask excitedly.

'No. I'm just amused. A little kid saw me and yelled out, "Hey, Dad, there's an old bloke here." But no. They don't know anything.'

I'm disappointed, but if Ken doesn't want to be found, it's his choice.

We visit some National Parks and I feel relaxed and comfortable with Dave. We talk about our lives and our childhoods and the effects of having been a homes kid. I marvel that any homes kid was brave enough to be a parent and raise kids well. Dave has a song for every occasion and, as I ask where he learnt each song, he tells me more about his life. It's fascinating. He has many hobbies similar to mine but I envy his confidence in all environments, including under the water, in the air, on mountain tops, in the bush or the desert. He attributes a lot of this to his Gunyabarai genes. His father's family were the original people of central western New South Wales.

We come home in time for school and my legs feel wobbly as we kiss goodbye.

I write a quick letter to Kerry to tell her we didn't find Ken. I guess she'll want to know. At school the new kids settle down. All is well. The phone rings during class and Kirsty answers.

'Phillip Johnson for you,' she says, looking hopeful. She knows what we've been waiting for. I don't know how Phillip got his call past the clerical assistant but I'm glad he did.

'Phillip Johnson here, Kate. I know you don't like calls at work but I don't think you'll mind this one.'

'The decision. You've got the decision?'

'Yes. It's as good as we hoped. The Board has accepted the recommendations of the Committee. Mr Tony Benton's name will be removed from the register for a period of three years.'

'Three years? Is that all?' I interrupt, disappointed.

'Don't worry,' Phillip continues. 'There are conditions upon his being accepted for reregistration.'

'He can reregister! But what if he starts all over again?'

'Hopefully he will have learnt his lesson. The conditions are intended to make sure that happens. He has to virtually retrain. It's not the most serious outcome they could deliver but it's pretty serious. You should feel entirely vindicated. Well done.'

'Well done to you. And thanks. It's all over now. Really over, isn't it?'

'He can appeal.'

'Oh no! Not another round!'

'He has three months. All we can do is wait and see.'

'I'm going to pretend it's over. I'd better get back to class, but thanks.'

'Ring me if you want to talk about it after you've read the decision.'

I hope this is the last time I cry about Tony Benton. Must pull myself together now. I wash my face and return to the kids, who hadn't noticed my absence.

'Good news?' Kirsty asks.

'Great news,' I say. 'Tell you later.'

At home I ring friends and supporters and spread the news. As I sit thinking how lucky I am to have so many friends, I find myself hoping Tony, good Tony, has too.

I ring Dave to tell him the news. He comes over with another bottle of champagne and we celebrate.

'Are you going to put all that in your book?' he asks.

'I don't think so. I doubt I'll ever get to book stage. I can't get any continuity, writing the way I do. You know, weekends and holidays. But now that interest rates are on the way down again I might be able to save and have a year off to do it.'

'If you move into my place you could have a studio to work in.'

I miss the point and say, 'I've got a whole house to work in. It's time that's the problem.'

'I'd like you to move in with me.'

This time I get it. 'I'm not ready for that yet. I need to recover and get my life back. Can we keep doing what we're doing for a while?'

'If you like. I don't want to pressure you. How long is a while?'

I want to take it slowly. It feels right, not like a cage. And I feel right too. I'm not afraid of Dave knowing the real me, but I need to know the relationship is real.

Meanwhile, I get the copy of the Board's decision with a letter saying it's not to be quoted anywhere because it's a confidential document. Unlike my journal. Unlike rape counsellor's notes.

Wait a minute! If no-one hears about Tony Benton being struck off, how have we actually protected the public and stopped him? If doctors don't know he's deregistered, how will they know to stop referring people to him? If someone sees his name in the phone book under psychologists, how will they be protected? Or a teacher who sees Tony's ad in the Federation magazine? Shouldn't there be a newspaper article, at least? I talk to a journalist friend and supporter who is interested in writing an article. We need to know if there are suppression orders and so on.

I put the questions to Josie, who can see my point, although she says nothing can be done until the appeal period is over. She'll ask around and let me know.

Soon her letter arrives informing me that I need to talk to the Registrar of the Board about the newspaper story. Josie also says that an annual newsletter goes out to psychologists, and the case, excluding Tony's name, will be reported there. She'll let me know what else she finds out.

The psychologist's newsletter reports:

. . . matter related to a psychologist about whom a complaint was made that he was guilty of professional misconduct in that he was guilty of improper or unethical conduct relating to the practice of psychology and that he was not of good character.

The psychologist's name was removed from the register for a period of three years. The Board also determined that restoration to the register was conditional upon the psychologist undertaking such educational courses during the period of his suspension as the Board determined appropriate and that he not practise therapy under any other descriptive title during this time. The Board also determined that restoration to the register would be contingent upon the psychologist accepting peer supervision for a further period of three years.

I know Tony needs some privacy to get on with earning a living, but his name needs to be published somewhere. How will psychologists know who the deregistered person is?

I discuss the issues with the Registrar. I'm told the newspaper article can be written as long as it doesn't identify Benton, or divulge anything confidential from the hearing or the decision document. Months later the Board gives permission for a short article to go in our local paper on the grounds that it will protect our community.

'I won't accept it without authority,' the editor says. 'We can't vilify someone or defame them. They have a right to earn a living like the rest of us.'

'Yes, he does. I understand that and I've got permission. Here's the number you can ring to confirm it. The community has a right to know.'

When it's published, I tell Thora, 'I hope your friend sees the article, even though it's not the same perpetrator. Oh, wouldn't it be great if that A person saw it too? That'd put the wind up him.'

Time to move on. I start writing about my childhood again. I see more of Dave and find myself looking forward very much to his company.

'Come and live at my place,' he says. 'We'll set you up with a studio. Then you'd get your story written.'

'Or yours,' I reply. 'Give me six months and then I'll know. It'll be my forty-sixth birthday present.'

'Good. I need to tell you this: I couldn't support you all the time but I could for a year, if you wanted to take that year off to write.'

'Thanks, Dave. That's so generous. Let's think about it. See how we go.'

We go well. I accept my birthday present.

EPILOGUE

Living with Dave shows me what connection is, what it is that I didn't have all those years ago, yet didn't understand. Mutual love and respect. And trust above all else.

I sit with Karen talking and reading to her while she dies. She can't accept it. 'Why now when I'm so happy and I've got friends and I love life?' She lapses into unconsciousness and I keep reading in case she can hear me, in case she can understand that she's not alone. I have breaks when other people come, and then I return to read to her again. When she draws her last breath I say, 'Goodbye, Cous. Give Freda my love.'

At home there's a shoulder to cry on as often as I need it. Dave has grown to care for Karen too and he grieves in his way. He doesn't need my shoulder. As one connection starts to fade, another is strengthened.

They are connections, not lifelines. My lifeline is inside me. It's my wholeness that I'd become disconnected from.

If single friends exclude me by saying, 'Oh, Kate. You're so lucky, though. You've got Dave,' I tell them I remember what being lonely is like. I will never forget.

But I am lucky too.

True to his word, Dave supports me during my year off teaching, and I write intensively. He gives me space where I can meet the child who Neroli taught me to love, not fear. I can draw back the curtain, lean my arms on the window sill and look right into my childhood. I meet the child face to face, day by day, and write her truth in *The Long Way Home*. I reconnect with my mother as I write about the visit to her grave.

The irony of Tony Benton having led me to that richest of experiences is not lost. Nor is my gratitude to Neroli who showed me how to trust again.

Letters arrive regularly from strangers thanking me for telling about the long way I took home to my wholeness. Letters arrive from Burnside kids telling me their stories and congratulating me on getting our lives documented. For many, especially the men, I've been too light. Their journeys through childhood were considerably darker than mine.

I speak at book groups and historical societies. Audiences laugh, cry, wonder and ask questions. There's one question that always comes up.

'What happened to you next? After you left Burnside.'

The support group Care Leavers Australia Network (CLAN) lobbies for an inquiry into the effects of being a homes kid on adult care leavers. This story will come too late for the Inquiry but others, whose stories make me proud, have told theirs to the senators.

'Do I want to write about what happened next?' I ask Dave, who knows me well enough now to know when I'm talking to myself.

I do.

Here you are at the end of it.

Don't leave me.

Unless you want to.

I'll be fine.

Note from the author

If you need to report abuse, gain support or you want to become an advocate for child protection, there are many organisations that can help. ASCA and CLAN have nationwide networks and the addresses below are their Head Offices.

Each state has its own Health Care Complaints Commission and these should be listed in your phone book.

CLAN
(Care Leavers Australia Network)
PO Box 164, Georges Hall, NSW 2198
tel: 02 9709 4520
website: www.clan.org.au
email: careleavers@hotmail.com

ASCA
(Advocates for Survivors of Child Abuse)
PO Box 141, Charlestown, NSW 2290
tel: 02 4943 9905
Info/support line: 1300 657 380
website: www.asca.org.au
email: asca@hunterlink.net.au

Mayumarri
(A healing centre for child and adult survivors of childhood trauma)
PO Box 361, Cessnock, NSW 2325
tel: 02 4990 9030
email: mayumarri@hunterlink.net.au

NSW Health Care Complaints Commission
Locked Mail Bag 18, Strawberry Hills, NSW 2012
tel: 02 9219 7444

The Long Way Home: The Story of a Homes Kid
by Kate Shayler
(Random House Australia)

A child separated from family is a truly disturbing prospect. Yet this has been the fate of many thousands of children in Australia's recent history.

The ordeals and triumphs of the Stolen Generations and British child migrants are now being exposed, but there is great silence about their white Australian contemporaries. How did these children cope in the institutions that housed them after separation from their families by court orders, abandonment or the death of parents?

Kate Shayler was born into a happy family that was soon devastated by the death of her mother. Four-year-old Kate was taken to the Burnside Homes to live a childhood of sorts. This is the story of her journey from dreadful loneliness, loss of identity and her father's betrayal, to rediscovering self-respect, dignity and her place in the world.

Far from being a litany of despair, *The Long Way Home* is a beautifully written memoir full of the hope of childhood. Hard to put down, even harder to forget, this is a timely reminder that every child deserves to be cherished.

Shortlisted for the Colin Roderick Award 2001

Also published by Random House Australia:

True Pleasures: A Memoir of Women in Paris
by Lucinda Holdforth
(Vintage)

'True pleasures for me can be found only in love, in Paris or in power.' GERMAINE DE STAËL

Meet the dazzling women of Paris: from Colette to Nancy Mitford; Marie Antoinette to Coco Chanel; Napoleon's Josephine to Edith Wharton. Rule-breakers and style-setters, these women were utterly diverse, yet they shared one common passion – Paris, the world's headquarters of femininity.

At a turning point in her life, Lucinda Holdforth journeys to Paris and takes a very personal tour through the lives, loves and losses of its celebrated women. She evokes the incarnations of the city from Louis XIV through the French Revolution, two world wars and the Paris of the new millennium. And, as she walks in their footsteps, Lucinda draws inspiration from the fascinating women who created and nurtured the world's most civilised city.

This enjoyable companion will seduce and delight – and inspire every woman in search of her own true pleasures . . .

Praise for *True Pleasures*:

'This is a treasure hunt of a book. Lucinda Holdforth's passionate portraits draw us deep into the lives of these supremely feminine characters and reacquaint even the most jaded Parisian with this

supremely feminine city. *True Pleasures* is an absorbing literary voyage – for Lucinda, we suspect, it's also one of self-discovery.'
CHARLA CARTER, PARIS EDITOR, *VOGUE AUSTRALIA*

'Living and loving in Paris – what more could any woman want? This enchanting memoir recalls the highs and lows of women through the ages – a splendid read.' MARGARET WHITLAM